Occupying Schools, Occupying Land

Recent Titles in

Global and Comparative Ethnography
Edited by Javier Auyero

Concrete Jungles
By Rivke Jaffe

Violence at the Urban Margins
Edited by Javier Auyero, Philippe Bourgois, and Nancy Scheper-Hughes

Soybeans and Power
By Pablo Lapegna

Occupying Schools, Occupying Land: How the Landless Workers Movement
Transformed Brazilian Education
Rebecca Tarlau

Occupying Schools, Occupying Land

How the Landless Workers Movement Transformed Brazilian Education

Rebecca Tarlau

OXFORD
UNIVERSITY PRESS

OXFORD
UNIVERSITY PRESS

Oxford University Press is a department of the University of Oxford. It furthers
the University's objective of excellence in research, scholarship, and education
by publishing worldwide. Oxford is a registered trade mark of Oxford University
Press in the UK and certain other countries.

Published in the United States of America by Oxford University Press
198 Madison Avenue, New York, NY 10016, United States of America.

© Oxford University Press 2019

First issued as an Oxford University Press paperback, 2021

Library of Congress Cataloging-in-Publication
Data Names: Tarlau, Rebecca, author.
Title: Occupying schools, occupying land : how the landless workers movement
transformed Brazilian education / Rebecca Tarlau.
Description: New York, NY: Oxford University Press, [2019] |
Includes bibliographical references and index.
Identifiers: LCCN 2018045717 | ISBN 9780190870324 (hardcover) |
ISBN 9780197584347 (paperback) | ISBN 9780190870355 (epub)
Subjects: LCSH: Movimento dos Trabalhadores sem Terra (Brazil) | Education—Political aspects—
Brazil | Education and state—Brazil. | Social movements—Brazil. | Land reform—Brazil.
Classification: LCC LC92.B8 T37 2019 | DDC 306.430981—dc23
LC record available at https://lccn.loc.gov/2018045717

3 5 7 9 8 6 4 2

Paperback printed by Marquis, Canada

I dedicate this book to Dona Djanira Menezes Mota (1948–2017) of
Santa Maria da Boa Vista, Pernambuco, and to the tens of thousands of
rank-and-file MST activists like her. Many of them will never hold an
MST leadership position, but their daily struggles keep the movement
an influential force throughout the country.

Dona Djanira with her daughter Edilane in their home on an MST settlement in Santa Maria da Boa
Vista. Edilane is a long-time activist in the MST state education sector. August 2011.
Courtesy of author (with permission from Edilane Mota)

CONTENTS

List of Illustrations *ix*
Acknowledgments *xiii*
List of Abbreviations *xvii*

Introduction: Education and the Long March through the
Institutions *1*

PART ONE: Constructing a National Educational Program

1. Pedagogical Experiments in the Brazilian Countryside *35*

2. Transforming Universities to Build a Movement: The Case of
   PRONERA *82*

3. From the Pedagogy of the MST to *Educação do Campo*: Expansion,
   Transformation, and Compromise *127*

**PART TWO: Regional Cases of Contentious Co-Governance of Public
Education**

4. Rio Grande do Sul: Political Regimes and Social Movement
   Co-Governance *177*

5. Pernambuco: Patronage, Leadership, and Educational Change *211*

6. Ceará: The Influence of National Advocacy on Regional
   Trajectories *246*

Conclusion: Social Movement Strategy, Education, and Social Change in
the Twenty-First Century *281*

Epilogue: What Is Left of the Brazilian Left? *303*

*Appendix A: First National Meeting of Educators in Areas of Agrarian
   Reform, July 1997—Manifesto of Educators of Agrarian Reform
   to the Brazilian People* *319*

Appendix B: Curriculum of the University of Ijuí Pedagogy of Land Program
        (1998–2001)   321
Appendix C: Curriculum of the UNESP PRONERA Geography Program
        (2007–2011)   325
Appendix D: Fourth National Seminar on PRONERA, November 2010—
        Final Document "Commitments for the Consolidation of
        PRONERA"   329
Appendix E: Second National Meeting of Educators in Areas of Agrarian
        Reform, September 2015—Manifesto of Educators of Agrarian
        Reform   335
Glossary of Portuguese Terms   341
Notes   343
References   365
Index   379

ILLUSTRATIONS

FIGURES

1.1   Collective Decision-Making Structure of MST Camps   48

1.2   Number of New Land Occupations, 1988–1998   60

1.3   Number of Families in New Land Occupations, 1988–1998   60

1.4   Number of New Families Issued Land Rights, 1988–1998   60

1.5   Regional Distribution of Families in Land Occupations, 1988–1998   61

1.6   Collective Decision-Making Structure of the MST's National Movement   64

1.7   Collective Decision-Making Structure of the MST Education Sector   65

2.1   PRONERA Budget, 1998–2010 (in millions of *reais*)   105

3.1   Number of Families in New Land Occupations, 1995–2010   141

3.2   Number of New Families Issued Land Rights, 1995–2010   141

3.3   The MST's Proposal for Institutionalizing *Educação do Campo* (Education of the Countryside) in the Ministry of Education   146

3.4   The Actual Institutionalization of *Educação do Campo* (Education of the Countryside) in the Ministry of Education   147

3.5   Number of Families in New Land Occupations, 2003–2016   162

3.6   Number of New Families Issued Land Rights, 2003–2016   162

MAPS

I.1   States in Brazil with Field Sites   *xxii*

2.1   Geographical Distribution of PRONERA Programs Completed, 1998–2011   *107*

3.1   Location of Baccalaureate and Teaching Certification in Education of the Countryside (LEDOC) Programs in 2015   *156*

4.1   Geographical Location of State Public Schools in Data Set in Rio Grande do Sul   *189*

5.1   Locations of Santa Maria da Boa Vista and Água Preta   *215*

5.2   Municipal Public Schools Serving MST Settlements in Santa Maria da Boa Vista in 2011   *221*

6.1   High Schools Built on MST Settlements in Ceará, 2009–2010   *261*

TABLES

I.1   Barriers and Catalysts to the MST's Contentious Co-Governance of Public Education   *14*

I.2   Case Studies of Institutionalizing the MST's Educational Program Within the Brazilian State   *26*

1.1   National MST Educational Initiatives, 1987–1996   *77*

1.2   Pedagogical Foundations of the MST's Educational Proposal   *79*

2.1   Number of PRONERA Programs Completed and Students Enrolled, 1998–2011   *106*

2.2   PRONERA Higher Education Programs Completed, 1998–2011   *108*

3.1   Conferences, Policies, and Coalitions Supporting *Educação do Campo* (Education of the Countryside), 1997–2012   *168*

5.1   Political Transitions and MST Educational Advances in Santa Maria da Boa Vista, 1995–2012   *219*

5.2   Political Transitions in Água Preta, 1988–2012   *234*

C.1   Barriers and Catalysts to the MST's Contentious Co-Governance of Public Education: Regional Cases   *291*

PICTURES

I.1   Students and educators from MST settlements and camps across the country protest in front of the Ministry of Education during the VI National MST Congress in Brasília. Their sign reads, "Little landless children against the closing and for the opening of schools in the countryside." February 2014.   4

I.2   A student from the municipality of Santa Maria da Boa Vista, Pernambuco, paints the walls of the Ministry of Education in protest during the VI National MST Congress in Brasília. Her sign reads, "Little Landless Children in Struggle." February 2014.   24

1.1   Students at IEJC/ITERRA perform a *mística* (cultural-political performance) celebrating the Soviet educator Anton Makarenko by recreating his image with beans and rice. September 2011.   75

1.2   Banner celebrating socialism hung on the outside walls of ITERRA/IEJC for the MST's twenty-five-year anniversary. October 2010.   81

4.1   An Itinerant School functioning in the state of Rio Grande do Sul even after the government mandated the closure of all Itinerant Schools. June 2009.   201

4.2   Educators and students from MST settlements and camps across the state protesting the closing of the Itinerant Schools. The banner reads, "To Close a School Is a Crime, Little Landless Children in the Struggle for Education." October 2010.   203

5.1   A teacher in front of a municipal public school in Santa Maria da Boa Vista, Pernambuco, located in the MST settlement Catalunha. The teacher is wearing her official municipal teacher uniform, which incorporates the MST's flag. May 2011.   227

6.1   One of the four new high schools built on MST settlements in Ceará in 2009 and 2010 and officially designated as *escolas do campo* (schools of the countryside), November 2011.   265

7.1   Educators and activists at the Second National Meeting of Educators in Areas of Agrarian Reform (ENERA). A picture of one of the MST's intellectual inspirations, Antonio Gramsci, is hanging in the back. September 2015.   283

ACKNOWLEDGMENTS

I arrived at my first MST settlement in June 2009 with a phone number and a notebook full of questions, and I embarked on the journey of a lifetime. Countless MST leaders embraced me as a fellow activist, put up with my endless questions and research requests, and welcomed me into their homes and at their meals. Among the many, I single out for special thanks Elizabete Witcel, Marli Zimmerman, and their families in Rio Grande do Sul; Cristina Vargas and her son Gabriel in São Paulo; Vanderlúcia Simplicio and her family in Brasília; Adailto Cardoso, Edilane Menezes, Erivan Hilário, and their families in Santa Maria da Boa Vista; and Flavinha Tereza, Alex Santos, and Elienei Silva in the *mata sul* region of Pernambuco. Alessandro Mariano became a close friend after I completed my data collection; however, our many conversations about the movement's educational program greatly shaped the current book. I also want to thank all of the Brazilian government officials who accommodated my research requests, answering my probing questions about state–society relations calmly and thoroughly.

Many others made my research in Brazil possible by providing practical and moral support. Bela Ribeiro and her mother Rita have been my second family in Brazil ever since I first studied there as an undergraduate student. I counted on Bela's home for food, rest, and comfort. Luis Armando Gandin and Bernardo Mançano Fernandes both served as my mentors while I was in Brazil. Lourdes Luna and Grupo Mulher Maravilha—a women's organization on the periphery of Recife—were a powerful support system. It was Lourdes and the other women of this organization who first taught me about the transformational potential of popular education. If our paths had not crossed, I might never have discovered my passion for education. I also want to thank the organizations whose generous grants funded this research: the Social Science Research Council, the Inter-American Foundation, the Fulbright Institute of International Education, and the National Academy of Education.

At the University of California, Berkeley, I had an amazing dissertation committee that included Peter Evans, Zeus Leonardo, Erin

Murphy-Graham, Harley Shaiken, and Michael Watts. I want to give a special thanks to Peter Evans, who took me on as his own, despite his retirement from UC Berkeley and my sociology-outsider status. Peter has been a part of every step of this writing process, offering critical advice on theoretical frameworks, research design, making sense of data, developing arguments, and much more. Other UC Berkeley faculty who shaped my thinking about theory, politics, and research include Patricia Baquedano-López, Michael Burawoy, Laura Enriquez, Gillian Hart, Mara Loveman, Tianna Paschel, Dan Pearlstein, Cihan Tuğal, and Kim Voss. Outside of the Berkeley world, Pedro Paulo Bastos, Ruy Braga, Miguel Carter, Aziz Choudry, Gustavo Fischman, Sangeeta Kamat, Steven Klees, Pauline Lipman, David Meyer, Susan Robertson, Ben Ross Schneider, Andrew Schrank, Wendy Wolford, Angus Wright, and Erik Olin Wright have all offered feedback on different stages of this book project.

My friends from the UC Berkeley Graduate School of Education—all on the front line of the struggle against the privatization and dismantling of public education—contributed to countless iterations of this research, always reminding me to connect my findings to the US educational context. My deepest gratitude goes to Rick Ayers, Liz Boner, Krista Cortes, Chela Delgado, Tadashi Dozono, René Kissell, Tenaya Lafore, Joey Lample, Cecilia Lucas, Nirali Jani, Kathryn Moeller, Ellen Moore, Dinorah Sanchez Loza, Bianca Suarez, Joanne Tien, and Kimberly Vinall. I am also grateful to my interdisciplinary group of friends and colleagues, Edwin Ackerman, Javiera Barandiaran, Barbara Born, Javier Campos, Brent Edwards, Dave DeMatthews, Fidan Elcioglu, Luke Fletcher, Ben Gebre-Medhin, Ilaria Giglioli, Gabriel Hetland, Tyler Leeds, Seth Leibson, Zach Levenson, Roi Livne, Kate Maich, Diego Nieto, Ramon Quintero, Leonardo Rosa, Jonathan M. Smucker, Gustavo Oliveira, Karin Shankar, Krystal Strong, and Rajesh Veeraraghavan. Among my many supportive peers, Alex Barnard, Carter Koppleman, and Liz McKenna have been especially helpful in the final revisions of this manuscript. I am moved and inspired by Effie Rawlings's dedication to making the MST's agrarian vision a reality in the US context. I am grateful to Pete Woiwode for pushing me to think about lessons for US movements. Robin Anderson-Wood, Laurie Brescoll, Anna Fedman, Kirsten Gwynn, Sara Manning, Katie Morgan, Ashley Rouintree, Julia Weinert, and Rob Weldon have all kept me sane by reminding me to look up from my books, laugh, live, and dance. Bill, Nina, Jill, Kim, Margot, Hilary, Jo, and their families have been a source of love and support.

Transforming a doctoral dissertation into a book is a huge endeavor. I am grateful to Stanford University's Lemann Center for Educational Entrepreneurship and Innovation in Brazil for the gift of time through a two-year postdoctoral fellowship. Martin Carnoy, my postdoctoral faculty sponsor, has been a huge advocate of this research. Georgia Gabriela da Silva Sampaio, a very talented Stanford undergraduate, was an enormous help in designing all of the book's maps and many of the figures. I also want to thank the Stanford Center for Latin American Studies for co-hosting a book workshop with the Lemann Center on a first draft of the manuscript. The feedback I received during the workshop led to a major revision of the book's theoretical contribution and a much-improved organization of its empirical chapters. My sincere thanks to Martin Carnoy, Alberto Diaz-Cayeros, Gillian Hart, Mara Loveman, Tianna Paschel, Doug McAdam, and Wendy Wolford for participating in that day-long workshop. In January 2018, I joined the faculty of Pennsylvania State University's College of Education and School of Labor and Employment Relations. I am thankful for the contributions and support of my new colleagues in the Lifelong Learning and Adult Education program and the Center for Global Workers' Rights, for the feedback I received from the PSU social movement reading group, and for the work of my two graduate assistants Hye-Su Kuk and Carol Rogers-Shaw for preparing the index. Finally, thanks to James Cook and Emily Mackenzie at Oxford University Press and Javier Auyero the Global and Comparative Ethnography series editor, as well as the four reviewers whose feedback greatly improved the manuscript.

My political commitments and intellectual curiosity are a direct product of the family I grew up in. My mother, Eileen Senn, has been fighting for workers' safety rights and racial justice her entire life, teaching me the importance of principled political actions. My father, Jimmy Tarlau, has been part of the labor movement for forty years, always showing through example how to build broad coalitions and support for economic justice. My stepmother, Jodi Beder, is a professional copy editor and offered feedback on every stage of writing, spending many hours helping me to find the means to communicate with nuance and clarity. Thanks also to my brother, Swami Adi Parashaktiananda, whose spiritual growth has been inspiring to watch.

As I prepared to turn in this final book manuscript, in July 2018, Manuel Rosaldo and I vowed our commitment and partnership to each other in the Santa Cruz redwoods in front of many friends and family, including nine MST activists. Manuel proposed two years before, in the home of educational activist Elizabete Witcel, in an MST settlement in the far southern state of Rio Grande do Sul. In his proposal he talked about the MST's inspirational achievements and how he learned through my experiences that research can be a means of forming powerful human connections. Manuel has been by my side during the entire process of writing this book, constantly reminding me of the book's political relevance. Manuel's *companheirismo*, his friendship, support, love, critical feedback, and advocacy, have helped to bring this book into fruition, while also making writing a more joyful process.

I want to end by thanking one more time all of the women, men, and children who compose the dynamic social movement we know as the Brazilian Landless Workers Movement (MST), and who have taught me so much about leadership, discipline, collective decision making, education, and the cultural aspects of political struggle.

ABBREVIATIONS

CEB	*Comunidades Eclesiais de Base* (Ecclesial Base Communities)
CNA	*Confederação Nacional da Agricultura e Pecuária do Brasil* (National Confederation of Agriculture and Livestock of Brazil)
CNBB	*Conferência Nacional do Bispos do Brasil* (National Conference of Brazilian Bishops)
CNBT	*Coordenação dos Núcleos de Base da Turma* (Class Coordinating Collective of Base Nuclei)
CNE	*Conselho Nacional da Educação* (National Education Advisory Board)
CNE/CEB	*Conselho Nacional da Educação/Câmara da Educação Básica* (Basic Education Committee of the National Education Advisory Board)
CONTAG	*Confederação Nacional dos Trabalhadores na Agricultura* (Confederation of Agricultural Workers)
CPI	*Comissão Parlamentar de Inquérito* (Congressional Investigation)
CPP	*Coletivo Política Pedagógica* (Political-Pedagogical Collective)
CPT	*Comissão Pastoral da Terra* (Pastoral Land Commission)
CRE	*Coordenadoria Regional de Educação* (State Department of Education Regional Office—Rio Grande do Sul)
CREDE	*Coordenadoria Regional de Desenvolvimento da Educação* (State Department of Education Regional Office—Ceará)
CUT	*Central Única dos Trabalhadores* (Central Union of Workers)
DEM	*Democraticas* (Democrats—previously the PFL)
DER	*Departamento de Educação Rural* (Department of Rural Education—of FUNDEP)

ENERA	*Encontro Nacional de Educadores da Reforma Agrária* (National Meeting of Educators in Areas of Agrarian Reform)
ENFF	*Escola Nacional Florestan Fernandes* (Florestan Fernandes National School)
FONEC	*Forum Nacional da Educação do Campo* (National Forum for Education of the Countryside)
FUNDEP	*Fundação de Desenvolvimento Educação e Pesquisa* (Foundation of Educational Development and Research)
IEJC	*Instituto de Educação Josué de Castro* (Educational Institute of Josué de Castro)
INCRA	*Instituto Nacional da Colonização e Reforma Agraria* (National Institute of Colonization and Agrarian Reform)
ITERRA	*Instituto Técnico de Capacitação e Pesquisa da Reforma Agrária* (Technical Institute of Training and Research in Agrarian Reform)
LDB	*Lei de Diretrizes e Bases de Educação Nacional* (National Educational Law)
LEDOC	*Licenciatura em Educação do Campo* (Baccalaureate and Teaching Certification in Education of the Countryside)
MAG	*Magistério, nível media, normal médio* (High School Degree and Teaching Certification Program)
MDA	*Ministério do Desenvolvimento Agrário* (Ministry of Agrarian Development)
MEC	*Ministério da Educação* (Ministry of Education)
MST	*Movimento dos Trabalhadores Rurais Sem Terra* (Brazilian Landless Workers Movement)
NB	*Núcleo de base* (Base Nucleus—small collective of families or students that form the organizational structure of camps and settlements and schools)
PDT	*Partido Democrático Trabalhista* (Democratic Labor Party)
PFL	*Partido Frente Liberal* (Liberal Front Party—changes name to Democrats in 2007)
PMDB	*Partido do Movimento Democrático Brasileiro* (Brazilian Democratic Movement Party)
PPP	*Projeto Político Pedagógico* (Pedagogical-Political Project—a school mission statement)
PRONERA	*Programa Nacional da Educação em Areas da Reforma Agrária* (National Program for Education in Areas of Agrarian Reform)

PSB	*Partido Socialista Brasileiro* (Brazilian Socialist Party)
PSDB	*Partido da Social Democracia Brasileira* (Brazilian Social Democratic Party)
PSOL	*Partido Socialismo e Liberdade* (Socialism and Liberty Party)
PSTU	*Partido Socialista dos Trabalhadores Unificado* (Unified Socialist Workers' Party)
PT	*Partido do Trabalhadores* (Workers' Party)
SECADI	*Secretaria de Educação Continuada, Alfabetização, Diversidade e Inclusão* (SECAD pre-2010—Secretariat of Continual Education, Literacy, Diversity, and Inclusion)
TAC	*Técnio na Administrão dos Cooperativas* (Technical Administration of Cooperatives)
TAC	*Termo de Compromisso de Ajustamento de Conduta* (Term of Commitment to Adjust Conduct)
TCU	*Tribunal de Contas da União* (Brazilian Federal Court of Audits
UnB	*Universidade de Brasília* (University of Brasília)
UNDIME	*União Nacional dos Dirigentes Municipais de Educação* (National Union of Municipal Secretaries of Education)
UNESCO	*Organização das Nações Unidas para a Educação, a Ciência e a Cultura* (United Nations Educational, Scientific, and Cultural Organization)
UNESP	*Universidade Estadual Paulista* (State University of São Paulo)
UNICEF	*Fundo das Nações Unidas para a Infância* (United Nations Children's Fund)

Occupying Schools, Occupying Land

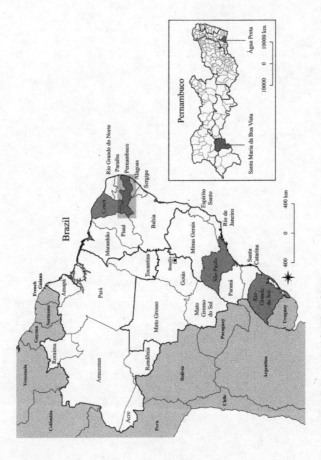

Map I.1 States in Brazil with Field Sites
Courtesy of Georgia Gabriela da Silva Sampaio

Introduction: Education and the Long March through the Institutions

How do we maintain this movement? Negotiating with the state without being absorbed.
—Antonio Munarim, *member of the National Forum for Education of the Countryside (FONEC)*
I would not call it co-optation but rather a type of institutionalization. If you are there in the school but you are also in the struggle and connected to the larger debates, then this is good. It is only co-optation if you stop being connected to the movement.
—Erivan Hilário, *national leader in MST education Sector*

"The Landless Children have arrived!" chanted some five hundred children, ages four to fourteen, as they stormed past armed security guards into the Brazilian Ministry of Education in the capital city of Brasília on February 12, 2014. They had traveled from rural communities across the country to defend *Educação do Campo*, Education of the Countryside, the right to schools located in the countryside with organizational, pedagogical, and curricular practices based on their rural realities. Over the previous two decades, this grassroots educational proposal, which promotes the sustainable development of rural areas and contests assumptions of the inevitability of rural-to-urban migration, has become institutionalized. In other words, the Brazilian state has formally adopted major components of the educational proposal through national policy, an office in the Ministry of Education, and dozens of federal, state, and municipal programs.[1] Nonetheless, despite official acknowledgment of this educational approach, governments at all levels continue to shut down rural schools and consolidate public education in large urban centers. The children held signs denouncing this trend: "37 thousand schools closed in the countryside." "Closing a school is a crime!" "Landless Children for the opening of schools in the countryside!"

The five hundred protesting children were the sons and daughters of activists from the *Movimento dos Trabalhadores Rurais Sem Terra*, the Brazilian Landless Workers Movement (MST). The MST is one of the most well-known and extensively researched social movements in Latin America.[2] The movement has become a reference point for left-leaning organizations around the world due to its success in occupying land and pressuring the government to redistribute this land to poor families. Since the early 1980s, the MST has pressured the state to give land rights to hundreds of thousands of landless families,[3] through occupations of privately and publicly owned land estates. These families live on agrarian reform settlements, where they have also won access to government services such as housing, roads, agricultural technical assistance, education, and health services. Additionally, tens of thousands of families continue to occupy land across Brazil, spending years living in plastic makeshift tents and fending off police attacks while waiting for the legal rights to this land.

The MST articulates its struggles in terms of three broad goals: land reform, agrarian reform, and social transformation. Although land reform is a central component of agrarian reform, the movement separates these two goals in order to highlight that the initial struggle for land through land occupations is only a first step in achieving agrarian reform—the resources for families to live sustainably on this land. Social transformation is the MST's struggle for socialist economic practices and what the movement refers to as a popular (grassroots) democracy. This is one of the most radical goals of the movement, as activists openly denounce capitalism and celebrate historical attempts to construct socialism, from the Bolshevik Revolution to the socialist governments of Cuba and Venezuela. The movement's vision of social transformation has also evolved over the past two decades to encompass women's rights, including equal gender participation within the movement, the defense of indigenous lands, racial equality, and more recently, the celebration of lesbian, gay, bisexual, and transgender (LGBT) working-class rights. Education is a critical component of achieving all of these political, economic, and social goals.

In the week before the children's protest, 15,000 MST activists from across the country had traveled by bus to the capital city of Brasília to discuss the movement's future at the MST's Sixth National Congress. The Congress, which coincided with the movement's thirtieth anniversary, exemplified the movement's practice of collective leadership, which Miguel Carter describes as "a multidimensional, network-like organization, composed of various decentralized yet well-coordinated layers of representation and collective decision making" (Carter 2015, 400). Delegations of a couple hundred to several thousand MST leaders arrived from twenty-four of the twenty-six Brazilian states.[4] Each state delegation organized itself into smaller collectives of several dozen activists, to oversee cooking, cleaning, and other basic tasks necessary to camp for the week. State delegations also sent members to participate in congress-wide collectives, with themes such as agricultural production, education, youth, communications, and international relations. The agricultural production collective set up a large market in the middle of the tent-city, where state delegates sold produce and artisanal products from their communities. The youth collective brought together young people to participate in a parallel conference appropriate to their needs and interests. The grassroots organizing collective—front of the masses (*frente de massa*)—planned the march that would occur in the middle of the week, to denounce the government's lack of support for agrarian reform. Other collectives focused on women's issues, health, culture, and security, while an international relations collective hosted 250 international delegates.[5]

The protesting children were a demonstration of the central focus that education has had in the movement. In the early 1980s, during the first MST land occupations, local activists began experimenting with educational approaches in their communities that supported the movement's broader struggle for agrarian reform and collective farming. These experiments included both informal educational activities in MST occupied encampments and alternative pedagogical practices in schools on agrarian reform settlements. As the MST grew nationally, these local experiments evolved into a proposal for all schools located in MST settlements and camps—which, by 2010, encompassed 2,000 schools with 8,000 teachers and 250,000 students. The MST also pressured the government to fund dozens of adult literacy campaigns, vocational high schools, and bachelor and graduate degree programs for more than 160,000 students in areas of agrarian reform, through partnerships with over eighty educational institutions. During the early 2000s, the MST's educational initiatives expanded to include all rural populations in the Brazilian countryside, not only those in areas of agrarian reform. The proposal became institutionalized within the Brazilian state through national public policies, an office in the Ministry of Education, a presidential decree, and dozens of programs in other federal agencies and subnational governments. By 2010, the MST's educational proposal—now known as *Educação do Campo*—was the Brazilian state's *official* approach to rural schooling. Nonetheless, the implementation of the proposal varied widely by state and municipality.

During the MST's Congress, the national education sector materialized the movement's educational approach by organizing a childcare center—the Center Paulo Freire—that engaged around eight hundred children in activities that touched on the themes of collective organization, work, culture, and history.[6] On the third day of the Congress, these five hundred *sem terrinha* (little landless children) learned about another component of the MST's pedagogy—struggle—by participating in their own direct action: occupying the Ministry of Education and declaring their right to locally based schools. While the children occupied the Ministry, the head of the *Educação do Campo* office—an office created in 2004 as a result of MST mobilizations—tried to convince the Minister to meet with the children, assuring him that he would not be in any danger.[7] After three hours, the Minister came outside and promised the children quality education in the countryside. The leaders of the national MST education sector were happy the children had the opportunity to see the power of their collective action; however, they also understood that the Minister's words were empty promises if activists did not continue to engage in similar actions across the country, to demand the implementation of the MST's educational program.

Picture I.1 Students and educators from MST settlements and camps across the country protest in front of the Ministry of Education during the VI National MST Congress in Brasília. Their sign reads, "Little landless children against the closing and for the opening of schools in the countryside." February 2014.
Courtesy of author

THE LONG MARCH THROUGH THE INSTITUTIONS, CONTENTIOUS CO-GOVERNANCE, AND PREFIGURATION

The MST's relationship with the Brazilian state—which in this book is understood as an assemblage of organizations, institutions, and national and subnational government actors that often have contradictory goals—is complex and fraught with tensions. Since the MST's primary demand is land redistribution, the movement has an explicitly contentious relationship with the Brazilian state, as families occupy land to pressure different government administrations to redistribute these properties to landless families. As the MST promotes agrarian reform through public resources, the MST also has a collaborative relationship with the state, promoting agricultural and educational policies that increase the development of rural settlements—an outcome that can help both the movement and the state itself. Finally, the relationship is fundamentally contradictory, as the MST pressures the capitalist state to support a project with the end goal of overthrowing or eroding capitalism, through the promotion of more collective, participatory, and inclusive political and economic relations. MST activists demand schools in their communities and communities' right to participate in the governance of these schools, with the purpose of promoting alternative pedagogical, curricular, and organizational practices—a process I refer to as *contentious co-governance*. These practices encourage youth to stay in the countryside, engage in collective agricultural production, and embrace peasant culture. These educational goals are an explicit attempt to *prefigure*, within the current public school system, more collective forms of social and economic relations that advance the future project of constructing a fully socialist society.

In the following chapters, I tell this story of how a social movement fighting for agrarian reform developed an educational proposal that supported its social vision, and how activists have attempted to implement this proposal in diverse economic and political regions throughout the country—transforming both the state and the movement itself.[8] Thus, the book is about how activists' contentious co-governance of formal state institutions can support their larger struggles. I follow the MST through what German student activist Rudi Dutschke termed the "long march through the institutions" (Dutschke 1969, 249).[9] Social movement leaders engage in the long march when they enter the state, helping to carry out the daily job of public service provision, while linking those actions to a broader process of social struggle and a long-term strategy for economic and political change. The goal is to work "against the established institutions while working within them" (Marcuse 1972, 56). This requires activists' technical and political skills in a wide range of areas, including production, communications, programming, health, and education.

Dutschke's inspiration for pursuing this strategy came from his engagement with the texts of Antonio Gramsci, an Italian Marxist intellectual and activist writing about political parties, revolution, and the state in the 1920s and 1930s. One of the central questions Gramsci was trying to answer is why—contrary to Karl Marx's predictions—revolution had succeeded in the less developed context of Russia but had failed in the more developed Western European nations. Gramsci sought to create a theory of the state that went beyond the traditional vision of the state apparatus as a unitary class subject; instead, he analyzed state power as a complex of social relations (Jessop 2001). Gramsci believed that while the Czarist regime in Russia had ruled based on pure domination and force, in most Western European nations the ruling class establishes hegemony: a combination of coercion and consent, whereby the ruling class convinces a range of social groups that its own economic interests are in the interests of all. This construction of consent takes place both through the realm of ideas and direct economic concessions.

Thus, rather than domination, the determining factor of hegemony is "intellectual and moral direction . . . the need to gain 'consent' even before the material conquest of power" (Santucci 2010, 155). Gramsci writes that "A social group can and, indeed, must already be a leader before conquering government power . . . even if it has firm control, it becomes dominant, but it must also continue to be a 'leader'" (Gramsci 1971, 57–58). Gramsci's concept of "intellectual and moral leadership" is critical for understanding the stability of any given hegemonic bloc, and why political organizations such as the MST must engage in a similar strategy to win over diverse groups to support their own economic and political goals.

Civil society, which includes but is not limited to political parties, print media, social movements, nongovernmental organizations (NGOs), the family, and mass education (Burawoy 2003, 198), is the most important sphere of ruling-class leadership. However, civil society also has a contradictory relationship to the state. As Michael Burawoy (2003) points out, "Civil society collaborates with the state to contain class struggle, and on the other hand, its autonomy from the state can promote class struggle" (198). Civil society is simultaneously a space of contestation where social organizations form and an arena of associational activity where daily life is experienced (Tuğal 2009). Gramsci suggests that rather than revolutionaries engaging in a war of movement—a direct attempt to take state power—in the "West" it is necessary to engage in a war of position: a long struggle in the trenches of civil society, to find allies who support their political project. Thus, rather than reject state engagement, a Gramscian question would be: "What institutions (schools, community organizations, work councils, etc.) best facilitate the transformation of common sense into political 'critical consciousness'?" (Adamson 1978, 432). In this book, I argue that schools, from preschool to tertiary education, are important institutions for social movements to engage in this Gramscian war of position.

MAIN ARGUMENTS

The MST's thirty-year engagement with the Brazilian state epitomizes this Gramscian strategy as the movement has attempted not only to redistribute land but also to integrate farmers into a process of contentious co-governance of their new communities through their participation in a range of state institutions. Leandro Vergara-Camus (2014) refers to this as a pragmatic strategy of putting pressure on the state in order to increase resources for the movement to build "autonomous structures of popular power" (295). Importantly, the MST not only embodies this Gramscian strategy, but activists also explicitly draw on Gramscian theory to justify their continual engagement with the Brazilian state. The MST's accomplishments have been astonishing, and although the movement is still far from achieving its goals of land reform, agrarian reform, and social transformation, it has arguably done more to promote alternative practices within a diverse range of state institutions than any other social movement in Latin America.[10] Therefore, anyone who studies or cares about social change should be wondering, *how did the MST do this*?

To answer that question, I analyze the MST's organizing in different regions over a thirty-year period, working with, in, through, and outside of the state. I focus specifically on educational institutions as a central node of the MST's broader political struggle, and how transforming schools allows the movement to develop local leadership and prefigure its social and political goals. Consequently, while this is a book about social movements, it also speaks to the structural constraints and conjunctural possibilities for transforming public education and the implications of this process for social change. While Gramsci's theories offer an accurate description of the MST's macro-strategy, his writings are more ambiguous about the exact mechanisms that facilitate the type of institutional change he advocates. Therefore, to answer the question of *how* the MST was able to transform Brazilian education, I turn to the scholarship on social movements.

Beyond Co-Optation: Social Movements' Contentious Co-Governance of State Institutions

The book's first argument is that social movements can increase their internal capacity by strategically engaging institutions. This directly contradicts a classical perspective on social movement development, which argues that movements inevitably become more conservative and less effective as they institutionalize. This enduring perspective can be traced back to Frances Fox Piven and Richard Cloward (1977), and their claim that disruptive protest is much more effective in achieving movement goals than organization and cooperation. This argument draws on Robert Michels's (1915) notion of the iron rule of oligarchy—the tendency for organizations to become more oligarchical and bureaucratic over time (Piven and Cloward 1977, xvi).

Scholars building on Piven and Cloward's and Michels's argument have often done so without a clear distinction between the three processes at the heart of this thesis: (1) the concentration of power within social movements, or the oligarchization of movements; (2) the deradicalization of movement goals; and (3) the institutionalization of movements' demands within state institutions. Darcy Leach (2005) makes an analytical distinction between the first two of these processes, what she refers to as the development of oligarchy versus goal displacement and bureaucratic conservatism. Leach argues that asking why an organization adopts less radical goals is not the same as asking how many people are ruling the organization. In fact, she argues, radical goals can be maintained even as organizations become more oligarchical. The second focus is conservatism or goal displacement. In the Piven and Cloward and Michels thesis, formal bureaucratic organization is seen as antithetical to the use of confrontational and radical goals. Kim Voss and Rachel Sherman (2000) contest this argument, illustrating that movements—in their case union locals—can break Michels's iron rule of oligarchy and become radicalized after decades of bureaucratic conservatism. Andrew Martin (2008) makes a similar argument, stating that "Movements do not automatically become institutionalized: they choose certain strategies based on specific environmental and internal considerations that may also reverse this process" (1093). These studies contest the idea that movements using less confrontational tactics are destined to do this forever.

The third strain of the Piven and Cloward and Michels thesis, which is central to this book, concerns the trajectories of social movements that engage in the institutional sphere. Piven and Cloward argue that the tendency to channel contention through institutions has a devastating effect on leaders' ability to organize future protests. Many scholars coming out of the US social movement tradition have complicated this argument, underscoring how movements advance their goals through both contestation and nonconfrontational strategies (Andrews 2004; Banaszak 2010; Ganz 2000; Johnston 2014; D. Meyer and Tarrow 1997). For example, David Meyer and Sidney Tarrow (1997) write that "if the definition of

movements depends on a sustained, conflictual interaction with other actors, they have seldom been very far from institutional politics" (5). Meyer
and Tarrow argue that we are living in a "social movement society," where
the institutionalization of protest through routines is becoming more
common. Nonetheless, there is still an implicit Piven and Cloward bias in
this argument, as the authors define institutionalization as containing rou-
tinization, inclusion and marginalization, and co-optation. This latter component forces movements to "alter their claims and tactics to ones that can
be pursued without disrupting the normal practices of politics" (D. Meyer
and Tarrow 1997, 21). Similarly, Tarrow (2011) defines institutionalization as the "movement away from extreme ideologies and/or the adoption
of more conventional and less disruptive forms of contention" (207). In
contrast, Lee Ann Banaszak's (2010) book on the US women's movement
illustrates that even when activists are located inside of the state, they often
employ nonconventional tactics; therefore, the deradicalization of a social
movement is not necessarily caused by movement–state interactions. All
of these authors help us move beyond Piven and Cloward, as they maintain that activists engaging in the institutional sphere can be an effective
method for achieving social movement goals.

A second perspective focuses on how activists transform state institutions.
A prominent example is Fabio Rojas's (2007) study of how the black power
movements of the 1960s led to the rise of Black Studies departments in
US universities. Rojas (2007) writes that once movement goals are institutionalized, outcomes can become examples of a countercenter: "a formalized space for oppositional consciousness in a mainstream institution"
(21). Tianna Paschel's (2016) study of black movements in Colombia and
Brazil illustrates how small groups of strategic activists can make tremendous changes to their national context, from expansive affirmative action
policies in Brazil to the titling of thousands of acres of land to black rural
communities in Colombia. Paschel pushes us to think beyond the notion of
movements as broad-based forms of collective action and, instead, examine
how movement leaders aligning with global discursive shifts can bring
about transformation in their national context (151). Similarly, Patrick
Heller (1999) has illustrated how working-class organizations in Kerala,
India, have institutionalized more democratic processes and redistributive policies, partially by maintaining high levels of mobilization when not
holding political power.

In literature on the Latin American feminist movement, scholars have
also contributed to this second perspective concerning if and how activists
can transform state institutions (Alvarez 1990, 1999, 2009; Lebon 1996;
Santos 2010). Sonia Alvarez (1990) argues that while the process of "taking
feminism into the state" often results in the co-optation of progressive gender

ideologies by dominant political and economic interests, this strategy can also produce concrete improvements in the conditions of women's lives (21). Alvarez argues that a "dual strategy," whereby activists continue to engage in contentious politics while also working with policymakers, allowed feminists to make important inroads within the state.[11] Alvarez (1990) describes how activists' participation in the elaboration, execution, and monitoring of women's health programs transformed the state's approach to health (194).[12] In a more recent discussion on Latin American civil society, Alvarez (2017) maintains that social movements can participate in the co-governance of public institutions with state actors, defining co-governance as "governing with social movements, producing radical democratic subjects" (327). Together, these scholars of state–society relations illustrate that there are different inroads and diverse access points through which movements can transform state institutions.

Nonetheless, despite this optimism, there are also real tradeoffs of activists engaging in institutional politics. For example, Paschel (2016) argues that black activist participation led to a process of social movement absorption, which ritualized activist engagement and made the movement vulnerable to the unmaking of black rights (223). Similarly, Heller argues that mobilized working-class populations were only able to become hegemonic in Kerala, India, by coordinating their interests with the interests of capitalists, what he calls class compromise.[13] Alvarez herself refers to the incorporation of women and women's issues into Latin American institutional politics as a "mixed blessing" (22), as women's institutions were "prone to manipulation by male-dominant politics" (268). Thus, all of these studies highlight both the possibilities and limits of social movement-led institutional change. Furthermore, none of these studies examine if and how these institutional changes might support the internal capacity of the movements themselves.

My research on the MST's educational struggle makes a new and controversial argument: *social movements can increase their internal capacity by strategically engaging institutions.* In other words, I am not only concerned with how movements transform state institutions, but how the transformation of state institutions sustains movements. This is not to say that there are no drawbacks to the MST's engagement with the Brazilian state. Throughout the book I highlight the many compromises that MST leaders are forced to make, as they attempt to transform the Brazilian public school system. Nonetheless, I also show the exact mechanisms by which formal institutions increase the MST's internal capacity: integrating new members into the movement through concrete tasks, allowing activists to practice and therefore refine their political and economic goals, and facilitating the accumulation of the expertise and technical skills that the movement needs for co-governance. Despite tradeoffs, I argue that the MST's three-and-a-half decades of engaging the Brazilian state through the long march through the institutions has been critical to its long-term viability.

Disruption, Persuasion, Negotiation, and Co-Governance

The second argument of the book is that although participating in formal institutions can help increase the internal capacity of a social movement, activists must still engage in a combination of disruption and institutional pressure in order to be effective. This point builds off the previous one, acknowledging that while activists' participation in formal institutions can help support the movement, the conscious use of state institutions to support movement goals is only possible through ongoing contentious actions. Thus, Doug McAdam's (1999) classical social movement definition, as "rational attempts by excluded groups to mobilize sufficient political leverage to advance collective interests through *non-institutionalized means*" (37, emphasis added), is still pertinent, as it highlights the protest and contestation that *allows* movements to gain and maintain institutional influence. When activists enter the state, and mobilization stops, this often *does* lead to the process of demobilization that Piven and Cloward (1977) caution against. However, while much of the social movement literature assumes a temporal shift from contentious to less disruptive forms of political action (Johnston 2014; Tarrow 2011), this move from the streets to the institutions is not necessary; both forms of political intervention can happen simultaneously over many decades.

I argue that movement activists are most effective when simultaneously combining disruption, persuasion, negotiation, and co-governance into their repertoires. Kenneth Andrews (2004) describes the first two of these movement strategies as "action-reaction" models, whereby movements organize "large-scale dramatic events . . . that mobilize more powerful actors to advance the movement's causes" (27). In contrast, the third strategy of negotiation, or the "access-influence model," assumes that "the determinant of movement efficacy is the acquisition of routine access to the polity through institutionalized tactics" (27). Building on these points, I offer a complimentary fourth strategy: the "co-governance-prefiguration" model, which highlights how participation in the daily governance of state institutions allows activists to engage in and implement alternative economic and political practices. "Prefigurative politics," a phrase coined by political scientist Carl Boggs, is the attempt to create "local, collective small-scale organs of socialist democracy" that help to build in the present the forms of social relations, decision making, and culture that are the ultimate goal of political struggle (Boggs 1977, 363).[14] Prefigurative politics is a type of praxis, the ongoing dialogue between theory and practice, and action and reflection. It is the act of taking an idea and making it a reality, and then allowing that reality to transform the original idea. Prefigurative politics, in particular, is the act of taking a utopian idea—for example, local communities' self-governance—and attempting to implement this utopian vision in a concrete context, what Erik Olin Wright (2010) refers to as "real utopias." The key to praxis, however, is allowing that experimentation to shape the theory, the broader utopian vision.

Generally, it is assumed that prefigurative politics is only possible outside of the state sphere, where movements have more autonomy to implement their social vision. However, I argue that activists can also prefigure components of their social vision within state institutions, despite the contradictory aspects of this process. The concept of "co-governance-prefiguration" represents this link between activists' daily participation in a variety of state institutions and their attempt to implement (or at least begin to practice implementing) alternative social and economic ideals in those institutions. This strategy of working with, in, and through the state is different than activists simply exerting influence on state officials through institutional access. Rather, this strategy involves activists becoming part of the state sphere while also maintaining their connection and loyalty to a mobilized movement.

Understanding this interplay between disruptive protest and institutional participation is particularly important in Latin America, where there is a rich history of participatory democracy. Leonardo Avritzer (2002) argues that traditional theories of democracy cannot account for the new institutional forms that developed in Latin America in the 1970s and 1980s, when activists both demanded new types of relationships with the state, which included direct avenues for participation and influence, but also defended the autonomy of their organizations in relationship to the state (99). Evelina Dagnino (1998) describes these developments as a shift from a classical Marxist perspective among left organizations, which saw the state as a "consolidation of power relations and the specific locus of domination in society" (35), to a Gramscian perspective of power as a "relationship among social forces that must be transformed" (37). Thus, in Brazil in the 1980s, the MST was only one of the many political organizations and social movements that became inspired by Gramscian ideas (Coutinho 2013). Dagnino refers to these shifts as the "new citizenship" that emerged as popular sectors demanded the democratic control of the state through direct participation.

In Brazil, the formation of the left-leaning Workers' Party (PT) in 1980 was itself a product of those participatory demands, as the combative union movement and urban and rural social movements structured the party to be accountable to grassroots decision making (Keck 1992). Another primary example of new institutional forms was participatory budgeting, a social movement demand, first implemented by a PT administration in the southern city of Porto Alegre (Abers 2000; Baiocchi 2005; Wampler 2007). Participatory budgeting "empowered local citizenry, fostered new activism in civil society, and created a novel form of coordination across the state-civil society divide" (Baiocchi 2005, 3). Not only did participatory budgeting expand rapidly across Latin America (Baiocchi, Heller, and Silva 2011; Gibson 2019; Goldfrank 2011; Hetland 2014), similar forms of institutionalized civil society participation developed in other spheres, including water basin councils, housing and health councils, and national policy conferences (Abers and Keck 2009; Abers and Keck 2013; Cornwall and Schattan Coelho 2007; Donaghy 2013). Gianpaolo Baiocchi (2005) argues that these participatory initiatives require a new "language for exposing relations across society and the state . . . and how social movements themselves can come to change the state" (17–18).

The MST's demand to participate in educational governance is part of this broader trend of participatory experiments across Brazil and Latin America, which I reference throughout the empirical chapters. However, in contrast to most of the literature on participatory democracy, in this book I discuss how a single social movement takes advantage of universal calls for participation to promote particular social and economic goals. The MST's ability to transform public schools over the past thirty years has always been contingent on a simultaneous combination of disruption, persuasion, negotiation, and co-governance. Once MST leaders institutionalize components of their educational goals within the state sphere, the mobilization of the movement's base is necessary to defend these gains. Therefore, the MST is continually engaging in *contentious co-governance*: overseeing and managing public institutions in coordination with state actors, while simultaneously engaging in contentious political actions and promoting practices within these institutions in direct conflict with the state's own interests. Again, this builds on Gramsci's theory of hegemony and the recognition that civil society is an ambiguous sphere that both protects the state from attack and is a terrain on which resistance is organized. Importantly, this framework helps theorize a movement's entrance into the state sphere as a contradictory process, which sometimes results in the absorption of activists' precious energy, but not as co-optation.

Government Ideology, State Capacity, and Collective Leadership

Finally, the book's third argument is that social movements can participate in the contentious co-governance of state institutions in diverse political

Table I.1 BARRIERS AND CATALYSTS TO THE MST'S CONTENTIOUS
CO-GOVERNANCE OF PUBLIC EDUCATION

		Political Orientation of the Government			
		Left-leaning		Right-leaning	
	High	Best context for co-governance	Many opportunities for co-governance	Difficult context for co-governance	Many opportunities for co-governance
Social Movement Infrastructure	**Low**	Difficult context for co-governance	Difficult context for co-governance	Difficult context for co-governance	Difficult context for co-governance
		High	**Low**	**High**	**Low**
		State Capacity for Educational Governance			

and economic contexts, including under extremely right-wing and conservative governments. In Part Two, I compare five school systems where the MST has had a strong presence, but where there has been a diversity of educational outcomes. [15] Based on this regional comparison, I find that activists' ability to participate in and transform public education hinges upon the interaction of three factors: the political orientation of the government, state capacity, and social movement infrastructure. Table I.1 shows how these three factors influence outcomes; in the Conclusion, I reproduce this table (as Table C.1), illustrating how each of the regional cases explored in Part Two map onto this framework.

Political Orientation of the Government

Unsurprisingly, the political orientation or ideology of the government directly influences a social movement's ability to engage the state and transform public institutions. This point builds on a long tradition of literature that examines how opportunities in the political arena, what is often referred to as the political opportunity structure, influences mobilization, organization, and eventual outcomes (Amenta 2006; Amenta et al. 2010; McAdam 1999; D. S. Meyer 2004; D. S. Meyer and Minkoff 2004). Although scholars most often analyze political openings at the level of the nation state,[16] in the case of Brazil's federal system, there are multiple access points for activists to engage the state at both the national and subnational level. Amenta et al. (2010) argue that "To secure new benefits, challengers will typically need help or complementary action from like-minded state actors" (298). Similarly, I find that the political ideology of the subnational government directly affects the availability of political opportunities, including access for participation and the presence of influential allies. In Brazil, left-leaning governments tend to be more open to the MST, as the movement has a close relationship to the left-leaning Workers' Party (PT). In contrast, right-leaning governments are most often openly antagonistic toward the movement.

State Capacity

Nonetheless, it was not simply the rise to power of the PT that allowed MST activists to participate in the public educational sphere. State capacity is the second factor that influences the movement's ability to engage in contentious co-governance. As I outlined earlier, in this book I am drawing on a Gramscian theory of the state, understood as a complex of social relations in which ruling classes maintain power by promoting their particular class interests as the general national interest, through both ideology and material concessions. From this perspective, the state is not simply an entity that possesses a monopoly on the legitimate use of physical force (Weber 1919), which can be seized. Rather, the state should be understood as an integral state, both including and forming civil society. The state is simultaneously a set of institutions, agencies, and people, as well as a messy and contested process of governing, or maintaining hegemony.

The capacity of different national and subnational states to implement intended policy goals differs drastically across Brazil and directly affects the movement's ability to participate in state institutions. Here, again, I am making a distinction between the government—the political actors who hold electoral power at any particular moment—and the state. Theda Skocpol (1985) argues that it is necessary to "explore the 'capacities of states' to implement official goals, especially over the actual or potential opposition of powerful social groups or in the face of recalcitrant socioeconomic circumstances" (9). In addition, different spheres of the state—for example, education and health versus defense—will have different capacities for policy implementation.[17]

I do not engage in a detailed discussion of the historical conditions that increase the state's capacity to pursue policy goals.[18] However, I do identify the subnational state's capacity to oversee the public education system—in terms of building the necessary school infrastructure, paying teachers adequate salaries and offering them professional development opportunities, retaining competent administrators, developing curriculum, and efficiently organizing student and parent participation—as a central factor influencing the possibilities for social movements to implement their educational vision. I refer to states' ability (or inability) to pursue intended policy goals in the educational sphere as high (or low) state capacity for educational governance. I argue that if a left-leaning administration is in power, then state capacity facilitates social movement participation; however, a right-leaning administration can use the same capacity of the state to opposite ends. If the state has a low capacity for governance, then the political orientation of the government is less determining of state–movement interactions.

Social Movement Infrastructure

The third factor that influences the MST's ability to participate in the public school system is the movement's own internal capacity, what Andrews (2004) refers to as "social movement infrastructure." Social movement infrastructure includes movements' access to resources, internal organizational structure, and the development of robust leadership. Although large mobilizations, protests, sit-ins, and other collective actions—what Charles Tilly (2008) calls "contentious performances"—are critical for social movements to win concessions from the state (Piven and Cloward 1977), social movement infrastructure is necessary to sustain movements.[19] Thus, the focus on internal movement capacity is a shift away from only examining levels of protest and mobilization, to a deeper understanding of what movements do when they are out of the public spotlight.

Leadership is one of the most critical components of social movement infrastructure. Surprisingly, as Marshall Ganz and Elizabeth McKenna (2018) note, leadership is not a central focus of most social movement studies. Yet, for those who participate in movements, it is clear that leadership is a central component of creating and sustaining mobilization. For example, developing local leadership was a central goal of what Charles Payne (1997) refers to as the "community organizing" tradition of the civil rights movement. Ganz (2018) defines leadership as "accepting responsibility to enable others to achieve shared purpose in the face of uncertainty" (quoted in Ganz and McKenna, 2018). In this study I focus on the development of *collective* leadership, or the extent to which movements can convince diverse and dispersed actors to take on the movement's political and economic goals and daily tasks as their own.

Gramsci's concept of the organic intellectual is helpful in conceptualizing collective leadership development within social movements. Influential movement leaders are organic intellectuals, not based on an official status they have as intellectuals in society, but because they (1) engage in the same economic activity of a given community; and (2) hold moral and intellectual leadership—that is, expansive influence—in those communities. In contrast to most social movements, the MST encompasses a very specific community, or grassroots base of families that have won land through land reform. Although not all families that win land rights remain connected to the movement—as Wendy Wolford (2010) has described in detail—the MST leadership is continually trying to link these families to the movement's broader political struggle. The MST is what Bernardo Mançano Fernandes (2005) has called a socio-territorial movement—attempting to transform entire geographical "spaces" and make them their own "territories" (30). While the boundaries of a settlement define a particular area, the MST's goal is to transform all of the social and economic relations in that territory; however, at any given moment, only a percentage of families are active in or sympathetic to the movement. There are also other actors constantly disputing those territories, such as the Evangelical church and agribusiness lobbies. For these reasons, Wolford (2010) argues that social movements should be seen as "competing discourses negotiating for the rights and ability to define who will represent the poor and how" (10).

From this perspective, social movements are not united and coherent entities with clear borders, but rather groups of core leaders, or organic intellectuals, who are constantly attempting to garner the consent of civil society to support their political and economic goals. Movement leaders are constantly in a dispute with other social groups for this moral and intellectual leadership, attempting to engage people's "common sense" and draw out the "good sense,"[20] which can serve as the basis for a common critique of capitalism and a justification for new forms of social relations. The concept of movement leaders as organic intellectuals highlights the subjective process of building the collective consciousness necessary to integrate people into these struggles, what McAdam (1999) has also referred to as "cognitive liberation."[21]

Throughout this book, I refer to MST leaders and activists interchangeably, to indicate people who self-identify not only as benefactors of the movement but also as active and often full-time participants. Being an MST leader (*militante*) does not simply mean participating in a protest, but rather identifying as part of the movement's collective struggle for land, agrarian reform, and social transformation. More practically, being an MST leader means participating in one of the movement's many regional and statewide collective leadership bodies (see Fig. 1.6 in Chapter 1). The MST's ultimate goal is to have every person living in a settlement or camp integrated into these leadership collectives; however, in reality, the cohesiveness of the MST's local leadership varies widely across Brazil, thus influencing the strength of its local social movement infrastructure. As I describe (particularly in Chapter 5), MST mobilization and leadership development are intimately linked, and it is difficult to have one without the other. Both collective leadership and mobilization are critical for MST leaders to be able to implement their educational proposal in and co-govern the public school system.

In summary, as Table I.1 illustrates, the best context for the MST's contentious co-governance of public education is under a left-leaning government, when there is a high level of state capacity for educational governance and a robust social movement infrastructure.[22] Nevertheless, the regional cases in this book illustrates that it is not necessary to have a supportive or left-leaning government for social movement co-governance. States with low levels of capacity for educational governance, independent of political leaning, may also be open to collaborating with movement activists in administering schools. In these contexts, governments with diverse political ideologies support the MST's educational initiatives because it avoids conflict and improves the quality of education. However, if a state is both hostile toward a movement and well resourced, it can effectively block activist participation. This provides a twist on the participatory democracy literature, showing how high state capacity can both catalyze and block civil society participation in the state sphere.

Finally, even when a left-leaning government is in power with a high level of capacity to implement policy goals, if the MST does not have its own internal capacity or local infrastructure to keep up with the rapid pace of reform, these state-led initiatives will tend to drift away from the original intentions. This underscores the importance of leadership in activists' ability to engage the state or, in Gramscian terms, capacity to garner the intellectual and moral leadership of diverse civil society actors—from settlement families to local government officials, university professors, and the wider rural community. The take-home point here is that movements can participate in and transform state institutions under a variety of conditions, with shifting strategies for political engagement, but the essential precondition is the mobilization, internal coherence, and local infrastructure of the movement itself. All of these arguments become clearer as we dive into the empirical cases.

THE TRANSFORMATIVE POTENTIALS
OF EDUCATIONAL STRUGGLE

While I discuss, broadly, how social movements engage formal institutions to support their political and economic goals, I examine these developments in one particular state sphere: the public education system. In this section, I explain why the education system is a particularly powerful state institution for social movements to garner influence. First, I outline the other types of educational initiatives that have been the focus of most social movement research, and why formal education has often been left out of the discussion. Then, I make an argument for how activists' attempt to offer formal educational access—public schools and other state-recognized educational programs—contributes to the long-term capacity of the movement.

Social movements incorporating alternative educational practices within their organizing efforts is not a new development. These initiatives can be divided into three broad categories: informal, nonformal, and formal educational practices. Informal education is the pedagogical experience of being part of a movement, the learning that comes from participating in a protest, joining a march, or coming to a collective decision in a meeting (Choudry 2015; Choudry and Kapoor 2010). There is an expansive literature that discusses these important forms of social movement learning (Hall and Turray 2006; Holst 2001). Nonformal educational practices are the opportunities for intentional study, reflection, and analysis that many movements offer, which can range from one-day seminars to several-months-long courses. In Latin America these nonformal educational practices, referred to as popular education, are frequently linked to the educational theories of Paulo Freire ([1968] 2000). Freire offered both a critique of traditional schooling practices and a theory for how to draw on the knowledge of oppressed groups to develop a collective political consciousness (*conscientização*[23]), in order to take action and combat political and economic inequality.[24]

In the MST, nonformal educational practices are referred to as *formação* (political training). Since the first land occupations in the southern regions of Brazil, the MST has promoted nonformal education among its leadership through study groups and courses at the movement's *escolas da formação* (political training schools). Statewide MST leadership bodies are responsible for organizing political education for people who have recently joined the movement; these courses allow new activists to learn about the major theories and practices that drive the MST's struggle. In addition, one of the movement's organizing principles is that all leaders, even seasoned activists, should be studying, either in formal education programs or in nonformal courses—in order to continue developing their intellectual capacity for analysis and critique.

Previous literature on education and social movements has focused primarily on the role of informal educational practices and nonformal education programs (Altenbaugh 1990; Arnove 1986; Delp 2002; Kane 2001; Payne and Strickland 2008; Perlstein 1990; Torres 1991). In contrast, in this book, I examine how engaging in the contentious co-governance of formal education serves as a generative sphere for movements to build internal capacity and social influence. Formal education takes place in public and private schooling institutions and educational programs that are recognized by the state and result in a diploma that has symbolic power in society. The role that schooling institutions play in both social reproduction and social transformation is a long-standing debate in the social sciences and among political activists. For critical educational theorists, formal educational institutions are most often associated with the reproduction of deeply embedded class, racial, and gender inequalities (Althusser 1984; Anyon 1997; Apple 2004; Bourdieu and Passeron 1990; Bowles and Gintis 1976). This perspective is often traced back to Marxist philosopher Louis Althusser (1984), who argued that the educational apparatus had replaced the Church as the most important institution for reproducing capitalist relations. Samuel Bowles and Herbert Gintis (1976) also contributed to theories of social reproduction by illustrating how the values, norms, and skills taught in schools correspond to those existing in the capitalist workforce. Pierre Bourdieu and Jean-Claude Passeron (1990) discussed schools as sites of social reproduction by introducing the idea of "cultural capital": the rules, relationships, and linguistic and cultural competencies that appear objective while actually representing the values of the dominant class. Together, these theorists offer a convincing argument for why schools in capitalist society function to replicate and deepen inequalities, rather than challenge them.

Nevertheless, from a Gramscian perspective, state institutions are an ambiguous civil society sphere that both protect the state from attack and represent a terrain for organizing resistance. This means that public schools are contradictory institutions that contain both oppressive and liberatory potential. Similarly, education scholars who theorize the state have often noted the limit of any government's control over its educational apparatus. For example, Roger Dale (1989) emphasizes the "inability of governments to effectively institute day-to-day control over every aspect of an apparatus's activities" and, consequently, that "state apparatuses are not directable at will" (33). Dale claims that, in particular, teachers enjoy a high level of autonomy in their classrooms and are not simply state functionaries. Amy Binder (2002) shows how challenger activists, in her cases movements for Afrocentrism and creationism in US school curriculum, attempt to influence bureaucratic decision making. Although school leaders were able to deflect most of these challenger efforts, outcomes varied depending on whether activists' demands resonated with local actors and the particular component of the curriculum that was in dispute. Martin Carnoy and Henry Levin (1985) write that schools are a product of the social conflict arising from two often contradictory educational goals: efficiency in preparing students for the workplace and constructing democratic, participative, and culturally aware citizens (24). Carnoy and Levin argue that the direction of educational policy is dependent on the strength of social movements at any particular historical moment, whose leaders challenge the assumption that schools are "legitimate instruments of social mobility" (108).

More recently, scholars who focus on the intersection of community organizing and educational reform have empirically illustrated this point (Anyon 2005; Mediratta, Fruchter, and Lewis 2002; Mediratta, Shah, and McAlister 2009; Shirley 1997; Su 2009; Warren and Mapp 2011). For example, Mark Warren and Karen Mapp (2011) document how "organizing groups work precisely to build a political constituency for a high-quality and equitable public education system, cultivating the participation and leadership of low-income people themselves in efforts to increase resource for public education and to redress the profound inequities faced by children in low-income communities" (259). Michael Apple (2006, 2013) also offers several concrete examples of how grassroots movements—on both the right and the left—have used educational institutions for political, economic, and cultural ends.[25] However, Apple is clear that the development of these alternative educational models "is best done when it is dialectically and intimately connected to actual movements and struggles" (41). Together, these implicitly Gramscian studies suggest that it is possible for social movements to interrupt social reproduction and link public schools to broader processes of economic and political change.

I argue that there are three reasons formal schools are strategic terrains for social movements to garner influence. First, movements' participation in public schooling can help recruit new activists and, in particular, youth and women to the movement. Public schools and universities are institutions where young people spend many hours each day and are therefore important spaces for investing in local leadership development—increasing students' interest in and capacity for social change. Although most youth initially enter school out of obligation or for their own individual advancement, while they are students in these institutions movement leaders have the opportunity to engage them in discussions about broader political, economic, and social goals. These discussions can also happen in other social movement–led training programs, such as popular education. However, the people who participate in these nonformal educational spaces are often already active supporters or at least sympathetic to the movements. In addition, schools have a steady flow of financial and institutional resources, and already bring together a wide range of community members at no additional cost to the movement. A social movement's participation in formal schooling can help convince youth, who may have never participated in a contentious protest, to become involved in these collective struggles.[26]

By politicizing childcare and education, the movement also opened a pathway for women and gay men to assume leadership roles. Both childcare and education are forms of "reproductive labor"—that is, work that reproduces the waged labor force.[27] Typically, such jobs are lowly remunerated, if at all, and carried out by women. In Brazil, gay men are also overrepresented in certain reproductive jobs such as teaching. This gendered division of labor is often echoed in social movements, in which women's unrecognized domestic labor facilitates male activists' participation in more public actions, such as protests and marches. As I will go on to describe, female MST activists recognized this gender imbalance from the very first occupations in the early 1980s. They thus demanded that their labor to provide childcare and education become a central part of the movement's struggle. Educational activism then became a *porta de entrada* (entryway) for women to occupy other movement leadership roles. The educational sector has thus helped the MST develop high levels of participation of women in other spheres of the movement. Similarly, many gay men also found an activist home in the educational sector, where they faced relatively less discrimination than in other heterosexual male-dominated spaces. And since 2011, gay activists have promoted and organized around a "queer landless" identity, an astonishing feat in the deeply homophobic Brazilian countryside.[28] I argue that the education sector was critical for the leadership development of these women and gay men.

Second, access to public education can help working-class activists obtain state-recognized degrees that enhance their power to negotiate with elite actors. As MST educational activist Maria de Jesus Santos explained, "Access to educational programs helped us because before these people [state officials] did not respect us, but when we all began to graduate, and hold higher education degrees, we could debate them as equals."[29] Although the informal learning, popular education, and training that occurs within movements may provide activists with similar opportunities for intellectual development, these courses do not help activists obtain the recognized degree necessary to increase their influence with state actors. State recognition is especially important in the case of professional degrees. Over the past two decades the MST national leadership has been able to access educational programs for local activists to become teachers, lawyers, agricultural technicians, and doctors. Once movement activists obtain these degrees, they are able to carry out professional tasks for the movement, reducing its reliance on outside experts. For example, the MST has sent over two hundred of its leaders to obtain medical degrees from Cuba, and now there is a large collective of MST activist-doctors who take care of health issues in the movement's settlements and camps. Similarly, hundreds of MST leaders are employed as teachers in schools on MST settlements or have been hired by state governments as technicians for the movement's agricultural cooperatives. These professional positions allow activists to sustain themselves economically, while also contributing to the movement's development and sustainability.[30]

Third, public schools are important locations where social movements can begin to prefigure, in the current world, the social practices that they hope to build in the future. For example, the MST's educational interventions are explicit attempts to prefigure in schools the decision-making processes, collective work practices, and agricultural production that the movement's leaders also promote in their communities.[31] The movement learns how to prefigure these alternative practices by building what Wright (2010) refers to as "real utopias": "utopian designs of institutions that can inform our practical tasks for navigating a world of imperfect conditions for social change" (6). In the MST's case, these practices include building social relations based on solidarity and mutual cooperation, developing collective work processes, creating cultural performances that respect peasant traditions, farming through agroecological methods, engaging in contentious politics, and of course, practicing participatory democracy. It is often difficult for the MST leadership to ensure that the families on agrarian reform settlements implement all of these practices, as a range of religious, political, and economic actors shape the development of these communities. However, if movements can develop a degree of influence in the public schools, then these state institutions can become real educational utopias—important examples for these communities that another world is possible. Again, as schools consume so much time from so many people and participation in schools is generally universal and obligatory, these institutions are important spheres for building real utopias. Transforming public schools thus becomes both a goal and a means of promoting social change.

STUDYING THE LONG MARCH: POLITICAL ETHNOGRAPHY, COMPARISON, AND POSITIONALITY

The following chapters offer a detailed account of how the MST developed an educational proposal to support its broader political and economic struggle, and how leaders in this movement worked with different state agencies and subnational governments to institutionalize components of this proposal in the formal public school system over the past thirty years. This book is what Javier Auyero and Lauren Joseph (2007) term a "political ethnography," which "look[s] microscopically at the foundations of political institutions and their attendant sets of practices ... [and] explain[s] why political actors behave the way they do to identify the causes, processes, and outcomes that are part and parcel of political life" (Auyero and Joseph 2007, 1). I explore both the contentious politics of mobilizations, occupations, and other noninstitutionalized actions and the everyday politics of backroom deals, state-civil society advisory boards, and teacher meetings. My goal is to understand how a social movement has been able to lead an expansive process of institutional change, with the broader goal of transforming society. Consequently, although the focus of my research is on the MST, I also spent half of my time shadowing and interviewing state actors, in order to highlight the dynamic relationship that exists between states and movements.

The comparative case study method is also a central part of the research design, as I analyze the factors that influence MST activists' impact on public education in different locations across the country. The MST is ideal for this case comparison, as it is a national movement, regionally dispersed, with activists attempting to implement similar pedagogical practices across the country, but with extremely different outcomes. Previous studies of the MST's educational struggles have either focused on one-off cases or national summaries (Arroyo 2004; Meek 2015; Souza 2002). My study, in contrast, provides the first systematic cross-regional comparison of the MST's

Picture I.2 A student from the municipality of Santa Maria da Boa Vista, Pernambuco, paints the walls of the Ministry of Education in protest during the VI National MST Congress in Brasília. Her sign reads, "Little Landless Children in Struggle." February 2014.
Courtesy of author (with permission from student and her family)

thirty-year educational struggle. As Andrews (2004) writes, the "insight—that movements are neither monolithic nor uniform in their distribution, strength, or impact—opens up new areas for exploring the outcomes that movements do generate" (20). In other words, exploring differences within movements is potentially more effective in understanding outcomes than comparing several different movements.

Furthermore, the Brazilian state is as diverse as the MST itself, with different levels of institutional capacity and norms in political practice. By focusing on one component of the movement's struggle—education—I am able to highlight some of these state differences and how they influence institutional change. Rather than treat the state as a unitary, coherent, and necessarily antagonistic actor, I analyze the state's heterogeneity and contradictory roles in contentious action. My goal in designing a comparative study, however, is not simply to isolate independent and dependent variables in each field site. Too often, comparative studies attempt to produce what Gillian Hart (2002) refers to as "ideal types," distorting and flattening complex realities by trying to isolate dependent and independent variables. Rather, following Hart's (2002) relational comparison, I examine the interrelationship of events, places, and social processes. While I draw lessons from similarities and differences between field sites, I also examine how the actions in one location affect the educational context in another, and how all of these developments are both embedded in and productive of national and international processes.

Most of my research was conducted in five school systems: the state school systems of Rio Grande do Sul, São Paulo, and Ceará, and the municipal school systems of Santa Maria da Boa Vista and Água Preta, in Pernambuco (see Map I.1). I chose locations where there was a concentration of MST settlements—in other words, the movement had been highly mobilized at some point in these areas—but where there were different outcomes in the MST's ability to transform the public school system. Thus, I purposively selected regions that had a baseline of movement activity, but where educational outcomes were quite different. This allowed me to trace the processes that led to these different outcomes, and also take nonevents seriously—by not selecting my cases based on instances of movement success.[32]

My unit of analysis is the state or municipal public school system, because this is where key decisions over policy are made. In Brazil, school systems cover massive swaths of territory, and I sometimes had to travel hundreds of miles to visit schools and government actors in the same bureaucratic jurisdiction. Nonetheless, in terms of my unit of analysis, I treat each school system as a single field site, or case. I also spent time collecting data on the implementation of the MST's educational goals in two federal agencies: the

National Institute of Colonization and Agrarian Reform (INCRA) and the Ministry of Education (MEC). My study of these agencies involved both visits to Brasília and ample research on the local implementation of these federal initiatives. I consider both the five school systems and the two federal agencies distinct case studies of institutionalizing the MST's educational program within the Brazilian state. Table I.2 overviews these seven case studies.

My data collection spanned twenty months, between 2009 and 2015, the majority between October 2010 and December 2011. In total, I spent eight months in Pernambuco (six in Santa Maria da Boa Vista and two in Água Preta), six months in Rio Grande do Sul, three months in São Paulo, two months in Ceará, and one month in Brasília. Although August 2015 was the official end of my data collection, I lived in the city of São Paulo between June 2016 and May 2017 and continued to attend some MST events and stay abreast of the MST's involvement in the major political changes that were taking place. These latter developments are the focus of the Epilogue.

I lived with MST educational leaders during most of the twenty months of research. This became one of the most important components of my data collection, as I was embedded in the day-to-day activities of the movement's educational collectives in each region. I participated in hundreds of informal and formal meetings, witnessed the decision-making processes that led to different political actions, and observed the daily interaction between

Table I.2 CASE STUDIES OF INSTITUTIONALIZING THE MST'S EDUCATIONAL PROGRAM WITHIN THE BRAZILIAN STATE

Case Study	Government Level	Region of Brazil	Focus of Analysis
National Institute of Colonization and Agrarian Reform (INCRA)	Federal agency	Nationally dispersed	National Program for Education in Areas of Agrarian Reform (PRONERA)
Ministry of Education	Federal agency	Nationally dispersed	Programs in the office for *Educação do Campo* in the Department of Diversity
Rio Grande do Sul	State school system	South	Public schools in MST camps and settlements
Ceará	State school system	Northeast	High schools in MST settlements
São Paulo	State school system	Central East	Public schools in MST settlements
Santa Maria da Boa Vista, Pernambuco	Municipal school system	Northeast	Public schools in MST settlements
Água Preta	Municipal school system	Northeast	Public schools in MST settlements

activists, teachers, and community members. I also spent dozens of hours in schools on MST settlements, as a participant observer of the daily activities of teachers, school principals, and students. This enabled me to gather first-hand evidence on indicators of the MST's influence in these schools.

I attended MST-led teacher trainings and educational seminars in each state. These events deepened my understanding of the MST's educational proposal, as the seminars and trainings were organized through the MST's pedagogical approach: collective living, shared work tasks, *mística* (cultural-political performances), and small base groups (*núcleo de base*, or NB) that were spaces of participatory decision making. It was often through these educational seminars that I made contacts with activists and teachers from other states and was able to get a sense of the educational context of MST communities beyond my field sites. I took extensive field notes on all of these experiences—in total, approximately 1,200 single-spaced pages over twenty months of field research.

Another important form of data collection were the 238 in-depth interviews I conducted with MST activists and state actors. The majority of these interviews lasted one and a half hours, while some were shorter and others much longer. Although I designed interview protocols for MST leaders and state officials, I tailored my questions to each person based on their experience and knowledge. These interviewees included sixty-five teachers and principals, fifty-five officials in state and municipal Departments of Education, thirty-one leaders in the MST education sector (although many teachers also fell into this category), seventeen university professors, twelve officials in the Ministry of Education, ten INCRA officials, eight current and ex-mayors, and a couple dozen other people, including members of other social movements and state agencies, MST leaders not involved in education, other prominent politicians, and some students.[33] Through these interviews, I determined the visions MST activists and government actors have for education in rural regions; the key factors that shift these visions; the characteristics of the negotiations between MST education collectives and government actors; the factors that affect these negotiations; the pedagogical practices in schools with different levels of MST influence; and the consequences of these MST practices for students. I use the real names of all elected and appointed government officials and pseudonyms for permanent state employees; I also honored the requests of teachers, principals, and activists who asked that their real names be used, and I have created aliases for those who preferred to remain anonymous.

A third source of data were hundreds of primary and secondary documents. These documents included movement correspondences, government laws and decrees concerning the MST's educational proposal, program textbooks, newspaper articles, magazines, historical archives about local politics, meeting agendas, conference programs, flyers, and activist study texts. Between 1990 and 2010, the MST education sector published approximately eighty-five texts about the movement's educational proposal, totaling more than 4,000 pages. I accessed hard or soft copies of the majority of these texts. I also drew on more than thirty books written about the MST's educational proposal and *Educação do Campo* (Education of the Countryside) by scholars not in the movement. Together, these primary and secondary documents helped to corroborate interviewees' claims, piece together dates and numbers, and compare official reports with the oral accounts of my many informants.

Finally, and importantly, my entry into the field was dependent on the MST's authorization. My initial contact with the MST was through the International Relations Collective (CRI), a group of movement leaders who oversee all of the MST's international relationships, including vetting research requests.[34] When I contacted the CRI about my research project, I was asked to write a justification of my research proposal and how it would contribute to the movement. I emphasized my background as an activist in the United States, and my belief that the MST could teach US social movements much about popular education. I also emphasized that I would be collecting data on both the Brazilian state and the movement, and I hoped that my findings about effective strategies for institutionalizing movement goals within different types of Brazilian states would be of interest to MST leaders. After several months, the CRI granted me permission to study the MST; without a doubt my involvement in US political organizing facilitated this access.[35]

Unlike the MST's centralized process of vetting research requests, obtaining access to state actors involved individually calling, emailing, or simply showing up at the doors of these many officials. I would explain that I was a doctoral student at UC Berkeley, studying social movements and education in the Brazilian countryside. Certainly, my affiliation with a prestigious US university facilitated their belief that I was an important visitor who deserved their attention. In addition, the data I collected as an ethnographic researcher—a researcher of both the Brazilian state and the MST—were always negotiated through my positionality as a young, white woman from the United States. This identity opened many doors throughout my research, and no doubt closed others. For example, it is likely that some state officials critical of the MST assumed from my whiteness and US identity that I was also disapproving of the movement. Alternatively, my US identity often meant that MST activists were initially skeptical of my intentions, and I had to continually earn the trust of local leaders. Nonetheless, I found that my foreignness—and as France Winddance Twine (2000) suggests, my more "authentic" US identity as blond and blue-eyed (17)—was a huge privilege that more often than not facilitated my research access.

OUTLINE OF CHAPTERS

In this introduction, I have outlined the three main arguments of this book: that engaging formal institutions can contribute to the internal capacity of social movements; that combining contentious and institutional tactics, including disruption, persuasion, negotiation, and co-governance is an effective movement strategy; and that the government's political orientation, the state's capacity for educational governance, and most important, a social movement's own internal capacity and infrastructure, condition the possibilities for institutional change. I have argued for an overall Gramscian perspective on social movement–state relations, which views state institutions as an ambiguous sphere that both protects the state from attack and is an arena for organizing resistance. I have also presented some of the basic goals of the MST's agrarian reform struggle, and how the movement's educational proposal is part and parcel of achieving those goals. In particular, I emphasized that engaging the public school system can integrate more youth and women into the movement, equip movement leaders with the professional degrees needed for self-governance, and allow activists to prefigure their social visions. Thus, while I am arguing broadly that the *contentious co-governance* of state institutions can build movements, I am also proposing that public schools are particularly important institutions for social movements to garner influence.

In Part One (Chapters 1–3) of the book, I analyze how local MST leaders developed a pedagogical proposal that supported their economic and social goals, and how they were able to institutionalize this proposal at the federal level. These chapters explore the evolution and expansion of the MST's educational proposal during four periods: dictatorship and political opening (1979–1984); democratic consolidation (1985–1990); neoliberalism and state–society conflict (1990–2002); and social movement participation and class compromise (2003–2013). Chapter 1 discusses the development of the MST's pedagogical approach during the first three periods. In Chapters 2 and 3, I analyze the implementation of the MST's educational program during the latter two periods, in two different federal agencies.

In Chapter 1, I analyze the pedagogical experiments that MST activists developed in the Brazilian countryside in the 1980s and 1990s. In the early 1980s, these educational experiments were largely isolated initiatives in dozens of different camps and settlements. There was room to experiment with pedagogical alternatives even under a dictatorship, partially due to the lack of state presence in these rural areas. In 1987, the MST leadership made education an official concern of the movement and founded the National MST education sector. Then, in the 1990s, MST leaders refined their educational proposal through their own teacher training programs, which became spaces for pedagogical experimentation and the prefiguration of alternative social and political values, what Wright (2010) refers to as "real utopias." These experiments took place under a conservative and antagonistic national government, illustrating the many avenues that exist for the institutionalization of social movement goals. In 1997, the MST published its first national education manifesto, summarizing the different components of its educational program.

Chapter 2 is about the MST's most important educational victory, the National Program for Education in Areas of Agrarian Reform (PRONERA), created in 1998 and put under the auspices of the National Institute of Colonization and Agrarian Reform (INCRA). I analyze the first PRONERA bachelor's degree program, which the MST helped to create, in order to show how the movement's pedagogical approach in this university setting enhanced the political and organizing capacity of the students and integrated them into the movement. I also explore the ways in which the MST's educational vision repeatedly came into conflict with established educational norms, even in a university with progressive and supportive professors. In the second part of the chapter I analyze the expansion of PRONERA and how its structure of triple governance within INCRA has allowed for ample social movement participation. I also describe an attack on this program in 2008, a story which illustrates that the institutionalization of social movement goals has to be constantly defended through contentious mobilization.

Chapter 3 presents a counterexample to PRONERA, illustrating how the institutionalization of movement goals can sometimes look like the process Paschel (2016) refers to as social movement absorption. In the late 1990s and early 2000s, the MST's local educational practices in areas of agrarian reform evolved into a national proposal for an alternative educational approach in the entire Brazilian countryside. This proposal, which became known as *Educação do Campo* (Education of the Countryside), was explicitly linked to an alternative vision of rural development. Between 2004 and 2012 this educational proposal was implemented in the Ministry of Education (MEC) through several laws, an office, and a series of programs. However, I show how the MEC's hierarchical organization, focus on best practices, and need to rapidly expand its educational programs undermined the MST's ability to participate—even with a national government historically aligned with the movement in power. During this period several powerful agribusiness groups also began to embrace the idea of *Educação do Campo* and influence the trajectory of these programs. The argument in this chapter is that although institutionalizing social movement goals can scale-up activists' initiatives, this process can result in more stakeholders laying claim over these programs and a watering down of initial intentions.

The goal of Part Two (Chapters 4–6) is to examine how the MST's regional efforts to transform state and municipal public schools played out in different contexts, during the four conjunctural periods highlighted in Part One. Chapter 4 on Rio Grande do Sul explores the start of the movement's regional engagement with education in the early 1980s, and how this shifted over different political regimes. Chapter 5 on Pernambuco analyzes the MST's attempt to transform public schools beginning in the late 1990s, after the movement had already developed a clear set of pedagogical proposals. Finally, Chapter 6 focuses on the MST's engagement with public schools in Ceará in the late 2000s, in a very different context, when the movement's educational initiatives were already recognized nationally.

In Chapter 4, I describe Rio Grande do Sul as an ideal case of state–movement cooperation, when well-organized MST activists helped a left-leaning PT government take power in a state with a high capacity for educational governance. I also show that once MST leaders institutionalize their proposal they can continue to co-govern these initiatives, even when the state withdraws its financial support. However, in the second part of the chapter, I illustrate that this is still a very fragile relationship, as the right-leaning government that came to power a decade later succeeded in directly attacking these educational programs and weakening the movement. The argument of this chapter is that a combination of disruptive tactics and institutional presence is critical to engaging the state, however, regime type can also directly affect movement outcomes.

In Chapter 5, I discuss the MST's attempt to participate in the public school system in a seemingly worst-case scenario: the pervasively clientelistic municipalities in rural Pernambuco. The goal is to offer a contrast to the previous chapter, arguing that regime type is not necessarily important in the context of states with low levels of capacity for educational governance. In the case of Santa Maria da Boa Vista, the MST's own increasing capacity for educational governance convinced multiple clientelistic regimes that it was worthwhile to collaborate with the movement. The second part of this chapter presents the case of Água Preta, which highlights the most important factor that determines social movement outcomes: the MST's own social movement infrastructure. Most important, a robust social movement infrastructure requires the integration of diverse civil society actors into local, collective leadership bodies. In this case, while the same political opportunities are open in Água Preta as in Santa Maria da Boa Vista, the internal divides within the settlements in Água Preta prevent local leadership development and thus hamstring activists' ability to participate in the public schools.

Finally, in Chapter 6, I bring together these different arguments and analyze one of the MST's most impressive examples of institutionalizing its goals in the educational sphere: the construction of a network of high schools on MST settlements in the state of Ceará in 2009 and 2010. Chapter 6 shows how the national context, while not determining of the regional trajectories, directly influences local relations between movement activists and local state actors. I describe this case as an example of Margaret Keck and Kathryn Sikkink's (1998) boomerang effect, in which a conservative government agrees to work with the MST due to increasing external pressure. As a counterpoint, I briefly mention how the state of São Paulo was able to deflect this national advocacy, illustrating that high capacity states can still override the influence of national trends. This chapter also shows the evolution of the MST's pedagogical practice, and what the movement's educational program looks like in the contemporary context.

I conclude by reflecting on the significance of the MST's educational initiatives for understanding states, social movements, and education. I revisit the theoretical claims I make in the introduction and explain why the study helps us to understand how activists' long march through the institutions sustains their movements. I also outline the exact mechanisms that facilitated the MST's ability to lead this massive process of institutional change. I end by noting the implications of this study for understanding social movements' contentious co-governance of state institutions in Latin America and globally. In the Epilogue, I reflect on the future of the MST's political struggle—and that of the Brazilian left more broadly—in the context of the 2016 ousting of the Workers' Party (PT) from the federal government and the 2018 presidential election of ultra-right conservative Jair Bolsonaro. Although we are living through a moment when global politics seems increasingly bleak, I hope these chapters can still serve as an indicator of the possibility, and indeed increasing urgency, to build mass, grassroots movements with savvy disruptive and institutional strategies.

PART ONE

Constructing a National Educational Program

CHAPTER 1

Pedagogical Experiments in the Brazilian Countryside

When people ask us, "What pedagogy does the MST follow?" we should respond that the MST does not follow a pedagogy; the MST has a pedagogy!
　　　　　—Maria de Jesus Santos, *national leader in MST Education Sector*
In the MST, your life, your family depends on the movement. . . . This is the Pedagogy of the MST.
　　　　　—Rosali Caldart, *national leader in MST Education Sector*

The Brazilian countryside is a space of contradictions. Representing one of Brazil's most important economic resources, it is also a territory of poverty, exploitation, and concentrated economic and political power. Historically, the Brazilian countryside has been controlled by local strongmen, colonels (*coronéis*), who owned vast areas of land and ruled these territories with an iron fist. Education for rural workers, if it existed, was dependent on the goodwill of local landlords, who would sometimes set up one-room schoolhouses for their workers' children. Over the past half-century, the Brazilian state has promoted agricultural modernization and industrialization, most often built on the back of poor rural wage laborers. With industrialization, the government also began to invest more in public services, including education; however, these resources were concentrated in urban areas. Although subnational governments maintained some public schools in the countryside, these schools had crumbling infrastructures, minimal resources, and mostly unqualified teachers, leading to a precarious rural education system that symbolized the state's abandonment of its rural populations.

Nonetheless, throughout Brazilian history the countryside has also been a place of resistance and struggle, with slave revolts, peasant leagues, and land struggles characterizing these rural regions. The strength of this rural resistance, including the literacy circles that were established throughout the poor northeastern part of the country, is one of the major reasons that elite and middle-class sectors supported the 1964 military coup. Although the military regime violently repressed rural activists, political organizing in the countryside continued throughout the dictatorship, often through clandestine communist organizations or under the auspices of progressive clergy in the Catholic Church. Then, in the early 1980s, rural organizing returned with a renewed force, leading to the founding of the Brazilian Landless Workers Movement (MST) in 1984.

In this chapter, I analyze the MST's early history and first decade as an established organization, as these broader economic and political changes took place across the country. I highlight three conjunctural periods–the coming together of broad political and economic developments–that characterize these moments: dictatorship and political opening (1978–1984); democratic consolidation (1985–1989); and neoliberalism and state–society conflict (1990–1996). First, I describe the land occupations that took place in the late 1970s and early 1980s, still during a period of military dictatorship, and how these early occupations led to the MST's founding in 1984. Next, I highlight how the MST developed its internal participatory structure over the following five years, as democracy consolidated in Brazil. Finally, as the country shifted in the 1990s toward a period of neoliberal economic policy and state–society conflict, I examine the MST's expansion, its national decision-making structure, and the evolution of the movement's three goals for land reform, agrarian reform, and social transformation.

Although much of this history has been written before, in this chapter I focus on an untold part of the story[1]: how MST leaders developed and institutionalized educational practices that reinforced and pushed forward their social vision. For each historical period, I analyze the evolution of the MST's engagement with education and schooling. This chapter illustrates the reflective relationship between Brazil's national context, the MST's evolution and expansion, and the movement's educational program. This chapter also shows how the story of a well-known social movement can look quite different, when examining a particular aspect of the movement. Specifically, by analyzing the evolution of the MST's education sector, I highlight the voices of the many women in the movement who were active during this early period, but who were not participants in prestigious decision-making bodies. As tasks were divided up in the occupied encampments and settlements, women often ended up responsible for childcare. These women organized on the basis of what Alvarez (1990) has referred to as women's practical gender interests, creatively transforming childcare and schooling into spaces that could support the MST's broader goals.

Finally, this chapter also shows how movement leaders can take advantage of the multifaceted state and implement their educational proposal in various institutional spheres, even during a period of dictatorship and intense state-society conflict. Local MST leaders were able to put their educational goals into practice by collectively monitoring the public schools in their communities. Then, after making education a national priority within the movement, MST leaders obtained the state's approval to establish their own educational institutions. These schooling spaces became what Wright (2010) calls "real utopias," which allowed MST leaders to "envision the contours of an alternative social world that embodies emancipatory ideals" (9). The institutions offered local activists both formal degrees and the opportunity to prefigure the MST's economic and political vision. Thus, this chapter illustrates the role that education can play in helping local activists learn about and practice alternative social and economic arrangements, and how these types of experiments can take place under antagonistic political regimes. The story of the MST's educational initiatives begins in the early 1980s; however, before describing this educational history, I offer a brief overview of Brazil's agrarian context leading up to this period.

BACKGROUND: THE BRAZILIAN
AGRARIAN CONTEXT

Landlessness in Brazil dates back to the early years of Portuguese colonialism in the 1500s. In 1536, King John III of Portugal (reign 1521–1557) divided the imense territory of his South American colony into 15 large tracts of land called *capitanias hereditárias*, which were donated to nobles trusted by the King. These were then subdivided into smaller areas known as *sesmarias* that were distributed to other colonists and conquerors who were supposed to cultivate this land. In many cases the beneficiaries did not cultivate the land, which led to these lands being occupied by small farmers and squatters who planted and harvested on the land but did not have land titles. After Brazilian independence (1822), this private land was supposed to be given back to the Brazilian state, as returned land (*terra devoluta*). However, through land grabbing and the production of false land deeds—known as *grilagem*[2]— local elites ensured that they could maintain ownership over their land, and also claimed the rights to indigenous territories throughout the country. In 1850, a new land law went into effect that made land available only through purchase. This law facilitated the consolidation of large-scale properties, made it difficult for small landholders to purchase land, and tightened restrictions on squatter communities (Wolford 2010b, 39).

Landlessness in Brazil is also a legacy of slavery, the largest slave trade in the Americas, only ending in 1888.[3] This legacy left a large population of landless Afro-Brazilians, especially in the northeastern region, where plantation owners used enslaved Africans and African-descenents for sugarcane production. The enslavement of Africans and African-descenents was also a labor practice throughout the country, not only in the sugar cane or coffee plantations for export, but also in the production of food for domestic consumption and in other economic activities. In the south of Brazil, there is a large white landless population, descendants of European immigrants who arrived beginning in the 1860s. Some of these immigrants received land plots, often too small for subsequent generations, while others were forced into exploitative labor relations and have always been landless (Wolford 2010b, 41).

Agricultural production was the most important motor of the Brazilian economy until the early twentieth century, with sugarcane dominating most of this period and coffee and milk becoming increasingly prominent in the late nineteenth century, especially in the southeast region.[4] In 1930, however, populist President Getúlio Vargas won a political contest against the coffee barons and began to implement policies to support industrialization, accelerating the rate of urbanization and decreasing slightly the political power of agricultural elites (Ondetti 2008, 11). In 1937, Vargas established an authoritarian regime known as the New State (*Estado Novo*), justified as a response to the threat of Communist Party organizing.[5] Vargas was known as the Father of the Poor for his social welfare programs, but he also established a system of union representation that ensured the state's control of workers. Industrialization and rural-to-urban migration continued. In 1945, Vargas announced the return of democratic elections and the Constitution of 1946 was passed, which stated that private land could be expropriated if it was not being used for social well-being; this ideal, however, remained "words on a page" (Ondetti 2008, 11).

During the late 1950s and early 1960s, there was a dramatic rise of rural mobilization, with tenant farmers in the northeast forming peasant leagues, the emergence of a landless movement in the south,[6] and rural workers' associations, radical literacy campaigns,[7] and other organizing efforts throughout the country. Two competing organizations, the Brazilian Communist Party (PCB) and the Catholic Church, were responsible for most of the mobilization. Protests were part of a broader trend of social unrest throughout Brazil, which led the president to resign in 1961. Left-leaning Vice President João Goulart became president and two years later Congress passed a Statute on Rural Labor, which legalized rural unions but also required that all rural unions be part of a new national labor confederation, the National Confederation of Agricultural Workers (CONTAG, discussed in Chapter 3). President Goulart also proposed the implementation of a national program for agrarian reform. These events scared middle-class wage earners, industrial sectors, and foreign investors, giving the military the support it needed for the 1964 military coup.

The military dictatorship in Brazil lasted for twenty years, during which the peasant leagues and other rural movements of the 1960s were destroyed, communist organizing had to go underground, and most other political mobilization was suppressed. Immediately after taking power, and in response to the rural unrest, the military regime passed a Land Statute that was extremely progressive on paper and emphasized land as a social good;[8] however, the law was "left vague enough to avoid any real responsibility for expropriation" (Wolford 2010b, 45); consequently, land concentration remained firmly in place. Nonetheless, the Land Statute laid the legal groundwork for the land occupations that began two decades later.

In 1965, the government implemented a two-party system, with the pro-military National Renovating Alliance (ARENA) and the opposition Brazilian Democratic Movement (MDB) parties—an attempt to feign a semblance of democracy. Although the first military president supported some freedoms, the regime took a more repressive stance during the late 1960s. In 1968, in an attempt to quell student rebellions, trade union activism, opposition groups in Congress, and more than anything else, the multiple guerilla organizations resisting the miltiary dictatorship, the regime approved the Fifth Institutional Act (AI-5), dissolving Congress, suspending the constitution, and declaring crimes against national security subject to military justice (Skidmore 2010). In 1969, a military hardliner became the president and used the AI-5 to implement policies that made torture commonplace and stamped out all of the remaining political opposition, resulting in hundreds of state assassinations and "disapeared" people throughout the country.

The first decade of the military dictatorship was also a period of rapid industrialization.[9] This so-called economic miracle was part of a state-led development strategy, which involved an alliance among local private entrepreneurs, multinational corporations, and state-owned enterprises (Evans 1979). These policies increased the uneven regional development that had characterized the first part of the twentieth century and created an even bigger divide between the rich and the poor. The military regime also invested in agrarian industrialization through subsidized credit to agribusinesses and the incorporation of new technologies, what became known as the green revolution.[10] Rapid agrarian development and technological change pushed thousands of people out of the agricultural workforce and, together with the expansion of the urban industrial sector, led to a sharp increase in rural-to-urban migration.[11] The outskirts of cities became expansive slums (*favelas*) with people living in shacks without water, electricity, or sewage disposal. The government essentially abandoned the population that remained in the countryside.

DICTATORSHIP AND POLITICAL OPENING
(1974–1984)

The first land occupations in the late 1970s, which eventually led to the founding of the Brazilian Landless Workers Movement (MST), were a response to these broader political and economic developments. In 1974, the military regime began a policy of political liberalization known as decompression (*distensão*), driven by a search for domestic and international legitimacy, as communism was becoming a less credible threat to national security and economic downturn had decreased the regime's popularity.[12] Among other consequences, the reforms increased the power of the opposition party and also led to a surge of political organizing around human rights. In 1977, the first student demonstrations in a decade erupted, as the military regime tried to backtrack on these political freedoms with a series of restrictions known as the "April packages" (Mische 2008). Then, in 1978, autoworkers in the industrial São Paulo region organized a series of strikes, garnering national attention. One of the most prominent leaders of this oppositional labor movement was Luis Inácio Lula da Silva, more commonly known as Lula, who would become president two and a half decades later. The labor unrest that erupted quickly spread to other states and worker groups.[13] Black organizers, who felt class-based movements did not focus enough on racial equality, came together to found the United Black Movement (MNU) in 1978 (Paschel 2016). Women were also mobilizing in the urban peripheries, creating groups ranging from self-help mothers clubs to radical, feminist movements (Alvarez 1990).

The Catholic Church played a particularly critical role in these mobilizations in the mid- and late 1970s. Traditionally in Latin America, Catholic priests were involved in charity projects, such as food drives, but were not involved in more political projects (Berryman 1987, 15). During the 1960s, religious leaders began developing a theology of liberation based on a preferential option for the poor: a shift in the Catholic Church to focus on improving the lives of poor populations. Priests following liberation theology began engaging working-class populations in discussions about poverty and power through local study groups, known as base ecclesial communities (CEBs). These CEBs were organized as traditional bible study groups, but the study was based in workers' own experiences and their ability to take political actions to improve their communities (Berryman 1987, 36). Many of these CEBs were inspired by the educational ideas elaborated in Paulo Freire's *Pedagogy of the Oppressed* ([1969] 2000). By 1981, there were 80,000 CEBs throughout Brazil (Moreira 1985, 177). The mere quantity and diffusion of CEBs, even during a period of dictatorship, was an indication of the church's capacity to influence and mobilize poor populations—through nonformal, grassroots educational initiatives.

Rural Organizing and the First Land Occupations

In 1975, the Catholic Church founded the Pastoral Commission on Land (CPT) to help defend the rights of rural workers. Initially, the work of the CPT was concentrated in the Amazon region; however, during the late 1970s progressive priests and nuns began to form chapters in other regions (Ondetti 2008, 54). The organizational and ideological support of the Church proved critical to the wave of land occupations that spread across the southern part of Brazil in the early 1980s.

One of the first land occupations took place in 1979, organized by primarily white, European-descendant families in the southernmost state of Brazil, Rio Grande do Sul. Although many of these European immigrants had received land when they arrived to Brazil, their adult children were considered landless as the 10–20 hectares (25–50 acres) of land they received was not considered sufficient to support their children's families.[14] Approximately 270,000 of these landless families were looking for a way to survive during the first decade of the military regime (Branford and Rocha 2002). The military regime had attempted to relocate the families to the sparsely populated Amazon Basin, but this colonization plan largely failed because of the rough living conditions, lack of health and sanitation services, and the settlers' inability to adapt to the region (Wolford 2010b, 45). By the mid-1970s, thousands of families in the south began accessing land by invading Indian reservations, an illegal act that the government chose to ignore (Branford and Rocha 2002, 6). This illustrated both the disregard many poor Brazilians had for indigenous territorial rights, and how the government's refusal to address land concentration often pitted different marginalized populations against each other.[15]

Of these thousands of families, two thousand were living on the Nonoaí reserve of the Kaingang Indians. On May 4, 1978, after protesting to the authorities for over ten years, the Kaingang Indians declared war against the settlers and expelled them from their land. A group of CPT religious leaders met with the landless families and offered their support to the settlers. At this first meeting an employee of the state Department of Agriculture, João Pedro Stédile, was also present (Ondetti 2008, 67). João Pedro would soon become one of the most important MST national leaders. The priests, nuns, and other allies began to discuss with the landless families the possible actions they could take, including the occupation of a large, unproductive land estate in the region. Ironically, religious leaders based their right to occupy this land on the military government's 1964 Land Statute, which designated land as a social good.

On September 7, 1979, 110 of the families expelled from the Nonoaí reservation occupied the unproductive plantation (*fazenda*) Macali, setting up make-shift tents and refusing to leave the area. After a year of resisting police eviction and an outpouring of public support, the state government agreed to give the families the rights to this land. After this initial occupation, the CPT helped to organize dozens of other land occupations that took place across the southern region of Brazil, with different degrees of success (Poletto 2015).

Meanwhile, other important political developments were taking place across the country. In 1979, a new military president continued the process of political opening (*abertura*). The most important reforms were the granting of amnesty to political exiles and more tolerance for protest and mobilization. The military regime also passed a Party Reform Bill in December 1979, which dissolved the two-party system. Although the government hoped that this reform would divide the increasing support for the one opposition party (Moreira 1985), the reform backfired, leading to the founding of a diversity of new political parties that transformed Brazil's political trajectory.[16]

In 1980, the oppositional labor movement, Catholic Church activists, progressive intellectuals, and leaders of the emerging social or popular[17] movements, including the landless movement, came together to form the Workers' Party (PT). Many of the landless activists who were involved in regional occupations in the south participated in the PT's founding congress. As Ann Mische (2008) writes, "The PT advocated a new, specifically Latin American brand of socialist struggle, committed to internal democracy, grassroots social movements, and increasingly, institutionalized democracy as the path to reform" (103). Two years later, the same grassroots leaders that founded the PT came together to create the Central Union of Workers (CUT), a new labor union confederation. The CUT became one of the most important organizing forces in Brazil over the next two decades.

In January 1981, in the midst of these national developments, one of the largest and most important occupations of the landless movement's early history took place, the occupation of another large *fazenda* in Rio Grande do Sul, Encruzilhada Natalino, with six hundred families. Local CPT leaders were central to the organizing of this occupation (Ondetti 2008, 68). Other politically active groups throughout the state also supported the camp, including union and student organizations. On July 25, ten thousand people participated in a solidarity march with the occupying families. Six days later, on July 31, the government sent two hundred soldiers to surround the camp, threatening violent action. However, the outpouring of public support deterred the military from evicting the families (A. Wright and Wolford 2003, 34). In June 1983, after more than three years, the state government agreed to "settle" (offer land rights to) the families. In the midst of the optimism following this victory, discussions began about creating a national movement.

In January 1984, a four-day meeting was held in the southern state of Paraná, bringing together all of the leaders of the dispersed land occupations taking place across the country. The dynamics of these land occupations differed significantly depending on the state or region. The CPT was the strongest organizing force in the southern region, while in other locations the rural union movement also played an important role. In 1983, the CPT's southern regional division had founded an entity called the Movement of Landless Workers of the Southern Region (MASTRO) (Ondetti 2008, 75), to coordinate the land occupations in the south. Thus, in January 1984, the landless movement already had a well-established network and some regional bodies, which had formed organically over the previous five years. The most important decision made during the January 1984 meeting was to found a new national autonomous organization, which would not be linked to the Church, a labor union, or a political party—the Landless Rural Workers Movement (MST). The slogan of the new organization was "Land for those who live and work on it."

The MST's Initial Educational Experiments

Before the MST's official founding in 1984, there was very little discussion among the leaders of the landless encampments about education. This was a period of intense conflict between the movement and the state, and leaders were primarily focused on resisting eviction and winning land rights. Nonetheless, local landless activists began to organize educational activities as a response to the demands of the parents living in the occupied encampments. As Alvarez (1990) writes about Brazilian society during this period, "As the 'wives, mothers, and nurturers' of family and community, women are the principal architects of the domestic strategies of the popular classes" (55). Consequently, the responsibility for organizing childcare fell primarily on women. Since the very first MST land occupations, women organized educational activities for the children living in the camps. Sometimes these were isolated activities with just a few families, but in some camps the women came together to establish camp-wide childcare offerings, with educational activities that taught the children about the landless movement and the struggle for agrarian reform.

Many of these landless activists already had experience with grassroots educational programs, through their previous participation in the Catholic Church's study groups (CEBs). Drawing on Paulo Freire's philosophy of literacy through reading the *word* and the *world*, religious leaders talked to landless families about their personal experiences and then progressed to broader discussions about inequality, the economy, and politics. Thus, Freire became a major educational reference for local landless leaders. Although discussions about educational theories were still minimal among the leaders of the landless occupations, the women who participated in these religious study groups began organizing Freirean initiatives in their camps. The following story of Salete Campigotto, known as the MST's first teacher, illustrates these connections between the Catholic Church, Freire, and these early educational experiments.

The MST's First Teacher: Salete Campigotto's Story

Salete Campigotto, born on April 29, 1954, is the daughter of a small land-owner in Rio Grande do Sul and spent much of her youth working on her parents' farm.[18] Her local school only went up to fifth grade, so Salete eventually had to leave her community and move to a nearby city to continue studying, completing high school in 1971. In 1975, at the age of twenty-one, she received a fellowship to attend a teacher training program, known as a *magistério*,[19] and the following year she began to teach first and second graders at the same elementary school that she had attended. In 1977, she met Father Arnildo Fritzen, a political activist and adherent of liberation theology who invited her to participate in a CEB. This informal study group met every week to reflect on religious and political texts. Salete recalls, "It was in the CEB that I learned to analyze the reality of small farmers, the reality of education in Brazil . . . it was through these experiences that I began to question what was happening and realized that how we organized learning did not help students reflect on their reality." In 1979, during the first land occupation in her region, Salete supported the camped families by bringing them food and other supplies.

In 1981, Salete decided to join a land occupation herself. She was the only person in the occupied encampment with a teaching degree. She describes her initial engagement with education as an activity that grew out of a concrete necessity: there were over a hundred children running around the camp without any structured learning environments, and two-thirds of the adults were illiterate. Salete and another woman began to organize educational activities for the children and many of these adults. However, she emphasized, they decided not to teach in the same way that they had been taught in school. Instead, they searched out educational methods that took into consideration the encamped families' local realities.

Salete's interest in developing a different type of educational approach in the occupied encampments was a direct result of her experiences in the

CEBs, where she had been introduced to Freirean educational practices. To add to this local knowledge, Father Arnildo, who became Salete's political mentor, and João Pedro Stédile, a local ally who helped to found the MST, invited two educators who had had been involved in Freire's literacy campaigns to visit the camp and work with Salete and the other volunteer teachers. Although Salete was familiar with Freire's educational practices through the CEBs—and would later pursue a graduate degree focused on Freirean pedagogy—she said that at this point her knowledge of his ideas was still superficial. Over a period of eight days, the educators introduced her to the main components of Freirean educational philosophy: building knowledge through generative themes; drawing on the language of the community; creating pedagogical activities based in students' realities; rejecting the traditional banking method of education (in which teachers simply deposit knowledge into the minds of the students); and promoting learning through dialogue.

After this training, Salete began to teach the alphabet with words that came out of the students' reality, for example, "A" for *acampamento* (camp) or "B" for *barraca* (tent). Then, she helped students reflect on each of these words by posing questions: What is a camp? Why are we camped? How do we organize camps? Why do we live in tents? What other types of construction exist for houses? How do poor people live? How do rich people live? How do landless people live? Salete taught geography by helping students identify where plantations were located in the region. To learn mathematics, she helped students estimate the size of the camp and the distance between tents. She continually experimented with various methods, always using Freire as her theoretical reference.

In 1983, Salete and the other people in the occupation won the legal rights to the land, and after more contentious protest they also won the right to a public school in their community. The school was the first public school in the country located within an MST settlement. In lieu of any qualified teachers who were willing to travel to the settlement to teach, the state government agreed to hire Salete to work at the school. Salete immediately began incorporating Freirean pedagogies into the classroom, despite the conservative national context. As she explains, "In a small school where you are the teacher and the principal . . . you have a lot of space to work. I worked during the dictatorship, and our school was watched because it was on a settlement, but I never had to stop helping students critically analyze their reality." As her story illustrates, local MST activists who became teachers were able to influence the public schools in their settlements early on, by incorporating alternative pedagogies into their classroom practice. In the afternoons, Salete visited MST camps to contribute to the movement's nonformal educational initiatives.

Salete's educational interventions illustrate that activists had room to experiment with pedagogical alternatives, even under a military dictatorship. Partially, this was because of the nature of teaching and the difficulty of knowing what is happening inside of a classroom. In addition, teachers like Salete, who were willing to teach in far-off rural settlements and proactively resolved any issues that emerged in their schools, increased the state's own capacity for governance. Finally, and perhaps most important, in the context of widespread social mobilization throughout the country, a few radical teachers were not seen as a major threat to the military regime.

DEMOCRATIC CONSOLIDATION (1985–1989)

When the official return to democracy came in 1985, activism and political organizing in Brazil was already at a peak. A primary goal of these grassroots groups was to transform the nature of the Brazilian state by bringing these organizations' participatory ethos inside state institutions. This was a period in which citizenship was being redefined beyond formal rights as a more active citizenship, which included engagement in social struggles *and* direct participation in state decision making. As Dagnino (1998) argues, this meant not a refusal to engage in "political institutionality and the state but rather a radical claim for their transformation" (47). Dagnino writes about this as a new form of citizenship, not limited to legal provisions, which called for more egalitarian forms of social relations at all levels (52). Wampler and Avritzer (2004) refer to these developments as "participatory publics."

The 1988 Constitutional Assembly was an opportunity for mobilized groups to institutionalize their demands for women's rights, racial justice, agrarian reform, housing, and much more. However, during this period conservative sectors of Brazilian society also began to organize. When the first civilian president took office in 1985, he announced a National Agrarian Reform Plan, which promised to settle 1.4 million landless people—a direct attempt to control rural unrest. The response of the agrarian elites was immediate, with the founding of the conservative Democratic Rural Union (UDR) that same year, which grew to tens of thousands of members by 1986. The goal of the UDR was to prevent the president from implementing his agrarian reform plan and to ensure that the new constitution did not allow for land expropriation. Consequently, the language concerning expropriation of private properties in the 1988 Constitution was more restrictive than the 1964 Land Statue (Ondetti

2008), a huge defeat for rural movements. There were similar attempts to block progressive reforms in almost all policy spheres. Thus, although the 1988 "Citizen's Constitution" brought more rights than ever before, it was a far cry from what the movements had initially demanded. Baiocchi and colleagues (2011) highlight three forces that shaped the 1988 constitution reform process: regional elites, social movements, and a debt crisis that led to an international push to transfer more responsibility to subnational governments. This combination of factors also led to a devolution of political power from the federal to the state and municipal level, creating more openings for both entrenched elites to consolidate power and civil society participation in local governance.

The MST's Internal Decision-Making Structure

The MST's first five years as an established organization were during this vibrant moment of civil society mobilization, leading up to the 1988 Constitutional assembly. The movement continued to organize land occupations, approximately fifty a year between 1985 and 1989, with tens of thousands of families. Although there were other groups also occupying land throughout the country, the MST was by far the most active group and the only one with a national scope.[20] During this period the government settled approximately 89,950 families, with an annual average of 17,990 families (Ondetti 2008, 148). After families received land rights, MST leaders encouraged them to continue participating in the movement, by both developing their own settlements and their active support for other families' land struggles in the region.

The MST also began to solidify its organizational structure during this period. Inspired by the liberation theology movement within the Catholic Church, the MST adopted an internal decision-making process based on small collectives, known as a base nucleus (*núcleo de base*, NB). As land occupations took place throughout the southern part of the country, local priests and nuns helped landless families organize themselves into small collectives of approximately ten families. These NBs were spaces of deliberation and debate, allowing families to make collective decisions about how to carry out the necessary tasks for their survival. Every camp also had a camp-wide leadership collective, with two coordinators from each NB.[21] This leadership collective was responsible for coordinating the day-to-day tasks of the camp. However, rather than representing the NBs, the camp leadership collective was meant to be an expression of the discussions and desires of the base collectives. Important debates in the camp leadership collective always had to be reported back to the NBs, before any final decisions could be made. In addition, general assemblies were held to ratify the most important decisions in the camp, allowing for everyone's direct participation. Figure 1.1 illustrates this collective decision-making structure of MST camps.

As Ondetti (2008) argues, the occupied camps were privileged spaces, where the MST leadership had a captive audience and could require encamped families to participate in the NBs and other work collectives needed for the camp to function. However, once families received official land rights on new agrarian reform settlements, the movement did not have the authority to require this level of sustained participation. This is where the MST's Gramscian strategy became even more important, as activists had to garner moral and intellectual leadership in these settlements and families' belief in the movement's political and economic vision. Movement activists also had to invest in the leadership capacity of people living in these settlements, in order to develop organic intellectuals who could link the communities to the MST's broader organizational structure. The MST's goal was to have all families in the camps and settlements participate in collective decision making, through their NBs. However, it was extremely difficult to integrate people into this form of self-governance. The participation of local families in education became an important strategy for exercising this local leadership.

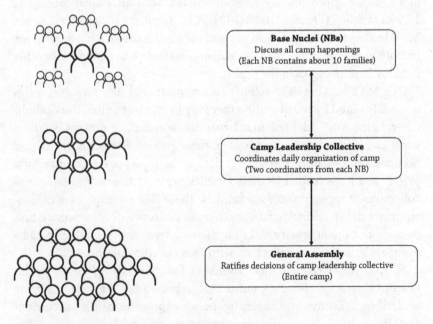

Figure 1.1 Collective Decision-Making Structure of MST Camps
Courtesy of author and Georgia Gabriela da Silva Sampaio

An Educational Approach to Support a Social Vision

Although the MST was officially founded in 1984, it was not until 1987 that the movement took an official position concerning education. Caldart (2004) writes that many MST leaders resisted the idea of public schools inside the settlements, because they had been previously marginalized and made to feel stupid in school. Additionally, in the mid-1980s, there was a tendency among the MST leadership to view public schools as an instrument of the capitalist state, with the sole purpose of reproducing capitalist social relations.

Nonetheless, as more families received land access, there continued to be a demand from the movement's base to construct schools in these new communities. For example, Sue Branford and Jan Rocha (2002) tell the story of one woman involved in an MST land occupation who described the following situation in her camp: "There were hundreds of children running wild, with nothing to do all day long, getting up to mischief. We carried out a survey and found there were 760 school-age children in the camp and twenty-five qualified teachers among the women. It made sense to set up a school" (114). At this particular camp, the issue came to a vote in a general assembly, and the majority of families decided they should ask the government to build a school.

Similarly, in other camps and settlements throughout the south of Brazil, families began to demand public schools for their children. By and large, government officials initially refused to build these schools, claiming that the children could be bused to nearby cities. In response, landless activists occupied education offices and organized other forms of protest until their demands for public schools were met. The decentralized public school system, heightened by the 1988 Constitution and the Brazilian economic crisis, created opportunities for the movement, as dozens of different state and municipal governments administered school systems with relative autonomy.[22] If a municipal government was antagonistic toward the encamped families, the movement could circumvent that government level and pressure the state government to build a school. As opposition parties (from the PMDB[23] to the PT) won an increasing number of mayoral and gubernatorial elections, there was also more opportunity for dialogue. Caldart (2004) writes that this was the first phase of the movement's struggle for public education: families mobilizing for educational access through direct actions that forced local governments to deliver on this public service.

This *first phase* of educational struggle solidified the most important aspect of the movement's educational vision: that schools should be located in rural areas, not consolidated in urban centers. Building schools within settlements and camps was the only way to ensure the movement's participation in these schools. Once the demand for educational access was met, the local landless leaders had to deal with a new problem: teachers commuting in from the cities who knew nothing about the MST or agrarian reform. Some of these teachers began telling students that their parents were illegal outlaws and that the purpose of education was to find a good job in the city. The educational debate within the movement shifted to how MST activists could make schools more sensitive to the needs of the movement. This began what Caldart (2004) describes as the *second phase* of the MST's struggle: organizing families to monitor the schools.

The active involvement of local families in the oversight of the public school system was critical to the movement's contentious co-governance of public schooling. One MST activist and teacher, Carmen Vedovatto, describes her own experience moving to an MST camp in Santana do Livramento, in the state of Rio Grande do Sul, in the mid-1980s. As soon as Carmen arrived at the camp she was invited to teach, since she already had a high school degree. At this point, the municipal government did not legally recognize the educational activities taking place on the camp. When her family finally won access to land on a new agrarian reform settlement, the local mayor refused to open a school. The families circumvented the municipal government by putting pressure on the state government to construct the school, through protests and marches in front of the State Department of Education Regional Office (CRE). This strategy succeeded, and on the first day of the school opening the community proudly hung an MST flag. When the state officials found out, they demanded that the flag be taken down. After multiple protests, the community won the right to keep the flag on the school walls. Carmen was appointed as the teacher, and the community set up a collective of families to support Carmen in her daily work and defend her if similar conflicts with the government arose.[24]

Salete Campigotto tells a similar story about how the community helped her with a legal issue she faced at her school. At that time in the mid-1980s, Salete's school was the only building on the settlement with electricity. In the afternoons, when the school closed for the day, Salete allowed the families to set up illegal wires (*gatos*) to stream electricity from the school to their homes. One afternoon, several state education officials arrived and saw these illegal wires. They were furious and left Salete a message demanding to meet, in order to legally prosecute her. Salete did not go to the meeting, and instead, a collective of parents from the settlement agreed to talk to the government officials. They explained their histories of poverty, their choice to occupy land, and their years of suffering in the camps. They asked the officials why they did not deserve to have electricity and threatened to organize protests if Salete was prosecuted. The families made such a commotion that the officials sent a letter to the state electricity company, demanding electric wires in the settlement. Salete recalls this event fondly: "I always use this story to show the importance of maintaining a strong community organization to watch over the schools. Imagine if I had been alone."[25]

Salete and Carmen's stories illustrate that from the very beginning of the MST's struggle, families have pressured the state for their right to participate in the school system. Regional collectives of families and teachers concerned about education began forming organically within the movement, even before a national MST education sector was established. These regional collectives were made up overwhelmingly of women.

Experimenting with a Freirean-Socialist Educational Approach

Many of the activists who occupied land in the 1980s were, like Salete, familiar with Freire's pedagogical approach. Freire offered MST activists a concrete set of pedagogies to employ in their classrooms, such as the incorporation of generative themes based on students' reality, problem posing, dialogue, and praxis—connecting theory and practice. Freirean theory also helped local activists understand that social change was not only possible but also ethically necessary. Furthermore, Freire taught the movement that education is never neutral; it is always either actively maintaining or transforming the status quo.

Perhaps most important, Freirean theory helped MST leaders reflect on the role of grassroots leadership in the movement and the pitfalls of vanguardism. One national leader in the MST education sector explained, "Paulo Freire taught us that we are the subjects of the process of social change, not objects. He believes in peasant workers. Some revolutionaries thought that vanguards would produce revolution. Paulo Freire taught us that revolution is not through vanguardism: everyone has to be an agent in their own liberation."[26] This notion of grassroots collective leadership has been critical to the practice of direct democracy that developed within the movement. MST leaders commonly say that everyone needs to learn how to coordinate and be coordinated: to efficiently lead a collective work process and also to follow the leaders who are put in charge of a certain task.

Despite these many valuable lessons, Freirean theory also had limitations for the MST's efforts in this early period. Most critically, while Freirean educational ideas were helpful in thinking about pedagogical practice and poor people's role as protagonists in their struggle, his writings never directly addressed how to reform the formal public school system. In addition to influencing teacher practice, the MST educational leaders wanted to transform the traditional hierarchical arrangement of the public schools—the relationships between government officials, bureaucrats, school principals, teachers, students, and community members. While not rejecting Freire's contributions to classroom pedagogy and political practice, MST activists began to search out other educational ideas. As Salete described, "We were looking for a new educational proposal for our schools, and we thought, where in the world have they attempted to create a school system for a socialist society?" One answer to that question was in the Soviet Union.

In the late 1980s, MST activists began to find inspiration for their pedagogical approach in the work of several Soviet theorists writing during the first decade after the 1917 Bolshevik Revolution.[27] How did these theories travel from the early-twentieth-century Soviet context to the Brazilian countryside? Importantly, the 1980s was a decade of widespread debate about socialism throughout Brazil, with prominent intellectuals and countless political groups taking their inspiration from the socialist and communist struggles of the previous century. Discussions about the Bolshevik Revolution and its significance for the Brazilian political struggle were common among the leaders of both urban and rural movements.[28] However, the incorporation of Soviet ideas into the MST's pedagogical proposal was not simply an imposition of an outside theory; rather, activists began to use these ideas because they resonated with practices already occurring in MST camps and settlements. The following story about the occupation of Fazenda Annoni illustrates how these Soviet theories reinforced values families already held about the relationship between education, work, and cooperation.

On October 29, 1986, fifteen hundred families occupied Fazenda Annoni, a large plantation in the north-central part of Rio Grande do Sul. This was the largest MST-led land occupation to date, and it drove the issue of land reform into the national spotlight. Salete started traveling daily from a nearby settlement to work with the children in this camp. Eleven of the people involved in the occupation of Fazenda Annoni had teaching experience. These teachers, along with some of the mothers, formed an education collective. Together, the group began to think more intentionally about the types of educational experiences they wanted to organize.

As the occupation of Fazenda Annoni received national media attention, other sympathizers of the struggle began to visit and offer their support. Among them was a master's student at a nearby university, Rosali Caldart, who would eventually become a leader in the national MST education sector. At Rosali's university there was a professor who specialized in Marxism and socialist pedagogy and had introduced Rosali to the work of the leading educational intellectuals of the Soviet Union. When Rosali visited the occupation of Fazenda Annoni, she was impressed by the practices that Salete and the camp's education collective had developed. In particular, she admired how the teachers incorporated cooperative work practices as a component of the children's educational activities. Rosali suggested that the education collective read the texts of several Soviet writers, including Nadezhda Krupskaya, the Deputy Minister of Education of the Soviet Union between 1929 and 1939 and Lenin's wife.[29] Salete Campigotto told a similar story, about her first introduction to these Soviet theorists:

> In the visit that Rosali made in the 1980s, we were already working in an education collective. I had developed practical activities with the kids. We had a rabbit farm, and the kids took care of the rabbits each day; they learned how to take care of them. Rosali came to see us, and I think she had studied some stuff before because personally I had never heard of Krupskaya. She said that we were developing a relationship between school and work . . . the focus on studying, but having children be responsible for work. This is an issue that Krupskaya wrote about, the connection between work and study. And this is how we began to learn about Krupskaya.

In the MST camp, everybody was working—growing food, building make-shift tents for shelter, taking care of animals. It seemed logical to Salete that her students should also have work related to the necessities of the camp. When Rosali introduced Krupskaya's writings to the education collective, Krupskaya's ideas about the educational purpose of manual labor resonated with the values of these encamped families.[30] Over the next few years, the collectives of educators and parents on MST camps and settlements continued to read Soviet theories, with the mentorship of allies such as Rosali. Two Soviet pedagogues in particular became major inspirations for the movement during the late 1980s and early 1990s: Moisey Pistrak and Anton Makarenko.

Educational Value of Manual Labor—Moisey M. Pistrak

Moisey Pistrak's theories about the educational value of work immediately resonated with MST activists. Pistrak, who was born in Russia and lived from 1888 to 1940, was influential in reforming the education system in the Soviet Union after the Bolshevik Revolution. In *Fundamentals of the School of Work* (*Fundamentos da Escola do Trabalho*),[31] Pistrak discussed his experiences constructing and implementing a pedagogical method in primary schools in the Soviet Union. He stated, "The revolution and the school should act in parallel, because the school is an ideological arm of the revolution" (Pistrak 2000, 30). In keeping with this belief, Pistrak emphasized labor as a cornerstone of a socialist school system—a way of teaching the principles of discipline, organization, and collectivity. "It is necessary to teach love and esteem for work. Work elevates the man and brings him happiness; it educates him in a collective sentiment, it ennobles the man, and because of this, work, and particularly manual labor of whatever type, is necessary as a means of education" (48).

Pistrak's idea that manual labor is an important educational process is at odds with the dominant assumption in society that the purpose of studying is for social mobility out of working-class and agrarian jobs. This separation between intellectual and manual labor—in Harry Braverman's (1998) phrasing, the divorcing of conception from execution—defined capitalist development during the nineteenth and twentieth century.[32] Such separation rejects workers' ability to envision the entire production process, as workers become executors of predetermined tasks. A major principle of the MST's pedagogical approach is to reject the separation between intellectual and manual labor and, instead, promote the idea of farmer-intellectuals who are both the engineers and laborers of the production process.

Rosali remembered that as local MST leaders began to read Pistrak's writings in the mid-1980s, they saw him as engaging in a task similar to their own: creating a school system that directly supported socialist economic practices. Pistrak's theory of a "school of work"—in which students engage in both manual labor and study at school—became one of the pillars of the MST's educational beliefs. Pistrak's writings offered activists a language to theorize the social benefits of the practices that they were already developing in work projects on their camps and settlements, such as Salete's rabbit farm. Pistrak's writings also helped the MST activists understand their educational initiatives in relationship to those of other socialist societies. The principal concept that MST leaders took from Pistrak's writings— that manual labor is an important educational process—became a central part of the movement's pedagogical proposal.

Self-Governance and Cooperation—Anton Semyonovich Makarenko

Anton Makarenko (1888–1939) was another Soviet theorist whose writings influenced the MST education sector during the late 1980s and early 1990s. Makarenko's writings became an important reference for how to promote collectivity within both the public school system and the movement itself. Makarenko was a Ukrainian educator who, in the early 1920s, set up a residence school for war orphans known as the Maxim Gorky Labor Colony[33] (Bowen 1962; Makarenko 2001, 2004). The Soviet leadership considered these orphans to be deviants and to lack socialist values; however, Makarenko believed it was possible to develop their personalities, character, and intellect (Bowen 1962). His solution to the educational difficulties these orphans had in the traditional school system was the creation of student collectives. He argued that students in a collective would dispense with individualism and strive for a greater social goal.

Makarenko's book *Road to Life* ([1933] 2001)—Pedagogical Poems (*Poemas Pedagogicas*) in Portuguese—is a first-hand narrative of his time as the director of the Gorky Colony. The book captured the imagination of MST activists, who related Makarenko's experiences to their own histories of landlessness. As MST educational leader Marli Zimmerman reflected, "I was drawn to Makarenko because of the population he was working with, the unwanted, the kids who were rejected from society. It was like the *sem terrinha* [little landless children]."[34] Makarenko wrote that a key aspect of constructing a collective is self-governance—allowing students to oversee the daily tasks in the school and determine their own solutions to all educational issues (Luedemann 2002). Makarenko's goal was to transform the relationship between students, teachers, and administrators. Rather than simply arriving at school and completing assigned tasks, students became agents determining how their schools should function.

MST activists embraced the idea of students' collective self-governance of their schools. Local leaders were already organizing the camps and settlements through base nuclei (NBs), which were the most important decision-making bodies within the movement. Creating NBs in the public schools—similar to Makarenko's student collectives—made sense to local MST activists. As MST educational leader Rubneuza Leandro explained, "For Makarenko the collective is a living social organism, and because of this, it possesses organs, attributes, responsibilities, correlations, and interdependencies between its parts. If this collectivity does not exist, then it is a crowd, a group of individuals."[35] By organizing students into collectives, the MST attempted to emulate Makarenko's vision of collectives as living organisms. The hope was for students to become something greater than the sum of their parts.

Founding an MST Education Sector

In July 1987, the MST leadership organized the First National Meeting for Educators in Areas of Agrarian Reform, held in the state of Espírito Santos. The national leadership organized this meeting in response to the bottom-up pressure from the families in the camps and settlements for the movement to support education. As one of the national leaders of the MST education sector, Edgar Kolling, described, "When we occupied land and created large camps there was a lot of pressure to have schools. The moms and teachers pressured the MST to be concerned with formal education."[36] Although the movement had already been investing in nonformal educational initiatives, and Edgar himself helped organize these political training schools (*escolas de formação*), the families in settlements also wanted formal educational access.

There were thirteen agrarian reform educators from four different states at the first national meeting. A document written by seminar participants sheds light on why they saw education as critical to the movement's broader agrarian reform struggle:

> We know that if the dominant class uses schools as one of their principle [sic] means of ideological control, to maintain order and sustain the capitalist system, the Landless Workers Movement has to try to transform this reality. We cannot stop believing in the fundamental importance of our educational work and investing seriously in the training of teachers. If teachers are at the margins of our struggle, they will continue to pass on the values and serve the interests of the dominant class. And we will be giving power to our enemies, allowing the enemy to grow inside our own territories. (MST 1987)

As this excerpt suggests, even in these early years, many MST leaders already had an explicitly Gramscian understanding of the relationship between the state and civil society. These activists believed that schools were institutions of social reproduction, which would pass on the values and serve the interest of the dominant class. However, rather than reject these institutions, the activists thought that it was necessary to win over the teachers for an alternative hegemonic project, through their presence and activism in these schools.

Although the MST's educational struggle was still marginal, the 1987 national seminar was a turning point when the movement leadership began to embrace the need to transform public education. The national seminar participants approved eleven proposals, including organizing a national education committee with representatives from each state to plan more meetings and activities and developing a national teacher training course. The movement considers this 1987 national seminar the de facto moment when a national network of MST educational activists formed, which became the national MST education sector.[37] The movement already had dozens of educational leaders, like Salete Campigotto, who arose organically from the camps and settlements and were implementing a range of alternative educational practices in their schools. These local leaders had access to these Freirean and socialist theories due to the political context of the 1980s, a period of a vibrant social movement mobilization, political party formation, and a society-wide emphasis on participatory governance. The national MST education sector would now help to coordinate these local efforts. Caldart (2004) calls this the *third phase* of the MST's educational struggle, when education was incorporated into the everyday preoccupations of the movement. This is when engaging the public education system became the MST's strategic goal.

NEOLIBERALISM AND STATE–SOCIETY CONFLICT (1990–1996)

The vibrant movements of the 1980s, and the hope they brought for promoting an alternative development model and a more participatory democracy, faced a huge disappointment in 1989 when Fernando Collor de Mello, a relatively unknown governor of a small, northeastern state, narrowly defeated the PT candidate Luis Inácio Lula da Silva. This had been the first direct election for president in almost three decades, and although a coalition of left groups had mobilized around Lula's candidacy,[38] the right-wing countermobilizations proved more effective. This election shifted the trajectory of Brazilian politics, leading to a decade-long era of neoliberal economic policies and state–society conflict, with cuts in social spending, trade liberalization, and financial stabilization policies. Collor's presidency also marked a new global context, as the fall of the Soviet Union in 1989 strengthened the argument that there was no alternative to capitalism.

In 1992, however, a corruption scandal broke that implicated Collor in a multi-million-dollar patronage ring, leading to the eruption of mass public demonstrations as hundreds of thousands of people took to the streets to call for Collor's impeachment.[39] On December 29, 1992, Collar resigned from office and Vice President Itamir Franco became president for the next two years, a period marked by hyperinflation. This is when the Minister of Finance, Fernando Henrique Cardoso of the Brazilian Social Democratic Party (PSDB), achieved national fame by developing the Real Plan (*Plano Real*) that stabilized inflation rates, leading to Cardoso's electoral victory in 1994 (once again against Lula). During Cardoso's administration, there would be a continuation of Collor's neoliberal economic policies and also an intensification of state–society conflict, especially with the rural landless movement (discussed in Chapter 2).

The 1989 election also redefined the internal dynamics of the left itself. A group of leaders vied for power within the PT who advocated for a more "pragmatic" party structure for winning elections, eventually achieving hegemony within the party in the mid-1990s. This meant increasing the number of PT members while investing less in the participatory processes that had previously characterized that membership (Keck 1992). In addition, PT politicians began forming more alliances with conservative politicians.[40] Throughout the 1990s, the candidates that ran on the PT's tickets were not ideological homogenous, but rather people with different relationships to grassroots movements and levels of support for participatory democracy and socialist politics. Thus, the conflicts that characterized this period were not only between a right-leaning, neoliberal economic paradigm and a left-leaning vision of participatory democracy and social development but, moreover, a bitter conflict about the left's own goals. The center of this conflict was about the compromises the PT needed to make, or not make, in order to garner the power necessary to implement reforms that could lead to real economic gains for the Brazilian working class.

It was in this context in the 1990s that the MST and other social movements succeeded in institutionalizing some of their demands within the Brazilian state. By this period, many of the movement leaders of the 1980s had established NGOs (Alvarez, 1999; Baiocchi 2005), while a minority, like the MST, maintained their identity as a popular (grassroots) movement. The decentralized federal system offered both the NGOs and the movements significant entry points to promote the transformation of state institutions. Furthermore, although Lula lost the presidency in 1989, the previous year many PT candidates had won their mayoral elections, and many of these political leaders still had deep relationships with social movements. This meant that the impetus for change often came from the state itself, as either left-leaning political candidates or dedicated reformers within the state pushed for new institutional designs. In the city of Porto Alegre, Mayor Olívio Dutra implemented a participatory budgeting system that became globally renown (Abers 2000; Baiocchi 2005; Goldfrank 2011a). In São Paulo, Mayor Luiza Erundina appointed Paulo Freire as the Secretary of Education (O'Cadiz, Wong, and Torres 1998) and promoted a series of other "solidarity economy" initiatives (Satgar 2014). In smaller cities throughout the country, social movement leaders became part of the municipal governments, either as elected or appointed officials (e.g., Gibson 2019). It is not surprising that Gramsci's theory of the state, civil society, and the war of position became part of popular discourse among grassroots groups during this period (Coutinho 2013; Dagnino 1998).

The MST in the 1990s: Land Reform, Agrarian Reform, and Social Transformation

As this period of neoliberalism, state–society conflicts, and participatory experiments evolved, the MST expanded nationally and solidified its organizational structure. First, the movement continued its practice of occupying large land estates.[41] With the goal of establishing a national organization, MST leaders from the south traveled to the northeast and north of the country to instigate land occupations in these other regions. Many of these regions had large Afro-Brazilian populations, with agrarian histories quite distinct from the small-family farming tradition of the south.[42] In these regions MST leaders organized sugarcane workers, day laborers, families living in semiarid climates, and people on the periphery of cities who had recently migrated from rural areas.[43] These land occupations were often successful, putting enough pressure on government officials that they agreed to redistribute this land and create new agrarian reform settlements.[44] Other groups learned from the MST's success and began to organize their own land occupations in different parts of the country. The National Confederation of Agricultural Workers (CONTAG) was one of the organizations that led a significant portion of the land occupations in the 1990s, achieving some important results (Sauer and Welch 2015).

Between 1988 and 1994, there were a total of 661 new land occupations involving 111,741 families, an average of 94.4 occupations with 15,963 families per year. The MST organized approximately 55 percent of these occupations, often with a much higher number of families participating than in the occupations of other, smaller and more isolated organizations. During Collor (1990–1992) and Franco's (1993–1994) presidencies, an average of 11,330 families were settled annually. The number of new land occupations and families issued land rights increased drastically during Cardoso's first term (1995–1998), with an average of 482 new land occupations per year involving 71,825.5 families. During these four years, an average of 75,204 families were issued land rights each year, a consequence of both social movements' mobilizations and the increased rural conflict (discussed in Chapter 2). Figure 1.2 shows the total number of new land occupations between 1988 and 1998, and Figure 1.3 illustrates the number of families involved in these new land occupations. Figure 1.4 shows the number of families that were issued land rights during this period. Finally, Figure 1.5 illustrates the regional distribution of the families involved in these land occupations and, importantly, the significant increase in the number of families participating from the poorer, northeastern part of the country during the course of the 1990s.[45]

A second characteristic of the MST during this period was the leadership's position that land alone was not enough to develop sustainable farming communities in the Brazilian countryside. To the contrary, without state support families did not have the resources to live and work on this land and would often abandon or sell their lots. To actually transform the agrarian structure, local MST leaders began demanding, beyond land reform, what they referred to as agrarian reform: the resources that would allow families to live a dignified and economically viable life on their land. These resources included seeds, farming equipment, technical assistance,

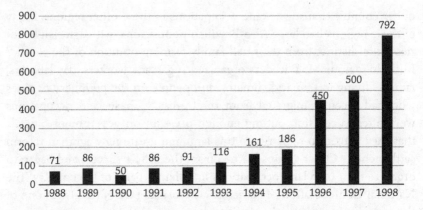

Figure 1.2 Number of New Land Occupations, 1988–1998
Source: *DataLuta: Banco de Dados da Luta Pela Terra: Relatório Brasil 2016* (NERA 2017)

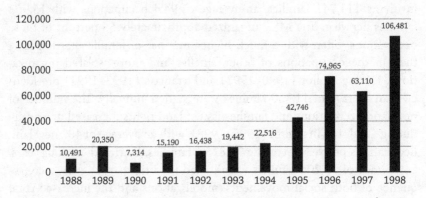

Figure 1.3 Number of Families in New Land Occupations, 1988–1998
Source: *DataLuta: Banco de Dados da Luta Pela Terra: Relatório Brasil 2016* (NERA 2017)

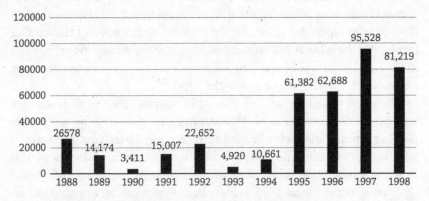

Figure 1.4 Number of New Families Issued Land Rights, 1988–1998
Source: *DataLuta: Banco de Dados da Luta Pela Terra: Relatório Brasil 2016* (NERA 2017).

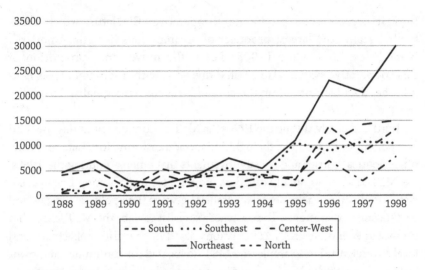

Figure 1.5 Regional Distribution of Families in Land Occupations, 1988–1998
Source: *Conflitos no Campo Brasil*, Pastoral Land Commission (CPT). Author compiled data from ten CPT reports on land conflicts from 1988 to 1998 (CPT 1989, 1990, 1991, 1992, 1993, 1994, 1995, 1996, 1997, 1998, 1999)

housing, roads, health services, cultural events, youth activities, and of course, public schools. Furthermore, the MST leadership took the position that although it was the state's responsibility to provide the resources for these public services, it was the community's right to collectively oversee their local implementation.

In 1992, the MST founded what would become another one of its most important thematic sectors: the agricultural production sector, later known as the production, cooperation, and environment sector. This sector was in charge of developing a strategy for collective agricultural production, and similarly to the education sector, coordinating at the national level the many local cooperatives that had already been established on the settlements. The MST promoted agricultural production cooperatives (CPAs) on all settlements, as well as state-level central agricultural cooperatives (CCAs) that collectivized marketing, transport, and the purchasing of inputs and machinery (Ondetti 2008, 125). The MST also established a national organization, the Confederation of Agrarian Reform Cooperatives of Brazil (CONCRAB), to coordinate the state-level organizations.

By 1994, the MST had more than forty CPAs, seven CCAs, and six regional cooperatives, often established with the help of government loan programs.[46] Furthermore, despite the neoliberal political climate of the 1990s, the MST was able to establish a range of agreements with the federal government and dozens of subnational governments to fund technical assistance programs for agricultural production. In 1997, the MST created its first organic seed production cooperative, BioNatur, which eventually became the largest producer of organic seeds in Latin America.[47] Nonetheless, as Ondetti (2008) notes, the movement's promotion of this cooperative system also created divisions within settlements, as families that decided not to join the cooperatives were marginalized from the movement (126).

Third and finally, during the 1990s the MST continued solidifying the third component of its struggle, the fight for social transformation. Like the many other political parties and social movements that emerged during the 1980s, the MST leadership openly called its proposal for transforming Brazilian society socialism, and activists drew parallels between their political struggle and past socialist experiments. To construct a socialist society, the MST leadership promoted economic and social relations based in solidarity, collectivity, and local sovereignty. For example, the MST advocated for communal land ownership. Although the MST did not have any legal authority to ask families to give up individual land rights, the leadership tried to convince these families to do so by invoking the values of solidarity and comradeship.[48] The MST also began to critique monoculture and the use of pesticides, and advocate for food sovereignty: "the right of peoples to healthy and culturally appropriate food produced through ecologically sound and sustainable methods, and their right to define their own food and agriculture systems."[49] In 1993, the MST helped to found The Peasant Way (*La Via Campesina*),[50] an international coalition of farmers' organizations promoting food sovereignty.

The MST also maintained the internal practice of forming base nuclei of ten to twenty families in all camps and settlements, which send coordinators to camp and settlement leadership collectives. As the MST evolved into a national organization, this structure was kept in place through additional regional, statewide, and national leadership bodies. In every state there are regional leadership collectives with representatives from all of the camp and settlement leadership collectives. The regional leadership collectives send several coordinators to participate in a statewide directorate: a more formalized leadership body with a specific number of representatives that determine the MST's priorities and actions in the state. Two activists from the state directorate also participate in the MST's national directorate. The MST's national directorate is the most important, ongoing, collective decision-making body in the movement. However, two other collective bodies determine the national directorate's major political positions and strategies: the national coordination and the national congress. The national coordination includes a couple hundred movement leaders from the state leadership bodies who meet every two years. The national congress takes place every five years and includes hundreds of representatives from each state; in 2014, it included approximately 15,000 people. The national congress is the most important "instance" of collective decision making within the movement.[51.]

In addition to the regional leadership collectives and state and national directorates, at each of the regional, state, and national levels, there are also "thematic sectors" that focus on specific issues within the movement. These thematic sectors include political training, education, grassroots organizing, finance, projects, agricultural production, international relations, human rights, communication, health, culture, gender, and youth.[52] These thematic sectors function in parallel to the regional leadership collectives and state and national directorates, while also participating in these broader leadership bodies. For example, the national directorate includes two representatives from each state directorate and two coordinators from each of the national thematic sectors. The national directorate also includes representatives from specific MST entities, including the Florestan Fernandes National School (ENFF; see Chapter 2), the Technical Institute of Training and Research in Agrarian Reform (ITERRA; see this chapter), and the MST offices in Brasília, Rio De Janeiro, and the national office in São Paulo. Figure 1.6 illustrates this collective decision-making structure of the MST's national movement.

The MST's national decision-making structure is an attempt to delicately balance three principles: collective governance, broad-based participation, and the division of tasks. The principle of collective governance is reflected in the fact that there are no individual leaders within the movement and all decisions are made collectively. The ideal of broad-based participation and division of tasks means that new activists are constantly integrated into these collective decision-making bodies within the movement and have real responsibilities over the movement's many spheres of action. Carter (2015) describes this as "various decentralized yet well-coordinated layers of representation and collective decision making" (400). This allows for an expansive base of activist participation throughout the country, where local leaders have real control to debate, coordinate, and carry out a wide range of movement activities.

This organizational structure is also a form of democratic centralism, as some critics have noted (Rubin 2017, 221). Although the MST leadership does not vocally proclaim democratic centralism as a principle of the movement, the MST's organizational structure is implicitly based on this ideal, as everyone adheres to the decisions made by the regional, state, and national decision-making bodies. Leaders refer to this as submitting your individuality to the collective, and it is assumed to be an important sacrifice in promoting a more collective, socialist society. Consequently, individuals who attempt to organize against these collective leadership bodies (*articular contra a direção*) can face expulsion from the movement. Rather than

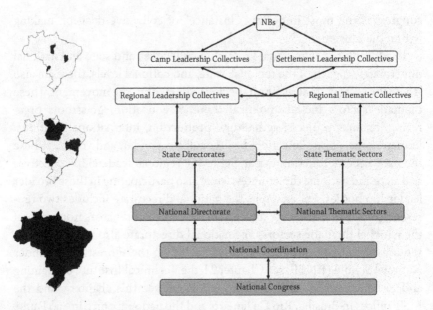

Figure 1.6 Collective Decision-Making Structure of the MST's National Movement
Courtesy of author and Georgia Gabriela da Silva Sampaio

mobilize against the collective decision-making process, MST activists are encouraged to discuss their disagreements in the collectives in which they take part—whether this is a base nucleus, a regional leadership body, or a thematic sector. In other words, as opposed to individual dissent, the movement's hope is to promote an ascending and descending democracy, whereby different levels of decision-making bodies are consulted and each person's voice is heard—through her or his collective.[53]

The MST education sector evolved similarly to the movement's national collective decision-making structure, with activists participating in decentralized yet well-coordinated regional, state, and national leadership bodies that organize the daily activities of the sector. Movement leaders recruit activists to participate in regional education collectives, who are then tasked with developing relationships with teachers and organizing educational activities for the children and adults in MST camps and settlements. In addition to the regional education collectives, there are also statewide education sectors or more formalized bodies of full-time activists that strategize about how to transform the school system in each state. Two members of each statewide education sector participate in the national MST education sector. Two leaders of this national body then represent the education sector in the MST's national directorate. Finally, there is also a smaller, executive education sector (not illustrated in Fig. 1.7), which includes several people from each of the five Brazilian regions and at least one person

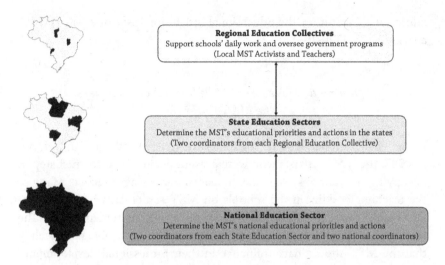

Figure 1.7 Collective Decision-Making Structure of the MST Education Sector
Courtesy of author and Georgia Gabriela da Silva Sampaio

representing each of the MST's educational foci: adult education, infant education, primary and secondary schooling, and formal schooling programs. In this way, the MST's education sector both reflects and is embedded in the movement's national decision-making structure. Figure 1.7 illustrates the collective decision-making structure of the MST education sector.

Theory in Practice: The Evolution of the MST's Educational Approach

The MST's first state-sponsored educational initiatives happened during the 1990s, as activists found diverse allies within different agencies and subnational governments who supported the movement's educational initiatives. The establishment of formal educational institutions increased the movement's knowledge and expertise about how to participate in and help govern the public education system. The educational programs also integrated new activists into the movement, especially women, equipping them with formal degrees that helped them negotiate with public officials and obtain jobs in other institutional spheres the movement wanted to occupy. In particular, four programs were central to the evolution of the MST's educational approach: the High School Degree and Teaching Certification Programs, or MAG programs (*magistério*), the technical administration of cooperatives (high school degree and technical certificate, or TAC programs), Freirean-based literacy campaigns, and the MST's first educational institution, the Educational Institution Josué do Castro (IEJC, also known as ITERRA).

Training a "Movement" of Public School Teachers: The MAG Program

At the First National Seminar for Educators in Areas of Agrarian Reform, in 1987, the MST activists who were present decided that the first step in occupying the school system was transforming teacher practice. Many of the teachers working in the schools on MST settlements had never finished high school. As educational leader Edgar Kolling remembered, "The teachers had some but not a lot of pedagogical training ... there was a feeling that the MST should have influence in their professional development." The MST education sector decided to prioritize the creation of secondary education programs for teachers working in areas of agrarian reform.

In the late 1980s, the MST was one of the many urban and rural social movements discussing how to create alternative institutions, such as schools, that embodied their political and economic ideals. In August 1989, the MST joined with a group of other social movements[54] in Rio Grande do Sul to establish a foundation that would provide educational access for their activists: the Foundation of Educational Development and Research (FUNDEP). In December 1989, the social movements that founded FUNDEP organized a seminar on Educational Experiences for Rural Development. Several groups were invited to talk about their educational initiatives, among them the family agricultural schools (EFAs). The EFAs were a network of schools inspired by an educational experience in the French countryside in late 1930s, which focused on teaching rural populations both academic content and agricultural knowledge. In 1968, the Catholic Church brought these practices to Brazil and set up the first EFA in the state of Espírito Santos. The educational proposal quickly expanded to other states. The distinguishing feature of the EFAs was the pedagogy of alternation (*pedagogia de alternância*), in which students studied intensively for several months and then returned to their communities to engage in applied research projects. This alternation between school periods (*tempo escola*) and community periods (*tempo comunidade*) allowed students to farm while studying. The pedagogy of alternation soon became a central component of the MST's educational approach.

Following this seminar, the MST proposed to create a high school degree and teaching certification program, known as a MAG program (*magistério*). The MAG program would take place under the auspices of FUNDEP's Department of Rural Education in the city of Braga, Rio Grande do Sul.[55]

The first MAG program began in 1990, with two cohorts of rural teachers (eighty total students). Drawing on the experience of the EFAs, the cohorts studied together for several months a year for two years. The pedagogy of alternation allowed the teachers to continue working, as the study periods were during summer and winter breaks. When the teachers returned home, they had to engage in local research projects in addition to their regular teaching responsibilities.

Although local government officials were often wary of the MST's educational initiatives, this was a moment when the interests of the movement and the state converged. Local mayors supported the teacher training program because the municipalities also had teachers without secondary degrees.[56] The Rio Grande do Sul State Education Advisory Board approved the MST's proposal to create the high school program for teachers, and several municipal governments requested to participate. Consequently, the first MAG cohorts included teachers from both areas of agrarian reform and the regular municipal public schools—illustrating how the MST's educational initiatives often developed in collaboration with local governments and the ways in which the MST's initiatives increased the state's own internal capacity.[57]

The MAG high school program was the first of many formal schooling programs that MST leaders would develop over the next two decades, with legal government recognition. As Edgar described, the goal of the MAG program was concrete, "to certify the teachers," but also to "debate about what type of school we wanted, and what was the necessary training to develop this relationship between work and school, education, peasant culture, and cooperation." For the MST, teacher training was not only important for improving effective classroom practice; it was about developing a collective of teacher-activists—what Gramsci (1971, 5) calls organic intellectuals—who would support the ideals of the movement in their local schools.

The MST education collective overseeing the MAG program incorporated the Freirean and Soviet educational pedagogies that local leaders had been experimenting with over the previous years. For example, when the teachers arrived in the school in Braga, they had to organize themselves into base nuclei (NBs) and divide up the tasks for the school to function. Students lived together and shared the responsibilities of cooking, cleaning, and childcare. The teachers were also required to complete two hours of work in the agricultural cooperatives each day, in addition to eight hours of study. Between study sessions, teachers put what they were learning into practice; and—like good Freirean practitioners—they were asked to reflect on these experiences during the next study period. Rosali Caldart, who by that time had become an organic member of the MST's national education sector, described the MAG program as "a laboratory, working with people who were in the classroom and trying to see if this or that worked." The MST's freedom to experiment with new educational practices turned the MAG programs into "real utopias" (Wright 2010), or in this case, real educational utopias, with the teachers not only reading Soviet and Freirean texts but also prefiguring these texts in practice. As Rosali says, "We made a lot of mistakes, but the MAG course had complete autonomy, we could do whatever we wanted."[58]

Thus, during the first half of the 1990s, while the federal government clashed with social movements and labor organizations nationally, the MST actively experimented with a socialist educational approach that could increase the internal capacity of the movement. Between 1990 and 1996, five cohorts of forty-five to fifty-five students from across the country—often teachers already working in MST settlements and camps—studied in the movement's MAG programs. I interviewed dozens of MST activists who received their high school degrees in Braga. For example, MST activists Elizabete Witcel and Marli Zimmerman never thought that they would achieve this level of educational access. In 1985 Elizabete was eighteen and only had an eighth-grade education, because her father did not believe girls needed to study. That year, she participated in the occupation of Fazenda Annoni and began to teach the five hundred children in her camp how to read and write. In 1990, she was invited to participate in the first MAG program.[59] Similarly, Marli only had an eighth-grade education when she went to visit her sister who was living in an MST camp. When Marli arrived, the camped families asked her to teach the children how to read and write. She agreed, and despite the fact that she had never occupied land, she was invited to participate in the third MAG high school program offered in 1991. Both Elizabete and Marli later became principals of public schools located in MST settlements.

The MST activists who graduated from the MAG programs talked about the important role these programs played in both their understanding of the movement's educational approach and their political consciousness. Vanderlúcia Simplicio, an MST activist from the state of Ceará who traveled to Rio Grande do Sul twice a year for three years to study in a MAG program, remembered reading Makarenko and realizing that the program was trying to imitate the Gorky Colony. She said that it was through the MAG program that she first learned the values of collectivity and its role in the movement's pedagogical approach.[60] Adilio Perin, who later became the principal of a large public school on an MST settlement, compared the MAG program to the organization of a settlement: the program incorporated self-governance, cooperation, and manual labor.[61] Similarly, Marli recalled that the program was based on a school as a cooperative model, and that the students actively participated in the governance of the program. Another MST educational leader, Ivania Azevedo, referred to the MAG program as an opening of the waters, when she first learned about the intentionality of education—à la Freire—and that an educator must always know for what purpose she is teaching.[62] The common theme in all of these reflections is that the MAG program helped MST leaders comprehend the movement's pedagogical approach by allowing them to experience it through practice. This form of praxis—implementing theory in practice and allowing these experiences to inform and transform the initial theory—also helped the MST national education collective refine their educational program. The activists who graduated from these real educational utopias took these experiences with them as they attempted to implement similar practices in their own schools.

From Training Teachers to Educating Farmers: The TAC Program

In 1993, the MST began offering a second type of high school program in Braga that focused on the administration of agricultural cooperatives. By the early 1990s, the MST agriculture sector was helping to construct cooperatives in settlements across the country. A discussion began about the need to train MST leaders with the technical skills to administer the agricultural cooperatives in the settlements. In February 1993, the MST leadership obtained permission from the Rio Grande do Sul Education Advisory Board to create a new high school program through FUNDEP/DER, known as the Technical Administration of Cooperatives (TAC) program. In June 1993, the first TAC program began with fifty-two students from nine Brazilian states, all activists in the MST agricultural production sector. A few months later, in October 1993, a second cohort of fifty-eight TAC students from eleven states also began studying in Braga.

The TAC program allowed these MST leaders to complete secondary education while earning a technical degree in cooperative administration. Liam Kane (2001) describes how the TAC program mirrored the MAG programs, but with a different purpose: "While it [TAC] is driven by the same educational principles, its aim is to help people in settlements survive economically. The course centres on 'co-operative firm management' and mixes 'education' with technical 'training'" (101). Edgar explained how Makarenko's work became especially important in the TAC high school program, as collectivity, self-governance, and cooperative organization were the principles of cooperative management. Through the TAC high school program, the MST's educational goals expanded beyond occupying the public schools to occupying other professional needs in the settlements.

Education thus became both the goal and the means of promoting agrarian reform.

In 1995, the same year that Fernando Henrique Cardoso of the center-right Brazilian Social Democratic Party (PSDB) took office, the MST received a prize in Education and Participation from the United Nations Children's Fund (UNICEF) for the MAG teacher certification program activists had developed. This award offered the MST's educational programs more public recognition, opening up opportunities to establish similar programs in other regions. While previously MST leaders had to travel to Rio Grande do Sul to access the movement's secondary education programs, by the end of the 1990s the MST was able to establish similar programs across the country through an array of university and government partnerships. The MST leaders who attended the courses in Braga became the coordinators of these other regional programs. The educational programs not only allowed MST leaders to achieve higher levels of education but also facilitated the movement's collective expertise and knowledge about how to administer a high school degree and teaching certification program. Through this iterative accumulation of expertise and skills, the MST activists were able to slowly expand their educational initiatives nationally.

Increasing Literacy: International Organizations and Universities Embrace the MST

Literacy was another central concern for the MST education sector in the early 1990s. During this period, illiteracy rates in the Brazilian countryside were extremely high, especially in the poor, northeastern region of the country. This was a result of the military regime's historical disregard for rural schooling (Plank 1996, 174–175) and the failed attempts to improve rural education throughout the 1980s (e.g., Harbison and Hanushek 1992). Rather than wait for the government's investment in rural literacy programs, in the 1990s the MST reached out to nongovernmental actors for support to run their own movement-led literacy campaigns. These programs allowed leaders to develop their Freirean approach to literacy, while also increasing the educational levels of the families living in areas of agrarian reform. Also, importantly, these literacy campaigns offered youth a concrete way to become involved in the movement as literacy trainers— often with financial compensation.

The MST led its first mass literacy program in Rio Grande do Sul, through a partnership with the Cultural Institute of São Francisco de Assis. The program ran for two years, beginning in 1991 and ending in 1993.[63] To prepare, in January and March 1991, the MST education sector trained one hundred educators in Freirean pedagogy at the FUNDEP/DER school in Braga. Then the educators were charged with teaching over one thousand adults to read and write over the course of two years. Paulo Freire attended the opening day of this literacy campaign, on May 25, 1991, in the MST settlement of Conquista de Fronteira in the far south of Rio Grande do Sul, Hulha Negra. When he arrived, he was asked if the drive had been difficult, given the muddy roads. Freire responded, "For a person that wrote a work called the *Pedagogy of the Oppressed*, it is not difficult to arrive where the oppressed are implementing this pedagogy" (MST 2001, 16). Then Freire proceeded to commend the MST's educational efforts: "This afternoon begins something that already started, that started the very first moment of your struggle . . . the right to knowledge, the right to know that you already know, and the right to know what you do not yet know" (MST 2003, 8). Freire's participation was another important moment that offered the MST's still nascent educational initiatives national recognition.

Over the next five years, the MST education sector led dozens of literacy campaigns in partnership with universities, state and municipal governments, and international organizations. For example, in 1995 the MST established a partnership with the Federal University of Sergipe as well as several municipal governments to administer a series of literacy trainings in the northeast region; that same year the MST signed a contract with the state Department of Education of Paraná to oversee literacy programs in this southern state (Souza 2002). These government officials were willing to support the MST's literacy campaigns because they increased the state's capacity to provide educational access in these rural regions. For these officials, the fact that the campaigns were based in Freirean pedagogies that taught farmers to critique inequality was less relevant than offering educational access to their constituents.

Although the federal government was more hesitant to establish a partnership with the MST, given the state–society conflicts across the country, relationships between MST activists and the Ministry of Education also developed. For example, in 1994 the MST was invited to participate in the National Commission on Adult Education in the Ministry of Education (MST 2003). Although this commission was terminated two years later, the MST's participation illustrated the movement's increasing influence in the public educational sphere. During this period, international organizations such as the United Nations Educational, Scientific, and Cultural Organization (UNESCO) and the United Nations Children's Fund (UNICEF) also began funding the MST's literacy campaigns (see Chapter 3). In 1996, several sympathetic professors at the University of Brasília convinced the Ministry of Education to sign a contract to allow the MST to train seven thousand literacy agents in agrarian reform regions (Carter and Carvalho 2009, 309).

Literacy campaigns were critical to building the internal capacity of the movement and the MST education sector for several reasons. First, the programs increased educational access for the rural workers in the settlements while raising these workers' political consciousness. Second, the campaigns offered youth a way of becoming more involved in the movement, with economic compensation. Third, the campaigns allowed MST activists to experiment with Freirean ideas and transform activists' scattered practices into a coherent approach toward adult literacy. A symbiotic relationship developed between the movement's adult educational practices and its other spheres of educational activism.

Building a Real Educational Utopia—IEJC/ITERRA

In 1995, the MST national leadership founded their first independent educational institution. The decision to create a school administered solely by the MST education sector was partially a response to the conflicts that were emerging in the TAC programs in Braga, between the MST leadership and the other social movements coordinating FUNDEP/DER. The conflicts concerned disagreements about the process of participatory governance in these programs and culminated in the MST's departure from FUNDEP in November 1994 (MST 2001). The MST leadership decided that they needed their own institutional space to develop educational programs independently from other movements. A few years earlier a clergyman from the Order of Capuchin Friars had visited Braga and had offered the MST leadership the use of the order's seminary building in Veranópolis, a relatively affluent city in the interior of Rio Grande do Sul. In December 1994, the clergy signed over control of the building to the MST for ten years.[64]

On January 12, 1995, the MST leadership founded ITERRA, the Technical Institute of Training and Research in Agrarian Reform. ITERRA became the new institutional host of the TAC programs. On January 25, 1995, the second cohort of TAC students—in their fourth study period—moved their course of study to ITERRA in Veranópolis. In March 1995, the first TAC cohort also moved to ITERRA. The conditions were initially difficult, as the building needed renovations to turn it into a space appropriate for a school. Furthermore, the MST leadership had decided to open the school with just a few volunteers, which meant that the majority of the work to maintain the school had to be completed by the students. A chronology of ITERRA's history notes, "There was no car, no telephone, and no easy access to make calls. There were no classrooms or infrastructure for studying. Some of the students began to demand the same conditions they had in Braga and did not accept that they had to be the ones to renovate the building. Other students pushed forward the process of constructing the school" (MST 2001, 37). The students' daily responsibility of renovating the physical structure of the school was what the MST education collective refers to as socially beneficial work[65]: labor that contributes to the betterment of the school community. A combination of socially beneficial work and study has remained a central component of the MST's educational approach.

Over the next decade, the MST's first independent school continued to evolve. In 1996, the MST obtained approval from the Rio Grande do Sul Educational Advisory Board for the creation of the Educational Institute of Josué de Castro (IEJC), a high school with the legal right to confer secondary degrees.[66] The IEJC replaced ITERRA as the institutional host of the MST's high school programs (although many MST leaders still refer to the school in Veranópolis as ITERRA). Then, in January 1997, the sixth MAG teacher training program officially moved to IEJC. This began the tradition of having several cohorts of students in different degree programs studying simultaneously at the school. A Political-Pedagogical Collective[67] (CPP) was established: a collective of MST leaders who lived permanently at the school and oversaw its administration. The CPP also began to develop other high school programs in community health, media communications, and accounting. Hundreds of MST leaders from around the country have obtained high school degrees through these IEJC courses, coming to Veranópolis for a several months to study and then returning to their communities to apply what they learned.[68]

When I visited IEJC for the first time in 2009, fourteen years after the school's founding, I was struck by the impressive physical infrastructure of the school. On the first floor there were administrative offices, a large dining room and kitchen, and a well-kept library with over 23,000 books. On the second and third floors were student dormitories. In the basement there was a bakery to make bread for the school and a factory to produce jams to be sold—teaching students how to manage small industries. There was a childcare center at the school, and everyone took turns babysitting, whether or not they were parents. In the front of the school was a large garden that produced most of the produce that the students ate. The IEJC had a relationship with a local butcher, who provided meat for the school in exchange for students' labor, while other food staples came from donations from MST settlements. The students also raised money through what is called in rural Brazil a *mutirão*: a collective effort to complete a project. For example, while I was in a course at the IEJC in August 2011, we all participated in a *mutirão* to clear the hillside of a local farm for planting. We spent five hours chopping down small trees and bushes, and weeds with machetes, and the money we earned was donated to the school. The idea was to learn the value of manual labor—à la Pistrak—while also contributing financially to the school.

In September 2011, a total of nine MST leaders were part of the CPP, overseeing the day-to-day tasks of the school in coordination with the students. There were three courses taking place: a cohort of students in a MAG high school program, a cohort in a community health high school program, and a group of seasoned MST educational activists taking a one-month course on the Pedagogy of MST. Each student cohort was divided into NBs of five to ten students who sent representatives to cohort-wide collectives (class coordinating collective of base nuclei [CNBTs]). The NBs and the CNBTs were in charge of the educational decisions concerning their programs, in coordination with at least one of the MST leaders in the CPP. Each of the program's CNBTs also sent two students to participate in a school-wide collective, which helped the CPP make decisions concerning the whole school. In addition, there were several school-wide work collectives and monthly general assemblies, with everyone in the school participating. The ultimate goal at the IEJC was to cultivate an authentic form of student self-governance, similar to Makarenko's Gorky colony, with the constant guidance of experienced MST educational leaders.

The establishment of the IEJC in 1995 has allowed the MST to experiment with different educational practices, while also offering professional training to local activists. Cleide Almeida, one of the nine MST activists in the CPP in 2011, explained that when the MST first founded the school, there was a big debate about whether the movement should be putting resources into this type of professional training. Many activists argued that this was the job of the government, not civil society. In the end, the MST leaders who were skeptical of the school realized that the MST was in dire need of people who could do the technical work required for the survival of the settlements.[69] If the movement did not train their activists, outside professionals with no notion of the MST's political vision would come to fulfill these technical needs. The MST decided to create IEJC with three interconnected goals: political formation—to train new activists; technical formation—to attend to the technical needs of the settlements; and high school access—to raise the level of educational access in the settlements and camps.

Between 1995 and 2010, more than three thousand students studied at ITERRA. Whether these activists graduate with a degree in teaching, cooperative administration, or community health, the combination of political formation and technical training that they receive contributes to the MST's struggle for social transformation in the countryside. Furthermore,

Picture 1.1 Students at IEJC/ITERRA perform a *mística* (cultural and political performance) celebrating the Soviet educator Anton Makarenko by recreating his image with beans and rice. September 2011.
Courtesy of author

although the majority of youth in MST settlements still access secondary education through the traditional public school system, the establishment of IEJC has given the MST an opportunity to refine its pedagogical approach—and its unique mixture of Freirean, Soviet, and organic movement practices—in a space where the MST has almost complete autonomy. For the MST, the IEJC is a real utopia, a space where activists can realize their educational vision. These educational practices might never be fully implemented in the public school system.[70] Nonetheless, the IEJC offers local activists inspiration to continue struggling for educational change in their communities, and a vision for that change. The MST's construction of the IEJC in 1995 was an accumulative product of the movement's other educational initiatives over the previous decade. Table 1.1 outlines the movement's first decade of educational initiatives, after establishing a national MST education sector in 1987.

"Systematizing," Publicizing, and Promoting the Pedagogy of the MST

Throughout the 1980s and 1990s, MST leaders drew on diverse pedagogical theories to develop their local educational initiatives (Table 1.2).

Freirean theory offered MST activists a concrete classroom pedagogy for working with children and adults, involving generative themes, problem posing, community research, and connecting academic content to the local context. In addition, the MST leadership took from Freire the idea of agency—that working-class people could be protagonists in constructing a new society. MST leaders began referring to the movement's educational approach as the Pedagogy of the MST, after Freire's *Pedagogy of the Oppressed*. Rather than constructing a pedagogy *for* the MST, the goal was to construct something *of* the MST, led by the movement itself. As MST educational leader Maria de Jesus Santos, says, "When people ask us, 'What pedagogy does the MST follow?' we should respond that the MST does not follow a pedagogy, the MST has a pedagogy!"

The MST also drew on socialist pedagogies, in particular the work of Moisey Pistrak and Anton Makarenko. From these writings, MST activists began to theorize the pedagogical value of manual labor and of students' participatory governance of public schools. Some of these practices were already taking place in the camps, for example, the involvement of all community members in work tasks and the formation of small collectives for internal decision making. Nonetheless, these Soviet theories helped MST activists give meaning to their local practices and think about how to implement these initiatives in their schools.[71] To many outside intellectuals, this combination of Freirean and Soviet theories often felt like a contradiction; the combination of a bottom-up, constructivist pedagogy with a more centralized, top-down approach based on collective discipline. Nonetheless, the movement's leaders refused to pick between these theories, declaring both central to their political and economic vision.

The MST's educational approach also evolved from the organic practices of the movement itself. For example, in the 1980s, MST activists began to incorporate into their educational activities *místicas*: cultural and political performances using dance, music, theater, plastic arts, video, or other cultural expressions to reflect on past and current political struggles.[72] Before every MST meeting or event, activists performed *místicas*, in order to feel the spirit of struggle before entering into an intellectual debate. Teachers in schools on MST settlements helped students produce their own *místicas*, creatively drawing on their local culture and making connections between the MST and other movements. By singing a song that came from a settlement's popular culture or reciting a poem about other socialist struggles, students embodied a collective history and began to understand the interconnections between the MST and other movements. Together these three theoretical inspirations—the *Pedagogy of the Oppressed*, socialist pedagogies, and the movement's own organic practices—began

Table 1.1 NATIONAL MST EDUCATIONAL INITIATIVES, 1987–1996

Educational Initiative	Initial Date and Location	Purpose and Participants	Institutional Support
First National Seminar for Educators in Areas of Agrarian Reform	July 1987, São Mateus, Espírto Santos	Share the experiences of developing MST educational initiatives in camps and settlements; thirteen educators from areas of agrarian reform in four states	MST national initiative
Founding of the national MST education sector	1987, first national seminar marks the founding	Coordinate attempts to transform Brazilian education	MST national initiative
Founding of the Foundation of Educational Development and Research (FUNDEP)	1989	Establish a school for popular movements in the countryside; social movement leaders in the state of Rio Grande do Sul, including from the MST	MST, Regional Commission of People Affected by Damns (CRAB), Women Rural Workers Movement (MMTR), Rural Department of the Central Union of Workers (DR-CUT)
High School Degree and Teaching Certification Program (MAG)	January 1990, Braga, Rio Grande do Sul	High school degree program for training teachers; 45–55 students per cohort; twelfth cohort in progress in 2010	Organized by FUNDEP/DER and the MST; course moves to IEJC in 1997
First MST Literacy Campaign	1991–1993, Rio Grande do Sul	Provide literacy training for families in camps and settlements; 2,000 people which involves 100 literacy educators; 10–20 students in each of the 100 cohorts	Partnership with the Cultural Institute of São Francisco de Assis, with funding from the Ministry of Education. Freire participated in launching
Training in Cooperative Administration (TAC) high school Program	June 1993, Braga, RS	High school degree program to administer cooperatives; 40–60 students per cohort; eleventh cohort in progress in 2012	Partnership with FUNDEP/ DER and MST; course moves to IEJC in 1995

(*continued*)

Table 1.1 CONTINUED

Educational Initiative	Initial Date and Location	Purpose and Participants	Institutional Support
National Seminar on Adult and Youth Education	November 1993, São Paulo	Reflection and debate about the ongoing MST literacy programs; hundreds of educators and students participating in the literacy programs	Program partners fund the seminars; three more seminars in 1997, 1998, and 1999
High School Degree and Teaching Certification Program (MAG) in central western Brazil	1995, Espírito Santos	Offer MST teacher training programs in more Brazilian regions; 50 students in first cohort. Program expands to dozens of other regions	Partnership with Federal University of Espírito Santos. Dozens of universities sponsor the program's expansion to other regions.
Educational Institute of Josué de Castro (IJEC)/ ITERRA	1995–present Veranópolis, RS	Provide access to high school degrees along with political and technical training to movement activists; 3,000 graduates (1995–2010) in a variety of programs	IEJC recognized as a high school degree-conferring institution by the Rio Grande do Sul State Education Advisory Board
National Adult Literacy Program	August 1996 to June 1997, multiple regions	Provide literacy training for families in camps and settlements; 7,500 people which involves 500 literacy educators; 10–20 students in each of the 500 cohorts	First official partnership between the Ministry of Education and the MST

to evolve into a comprehensive educational proposal for rural schooling. Table 1.2 summarizes these pedagogical foundations.

By the early 1990s, there were also multiple universities and international organizations funding the MST's educational initiatives. One of the major reasons that the MST's educational approach received so much national and international recognition in the 1990s was the priority the MST education collective gave to writing about and analyzing their educational experiences. The MST refers to this as systematizing, or systematical summarizing and analyzing for the purpose of sharing. In 1990, the MST education sector published its first educational text, "Our Struggle Is Our School," which includes testimonies of teachers working in schools on MST settlements throughout the 1980s. Another important text, "Basic

Table 1.2 PEDAGOGICAL FOUNDATIONS OF THE MST'S EDUCATIONAL
PROPOSAL

Pedagogical Foundation	Specific Authors and/or Theories	How These Ideas Were Introduced to the Movement
Pedagogy of the oppressed	*Paulo Freire*; critique of "banking" education; promotion of generative themes, problem posing, drawing on students' knowledge; critique of vanguardism	Activist participation in base ecclesial communities (CEBs); Freirean educators also helped to train local MST activist-teachers
Socialist pedagogies	*Anton Makarenko, Moisey Pistrak, Nadezhda Krupskaya*; student self-governance, cooperation, educational value of planning and carrying out collective manual labor tasks, collaboration and work	Outside intellectuals introduced these theorists to activists in the mid-1980s and their ideas resonated with the movement's local practices; in the 1990s the MST also studied Cuban literacy campaigns and infant circles
MST practices	Collective agricultural practices and agroecology in schools; cultural traditions, including *mística*; integration of students into social struggles	In the late 1980s the MST began to perceive its own practices as sources of knowledge and consciously incorporated these practices into their educational program

Document of the MST," published in February 1991, articulated for the first time the MST's goal of transforming public education. In 1991, the MST also launched two different notebook series on education: *Boletim da Educação* (Education Bulletin) and *Caderno de Educação* (Education Notebook). These publication series included practical guides for teachers implementing the MST's educational proposal, such as "How to Create the School That We Want," "How to Teach Children *Mística*," "Adult Education and Math," and "A Proposal for Fifth Through Eight Grade." In November 1994, the MST added a new education series on Making History (*Fazendo História*), which includes children's stories of Brazilian social struggles (e.g., the history of Brazilian slave rebellion) that teachers can use in their classroom.[73]

In 1996, the MST education collective published its eighth issue of the *Caderno da Educação*, an important text on the "Principles of Education in the MST" that summarizes the MST's core philosophical and pedagogical approaches to education. Thus, by 1996 the MST had put into writing a coherent educational proposal—the "Pedagogy of the MST"—both for study and for implementation in camps and settlements throughout the country. These MST publications served as study texts for teachers working in schools on settlements and camps. In addition, teachers used the publications geared toward children as curricular offerings in their schools. At the same time, the publications summarized the MST's educational approach for a broader audience, illustrating to the public the different components of the MST's educational proposal. These publications also showed Brazilian society the value that the MST placed on reflection about and improvement of their educational practice.[74]

CONCLUSION

In summary, the Pedagogy of the MST evolved over the course of the 1980s and 1990s because the movement developed concrete initiatives that allowed activists to experiment with the educational theories that they were studying. During the period of military dictatorship, local MST activists began organizing alternative educational practices, often based on their experiences with Freirean education within the Catholic Church. Then, as the country began to consolidate its new democracy, activists engaged other texts written by Soviet educational theorists and a national education sector was established. In the 1990s, even as the country shifted into a period of neoliberal economic policies and state–society conflict, the movement was able to establish a range of high school and literacy programs that raised the educational level of MST members, integrated more women and youth into the movement, and allowed local activists to prefigure the movement's economic, political, and social goals.

The 1990s was also a period when calls for participatory governance were growing across the country. Sometimes the MST's educational demands overlapped seamlessly with these broader calls for participatory governance, while at other times these initiatives sat in tension. Benjamin Goldfrank (2011b) writes about two visions within the Brazilian left: the "radical democratic position," which saw the municipal government as a site for demonstrating civil society capacity to govern effectively and consolidate local power; and the Leninist vision, which saw participation as an attempt to create parallel power structures that could support a revolutionary transformation of society (164). The MST embodied both of these visions, promoting broad-based civil society participation in state institutions, as well as a particular socialist agrarian program. Dagnino (2007) refers to the "perverse confluence" that took place in the 1990s, as neoliberal visions of decentralization overlapped with radical calls for participatory democracy. Similarly, the MST's promotion of socialist practices in state institutions converged with the calls for participatory democracy that became embedded in diverse Brazilian institutions during this period. Political opportunities were abundant, and the MST's leadership had the capacity to take advantage of these opportunities at multiple levels. The

Picture 1.2 Banner celebrating socialism hung on the outside walls of ITERRA/IEJC for the MST's twenty-five-year anniversary. October 2010.
Courtesy of author

MST's real educational utopias became important spaces for leaders from across the country to live the movement's theories and ideas in practice.

In the next chapter, I analyze the violence that erupted in the Brazilian countryside in the mid-1990s and how this led to the MST's most important educational victory in 1997, the National Program for Education in Areas of Agrarian Reform (PRONERA). This chapter will show that it is possible to institutionalize radical goals within the state, even during an unfavorable national context, and how the MST's institutionalization of its educational program through PRONERA has contributed significantly to the internal capacity of the movement.

CHAPTER 2

Transforming Universities to Build a Movement

The Case of PRONERA

This is a dream for us—we never imagined that we would have access to higher education.
    —Vanderlúcia Simplicio, *national leader in MST Education Sector*

Now we have pedagogues, agronomists, lawyers, journalists, all of these professions in the countryside that are important for the working class.
    —Maria de Jesus Santos, *national leader in MST Education Sector*

In this chapter, I describe one of the MST's most important educational victories: the National Program for Education in Areas of Agrarian Reform (PRONERA). This case illustrates that social movements can increase their internal capacity by strategically engaging institutions, and that it is possible for activists to institutionalize their goals within the state apparatus, without being co-opted and demobilized. To the contrary, PRONERA has directly contributed to the MST's internal social movement infrastructure and ability to renew its leadership. These achievements, however, have required ongoing political advocacy and contentious protest.

Created in 1997 by center-right President Fernando Henrique Cardoso, PRONERA has allowed thousands of MST leaders access to higher education, while also increasing funding for literacy and high school degree programs in areas of agrarian reform. PRONERA has also deepened the relationships between MST educational activists and university professors, as well as with other social movement and union leaders who began taking courses through the program. Furthermore, PRONERA's governance structure and its location within the National Institute of Colonization and Agrarian Reform (INCRA) has allowed the MST to maintain a high degree of control over the program. Again, the case of PRONERA is a clear illustration that it is possible for a social movement to institutionalize radical initiatives, and that engaging formal institutions can increase a movement's internal capacity to achieve its social and economic goals. In promoting an educational program tailored to areas of agrarian reform, the MST embodies a Gramscian political strategy, attempting to cultivate the movement's own organic intellectuals to take on the necessary tasks the movement needs to sustain itself—and utilizing the temporary openings within the state to offer these alternative educational programs to activists.

I discuss the founding and expansion of PRONERA during two different periods: first, the continuation of a period of neoliberalism and state–society conflict during the two presidential mandates of President Fernando Henrique Cardoso (1995–2002), and then, through a period of social movement participation and class compromise, beginning after President Luis Inácio Lula da Silva (2003–2010) took office. During the first period, public outrage provoked by the government's massacre of dozens of landless activists created a political opportunity for the MST to push through a national education program for areas of agrarian reform, PRONERA. Through PRONERA, the MST was able to develop its first bachelor's degree program, which became an important space for the MST to continue refining its educational approach. This program also illustrated to the MST the many conflicts that emerge when trying to implement the movement's educational proposal in the elite university system. I describe these conflicts and how they shaped the MST's relationship to future university partners. The first bachelor's degree program is also representative of a real tension that continues to characterize the movement's educational approach between students' individual rights and the MST's collective discipline.

In the second part of the chapter, I discuss PRONERA's expansion and the dynamics of the long march through the institutions under a progressive political regime. The Workers' Party (PT) invested much more money than the previous administration in agrarian reform settlements through programs like PRONERA. A system of triple governance developed that involved collaboration between state, university, and social movement actors, allowing the MST to maintain a high degree of control over PRONERA programs. Nonetheless, I argue that even with a left-leaning government in power, the MST activists had to engage in both institutional and disruptive tactics in order to advance their educational goals. To illustrate this point, I describe the challenges the MST confronted developing a geography degree program at the State University of São Paulo (UNESP). Then, I analyze an attack on PRONERA that took place between 2008 and 2010, and how the relationships the MST built with university and state actors became critical to securing the program. The multiple attempts to end PRONERA illustrate the challenges and possibilities of defending institutional spaces that directly threaten elite interests.

RURAL VIOLENCE AND STATE CONCESSIONS IN AN ERA OF CONFLICT (1995–2002)

As I discussed in Chapter 1, in the mid-1990s conflicts between social movements and the Brazilian state intensified. Globally, and in particular in Latin America, governments pushed through neoliberal policies that promoted decreased social spending, eliminated tariffs, and opened up domestic markets to financial investment. In Brazil, President Fernando Henrique Cardoso of the center-right Brazilian Social Democratic Party (PSDB) took office in 1995. Although Cardoso created some new social programs, his administration's main concern was maintaining economic stability through fiscal austerity and a conservative monetary policy. He also implemented a series of market-oriented reforms, including cuts to the public service sector and the pension system, privatization, and trade liberalization (Ondetti 2008, 144).

In 1995, as President Cardoso took office, the MST held its Third National Congress, with 5,226 delegates from twenty-two states. The moto of the Third Congress was "Agrarian Reform, a Struggle for All," an attempt to demonstrate that agrarian reform not only benefited rural workers, but urban ones as well, by increasing food production and decreasing housing costs in cities (MST 2015, 45). The MST also began organizing more land occupations across the country. Although Cardoso had promised to implement an agrarian reform program during his 1994 campaign, as president he critiqued land occupations. This emboldened the entrenched agrarian elite that opposed agrarian reform. Incidents of violence against rural workers increased throughout the country. On August 9, 1995, in the northern state of Rondônia, military police, under state jurisdiction, entered an occupied encampment and killed ten landless people, including a seven-year-old girl. Three of the landless leaders were reported to be executed and several tortured (Ondetti 2008, 150).[1] These events spurred a series of national protests.

Then, on April 17, 1996, military police massacred nineteen MST activists in the northern state of Pará. On April 17, two thousand families had been camped alongside a road in the municipality of Eldorado dos Carajás, when two groups of military police descended on the families. The military police had orders from Governor Almir Gabriel (also from Cardoso's PSDB party) to "eliminate the encamped families" (MST 2015, 47). The police opened fire and nineteen workers were immediately killed. Two men died a few months later and more than seventy others were injured.[2] The massacre was caught on camera, sparking international outrage.[3] Ironically, the massacre created a political opportunity—as McAdam (1999) defines it, an event that "serves to undermine the calculations and assumptions on which the political establishment is structured" (41)—as public dismay at the government's actions increased national sympathy for the movement and for agrarian reform. A week after the massacre, the President expropriated dozens of land estates, including the area occupied by the activists killed in Pará, offering the rights to use this land to thousands of encamped families (Ondetti 2008).

The 1997 massacre also sparked a surge of support for agrarian reform throughout the country. In February 1997, the MST organized a National March on Brasília for Agrarian Reform. Three groups, each with a few hundred MST leaders, left from different parts of the country and marched for two months to the capital, around 620 miles. They organized meetings and educational events with local communities as they marched. The march, together with the sympathetic media coverage and the national and international attention, helped the movement garner even more support. When the activists arrived to the capital on April 17, the one-year anniversary of the Eldorado dos Carajás massacre, over 100,000 people from a variety of social movements, unions, universities, and other organizations joined the marchers to demand large-scale agrarian reform. Under this pressure, Cardoso was forced to follow through on his promise to implement agrarian reform. By 1998, the end of Cardoso's first term, the state granted more than 300,000 families land access—double the amount given in the previous decade. In Chapter 1, Figures 1.2, 1.3, and 1.4 illustrate these spikes in the number of land occupations and families participating during this period, and the amount of new families issued land rights.[4]

Creating the National Program for Education in Areas of Agrarian Reform (PRONERA)

By the late 1990s, the national MST education sector already had developed dozens of educational initiatives with state and municipal governments across the country, including multiple literacy campaigns and teacher training programs. However, according to national MST leader Edgar Kolling, in the late 1990s the movement's educational proposal expanded as it received a free ride (*carona*) with this larger movement for agrarian reform. In July 1997, a few months after the national march and the 100,000-person rally in Brasília, the national MST education sector organized a National Meeting for Educators in Areas of Agrarian Reform (ENERA). Over seven hundred educators participated, nearly double the originally anticipated attendance (Kolling, Vargas, and Caldart 2012, 503). The meeting was a week of debate and discussion about the MST's pedagogical proposal, with lectures from MST leaders, university professors, and other invited allies. The hundreds of teachers at the event had the opportunity to share about their experiences teaching in MST settlements and camps. A childcare center, known within the MST as a *ciranda*,[5] was set up for the children at the conference to ensure the full participation of all parents. The days began with regions performing *místicas* (see Chapter 1): theatrical presentations using poetry, music, and dance to touch on themes related to the Brazilian countryside, education, and social struggle. Other cultural activities—musical presentations, dance performances, theatrical interludes—were integrated throughout the week.

The major demand that came out of the meeting was for the federal government to create a national education program specifically for areas of agrarian reform (settlements and camps). In October 1997, several professors from the University of Brasilia (UnB)—one of the institutions coordinating the ENERA conference—organized a meeting with representatives from six universities to discuss how their institutions could support the MST in creating this program.[6] Many of these professors were already familiar with the MST's educational approach because they had partnered with the movement to organize literacy programs during the previous decade. The advocacy of these university professors proved critical, offering the movement's demand more legitimacy. For example, according to University of Brasília professor Monica Molina, her university provost had connections within the Cardoso administration and helped facilitate support for the MST's proposed program.[7]

Although the Ministry of Education (MEC) generally administers all federal education programs, the MST leadership opposed putting their new program in this large and bureaucratic agency. During the Cardoso administration, the MEC had prioritized national assessments, standardization, and teacher accountability, not diversity and inclusion. Furthermore, collaboration between civil society and the MEC was minimal. As Edgar explained, "Up until that point, we had never been able to meet with any MEC officials, unless a senator or congressional representative intervened. For us, the MEC was a cloister, something that was closed and not willing to have a dialogue. We would never propose that the MEC administer one of our programs, given that we could not even set up a meeting there!" The

MEC, a well-funded, centralized, and important agency in policy debates, reflected closely the ideals of the right-leaning federal government.

In contrast, the National Institute for Colonization and Agrarian Reform (INCRA), the agency overseeing the judicial, technical, and administrative aspects of agrarian reform, was underfunded and relatively neglected in national politics. After the 1996 massacre, President Cardoso had removed INCRA from the jurisdiction of the conservative Ministry of Agriculture and put the agency under the umbrella of an Extraordinary Ministry of Agrarian Issues, which in January 2000 became the Ministry of Agrarian Development (MDA). While the Ministry of Agriculture continued to promote large-scale agribusiness and a primary export model, the MDA was charged with supporting family and small-scale farming. The fact that INCRA was now under the umbrella of the MDA meant that there was more support for agrarian reform. In addition, MST leaders already had many personal relationships with INCRA officials. Consequently, the MST leadership fought for INCRA—an agency they perceived as more aligned with their political objectives—to administer the new national education program.[8]

On April 16, 1998, the day before the two-year anniversary of the massacre of Eldorado dos Carajás, President Cardoso officially created the National Program for Education in Areas of Agrarian Reform (PRONERA) and put it under INCRA's jurisdiction. President Cardoso created this program because of the political pressure he faced to make amends to the landless movement after the 1995 and 1996 massacres, the increased support for agrarian reform among the broader population, and the universities' internal maneuvering. PRONERA was a clear concession to the movement, an attempt to quell the rural unrest. Initially, the federal government had intended for the program to only fund literacy initiatives; however, the MST leaders had other plans: they wanted to use PRONERA to occupy the public university system.

THE MST'S FIRST BACCALAUREATE PROGRAM
(1998–2001)

By the time PRONERA was created in 1998, hundreds of the MST's national and state leaders had already graduated from the movement's formal schooling programs. A large portion of these MST activists had traveled to Rio Grande do Sul to study in the movement's High School Degree and Teaching Certification (MAG) and Technical Administration of Cooperatives (TAC) programs (see Chapter 1). Others had been students in the many literacy and adult education programs that the movement had developed in partnership with universities, state governments, and the Ministry of Education. However, in 1998, very few of the thousands of MST activists in the movement's national and statewide leadership bodies held a college degree.

Although these leaders were constantly studying, reading, and learning through nonformal movement courses and meetings—which took place in the movement's political training schools (*escolas da formação*)—in the eyes of the Brazilian state they were still only high school graduates. The MST leadership had no way to offer formal education beyond high school. Furthermore, activists found it difficult to pursue bachelor's degrees on their own because entrance exams to attend the free public universities were notoriously difficult, and pursuing higher education would leave them with little time to dedicate to the movement. Rubneuza Leandro, an educational activist from Pernambuco, explained why obtaining higher education was important for the MST during this period:

> When you are in the movement, you are an activist twenty-four hours a day; you are always at the disposal of the movement. It is hard to fit in the routine of formal education, because you would have to stop your activism to study. Lots of people were doing this, leaving the movement because we had reached a ceiling for the level of education that activists could attain. . . . The professors at universities would also not respect us—we had hit a limit because we did not have higher education. However, we did not want to study in any type of university. We started analyzing how we could offer higher education to our activists.[9]

In 1997, the year before PRONERA was approved, the MST began approaching dozens of public universities, proposing the creation of a bachelor's degree program in pedagogy for educators living in agrarian reform communities. The MST contacted university professors who had been allies of the movement, telling them about PRONERA and asking for help. Although some professors supported the idea, other faculty and all of the provosts at these universities rejected the MST's proposal. While many of these provosts were supportive of the MST's educational initiatives, especially the movement's literacy campaigns, none of them were willing to offer a university-level degree program specifically for and in partnership with the movement. Edgar interpreted this reluctance as an indication that although the MST was continually invited to talk at these universities about their educational initiatives, "the idea that *sem terra* [landless people] could come to the university to study, as peers, was intolerable."

Finding the University of Ijuí

The MST's attempt to provide higher education to its activists might have ended in 1998, if not for a small private university located in the southern state of Rio Grande do Sul—the University of Ijuí.[10] As one University of Ijuí professor, Dinarte Belato, explained, the university already had had a long history of activism, which traced back to the early 1960s.[11] During this period, society was "boiling" with grassroots organizing—there was a huge student movement, progressive Catholic groups were strong, Freirean popular education was proliferating—and University of Ijuí professors were part and parcel of this organizing. This grassroots activism came to an abrupt halt in 1964, with the military coup. However, even under this repression, professors at the University of Ijuí developed clandestine education projects. For example, Dinarte taught Freirean literacy classes for construction workers, helping them to read and write while also reflecting on the reasons for their poor working conditions. The fact that the university was private facilitated the ability of faculty members to engage in this covert work, illustrating how institutions can protect activists under hostile, authoritarian regimes.[12]

During the democratic transition in the early 1980s, there was another explosion of protest and activism throughout Brazil. The professors at the University of Ijuí were well positioned to help these emerging movements, given their two decades of underground organizing during the dictatorship. They developed meaningful connections with local activists, including the landless movement, and maintained those connections over the next decade. At the end of 1997, after the MST's proposal for creating a bachelor's degree program in pedagogy was rejected by dozens of public universities, MST activists contacted several University of Ijuí professors. Dinarte remembered this moment: "The MST asked, who can help us create a bachelor's degree program? What university has a pedagogical proposal that allows them to do this? And we told them, we are able to do this! We already had these past experiences . . . and we knew the professors at our university would embrace the program." Although public university professors were cautious about supporting the MST, the University of Ijuí professors were enthusiastic.

Once the professors agreed to develop a baccalaureate program in partnership with the MST, the next step was elaborating a proposal for the four-year program, which had to be approved by the university administration. The proposal included an explanation of the need for the program and a description of its pedagogical approach, its structure and curricular requirements, and the role of the different partners in the program, including the MST education sector. The objective of the degree program was to train teachers to work in fifth- through eighth-grade classrooms on agrarian reform settlements. The proposal identified the University of Ijuí as the appropriate institution to create this program, due to its history of dedication to social movements. The university approved the proposal and the program became known as the Pedagogy of Land, indicating the relationship between pedagogical training and agrarian reform.

On January 20, 1998, fifty-eight students from MST settlements and camps from thirteen states traveled to Ijuí for the first semester of the Pedagogy of Land bachelor's degree program. Many of the students were already prominent leaders in the MST education sector, and although the majority of the students came from Rio Grande do Sul, the fact that thirteen different states were represented illustrated the reach of the movement's educational program. Fifty of the fifty-eight students were women, also reflecting the dominant role of female activists in the MST education sector. The Cardoso administration had announced its intention to create PRONERA later that year; however, the MST leadership decided to launch the bachelor's degree program early with their own resources, to increase pressure on the government to fulfill its promise. After PRONERA was officially established in April 1998, INCRA began funding all of the costs of the program. Thus, PRONERA itself did not create more educational access for the MST; rather, the MST education sector creatively used this new institutional legitimacy to convince university professors to develop an educational program specifically for the movement.

The MST's Pedagogical Approach at the University of Ijuí

In addition to training teachers to work in settlement schools, the MST sought to use the first bachelor's degree program to refine the movement's pedagogical proposal, through the serious study of educational theories and the prefiguration of those theories in practice. The MST leadership understood this process as a form of praxis, or the ongoing dialogue between theory and practice, action and reflection. In what follows, I describe six of the pedagogical and organizational practices that became central to the Pedagogy of Land program.

Pedagogia da Alternância

The most unique aspect of the Pedagogy of Land program was that the university offered the program through the pedagogy of alternation (*pedagogia da alternância*), the rotation between study periods lasting one to two months and community periods of four to six months. The students traveled to the University of Ijuí for seven study periods (January–February and July) over the course of four years, when the majority of the student body was not in class. PRONERA funded the housing, food, and other basic necessities while the students were at the university, as well as travel to and from the university twice a year. This meant that the students could fulfill their activist tasks and teaching responsibilities in their home states as they pursued their degree.

Beyond such logistical concerns, the MST's embrace of the *pedagogia da alternância* also reflected the movement's commitment to integrating theory and practice. During the study periods, the students were in class the entire day and had a rigorous schedule, taking up to ten classes per one-to-two-month semester (see Appendix B for full curriculum). Then, in the community periods, the students put the theories they learned into practice through local community assignments. For example, in a class about infant education at the University of Ijuí, the students theorized the role of play in young children's educational experience. To complete their activity hours for the course, they returned to their communities and set up playgrounds in their local schools that were pedagogically appropriate for young children. Sometimes the students were able to integrate activity hours for several courses into a single project, for example, implementing Freirean pedagogies in their school classrooms or putting educational theories into practice through their activism in the MST education sector.

Research

For the MST, research is a central principle of education, allowing students to investigate their reality, register local histories, question appearances, and understand social processes. In the Pedagogy of Land program, students had to complete final thesis projects, collecting primary data in their communities on an educational topic. For example, MST leader Rubneuza Leandro wrote her final social studies project on the lack of participation of teachers from the sugarcane regions of Pernambuco in the MST's educational activities.[13] She interviewed dozens of teachers, trying to understand the political, economic, and cultural reasons why teachers resisted the MST's pedagogical support. Additionally, Rubneuza analyzed the history of the region's sugarcane production and political violence, and their effects on education. This research project contributed to both Rubneuza's intellectual growth and the MST's educational decisions in this region, thus directly increasing the strategic capacity of the movement.

Student Self-Governance

Another central part of the Pedagogy of Land program was the prefiguration of the MST's principle of self-governance (*auto-gestão*). The practice of self-governance was a rejection of the traditional hierarchy whereby students simply come to the university to learn and professors to teach. Instead, with self-governance, the students became the center of every decision-making process. The Pedagogy of Land cohort adopted the organizational structure of the MST's camps and settlements, dividing themselves into small collectives, or base nucleus (*núcleo de base*, or NBs, explained in Chapter 1), of five to eight students. Since the Pedagogy of Land cohort had a range of experiences participating in the MST's other collective spaces, the NBs always included a combination of newer and more experienced activists. The NBs were in charge of carrying out many of the logistical, organizational, and pedagogical tasks during the course of the Pedagogy of Land program. For example, during each class an NB was responsible for taking attendance, facilitating discussion, and administering classroom discipline.

At the end of each study period, the NBs collectively evaluated the courses they had taken, including the professors' pedagogies and the readings that they had been assigned. The cohort also met for critique and self-critique, evaluating each other's contributions one by one. Ivori Moraes, an activist from Rio Grande do Sul in the first cohort reflected: "This process of critique and self-critique is important, because if you are going to live in a collective, airing grievances about each other is necessary . . . I am a teacher in a school now, and if I say anything bad about someone, I become their enemy. This does not help us grow collectively."[14]

Also, central to the students' self-governance was the class coordinating collective, which included a representative from each NB. The coordinating collective made decisions for the entire cohort, based on the NBs' discussions. The coordinating collective was also responsible for organizing the daily logistics of the program with the university professors. If the students decided that they wanted to have an extra day to complete a homework assignment, the coordinating collective would bring this request to the professor and negotiate a new timeline for turning in the assignment. After the collective evaluation of each study period, the coordinating collective would bring suggestions to the professors overseeing the program. Ivori was a member of the coordinating collective. He remembered that one time they demanded a new professor for their research methodology class, because the NBs had all criticized the teacher's syllabus and his pedagogical approach. The University of Ijuí assigned a new person to the class the following study period. The MST activists' contentious co-governance and outspoken critiques allowed them to have an unusual degree of influence over their educational experience—perhaps to the detriment of some faculty's own desires.

The Political-Pedagogical Collective

Several MST activists who were not students in the program also participated in each study period to offer advice, guidance, and support. This support collective, which is a central part of all of the MST's formal and nonformal educational programs, is called the Political-Pedagogical Collective (CPP).[15] Rosali Caldart and Edgar Kolling were two national MST educational leaders in this support collective, responsible for visiting the cohort each study period. Rosali and Edgar made sure that the program was completing its political goal: training a cohort of MST activists who could more meaningfully participate in the movement. They met regularly with the NBs each study period, reflecting on any challenges that emerged within the cohort or issues that the cohort had with the university professors. Rosali and Edgar also organized extra moments for study and debate on topics that were particularly relevant to the movement. For example, during one study period they invited national MST leader João Pedro Stédile to teach for three days on the contemporary agrarian context in Brazil—a noncredit class that was not part of the official curriculum. Edgar and Rosali also shared information with the cohort about the MST's national activities, such as the number of land occupations that month or preparations for the World Social Forum in 2001. However, as Vanderlúcia Simplicio, an activist from Ceará, emphasized, "Students really coordinated the day-to-day aspects of the course and developed the relationships with the university."

Collective Living and Collaborative Work Practices

One of the MST's most important educational principles is that of collectivity and collaboration. In order to promote collectivity among the cohort, the national education sector decided to have the students live together in a local boarding house. The Pedagogy of Land cohort organized life in the boarding house collectively, cooking together, eating together, and studying together. This form of collective living was already familiar to most of the students, as they had collectively governed their camps and settlements for years. By living together, the MST also had many opportunities to put collective resistance into practice. For example, an elderly German man, Mr. Schultz, owned the boarding house they were living in and was accustomed to taking advantage of the students who lived there by offering only the cheapest accommodations. The cushions that Mr. Schultz provided were stuffed with cattle feed, and several of the students got rashes all over their bodies from sleeping on them. During one study period, several of the Pedagogy of Land students marched to the backyard of the boarding house, dragging three cushions and setting them on fire, demanding that Mr. Schultz invest some of his money in new cushions. Mr. Schultz, unaccustomed to collective demands from his tenants, agreed to buy new cushions for his establishment. This story illustrates how the MST's presence in this university town, and the students' willingness to engage in contentious political action, influenced the wider community.

The collective living arrangement also helped the students overcome the financial difficulties they faced. An MST leader from Rio Grande do Sul, Elizabete Witcel, explained, "PRONERA was supposed to pay for everything, the professors, the university, food, and housing, but the money sometimes did not arrive. . . . We had to collect money through raffles and share our incomes. . . . We found it hard to survive, but possible, because we were acting collectively." In one case, the severely underfunded students pled for help from a local principal, who let them sleep in her school for the entire study period.

Childcare was also a collective responsibility. While women in conventional university settings often drop out of school when they have children, the women in the Pedagogy of Land cohort were able to continue with their schooling uninterrupted because the cohort organized a collective childcare center (known as a *ciranda* within the movement). The cohort found an activist in the MST education sector who, for a small stipend, cared for the children while they were studying. The students negotiated with the university to be able to use an empty classroom on campus for the childcare. The childcare initially caused resentment among the other students, who thought that the administration was offering special privileges to the movement. However, as Ivori explained, some of these students began to realize that it was the MST's collective organizing that had forced the university to offer this space to the students. These students began mobilizing around similar demands. For the MST activists, the incorporation of collective housing and collaborative work tasks was a way of bringing the movement's organizational principles into the university, which had implications beyond their own cohort.

Cultural Practices and Political Struggle

Finally, the MST prioritized the integration of their cultural and political practices into the university sphere. Every morning the students performed a *mística*, using poetry, theater, music, and dance to express an aspect of social struggle in the countryside. Saturday evenings, after six days of intensive study, the movement organized large social gatherings known as cultural nights at the boarding house, cooking traditional foods and playing music from their communities. These cultural nights also began with an elaborate *mística* that incorporated a particular political theme, such as a tribute to the Cuban Revolution or a denunciation of the killing of an MST leader, followed by a dance party that lasted late into the night.

The Pedagogy of Land cohort also participated in actual political struggles while they studied at the University of Ijuí. For example, the cohort supported local political events and engaged in discussions with the University of Ijuí student government and other groups on campus. In July 1998, the second study period, the entire cohort took a bus to Brasília to participate in the First National Conference for a Basic Education of the Countryside (described in Chapter 3), presenting the opening *mística* at the conference. One study period the entire cohort even participated in an occupation of a Monsanto plantation, where genetically modified soy was being grown. Participating in a land occupation imbued a new, combative meaning to the pedagogies of land they were studying.

Conflicts Between the MST and the University of Ijuí

During the four years that the MST activists studied at the University of Ijuí, the faculty overseeing the program broadly supported the students and their pedagogical innovations. Nonetheless, conflicts and tensions developed between the institutional norms of the university and the MST's own political goals. These conflicts were not particular to the University of Ijuí, but rather, representative of the tensions that would continue to emerge as the MST occupied the university sphere. Adilio Perin, an MST activist from Rio Grande do Sul, recalled, "There was one math class where the professor taught a lot of information that had nothing to do with our reality. He would just enter, give his lecture, and leave everything on the board for us to study. He would not even talk to the class. He did not care who we were." While the MST wanted the professors to connect the content they were teaching to the lives of the students through debate and dialogue, many of the professors just gave the same lectures that they had developed for the general student body. Another student from Rio Grande do Sul, Rita de Cascia, recalled that the Pedagogy of Land cohort wanted professors to participate in their collective evaluations.[16] Some refused to participate in this process as it subverted the traditional teacher–student power hierarchy.

The institutional norms of the university thus came into conflict with the MST's practice of collectively evaluating their educational experience.

As described earlier, the MST leaders also wanted to make sure the program's curriculum included the educational theorists who made up the backbone of the movement's pedagogical proposal, such as the Soviet theorists discussed in Chapter 1 and the movement's own publications. The professors, however, demanded that the students adhere to the classical educational canon. Consequently, the students had to read these movement texts in the evenings or on weekends. Elizabete remembered these extra sessions. "We were busy studying and did not have time for additional meetings and political discussions, but we had to ask ourselves, do we value the education in the academy more than our own reality?" In practice, the students were studying two parallel curricula. Rosali Caldart explained, "The basis of the program was the university's curriculum, but all of the extras, the spices, were from the movement."

The movement's insistence on extra studying offended some of the university professors, who felt that inviting outside speakers to teach the students was disrespectful to the body of faculty already working at the university. The professors claimed that the Pedagogy of Land students were not interested in receiving an education from the University of Ijuí—they were just using the university to their own ends. Edgar recounted another conflict that developed with the faculty members who supported the "postmodern" turn in the academy: the rejection of grand theories and ideologies, including Marxism, and the focus on deconstruction and criticism. From the perspective of many MST activists, these postmodern ideas were not helpful because they rejected the unifying theory of class struggle that the movement promoted, while also denying the importance of social movements and collective resistance by focusing on the "deconstruction" of social categories. Edgar explained, "This theoretical perspective does not work with our outlook because we think that movements can transform the world through struggle." Other MST leaders echoed the belief that the academy value many theories that deny the agency of working-class populations.

Some students within the Pedagogy of Land cohort, however, resented the extra work that the MST required them to complete. This created yet another conflict within the university, as professors disregarded the MST's collective practices and supported students' individual choice not to complete the extra tasks. Elizabete told a story of a fellow student who wanted the Pedagogy of Land program to "enter the rhythm of the university." The student thought that the MST leaders in the coordinating collective were overstepping their authority by organizing the program differently than the rest of the university. Ivori remembered how stressful the situation was "because the student did not want to be part of the organization of the program. He did not want to be bothered with helping with childcare. He just wanted to be a student." The coordinators said he had to participate in the cohort's collective organization or leave the program. The University of Ijuí professors supported the student's decision to enroll in a normal pedagogy program, which did not include additional studying, collective living, or classes separate from the rest of the student body. Reflecting on the professors' support of the student's decision, Elizabete said, "In that moment, we realized that the university did not understand us or our proposal, because they supported and valued his decision one hundred percent." Neyta Oliveira, one of the University of Ijuí professors, also reflected on these events: "There is a limit. The university cannot just kick out a student. It is difficult to expel a student. So we resolved to transfer the student to the regular pedagogy program."[17]

While the university professors were protecting the individual rights of this student, the MST leadership was concerned about the precedent the Pedagogy of Land program would set for future PRONERA bachelor's degree programs. Ivori reflected in more detail:

> We seemed like monsters, Stalinists, anti-humanist, but this was not a personal question. We were setting the path for thousands of landless people to have access to university education. Legally, we already had the right to enter a university. But without a place to live, food to eat, childcare, landless people were not accessing this right. . . . We knew the Pedagogy of Land program would be a model for how to provide this access, and we knew we had to guarantee the movement's organizational and collective principles in the program.

The Pedagogy of Land cohort was rigid with their collective discipline, because they believed that transforming the traditional structure of the university system would be necessary to open up higher education access to poor, rural populations. For the MST activists, their entire educational project was at stake, which overshadowed concern for the individual rights of one student.

Despite these challenges, Dinarte and the other professors overseeing the Pedagogy of Land program continued to support the majority of the MST's initiatives. However, during the last study period, an unresolvable conflict developed between the students and the professors who had been their most adamant supporters. In the late 1990s, the Brazilian Ministry of Education began requiring that all private and public universities administer standardized tests to allow for national rankings of university program offerings. The national student movement had called for a public boycott of these tests, on the grounds that the quantitative assessment would diminish the purpose of higher education and produce competition be-tween institutions. Nonetheless, for the professors who went out on a limb to create the first PRONERA program—like Dinarte—the exam was crit-ical for the national legitimacy of the Pedagogy of Land program and the university itself. The Pedagogy of Land cohort debated the issue and made the collective decision that, despite the concerns of the faculty, they should align with the student movement. However, instead of boycotting the test—an action the University of Ijuí could have used to deny the students their diplomas—they sat for the exam but left all of the questions blank. Putting salt on the wound, they did not warn the professors about this de-cision. Although other students at the University of Ijuí also refused to take the test, the Pedagogy of Land was the only program where an entire cohort collectively decided to fail the test.

The professors in the Pedagogy department were outraged. The failed exams would seriously affect their department's national reputation, poten-tially reducing their enrollment and access to resources. Professor Neyta Oliveira said, "We agreed to work with the practices of the movement; we did what the movement wanted, but the movement refused to work with the practices of the university." Neyta criticized the activists' refusal to make strategic short-term compromises in order to promote the long-term national success of the program. Dinarte, one of the most important actors in convincing the University of Ijuí to develop this first PRONERA bacca-laureate program, was so insulted by the students' actions that he refused to attend the Pedagogy of Land graduation. The MST's political values had come into conflict with the requirements of the university, even at a pro-gressive university with professors dedicated to social change. The MST never developed another PRONERA program at the University of Ijuí.

The story of the MST's first bachelor's degree program is important both for its historical role helping the movement refine its pedagogical ap-proach, and as a representative case of the constraints, opportunities, and tensions that the MST faces when attempting to implement its educational proposal within the university sphere. First, the case illustrates why cer-tain institutional actors are more willing to experiment with alternative practices. While administrators and professors of public universities were wary about partnering with the MST, especially in the context of an an-tagonistic federal government, the University of Ijuí community embraced the proposal. The University of Ijuí was a private institution relatively insu-lated from the federal government, with professors who had long-standing ties with social movements and a common political mission. Second, the case illustrates that the process of institutionalizing social movement goals within the state is an active and dynamic process, not simply a moment when the movement's goals become frozen into a state structure. To the contrary, once PRONERA was created, the MST leadership had to use the program creatively to promote its educational goals, by seeking out university allies and helping to build an educational program that adhered to the movement's ideals. Third, this was an inherently contentious process, with different world visions and practices coming into conflict. Although the MST education sector and the university professors had many points of commonality, the movement's refusal to compromise its ideals led to tensions and ruptures. Fourth, these conflicts became an important process of learning. Although the MST already had an established educational proposal, putting this theory into practice at the university level led movement leaders to reconstruct some of their previous theories, a form of praxis. This process was particularly important for the first Pedagogy of Land cohort because, as the next section discusses, the graduates from this program would go on to become prominent leaders of MST education collectives throughout the country, implementing similar degree programs in their local universities.

How Institutions Build Movements: Reflections from the University of Ijuí Graduates

To what extent did this university program support the MST's movement infrastructure, defined by Andrews (2004) as its collective leadership capacity, organizational structure, and access to resources? In this section I draw on interviews with twenty graduates from the Pedagogy of Land cohort, from seven different states, to show how the program helped "build" the movement. In terms of leadership capacity, the program increased activists' know-how and ability to navigate the conflicts and tensions of engaging the institutional sphere. The MST's organizational structure also benefited, as students who were not previously involved in the movement became integrated into the MST's different thematic sectors and collective leadership bodies. Finally, the program offered material resources, equipping activists with the degrees necessary to seek formal employment, which they used to sustain themselves financially, while also often sharing their salaries with the movement. The funding for the activists to travel twice a year to study was also a resource, allowing leaders in far-off states to participate in face-to-face debates and dialogue about the movement. As Edgar Kolling commented, "These educational programs are pedagogical laboratories. They are privileged spaces because in no other space are activists together for an extended period of time, discussing and creating theories for the movement."

Of the forty-seven MST student-activists who received their bachelor's degrees in the Pedagogy of Land from the University of Ijuí,[18] thirty-four of the graduates—approximately two-thirds of the cohort—were still involved in the movement in 2011.[19] Nineteen of these activists participated in one of the movement's national or statewide leadership bodies or thematic sectors, including the education, political training, and gender sectors. The other fifteen of these activists were regional leaders, most often teachers or principals in local schools, but still active in the movement.[20] Finally, thirteen of these graduates no longer had any direct participation in the movement, although five of the thirteen were teaching in schools on agrarian reform settlements. The twenty interviews I conducted with graduates were with a combination of national and statewide leaders, regional activists, and nonparticipants. While the interviews with MST leaders shed light on how the Pedagogy of Land program increased the movement's internal infrastructure, the latter interviews highlight the conflicts that emerged within the cohort and why the movement's collective discipline led some activists to leave the movement entirely.

Reflections from MST National and Statewide Leaders

In my interviews with statewide and national MST leaders, one common theme was how the Pedagogy of Land program increased their ability to communicate as equals with public officials. For example, Vanderlúcia was from the poor rural interior of the state of Ceará and had only completed fourth grade by the time she turned twenty, in 1992. During this period, she became an MST activist and she had the opportunity to finish primary and secondary school through MST adult education and high school programs. In 1997, she was chosen to attend the bachelor's degree program at the University of Ijuí. She described the opportunity as a dream; activists in the MST had never thought they would achieve access to higher education. Shortly after graduating she moved to the federal capital and was put in charge of talking to public officials about the MST's educational initiatives, now equipped with a new college degree.

Maria de Jesus Santos is another activist from the state of Ceará who graduated from the first Pedagogy of Land program. In 2011, Maria de Jesus was one of the two representatives from her state in the MST national directorate (see Fig. 1.6 in Chapter 1). She also mentioned the role PRONERA had played in fortifying the relationships between activists and public officials. "Before these people did not respect us, but when we all began to graduate, and hold higher education degrees, we could debate them as equals." Unfortunately, Maria de Jesus said, these degrees have also caused divisions within the movement. She remembered that the Pedagogy of Land graduates were often treated like the "academics of the MST." She said, "We did not like this; it caused a big debate because, yes, we were students, but we wanted to access higher education to contribute to the movement. We did not want to be considered the intellectuals of the MST." Maria de Jesus celebrated the respect activists had earned, while lamenting the hierarchies that university degrees produced.

Another theme that emerged in the interviews was the role the program played in helping the movement develop its educational approach. As many of the activists expressed to me, the cohort arrived at the University of Ijuí wanting to transform the university, but no one knew exactly what that meant. At first, the MST activists tried to control all aspects of the university program, critiquing the professors every time they assigned a reading that did not resonate with the values of the movement. This generated a lot of resentment among the faculty, and the movement had to rethink how to implement their pedagogical proposal without damaging their relationships with allied professors. They began to see their pedagogical proposal as adding to the university's extant curriculum, rather than replacing it. Ivori reflected on the falling-out the cohort had with professors, like Dinarte, who had supported the program:

> Our actions had serious consequences; it hurt the relationship between the movement and our long-time supporters at the university.... I do not want to defend the academy, but I do think that the professors had a point. At the very least we could have boycotted the exam completely, which would not have hurt the department's national ranking. We might not have received our diplomas right away, but this would have been the more principled action.

The conflicts that emerged in the Pedagogy of Land program were a process of learning. Instead of always taking an antagonistic stance, movement activists started to think about how to integrate faculty into the movement's process of collective governance. Ever since the first Pedagogy of Land program, the movement has included several professors in the CPP, in order to involve faculty in the cohort's collective decision-making processes. This first experience in a university setting helped MST national and statewide leaders learn what was worth a fight, and what was not.

Reflections from Regional Activists

For the MST regional activists who participated in movement activities but did not hold statewide or national leadership positions, the most common theme in our interviews was how the Pedagogy of Land program expanded their professional opportunities. For example, in 2000 and 2002, two civil service exams opened for new teachers to enter the official statewide teaching network in Rio Grande do Sul.[21] Eight of the Pedagogy of Land students from Rio Grande do Sul took this exam, passed, and became part of the official state teaching network. Marli Zimmerman remembered, "I had taken a lot of public exams, but I had never passed. I only passed the state exam in 2002 because I had just graduated from the Pedagogy of Land program. Everything was fresh in my head." Once Marli became a teacher, she had a salary that sustained her financially, while also continuing to be active in the movement.

The Pedagogy of Land program also increased regional activists' understanding of the MST's educational proposal and integrated these activists into the movement. For example, Carmen Vedovatto, a teacher in Rio Grande do Sul, worked with a group of small children on her settlement for her final thesis project, organizing a collective artisan work project. She then interviewed the children about what this collaboration and manual labor meant to them, helping her to improve future iterations of the project. Mauricéia Lima was a regional activist in the state of Pernambuco when she entered the program, but she had never held a statewide leadership position. She was intimidated by the presence of the many prominent MST leaders in the cohort. She said, "I did not speak much because I was surrounded by the cream of the education sector, the people who created the MST education sector."[22] Mauricéia grew politically from the experience, and after graduating she took on more prestigious leadership positions within her state. Rosangela do Nascimento, another teacher from Rio Grande do Sul, said that the program helped her understand her role in the movement. She said, "I will always be an MST activist, but I am an activist who works in the schools."[23]

Reflection from Graduates Who Left the Movement

Finally, I also spoke with two graduates who were MST activists when they entered the program, but who left the movement because of the conflicts that developed.[24] Bernadete Schwaab and Jussara Reolon were the principal and vice-principal of a school located on one of the largest MST agrarian reform settlements in the region, Fazenda Annoni (discussed in Chapter 1). At this school, unlike most schools I visited on MST settlements, I did not see any signs of the movement—no MST flags, no quotes about social justice on the walls, no pictures of agrarian reform struggles. Bernadete and Jussara had been activists in the MST regional education sector in the late

1990s, which is why they entered the Pedagogy of Land program. Although Bernadete and Jussara said they learned a lot about education through the program, in our conversation they emphasized the conflicts.

For example, although they lived only an hour from the city of Ijuí, they were not allowed to go home on the weekends because the cohort had to do everything collectively: since students from the northeast region could not go home, they were also not allowed. However, Bernadete said, she had to go home some weekends because she was working for her municipal Department of Education. She said, "I was critiqued and critiqued and critiqued." Bernadete believed that the activists in the program were only concerned with showing the strength of the MST, not with other aspects of the experience, such as learning how to improve their classroom pedagogy. Bernadete and Jussara kept referring to the radicalization of the program and stated that they were "tortured on the weekends," forced to sit through boring lectures on politics.

When I met Bernadete and Jussara in 2010, they were still teaching at the same public school they had taught at when they entered the Pedagogy of Land program. In my visit, I observed them incorporating many aspects of the MST's pedagogical program into their school, such as group work and community research. However, Bernadete and Jussara were trying to isolate the school from the more political aspects of the movement. For example, they took down the MST flag from the school's entrance. They also stopped promoting the MST's cultural practices, such as *mística*, and they no longer took students to local protests. They did not feel a need to push the struggle on students, because "kids need to be kids and play." They disagreed with activists "who talk about socialism at every moment." They preferred to construct a quality education not overshadowed by political debates.

Bernadete and Jussara are two of the thirteen graduates of the Pedagogy of Land program who received their bachelor's degrees through the MST's political maneuvering but have chosen to leave the movement. These two teachers exemplify some of the contradictions of the movement's educational approach: while the movement leaders promote an educational experience that is more participatory than the traditional school system, they also support a form of democratic centralism, in which collective decisions become more important than individual desires. This pushed some activists to abandon the movement. However, it could be argued that Bernadete and Jussara have not left the movement completely behind, as they continue to incorporate aspects of the MST's pedagogical proposal into their classrooms. Nonetheless, these practices are now disconnected from a broader social movement struggling for political and economic change.

PRONERA'S INSTITUTIONALIZATION UNDER THE
WORKERS' PARTY (2003–2010)

The first PRONERA baccalaureate program was a turning point in the MST's educational struggle, as it became the movement's institutional entry point into the public university sphere. Despite the fact that the University of Ijuí was private and also not highly ranked, its work with the MST made professors at other universities more comfortable creating similar programs at their own institutions. Over the next decade, dozens of more universities—almost all public—sponsored bachelor's and graduate degree programs through PRONERA. This is additionally surprising, as PRONERA was not initially intended to support university degree programs. Nonetheless, the MST used the program to legitimatize and fund this sphere of educational access. PRONERA became a wedge for the MST to open the doors to other institutions, transforming the program into something bigger than the government had intended. Thus, institutionalization was not a passive, monolithic process, but rather an active struggle, one of ongoing contestation, setbacks, and advances.

The presidential election of left-leaning PT candidate Luis Inácio Lula da Silva's in 2003 created new opportunities and challenges for PRONERA's institutionalization and expansion. Lula's presidency initiated a period of both more social movement participation at the federal level and class compromise (a political shift that I discuss in more detail in Chapter 3). The PT's incorporation of agribusiness as an important part of its governing coalition meant that the administration was constrained in terms of its ability to implement large-scale agrarian reform. Thus, the administration's strategy became investing resources in already established agrarian reform settlements. This allowed the PT administration to maintain a delicate balance between the party's support of industrial agriculture and its promotion of social policies in areas of agrarian reform. PRONERA was one of the many agrarian reform programs that received a dramatic increase in funding during this contradictory PT era. Furthermore, the PT's appointment of movement allies within INCRA helped to facilitate the institutionalization of a new form of state-university-movement co-governance, what became known as triple governance. Triple governance meant that PRONERA programs adhered closely to the MST's political and economic goals. However, perhaps unsurprisingly, this social movement participation also left the program more vulnerable to conservative attacks. Thus, the MST's continual mobilization was critical to defend the federal program, even under a nominally sympathetic presdential administration.

Increased Funding and Tremendous Growth

During President Cardoso's second term, between 1998 and 2002, the operational office of PRONERA had a minimal structure and the institutional relations between INCRA officials and the MST leadership were precarious at best. The government had created PRONERA in 1998 with the stated goal of eliminating illiteracy in agrarian reform settlements by 2004. Researchers (Andrade et al. 2004) estimated that this would be possible through an annual investment of 21 million reais (about 18.5 million US dollars in 1998[25]); however, PRONERA began its first year of operation with a budget of only 3 million reais (about 2.6 million US dollars in 1998). This budget increased slightly over the next three years. According to Clarice dos Santos (PRONERA director, 2007–2013), the program would not have had any budget during these four years were it not for a few PT congressional representatives who amended the proposed congressional budget each year and put aside money for the program.[26]

Lula's election in 2002 was an important turning point for PRONERA, financially, institutionally, and substantively. Financially, the program's budget increased rapidly under the new PT administration. Figure 2.1 illustrates the humongous increase in PRONERA's budget over the course of Lula's two terms in office (2003–2010).[27] Institutionally, the PT administration appointed allies of the movement to administer the program. Monica Molina, a professor at the University of Brasília and long-time ally of the MST, became the director of PRONERA in 2003. Monica's entire personal trajectory was connected to the struggle for agrarian reform and her

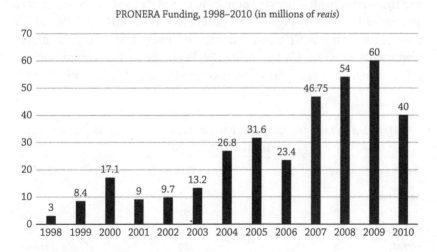

Figure 2.1 PRONERA Budget, 1998–2010 (in millions of *reais*)
Courtesy of author based on interviews and primary documents

dissertation had been an assessment of PRONERA's first four years of operation. Substantively, the types of PRONERA programs also began to diversify. As Monica Molina described, "This was the period when we started to talk about developing graduate programs in history, law, agroecology. PRONERA began expanding its technical and disciplinary offerings." This was significant, because it increased the professional opportunities available for students in areas of agrarian reform.

Nonetheless, despite these changes, PRONERA's operation was never easy, even under a PT administration. For example, Monica said that many INCRA officials believed that the program should be under the jurisdiction of the Ministry of Education. Monica had to constantly defend PRONERA's existence within the agency. Nonetheless, Monica's advocacy as the director, her dialogue with the movement, and the MST's continual mobilizations advanced the program.

PRONERA programs fell into three categories: adult education, high school, and higher education. Adult education programs represented around half of all PRONERA programs completed between 1998 and 2011 (a total of 167 programs), but more than 90 percent of the students (a total of 154,192 students, see Table 2.1).[28] These were massive programs, each involving one to two thousand students and hundreds of teachers, who traveled to the settlements and camps to offer literacy training and accelerated primary education to adults. The second largest category of PRONERA programs were at the high school level. By 2011, a total of ninety-nine high school programs were completed with 7,373 students enrolled. All of these high school programs used the pedagogy of alternation, with students living for several months a year at the educational institution hosting the program, and then returning to their community to complete local research projects. Ten of the first twenty high school programs funded through PRONERA took place at the MST's own educational institution, the Educational Institute of Josué de Castro located in Veranópolis, Rio Grande do Sul (IEJC, also known as ITERRA, discussed in Chapter 1). Thus, PRONERA

Table 2.1 NUMBER OF PRONERA PROGRAMS COMPLETED AND STUDENTS ENROLLED, 1998–2011

Category of PRONERA Program	Programs Completed	Students
Adult Education	167	154,192
High School	99	7,373
Higher Education	54	3,323
TOTAL	320	164,894

Source: *Relatório da II Pesquisa Nacional sobre a Educação na Reforma Agrária* (INCRA 2015).

helped the MST fund the high school programs that the movement had already been offering for the previous decade, and expand these high school offerings to other regions of Brazil.

Higher education programs were the rarest and most difficult type of PRONERA program to approve, as these required the endorsement of university governance bodies for the new degree programs. Nonetheless, by 2011, fifty-four higher education programs had been completed, involving 3,323 students, 2,635 in baccalaureate and 688 in graduate specializations.[29] These higher education programs were also offered through the pedagogy of alternation and took place at the actual university or a partnering institution. The students had to complete the same number of course credits as the other students at the university and, in addition, assignments during the community periods. A final research project was also a central part of these programs. Table 2.1 lists the total number of PRONERA programs completed between 1998 and 2011, and Map 2.1 shows the geographical distribution of these programs.

In 2003, the MST developed a proposal for the first PRONERA graduate program, a specialization in Education of the Countryside offered by the University of Brasília. In 2003 and 2004 the MST proposed two bachelor's degree programs in agronomy, through partnerships with the Federal University of Pará and the Federal University of Sergipe. Also in 2004, the

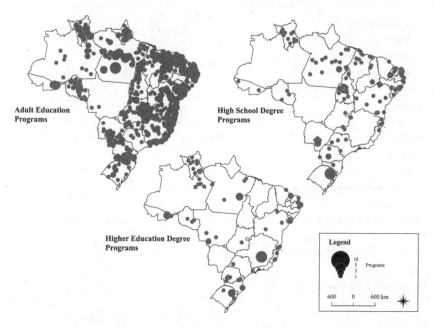

Map 2.1 Geographical Distribution of PRONERA Programs Completed, 1998–2011
Courtesy of *Relatório da II Pesquisa Nacional sobre a Educação na Reforma Agrária* (INCRA 2015)

MST created the first PRONERA higher education program outside of the disciplines of pedagogy and agricultural studies: a baccalaureate program in history sponsored by the Federal University of Paraíba. This illustrated a demand for training in a wide range of professions in areas of agrarian reform, not only teaching and farming. Table 2.2 lists all of the PRONERA baccalaureate and graduate programs completed between 1998 and 2011. The MST proposed eighty percent of these higher education programs (fifty-four programs) and all of the higher education programs outside of the areas of pedagogy and agricultural studies.

Since 2011 the diversity of PRONERA higher education programs has increased rapidly, with PRONERA baccalaureate and graduate programs created in journalism, arts and music, math, administration, veterinary studies, social and human sciences, and social work, and a baccalaureate program in law.[30] In 2012, the MST, in coordination with the State University of São Paulo (UNESP), created the first-ever PRONERA master's program in "Territorial Development in Latin America and the Caribbean".[31] As a consequence of these PRONERA higher education programs, the MST

Table 2.2 PRONERA HIGHER EDUCATION PROGRAMS COMPLETED, 1998–2011

	Number of Programs	Total Number of Students Entered (Graduated)
Baccalaureate-Level Programs		
Pedagogy of Land	30	1,997 (1,682)
Agronomy, Agroecology, or Cooperative Management	6	299 (273)
History	2	120 (106)
Literature	2	160 (121)
Geography	1	59 (45)
TOTAL	**41**	**2,635 (2227)**
Graduate-Level Programs		
Agrarian Residency	6	315 (266)
Specialization in Education of the Countryside	2	176 (121)
Specialization in Adult Education	1	44 (34)
Specialization in Agroecology, Family Agriculture, or Cooperatives Management	3	122 (77)
Specialization in Economics and Agrarian Development	1	31 (29)
TOTAL	**13**	**688 (527)**

Source: Relatório da II Pesquisa Nacional sobre a Educação na Reforma Agrária (INCRA 2015).

leadership transformed, in a little over a decade, from a group of leaders with, at most, high school degrees, to a movement of college graduates.

A Unique Form of Triple Governance

Another significant development during Lula's administration was the formalization of relationships between social movements, INCRA officials, and university sponsors, which became known as a system of "triple governance." The idea behind triple governance was that the state should *not* be responsible for deciding what educational programs to offer; rather, communities should propose new programs based on their local needs. Furthermore, universities and other educational institutions that offer PRONERA programs should do so with the active participation and oversight of the communities they are serving. A group of researchers who worked with PRONERA explained the triple governance process as follows:

> The institutions of higher education have a strategic function in the program, as they play the role of mediating the relationship between the social movements and the National Institute of Colonization and Agrarian Reform (INCRA), overseeing the administrative and financial components of the program, and coordinating the pedagogical approach. The social movements respond to the demands of the communities, while the INCRA regional offices are in charge of finances, logistical support, and inter-institutional connections. (Andrade et al. 2004, 22)

A National Pedagogical Commission, which included government, university, and civil society representatives, was also established in order to vet all PRONERA program proposals.

PRONERA's triple governance has allowed for a centralized process of decentralized program development. The program is decentralized because groups of social movement activists or rural unionists, in partnership with a university, must participate in the development of every new PRONERA program. For the first three years after PRONERA was created, the MST was the primary organization submitting PRONERA project proposals. Other rural organizations, in particular the rural union movement, began developing their own proposals independently of the MST in the 2000s. However, the MST still proposed 190 of 320 programs completed between 1998 and 2011, either on its own or with other rural organizations.

The process of developing a PRONERA program is also centralized, as every new program proposal must pass through a central office in Brasília and be approved by the National Pedagogical Commission. However, bureaucrats in Brasília are not allowed to develop these proposals; rather, the university professors in partnership with local activists propose new programs. Clarice dos Santos summarized how this centralized decentralization plays out:

> The fundamental difference in PRONERA [from the Ministry of Education] is that our projects are a permanent demand from below. Social movements come together with the universities to present a proposal to INCRA. We do not do a public call for a proposal; we could, but we do not. The fact is that the demand comes from the social movements, from the actual settlements. These local leaders take the initiative to propose a course *to* the university; and they are not just proposing a course but also how they are going to oversee that course. . . . Therefore, the students do not go to the university just to take a class; they are part of constructing the educational process. This is an important component of the program, that the students take agency over governing their education.

PRONERA fosters direct civil society participation because every new course comes out of a proposal from regional groups of activists, who also help administer the course that they propose. However, this means that the ability to scale up programs across the country is limited. Once a PRONERA program is completed and the cohort has graduated, the social movement and the university must submit a new proposal, even for offering the same program to a new cohort. Thus, ongoing collaboration between activists and university partners has been essential for the program to function. The following account of approving a bachelor's degree program in geography illustrates both the benefits and challenges of this triple governance process, and the importance of continual mobilization when proposing new PRONERA programs.

An Example of Triple Governance: Proposing a Bachelor's Degree Program in Geography

In 2005, MST national leader Edgar Kolling approached Bernardo Mançano Fernandes, a professor of geography at the State University of São Paulo (UNESP) and a life-long collaborator with and researcher of the MST (Fernandes 1996, 2000, 2008).[32] Edgar asked Bernardo to help the MST propose a PRONERA bachelor's degree program in Geography at the UNESP.[33] Bernardo knew that approving a PRONERA program for MST leaders would not be easy at a prestigious university in the conservative state of São Paulo. The three most prominent state universities in São Paulo (UNESP, the University of Sao Paulo, and the State University of Campinas) had been notoriously resistant to affirmative action programs, such as quotas for Afro-Brazilians and low-income students (Johnson and Heringer 2015). A PRONERA program would fall into this category of affirmative action, as only students living in areas of agrarian reform would be able to enroll. Despite the uncertainties, Bernardo agreed to develop a proposal for the new program: a Baccalaureate and Teaching Certification in Geography with an Emphasis in Rural Development.

The process of writing the proposal took a full year, as the degree program was considered a new university offering and had to include a detailed account of all of the classes, activities, assignments, and evaluations. The proposal outlined the structure of the program, which would take place through the pedagogy of alternation over a period of five years, with a total of 3,465 hours of study, including classroom hours, community activity hours, and classroom activity hours (for full curriculum see Appendix C). Sixty students from areas of agrarian reform would be able to enter the program through a special university entrance exam. The UNESP College of Science and Technology would be the program's official sponsor, with the faculty in the geography department in charge of teaching the courses and handling administrative work.

PRONERA's triple governance structure was clearly outlined in the proposal, with lists of the different responsibilities of the university faculty, INCRA officials, and social movements:

The university faculty was responsible for

- developing the program proposal,
- selecting the students,
- assessing the learning of the students,
- organizing the curriculum and choosing the professors that would teach each course,
- issuing diplomas for the students,
- coordinating the program "together with representatives from the social movements,"
- providing infrastructure, and
- choosing the students who would receive fellowships.

The social movements were in charge of

- publicizing information about the program and mobilizing people to apply,
- ensuring the appropriate infrastructure,
- helping with the student assignments,
- supervising the students' projects during their community periods,
- overseeing the budget,

- evaluating the program along with the professors,
- participating in the "pedagogical coordinating collective" of the program, and
- suggesting professors to teach in the program.

The regional INCRA officials were responsible for

- divulging information about the program,
- helping to establish and maintain institutional partnerships,
- overseeing the process of evaluation with the other partners,
- ensuring the proper use of financial resources, and
- verifying that students are from areas of agrarian reform.

One of the most unique components of the program proposal was that the study periods would alternate between the UNESP campus in Presidente Prudentes and the MST's Florestan Fernandes National School (ENFF) in Guaranema, São Paulo. The ENFF is one of the MST's political training schools (*escolas da formação*), founded in 2005 to support the internal training and political education of MST activists and other social movement leaders across Brazil and Latin America. Unlike many of the MST's other educational institutions (e.g., IEJC/ITERRA discussed in Chapter 1), the ENFF is not connected to the state and the courses offered at the school are not formal degree programs. Nonetheless, the university professors and MST activists writing the proposal wanted the UNESP geography department to partner with the ENFF to host half of the classes. Partially, this was because there was not the appropriate infrastructure for sixty students to live and study together at the UNESP campus for several months each year. More important, the location of the program at the ENFF would give the MST leadership a high degree of influence over the program.[34]

After finishing the elaboration of this proposal in January 2006, the next step of the process began: obtaining UNESP's approval for the new program offering. The proposal was read by and voted on in four different university bodies, a process that took about seven months. First, the geography department voted on whether to approve the proposal, and it passed unanimously in the first meeting. Next, the College of Sciences and Technology and the Deans' advisory boards voted. Garnering support for the proposal at these two levels was more difficult than at the department level. There was a group of faculty and student representatives who opposed the program, on the grounds that it privileged certain sectors of the population over others and that the university's role was to offer universal educational access.

Despite this resistance, the proposal passed both governing bodies and was sent to the final and most challenging level of approval: the university-wide advisory board, which included eighty faculty, staff, student, and administrative representatives. As Bernardo recounted, "We brought the proposal to the advisory board two times, and both times the board delayed the vote, asking for more time to read the proposal." Both Bernardo and the MST activists were worried that the proposal would not pass. After the proposal was delayed the second time, they brought Senator Eduardo Suplicy (PT, São Paulo) to talk to the university faculty about PRONERA's positive contributions. They also organized several demonstrations to pressure the university advisory board to approve the program proposal. When the proposal finally came up for a vote, in June 2006, it passed by the slimmest of margins, forty-one votes.

In July of 2007, over two years after Edgar first approached Bernardo, the PRONERA bachelor's degree program in geography began with sixty students—forty-nine MST activists and eleven members of five other rural social movements.[35] The program would be a one-time offering, and if UNESP wanted to create a similar program in the future, the professors and activists would have to go through this same process, once again.

In July 2009, Bernardo invited me to observe a week of the UNESP geography program, at the Florestan Fernandes National School (ENFF).[36] When I arrived, the geography students were eating breakfast in the ENFF cafeteria. Shortly after breakfast, at 7:30 AM, we gathered in a patio, and a small group of students, members of one of the student collectives (NBs), performed a reenactment of a land occupation and farmers resisting eviction by the police. This *mística* ended with a man playing guitar and everyone singing a song about agrarian reform. Two students hoisted the MST flag up a pole in the center of the patio, and then everyone sang the movement's anthem. Each of the NBs announced their presence with a chant about social struggle. At 8 AM, we went to class.

That morning, Bernardo, the UNESP professor in charge of class that week, discussed the difference between land and territory. He explained that land is a physical location, while territory is the totality of social and economic relations in that area. The class was dynamic, with students interrupting and asking follow-up questions throughout the lecture. At one point, a student raised his hand and said, "We are not fighting for land, we are fighting for territory!" Bernardo nodded enthusiastically. One of the NBs was in charge of organizing classroom discussion and discipline. These NB coordinators called on students to speak, reminded us to avoid side conversations, and announced when it was time for a twenty-minute break.

After four hours of class, we went to eat lunch, where several NBs were in charge of serving food and washing the dishes. After lunch, all of the students participated in the ENFF's work collectives, helping out in the school garden, cleaning bathrooms, washing clothes, and decorating the school. At 4 PM, we all met again for class. Bernardo gave the students one individual and three small-group assignments to complete that afternoon, plus an extra assignment for students who had missed class earlier that week. The students worked late into the night, even after dinner was finished, reading and debating about territory, land, and agrarian reform. In a single day, the group of activist-students had presented a cultural performance, participated in the governance of their classroom, completed several different manual labor tasks, and studied both individually and collectively. Although this cohort would graduate with the same bachelor's degree in geography as other UNESP students, they were clearly part of a very different educational experience.

PRONERA's higher education programs have been critical in offering youth in areas of agrarian reform an access point into the public university system, with the resources to study for four years and a class schedule that allows them to maintain a connection to their rural communities. In the words of national MST leader João Pedro Stédile, "PRONERA is one of the most valuable experiences we have. It is fighting against ignorance throughout the Brazilian countryside."[37] The program has increased the movement's internal capacity by training hundreds of activist-professionals—from lawyers to veterinarians—who take on the internal tasks of the movement. The program also allows these students to learn about and prefigure the movement's social and political vision, including collective leadership and self-governance. It was precisely the MST's ability to use PRONERA to support its agrarian reform struggle that opened the program up to a judicial proceeding, as described in the following section.

SOCIAL MOVEMENT CRIMINALIZATION AND A FRONTAL ATTACK AGAINST PRONERA (2008–2010)

In 2005, the State University of Mato Grosso (UNEMAT) agreed to sponsor a four-year PRONERA baccalaureate program in agronomy, a proposal that the MST helped to develop, for sixty students living in areas of agrarian reform. The sixty students who formed the cohort were from seven different states and four different social movements.[38] At the program's opening ceremony, in January of 2006, the Dean of Research and Graduate Studies declared the program to be a "revolutionary space,"[39] suggesting a general awareness among both activists and university professors of the unique role that PRONERA was playing in offering rural social movement leaders access to higher education.

Like other PRONERA programs, the four-year UNEMAT agronomy degree was organized around the values of collectivity and collaboration. All of the students lived together at the university for intensive two-to-three-month study periods, and then returned to their communities to complete research projects based on what they were learning. While living at the university, the cohort divided itself into small student collectives (NBs) in charge of cleaning, cooking, studying, and completing other day-to-day tasks necessary for the program to function. The cohort also organized several political events, including a March for Agroecology and Socio-Economic Solidarity, thus generating debate at the university about agroecological alternatives.

In 2008, one student refused to participate in the collective organization of the program, claiming that the movement leaders overseeing the program were imposing unnecessary requirements on the cohort. The other students thought that this was unacceptable, and they decided in a general assembly to ask the student to leave the program. Clarice dos Santos, the coordinator of PRONERA during this period, explained, "The other students decided they would kick him out. But you cannot just kick someone out of the program. He had taken an entrance exam and had a right to stay." Nonetheless, the other students in the cohort effectively forced the student to drop out. In response to his expulsion, the student wrote a complaint to the Federal Public Ministry, denouncing INCRA for allowing the MST to have so much influence administering the program. The Federal Public Ministry's lawyers sent the student's denunciation to the Brazilian Federal Court of Audits (TCU), the auditing branch of the Brazilian congress that ensures the proper use of the federal budget. The TCU is a prestigious and powerful institution within the Brazilian bureaucracy, with nine ministers in charge of auditing congressional spending.[40] One of the TCU ministers decided to take on the investigation of the UNEMAT program, because if federal money was going toward a private actor, such as the MST, this was a misapplication of the federal budget.[41]

The TCU minister in charge of the investigation quickly discovered that the bachelor's degree program was called "Agroecology and Socio-economic Solidarity for Social Movements of the Countryside." This created alarm because, although PRONERA's mandate was to serve students in areas of agrarian reform, legally these students did not have to be associated with a social movement as this name suggested. The TCU minister visited the UNEMAT campus and talked to dozens of university faculty, including professors who had not been directly involved in or supportive of the PRONERA agronomy program. Many of these professors described the influential role MST leaders had in establishing the program at the university and selecting faculty who were sympathetic to the movement to teach in the program.

On November 19, 2008, the TCU minister issued a scathing judgment (*acordão* 2653/2008) that PRONERA was being administered "without a public call or open selective process, which allows professors to be chosen by an organization that is external to public oversight, the MST, which abuses the principles of impartiality and morality."[42] The TCU argued that although the funding from PRONERA was technically going toward the university, not a third party, the leaders of the MST were effectively administering the program. The TCU judgment required that PRONERA programs be administered through contracts, placed a ban on paying university professors extra money for teaching in PRONERA programs, and prohibited the participation of social movements. Although the TCU ministers did not forbid PRONERA from continuing to function, these requirements effectively paralyzed the program.[43]

The biggest challenge for PRONERA's functioning was the new requirement to use contracts, instead of the previous practice of using institutional partnerships. Leonardo Kauer, a lawyer who worked with the MST in 2010, explained to me the significance of this change:[44] When a government wants to implement a program that requires a third party, it can work through two different mechanisms. The first is a contract, which requires an open bidding process. For example, if the federal government wants to construct a new building, dozens of companies can bid for the contract and the one with the best offer receives the job. A second option is for the government to create an institutional agreement with a third party, which is allowed if there is no profit involved and a common interest exists between both parties. For education, the government frequently uses institutional partnerships, as they allow the transfer of money to nonprofit entities with the common interest of offering educational access to the Brazilian population.

Until 2008, all PRONERA programs were developed through institutional partnerships between INCRA and universities or other educational entities. Now, INCRA was required to issue an open call for each new educational program and then select the most efficient entity to administer the program—regardless of that entity's public or private status. Federal universities would not be able to enter into this bidding process, as they were part of the same public administration level as INCRA and therefore could not be issued a contract. This open bidding process would also effectively end the civil society participation that had previously characterized PRONERA's governance, as INCRA was now required to define which programs to implement in a top-down decision-making structure.

Unsurprisingly, the reforms provoked resistance both within INCRA and among social movement leaders.

Technical Requirements Versus a Political Attack

I visited the TCU offices in Brasília in November of 2010 to learn more about the judgment and the debates over PRONERA's administration. I met with TCU official Paulo Nogueira de Medeiros, who was an interlocutor between the Congress and the TCU ministers.[45] I asked about the history of the PRONERA case and Paulo quickly explained his perspective: "Everything in the program is outsourced, and when federal programs are outsourced, there has to be extra caution to ensure fraud does not happen."[46] This is why, he continued, outsourcing through contracts is always preferable to institutional partnerships, which involve no accountability or transparency as to which entities are receiving federal money. In the case of PRONERA, he said, social movements were choosing which universities participated in the program. Paulo insisted that the TCU did not investigate PRONERA because of any political contempt for the MST. The goal of the TCU, he said, was simply to ensure the proper use of federal money. Another lawyer who worked for the state-level TCU in Rio Grande do Sul, Jorge Martuis, also described the TCU as a technical, apolitical entity:

> There are hundreds and hundreds of audits that the TCU does every year, almost thousands. This does not depend on the TCU's preferences; we choose based on a technical need. There are no politics involved in the choice of what is going to be audited. The selection is based on the amount of money in question and social relevance. Issues such as education and agrarian reform have more social relevance.[47]

Both Paulo and Jorge were doing what Tania Li (2007) refers to as "rendering technical": representing political conflicts as problems with technical solutions. For the TCU officials, the problem in question was potential corruption in the outsourcing of federal money. The technical solution was ensuring that no third party could have undue influence in this outsourcing process, by requiring open bidding for contracts between INCRA and third parties.

Unlike the TCU congressional assistant, Clarice dos Santos interpreted the sanctions on PRONERA as an overtly political—not technical—process. She believed that the right-wing had been waiting for years to find an excuse to attack PRONERA. Once the incident occurred at UNEMAT, conservative officials used the TCU investigation to shut down the program.

The contractual bidding process appeared to be a neutral technical solution, but it rendered PRONERA unfeasible. This is because, Clarice explained, PRONERA programs emerged from specific community demands, and the goal was for these communities to have agency in their development and administration. What would happen, she asked, if university professors and activists developed a pedagogy program for communities in Pernambuco, but a private foundation in São Paulo that knew nothing about the northeast region won the contract? Clarice believed this would destroy the program. Due to the difficulties of establishing contracts, INCRA did not approve any PRONERA programs between 2008 and 2010, while this ban was in effect.

MST Countermobilization

In response to the TCU's judgment, between 2009 and 2010, MST leaders reached out to allies and political supporters, in order to publicly shame the TCU ministers and pressure the agency to reverse its decision. Critical to this coalition were the university faculty and administrators who had grown to support PRONERA. Even though only a decade before, none of the public universities in Brazil had been willing to sponsor a bachelor's degree program funded through PRONERA, by 2009 hundreds of professors and dozens of provosts had come to embrace these programs as an alternative way of offering university access to poor rural populations. These university supporters became part of a broad-based movement that contested the TCU's judgment and defended PRONERA's importance for the Brazilian countryside.

This coalition employed a dual strategy (Alvarez 1990) to pressure the TCU ministers to rescind their decision: contentious protest and political advocacy. First, the MST leadership mobilized hundreds of people to support PRONERA through rallies, marches, and building occupations. For example, in June 2009, there was a protest in support of PRONERA in Pernambuco's capital city of Recife. Pamphlets were given out that stated:

PRONERA has been responsible for educating 600,000 youth and adults in settlements. . . . This program has contributed to the quality of life of people in the countryside and their choice to stay in the countryside. Nonetheless, last year INCRA suspended all new courses and cut 62 percent of PRONERA's budget. We are fighting for reinstating the budget, allowing institutional partnerships, and paying professors and coordinators. In defense of PRONERA educators and the Landless Workers Movement: School, Land and Dignity![48]

For two years, similar mobilizations brought activists, students, and sup-portive university actors together in the streets. The participation of dozens of prominent faculty and provosts, who openly declared their support for PRONERA at these rallies, illustrated the substantial degree of respect the program had garnered across the country.

The national coalition also developed less contentious strategies for political advocacy, such as letter-writing campaigns and government meetings. One letter sent to the TCU on July 13, 2010—with signatures from a diverse group of civil society and government actors from Ceará—outlined the history of PRONERA and social movements' participation in the program:

> The social movements and unions are important agents, as legitimate representatives of rural workers, in creating this initiative and repairing the historical negation of rural people's right to education. The participation of these movements in the identification of local educational demands, in the search for partnerships, and in the construction of a pedagogical process for these populations has been essential for the development and success of this program.[49]

The document goes on to state, "The [TCU] decision to require a bidding process instead of institutional partnerships puts education in the same cat-egory as a commodity." Letters such as these, signed by civil society groups, public officials, and faculty, disputed the TCU's legal justification for the judgment. While the TCU claimed this social movement participation was illegal, this coalition embraced the right of movement activists to co-govern higher education.

The Mobilizing Climax

Civil society groups and government and university supporters came to-gether in Brasília in November 2010, for the Fourth National Seminar on PRONERA. I flew to Brasília to participate, arriving at a conference center with dozens of MST activists from across the country.[50] The con-ference brought together all of the supporters of PRONERA to engage in a joint effort to pressure the TCU to rescind its judgment. The attendees included over six hundred students and university professors who had par-ticipated in PRONERA programs over the previous decade. There were also dozens of MST activists, INCRA officials from every state, federal and state legislators, and representatives from the other rural social movements that had helped to organize PRONERA programs, most significantly the National Confederation of Agricultural Workers (CONTAG, more details in Chapter 3). Multiple university provosts were also present at the meeting, as well as the president of INCRA and representatives from the Ministry of Agricultural Development and the Ministry of Education. The conference took place in one of the Brazilian Congress's legislative auditoriums, which helped to put the event in the public spotlight.

The opening ceremony began with an elaborate musical and cultural performance, an MST *mística*. The performance involved dozens of people wearing straw hats entering the room and slowly walking to the front, while miming the actions of farmers clearing fields with machetes, digging with hoes, and picking food for the harvest. While this was happening, a few of the performers read aloud poems about the importance of education for agrarian reform. Right after the performance a band of young children from an MST settlement in Ceará sang several songs about education of the countryside, accompanying themselves with instruments made out of recycled materials. A student in a PRONERA Pedagogy of Land baccalaureate program had helped the children create this band as his final community project. The refrain of one song declared, "I am not going to leave the countryside to be able to go to school. Education of the Countryside is a right and not charity." This refrain encompassed the general sentiment of the conference: the need for more access to quality education, at all levels, for rural populations.

After this performance, all of the university, social movement, union, and government representatives spoke. The speeches of the politicians emphasized the work they were doing to advocate for PRONERA within the federal government. Congressman Valmir Assunção (PT, Bahia) spoke about the meeting government officials had scheduled the next day with the TCU's president. Their plan was to convince the TCU minister that PRONERA bidding contracts were not feasible. Congressman Dionilso Marcon from Rio Grande do Sul said, "Tomorrow we are going to try to have a dialogue, and we are going to talk to the TCU. They need to understand the amount of learning that is happening in these PRONERA programs and the importance of working with both universities and social movements."

The many university provosts at the PRONERA conference also increased public pressure on the TCU. The provost of the Federal University of Goiás, Edward Madureira Brasil, spoke about the PRONERA law degree program that was offered at his university, which had been critiqued by both the TCU and the Federal Public Ministry as unnecessary for agrarian reform populations. He expressed his disagreement with the idea that rural populations only needed educational programs that focused on agronomy and pedagogy, as though farming and teaching were the only professions in the countryside. The provost affirmed the importance of training lawyers to work in these rural communities. He told us about a document that fifty-nine university provosts had signed in support of PRONERA. "We are thinking about the social role of the university . . . The TCU is being absurd. Forcing a contract bidding process is ridiculous, not possible. Education is not a commodity. The central question is the autonomy of the university." The public declaration of support for PRONERA by fifty-nine provosts helped legitimize the participation of social movements in these university programs. Their support was a powerful message that these were high-quality programs that did not involve the misuse of federal money. The Brazilian constitution's defense of the autonomy of universities was further reason to question the TCU's judgment.

These collective efforts culminated on the second day of the conference, November 4, 2010, when President Lula signed a decree that made both *Educação do Campo* (see Chapter 3) and PRONERA official public policies.[51] The MST and other rural social movements had put pressure on Lula to sign this decree, as one of his final acts as president. The 2010 presidential decree states that PRONERA "will be governed within INCRA with the oversight of a National Pedagogical Commission," which will include "representatives from civil society and the federal government, with the goal of defining political and pedagogical guidelines, offering technical and pedagogical support for the courses and projects, and overseeing and evaluating all PRONERA programs."[52] This affirmation of civil society's right to participate in PRONERA directly contradicted the TCU's judgment. Furthermore, the decree raised PRONERA from the status of a government program to that of a public policy. The distinction, according to the state actors and movement activists with whom I spoke, was that if a new government came to power, they could not simply eliminate the program. However, as a lawyer at INCRA Gilda Diniz dos Santos, explained to me a few days later, the decree did not actually legally permit INCRA to start implementing any new programs through institutional partnerships.[53] She claimed that the decree was only important insofar as it influenced the TCU, as INCRA was legally bound by the TCU's judgment. Gilda insisted that other actions, such as the advocacy of the congressional representatives, were as equally important for convincing the TCU to revoke the judgment.

On the last day of the Fourth National Seminar on PRONERA, the 667 participants approved a final declaration: Commitments for the Consolidation of PRONERA. The document reaffirmed the importance of PRONERA as a program that "opened the door of the universities to workers" and emphasized social movements' and unions' participation in the construction of the program (see full document in Appendix D). The end of the declaration includes sixteen demands, including rescinding the TCU judgment and increasing funding for PRONERA. This conference declaration, Presidential decree, meeting between TCU and congressional representatives, and the statement from the university professors—all of which took place in November 2010—formed a collective mobilizing effort to force the TCU to rescind its judgment.

The Social Movement "Wins"

On December 1, 2010, the TCU passed a new judgment (*acordão* 3.269/ 2010) that lifted many of the restrictions that had been placed on PRONERA. Most significantly, the requirement to implement new programs through contracts and an open bidding process was repealed. This was a huge victory for the supporters of PRONERA and, in particular, for the MST. In a public statement issued by INCRA, Clarice dos Santos attributed this decision to public pressure, the "intensive mobilization of universities, state governments, secretaries of education, and workers' movements asking the tribunal to reconsider its previous position."[54] Clarice declared this a "victory for the social forces struggling for education in Brazil." Two years later, in 2012, this coalition of civil society, university, and government groups won another legal victory: the right to pay professors additional honorariums (beyond their university salaries) to teach in the PRONERA programs and the funding of student scholarships.[55]

Nevertheless, the TCU did not rescind all restrictions on social movement participation in the program. The new judgment required INCRA officials to rewrite the PRONERA manual and explicitly outline the limits to social movements' involvement in the program. The new 2012 manual stated that although activists could help identity local educational needs and offer suggestions about the pedagogical process, they could not be official partners of the PRONERA programs (MDA 2012, 24). In addition, the manual explicitly banned "restricting the participation of students that do not belong to social movements . . . attempting to train activists . . . and selecting professors based on political, partisan, philosophical, or ideological criteria" (MDA 2012, 19). In September 2015, I was able to interview Clarice again, a year after she had left her position as the coordinator of PRONERA. I asked her to talk about the TCU's judgment and the effects the new regulations had on movement participation in PRONERA. Clarice explained, "We took social movements out of the administrative part of the program and put them as advisors for the pedagogical components of the program." MST leaders criticized Clarice for agreeing to make this change, but she had assured them it would not change their actual participation in program.[56] She said, "Now, the MST agrees that nothing has changed about the program's governance structure." According to Clarice, despite the TCU restrictions, activists continue participating in developing, over-seeing, and evaluating PRONERA programs.

Critical to this process has been the MST's ability to win over allies both within INCRA and among the university partners, who support the movement's participation. For example, although the MST cannot official write new PRONERA program proposals, the movement can put univer-sities allies in contact with INCRA officials to develop a new program. Similarly, although the MST leadership cannot choose the students who enter each new program cohort, the movement's leaders can mobilize their own activists to apply once a new program is announced. The movement can also offer its own courses to help prepare these activists for the entrance exams. Finally, although MST activists cannot be paid to help coordinate these programs, if the professors are sympathetic to the movement, they encourage leaders to participate and informally offer financial compen-sation. Thus, although there are some limitations, MST activists are still involved in the co-governance of PRONERA programs. The key to the MST's ability to participate in PRONERA, under conditions of increased state regulation, is the expansion of its movement to include the state and university allies that are officially running the program.[57] This is essentially what Gramsci refers to as a "war of position," garnering the consent of di-verse institutional actors for an alternative hegemonic project.

Despite these high levels of social movement mobilization and partic-ipation, in 2015 Clarice claimed that the TCU judgment still had grave effects on the program.[58] One effect was the time it took for universities to offer PRONERA programs again. When the TCU judgment took effect in 2008, dozens of universities had program proposals accepted with students enrolled, which had to be put on hold for three years. In 2011, when INCRA was finally ready to move forward with these programs, many professors were no longer interested in being involved and the students had already enrolled in other programs. She gave the example of the State University of Piauí, which had several bachelor's degree programs approved in 2008 that all had to be cancelled. "The social movements in Piauí had to go through a process of mobilizing everyone again, finding out what types of programs were in demand and establishing relationships with professors to offer these programs." She said that all this mobilization only paid off in 2015, when the State University of Piauí opened three new bachelor's degree programs through PRONERA (in geography, agronomy, and pedagogy). "So what was the effect of the TCU judgment? For seven years, from 2008 to 2014, we functioned with fewer programs."

Clarice also said that the employees inside INCRA are now scared to work with PRONERA. When the TCU judgment was issued, Clarice and her staff were fined for financial mishandling. Although they never ended up paying the fines, all of the INCRA employees became wary of putting their names on PRONERA program proposals. Now, Clarice explained, everything related to PRONERA moves more slowly: "If there is a comma out of place, program proposals do not move forward." The TCU judgment also affected the size of PRONERA's budget, which had grown to 60 million *reais* by the 2009 fiscal year (about 26 million US dollars in 2009[59]). The 2008 TCU judgment prevented Clarice from executing this budget. "The President of INCRA came to talk to me at the end of 2009 and said, 'Clarice, since you only spent 40 percent of your budget, you are only going to be allotted 40 million *reais* next year.' And then since we could not even spend those 40 million in 2010, he said, 'Now your budget allotment is going to be 15 million.'"

Thus, when the TCU judgment was reversed in December 2010, PRONERA had a smaller budget, more bureaucratic foot dragging, and no universities with program proposal ready to be submitted. It was only five years later, through the advocacy and mobilization of the MST and other movement, state, and university actors, that PRONERA was back in full swing.

CONCLUSION

In this chapter, I explored one of the MST's entry points into the state, the National Program for Educators in Areas of Agrarian Reform (PRONERA). The case of PRONERA illustrates two of the principal arguments of the book: it is possible for social movements to co-govern public institutions as long as they continue to engage in contentious mobilization, and that occupying formal institutions helps to build movement's organizational and leadership capacity and resource base. Similarly to other scholars who analyze social movements' long march through the institutions and dual strategy of working inside and outside of the state (Alvarez 1990; Paschel 2016), I argue that a strategic group of movement activists were able to make tremendous gains in the state sphere—without demobilizing. To the contrary, MST leaders expressed a fear that the movement might lose many of their activists if they did not provide higher education to their social movement base. This was an explicit Gramscian strategy to develop organic intellectuals within the movement who could attend to the agricultural, educational, legal, and health needs of the settlement and camps.

The story of PRONERA's creation and expansion supports the argument that social movements' effective participation in formal institutions requires a combination of political advocacy and contentious protest. The starkest example of this is the initial approval of PRONERA itself, which only occurred after the movement organized a national march in Brasília with 100,000 participants. The movement organized this march after a shift in what social movement scholars call the political opportunity structure (McAdam 1999; Tarrow 2011). More specifically, the massacres of landless activists in 1995 and 1996 increased national support for agrarian reform and put pressure on the federal government to offer a series of concessions to the landless movement, including PRONERA. The MST then used PRONERA to justify activists' entrance into a new sphere of educational access: higher education. However, in a context of intense state–society conflict, the MST education sector had difficulties finding a university to support this initiative. It took a particular type of institution—private, with a long history of social mobilization—to risk hosting the MST's first bachelor's degree program. Even after the left-leaning PT took power and PRONERA had more funding and support, the MST had to continue mobilizing its base to pressure universities to approve new degree programs, as the case of the geography program illustrated. Thus, institutionalization was never a freezing in time of the MST's educational proposal, but rather, a dynamic process that required both mobilization and political maneuvering to push forward institutional goals.

The MST's first bachelor's degree program at the University of Ijuí is illustrative of both the evolution of the MST's educational proposal and the conflicts that emerge when activists enter the university sphere. Students were able to maintain many of the movement's educational ideals in the program, including the rotation between study and community periods, cultural practices, collectivity, self-governance, a pedagogical coordination collective, and research. However, this process was also full of tensions and conflicts, and in the end the MST leadership's refusal to compromise ruptured their relationship with the university professors who had gone out on a limb to support the movement. Nonetheless, this was a process of learning for both the MST and the university, which helped the MST educator sector refine its educational approach and the types of relationships they would build in the future with university and state actors. The vast majority of students in this first cohort are still activists, but they are now equipped with degrees, professional opportunities, and a clearer understanding of the MST's educational vision.

Importantly, the case of PRONERA also shows the contradictions inherent in social movements' contentious co-governance of public institutions. The Federal Court of Audits' (TCU) judgment against PRONERA in 2008, whether or not politically motivated, stemmed from a tension between the state's defense of individual rights and the MST's collective practices. For the TCU ministers, their judgment ensured universal access to public resources. For the MST, the judgment undermined communities' right to participate in the governance of their educational services. MST activists and their university and government allies engaged in a united attempt to pressure the TCU to rescind the judgment. This campaign was successful because the MST had garnered the consent of a wide range of civil society and state actors for its educational goals. The TCU ministers were forced to amend the judgment. Although social movements still face some restrictions, activists have found ways to continue participating in the development, oversight, and implementation of PRONERA programs. Nonetheless, the state's funding of PRONERA is necessarily tenuous, as the program supports the goals and desires of a particular segment of the population. Consequently, defending PRONERA will require the support of a diverse coalition of civil society, university, and government actors.

Finally, the case of PRONERA illustrates that among the diverse types of institutions that social movements can try to influence, higher education is an especially important sphere. The Brazilian public university system is notoriously elite, with difficult entrance exams, forcing poor youth to pay for low-quality private institutions. For almost all of the MST activists I spoke with during twenty months of field research, enrolling in a public university was a dream, something that nobody in their community had been able to attain. Although some youth were MST activists when they entered these university programs, many others had little contact with the movement and enrolled to improve their individual career opportunities. Like the secondary education programs that the MST developed in the early 1990s, these PRONERA higher education programs introduced these students to the MST's agrarian reform struggle and allowed them to prefigure, in the current social world, the economic and political practices that the movement hoped to build in the future. Many students became organic intellectuals, using their new technical and intellectual capacities to contribute to the movement.

In August 2012, forty-seven students graduated from a PRONERA bachelor's program in law. Although not all of these graduates have continued to participate in the movement, many are now activist-lawyers taking on legal tasks that the MST had previously relied on outside allies to complete. In a short decade, thousands of MST leaders obtained higher education degrees. The existence of PRONERA defies the claim that "it is not possible to compel concessions from elites that can be used as resources to sustain oppositional organization over time" (Piven and Cloward 1997, xxi). To the contrary, PRONERA integrates new activists into the movement, contributes to their professional and intellectual growth, and directly supports the economic development of agrarian reform settlements. In the next chapter I describe the institutionalization of the MST's educational goals in another federal agency, the Ministry of Education, a process that had very different outcomes for the movement.

CHAPTER 3

From the Pedagogy of the MST
to *Educação do Campo*

Expansion, Transformation, and Compromise

Educação do Campo was born within the MST, but it no longer belongs to the MST.
—Bernardo Mançano Fernandes, *professor at the State University of São Paulo (UNESP)*
Sometimes I feel that in the Ministry of Education we are just there for show; we are forced to appear as though we support everything, even though we critique their programs.
—Vanderlúcia Simplício, *national leader in MST Education Sector*

In the previous chapter, I told the story of how the MST implemented its educational approach at the federal level during the late 1990s and 2000s, through the Program for Education in Areas of Agrarian Reform (PRONERA). PRONERA helped the movement solidify its educational approach, by allowing MST leaders to experiment with alternative pedagogies in the university sphere. PRONERA's location within the National Institute for Colonization and Agrarian Reform (INCRA) permitted the movement a high degree of control over the program; however, the movement's ability to approve new courses was a lengthy process that always required a delicate balance of political advocacy and disruptive protest. Furthermore, the movement's entrance into the university sphere was full of tensions and conflicts, transforming both the movement and the universities themselves.

For the MST, access to higher education through PRONERA integrated new activists into the movement, introduced them to the MST's political vision, and equipped them with the technical skills and professional degrees needed for self-governance. Movement leaders also learned how to pick their battles and strategically compromise on some issues and not on others. As for the universities, contact with the movement transformed many professors and administrators into advocates of the MST's educational proposal, integrating them into a broad-based social movement defending the program. For other university faculty, PRONERA reinforced their perception that outside actors should not be allowed to influence higher education. Although PRONERA maintains a fragile space within the Brazilian state apparatus, MST activists continue to be real protagonists in this institutional sphere, developing educational programs that directly serve the needs of their communities and the movement.

In this chapter, I discuss the transformation of the MST's pedagogical approach into a general proposal for the entire countryside in the late 1990s—*Educação do Campo* (Education of the Countryside)—and the trajectory of this educational program in the Ministry of Education (MEC) between 2004 and 2014. This chapter presents a counternarrative to the story of PRONERA. While PRONERA facilitated small-scale movement-led initiatives, the promotion of *Educação do Campo* in the Ministry of Education was more expansive and state led, with less direct movement involvement. This rapid expansion led to more stakeholders laying claim over these initiatives and a watering down of the original proposal. These developments force us to reflect on the meaning of success when discussing the MST's educational proposal. On the one hand, success could be defined as the degree of expansion of the MST's program initiatives, the amount of resource invested in these programs, and their geographic and numerical reach. On the other hand, the MST leadership would be more likely to define success as the movement's direct participation in these educational programs and the extent to which the programs succeed in supporting the broad goal of constructing socialism in the Brazilian countryside. The MEC's embrace of *Educação do Campo* is a unique case to reflect on these diverse social movement outcomes and different visions of success.

The origins of *Educação do Campo* trace back to 1998, the last year of President Fernando Henrique Cardoso's first mandate. During this period, several international organizations encouraged the MST to expand its educational program to other rural populations not living in areas of agrarian reform. Partially, this was a strategic proposal, as the federal administration was antagonistic to the MST and it was unlikely that education only for agrarian reform settlements and camps would garner more national support. However, this change also reflected a realization among the MST leadership about the importance of constructing an educational program for all working-class populations in the countryside, and of building relationships with other rural organizations. The shift in framing from the Pedagogy of the MST to *Educação do Campo* (Education of the Countryside) resonated with dozens of other civil society groups, a process that social movement scholars refer to as "frame alignment" (D. A. Snow, Rochford, Worden, and Benford 1986). Most important, the large and powerful National Confederation of Agricultural Workers (CONTAG) became a central player in the national *Educação do Campo* coalition. These developments strengthened the force of the educational proposal but also had deep implications for the MST's ability to control the content of these educational initiatives. Nonetheless, the contentious partnership that developed between the MST and CONTAG—organizations with distinct historical trajectories, contrasting political strategies, and competing membership bases—succeeded in pressuring the government to pass legal guidelines supporting *Educação do Campo* in 2001. However, this law remained words on paper until Workers' Party (PT) candidate Luis Inácio Lula da Silva became president in 2003.

In 2004, the Ministry of Education (MEC) created a new office for *Educação do Campo*, with an advisory board that offered movements a direct point of access to participate in state decision making—a participatory space typical of the new PT administration. The office for *Educação do Campo*, in coordination with the advisory board, hosted seminars in every Brazilian state in order to promote this new educational approach. This led to multiple conflicts while also deepening the connections between local MST activists, state educational officials, university professors, and other rural movements. *Educação do Campo* began to take on a life of its own, with universities institutionalizing the concept through new degree programs; state departments of education establishing *Educação do Campo* offices; and a range of groups embracing these educational ideas. The office for *Educação do Campo* implemented a series of new programs that expanded education in the rural countryside to an unprecedented degree; however, these programs were a far cry from the MST's original intentions. I analyze two of these programs to illustrate how the MEC's tendency toward implementing large-scale and universal solutions to educational access created barriers to the movement's co-governance.

The last part of this chapter analyzes the trajectory of *Educação do Campo* during Dilma Rousseff's first presidential term (2011–2014). I critically assess the meaning of *Educação do Campo* during this period, given the PT's lack of political capacity and/or will to implement agrarian reform. The MST still actively participated in debates about *Educação do Campo*, but it was now only one of the dozens of groups laying claim over the meaning, content, and purpose of these educational ideas. Even elite agribusiness groups began to embrace the educational approach as a solution to the schooling and training needs of rural workers. *Educação do Campo* had not only been institutionalized; it had also become hegemonic.

In referring to hegemony, I draw on Gramsci's definition of the term as a governing alliance that maintains power through a combination of both coercive force and willing consent, the latter of which requires both concessions and moral and intellectual leadership (Gramsci 1971, 258). After *Educação do Campo* became common sense for a multiclass coalition,[1] these programs partially served to reinforce the dominant, capitalist mode of economic production in Brazil—despite the education proposal's socialist origins. From this perspective, the PT era represented two phenomena: (1) a successful war of position—whereby MST organic intellectuals convinced a wide range of civil society groups and state actors to embrace their educational ideas; and (2) a passive revolution, or an absorption of this proposal into the ideological milieu of the hegemonic bloc. Tuğal (2009) refers to passive revolution as "one of the convoluted, sometimes unintended, ways the dominant sectors establish willing consent ('hegemony') for their rule" (3–4). This process of passive revolution was not simply co-optation, as the MEC's embrace of *Educação do Campo* had real positive implications for poor populations in the countryside, offering thousands of rural people more educational opportunities. However, the support for *Educação do Campo* also reinforced a class alliance between the federal administration and large agribusiness. Thus, while this is clearly a story of the transformation of rural education, the process did not unfold in the exact ways or forms that the MST leadership had hoped. In order to understand the incredible rise of *Educação do Campo* to national prominence, it is necessary to return to the 1990s and the series of events that laid the foundation for the emergence of this national educational proposal.

NEOLIBERALISM AND STATE–SOCIETY CONFLICT (1998–2002)

Powerful Allies: UNESCO, UNICEF, and University Supporters

When the MST began to participate in the public educational sphere in the early 1980s, it was out of a concrete necessity: the existence of thousands of children and youth living in settlements and camps that were out of school. In addition, MST activists were motivated to engage in this struggle due to the contrast between the movement's vision for the countryside—of vibrant, intellectual communities of small farmers and collective agricultural production—and the traditional vision teachers held of education as a path for youth to leave backward rural areas. MST leaders wanted to develop new leaders from among the youth, not witness a mass rural-urban migration. Illiteracy was also rampant in agrarian reform communities, leading MST activists to organize several large-scale literacy campaigns.

At the same time, in the early 1990s, international organizations such as UNESCO, UNICEF, and the World Bank were becoming dominant voices in global educational debates (Klees, Samoff, and Stromquist 2012; Samoff 1999). These organizations focused on eradicating illiteracy and providing universal access to primary education in high-poverty countries. International program coordinators often criticized the priorities of national governments and tried to circumvent corrupt and inefficient bureaucracies by working directly with local communities. This was partially a consequence of a neoliberal perspective becoming dominant in educational development discourse, which promoted the devolution of school authority to local governing levels that were considered more efficient and accountable (Bray 2003). In this context, UNESCO and UNICEF began to fund the MST's educational initiatives. These international organizations invested in the MST, despite its radical political and socialist goals, because the activists were organizing the most massive educational programs in the countryside.

The head of the educational unit of UNESCO-Brazil in 2014 explained the funding relationship that the agency developed with the MST during this period: "The MST was the only group working in the settlements . . . it is hard to work in these areas if you are not connected to the MST; these are very poor areas. The MST created the infrastructure for these programs, and the families living in the settlements already had a relationship with the MST."[2] As the UNESCO official suggested, the imperative for expanding educational access in high poverty areas overshadowed ideological differences between the program coordinators and the movement. Given the MST's organizational networks in these communities, it made sense to ask for the movement's help in the agency's literacy campaigns. In 1995, the MST also received an Education and Participation prize from UNICEF for the teacher certification courses activists had developed for rural teachers (the MAG program, described in Chapter 1). The fact that an internationally respected organization would give such a prestigious award to a confrontational movement was significant, offering the MST more public legitimacy. Thus, the MST's socialist mobilization and international organizations' educational mandate became linked together in complex ways.

By the mid-1990s, the MST's educational initiatives were ripe for expansion. First, the MST had developed concrete practices that represented a comprehensive approach to rural schooling. Second, international organizations recognized these educational practices as legitimate through funding and awards. Third, the MST had cultivated dozens of partnerships with university professors across Brazil, who actively promoted and sponsored MST-literacy programs. Fourth and finally, the federal government faced increasing pressure to provide a solution to the country's dismal rural education system. This political conjuncture set the stage for a surge in federal support for the movement's educational initiatives.

Framing and Coalition Building under Conditions of State–Society Conflict

The year 1997 was a turning point for the MST's educational struggle, as described in Chapter 2. The two massacres of dozens of rural landless activists in 1995 and 1996 increased national support for agrarian reform and the number of land occupations across the country. In July 1997, the MST organized the First National Meeting of Educators in Areas of Agrarian Reform (ENERA), in partnership with UNICEF, UNESCO, the University of Brasília (UnB), and the National Conference of Brazilian Bishops (CNBB). Out of these discussions came the proposal to create a National Program for Education in Areas of Agrarian Reform (PRONERA), which would fund hundreds of adult education, high school, and university programs in areas of agrarian reform over the next decade.

Up until this point all of the MST's educational initiatives, including PRONERA, were directed toward populations in areas of agrarian reform, which included settlements and camps. However, these areas of agrarian reform only represented a fraction of the rural population. During the 1997 ENERA meeting, a representative from UNESCO, Ana Catarina Braga, challenged the five organizations that coordinated the event to think about a broader proposal for education in the entire countryside (Kolling et al. 1999, 13–14). This proposal would include other rural groups, such as indigenous peoples, black rural communities (*quilombos*), people displaced by dams, small farmers, and farm workers. The MST activists were open to this new initiative, as a strategic opportunity to demand more financial support for their educational proposal and also to influence the broader working-class population in the countryside.

In August 1997, representatives from UNESCO, UNICEF, the UnB, the CNBB, and the MST met to plan another national conference to stimulate this broader debate: the First National Conference for a Basic Education of the Countryside (*Conferência Nacional por uma Educação Básica do Campo*). The phrase "*Educação do Campo* (Education *of* the Countryside)" was deliberate, indicating a proposal not simply *in* the countryside or *for* rural populations but, rather, a proposal *of* those rural populations, implemented by them according to their realities. This phrasing was linked to Paulo Freire's idea of a "Pedagogy *of* the Oppressed" not *for* the oppressed, or in other words, created for them without their participation. The goal of the 1998 national conference was to debate *Educação do Campo* and, in particular, the relationship between this educational proposal and a sustainable development model in the countryside based on small-farming and collective agricultural production. To stimulate these discussions, the organizers of the conference wrote a study text about *Educação do Campo* and its relationship to rural development. It states, "There is a dominant tendency in our country, due to exclusion and inequality, to consider the majority of the population in rural areas as backwards and outside of the project of modernity" (Kolling et al. 1999, 21). In contrast, *Educação do Campo* supported a new vision of rural development encompassing agrarian reform, family-led agriculture, agroecology, agrarian cooperatives, food sovereignty, and the commercialization of local produce (22).

During the six months leading up to the national conference, this study document became the basis for twenty-seven state seminars on *Educação do Campo*. At each seminar, participants included representatives from a broad range of rural populations and grassroots organizations. The coordinators of these state seminars were responsible for highlighting local educational experiences that could be shared at the national conference.[3] On July 27, 1998, 974 delegates from these state seminars traveled to Brasília for the First National Conference for a Basic Education of the Countryside. Participants at the conference included nineteen federal and state universities, several government agencies, and more than a dozen rural social movements and nongovernmental organizations (NGOs). The meeting consisted of a week of debate about the relationship between rural development and education, the status of rural education in Latin America, educational financing, indigenous education, and sustainable rural development. There were also cultural performances, which brought to life the traditions of the different rural communities present at the conference. The Pedagogy of Land cohort in the PRONERA bachelor degree program at the University of Ijuí (described in Chapter 2) organized the opening cultural performance, known as a *mística*, which was an elaborate presentation of poetry, song, and theater pertaining to social justice in the countryside.

At the end of the conference the attendees approved a text, "A Basic Education of the Countryside: Challenges and Proposal for Actions," which states in part:

> The discussion in this conference proved that it is only possible to work towards a basic education of the countryside if it is connected to the process of constructing a popular

project for Brazil, which necessarily includes a new development proposal for the countryside and the guarantee of educational access for all populations in the countryside. . . .
This debate must include the social movements, unions, universities, churches, and base
communities . . . through the creation of local collectives to discuss their educational
proposals for the Brazilian countryside. (Kolling et al. 1999, 77–78)

The final conference document emphasized the link between *Educação do
Campo* and a new development proposal based in small farming traditions,
agroecological food production, collective work, and participatory democracy. The document identified rural communities as the principal agents in
developing and implementing these educational and economic alternatives.

After the 1998 conference, the MST education sector began to shift from
referring to its educational approach as the "Pedagogy of the MST" to a more
general call for "*Educação do Campo*" (Education of the Countryside). The
MST's new use of this phrase is similar to what social movement scholars
refer to as frame alignment, or the linking of the movement's "interests,
values, and beliefs" to the ideologies and goals of other movements (D.
A. Snow et al. 1986, 464). Several MST leaders explain:

The MST began to understand that to advance its struggle it needed to join with other
working-class populations in the countryside, to pressure the state for broader public
policies . . . [for example] in order for MST activists to convince the state to build
middle schools and high schools in their communities, it was necessary to build this
bigger coalition with the other communities in the countryside that would attend these
schools. . . . It was for these reasons that the MST began to advocate for *Educação do
Campo*. (Kolling et al. 2012, 502)

The concept of *Educação do Campo* resonated with a wide range of social
movements, union leaders, NGOs, and academics working in the countryside but not connected to agrarian reform.

Uniting the Landless and Rural Workers

Despite these advances, there was one group conspicuously absent from
the First National Conference for a Basic Education of the Countryside in
1998, the National Confederation of Agricultural Workers (CONTAG).
This union confederation is made up of dozens of federations comprising
thousands of unions representing more than 15 million rural workers.
CONTAG members include wage workers (with no autonomous control over land); small holders and sharecroppers (with modest access to
land they used to plant subsistence and cash crops); and homesteaders
or squatters (*posseiros*) (Maybury-Lewis 1994, 56). The absence of an

organization representing millions of rural workers meant that convincing the federal government to support an educational policy for the entire country-side would be unlikely. This raises the question: Why was CONTAG not yet willing to take up the cause for *Educação do Campo*?

Under pressure from rural social movements, President João Goulart created CONTAG through a presidential decree on January 31, 1964. This meant that the processs of unionization for rural workers was now legally regulated by the Ministry of Work, strengthening the struggles and demands of rural workers nationally. CONTAG experienced its biggest growth during the twenty-one year dictatorship when the number of agricultural unions grew from 266 in 1963 to 2,144 in 1980 (Anthony Pereira 1997, 58). The military government purposely stimulated the growth of the rural union movement in an attempt to increase agricultural production, foster national integration, and incorporate rural labor into national society (Houtzager 1998). Rural oligarchs still ruled the countryside, and the military government wanted to curb their power by having a presence in remote regions. Turning the union into the distributional arm of the state could achieve this goal, as social welfare programs became a link between the federal government and dispersed rural populations.[4] For the MST, this history illustrated that CONTAG was simply a *pelego* (co-opted) union, functioning as an appendage of the military government.

However, this was not the whole story. Although most union locals functioned as social service providers, some unionists took advantage of the limited space they had in order to wage a national campaign for workers' rights. These were primarily the activists who had been organizing closely with the Catholic Church prior to the coup. In contrast to Communist Party activists, who had largely been purged from their unions, these unionists

> understood that excessive provocation of rural elites and the authorities, given the power relations in the countryside, would hurt them and set back their organization drive....
> They learned the value of respecting the law. Indeed, the unionists became champions of the law, pushing for enforcement of policy on the books ostensibly to protect their rights. (Maybury-Lewis 1994, 73)

In 1968, a group of unionists that came out of this organizing tradition took control of CONTAG. Although their ability to act was constrained, their presence resulted in important benefits for rural workers: "Precluded from mobilizing rank and file and engaging in any form of collective action, CONTAG undertook instead a 'campaign for rights' in which unions would educate workers about their legal rights and encourage them to bring individual cases before the labor courts" (Houtzager 1998, 132). This legal strategy resulted in concrete gains for workers during a highly repressive period. The downside of this strategy was that an entire generation of labor activists became accustomed to nonconfrontational approaches to unionism. In addition, while some committed activists organized workers' rights campaign, almost two-thirds of unions were still involved exclusively in service delivery (Houtzager 1998).

In 1979, in the context of a more general political opening, union leaders affiliated with CONTAG initiated a series of annual strikes in Pernambuco and began calling for large-scale agrarian reform (Maybury-Lewis 1994, 76; Welch 2009). By this time, other rural organizations were also beginning to engage in direct action in the countryside. Among these was the Pastoral Land Commission (CPT), founded in 1975. The CPT was critical in helping workers occupy land in the early 1980s, leading to the founding of the MST in 1984 (discussed in Chapter 1). These religious and landless leaders joined with urban movements, neighborhood associations, and militant unionists to help found the PT in 1980 and the Central Union of Workers (CUT) in 1983. In contrast, the national CONTAG leadership "made a virtual religion out of its autonomy from political parties" (Houtzager 1998, 135).

Nonetheless, the relationship that developed between local CONTAG leaders and the emerging landless movement was complex and full of tensions.[5] Many local unionists developed connections to the CPT, the MST, and the PT, and with the help of these social movements they took over their local unions (Maybury-Lewis 1994, 173–197). In Pernambuco, in the early 1990s, CONTAG activists hosted MST leaders in their headquarters and helped the movement organize its first occupations in the sugarcane region. This eventually led to the state union federation in Pernambuco leading its own land occupations in the mid-1990s—despite a deeply embedded culture of "following the law" (Rosa 2009, 471–472).

At the national level, however, there were deep ideological divides between CONTAG and the CUT, CPT, and MST leaders. For example, CUT activists believed that the union movement should reject federal funding, while CONTAG felt that this would create more hardship for rural workers (Maybury-Lewis 1994, 242). In many local unions, a competitive relationship developed between CONTAG and CUT, as CUT activists—often in tandem with the MST and the CPT—ran their own candidates in local union elections. This fed into a general mistrust between the national MST leadership and CONTAG, in addition to other ideological disputes.

A critical shift occurred in 1995, at CONTAG's VI National Congress. CUT unionists had won enough local elections that they tipped CONTAG's internal power balance, leading CONTAG to affiliate with CUT. At this congress, delegates also began to discuss a proposal for broader social policies in the countryside that became known as the Alternative Project for Sustainable Rural Development and Solidarity (PADRSS).[6] The PADRSS proposal represented a new focus within the confederation on broader public policies for the countryside. The plan emphasized agrarian reform, family agriculture, environmental conservation, food sovereignty, biodiversity, territorial sovereignty, women's rights, and racial equality—issues that closely aligned with the MST's own agrarian vision. At CONTAG's VII National Congress, in 1998, the delegates passed the PADRSS proposal.

The approval of the PADRSS proposal transformed CONTAG's engagement with rural education, turning schooling into a central concern of the union movement. Consequently, although the union confederation did not participate in the First National Conference for Basic Education of the Countryside in 1998, two years later CONTAG was at the forefront of the national coalition for *Educação do Campo*. A leader in the CONTAG federation in Pernambuco, Sônia Maria dos Santos, explained how the PADRSS proposal motivated the confederation's involvement in education: "In 1995 we discussed the alternative project we were trying to construct . . . we wrote the PADRSS proposal . . . it was a document that discussed the public policies we wanted for the countryside, and education became an important part of those policies."[7] The combination of the new PADRSS proposal and the attention rural education was receiving nationally led CONTAG's leadership to take a stance on the issue of *Educação do Campo*.

Passing Legislation to Support *Educação do Campo*

By the time the Second National Conference for Education of the Countryside took place in 2005, CONTAG was one of the most important participants in the national struggle for *Educação do Campo*—at times surpassing the role of the MST itself. Many scholars have shown how the process of framing can expand a movement's network of allies (Benford and Snow 2000; McCammon, Muse, Newman, and Terrell, 2007; D. Snow 2004). However, less often emphasized in this literature are the other implications of the framing process. In this case, as more civil society organizations began internalizing the struggle for *Educação do Campo*, the MST became only one of the many groups laying claim to the meaning of these educational ideas. In addition, CONTAG activists did not take on the struggle for *Educação do Campo* simply because MST activists shifted their frame. This alliance occurred at a particular historical moment when a series of internal changes within CONTAG opened up the possibility for the confederation to take a position on the issue of rural schooling.[8]

Despite the changes that occurred within CONTAG between 1995 and 1998, decades of practice with a legalistic approach to workers' rights was still engrained within the organization. Consequently, as soon as CONTAG activists decided to take on the issue of *Educação do Campo*, their first step was to work with President Cardoso's administration to pass through a law in support of this educational approach. The MST, whose relationship with the Cardoso administration was much more confrontational, did not directly participate in this process. Again, these interactions illustrate the ways that movements, with different histories, transform each other through their interactions. The MST's reframing of its educational struggle pushed CONTAG to take a position on rural education. CONTAG unionists, who still approached workers' rights through legislative interventions, applied this approach to *Educação do Camp*.

Between 2000 and 2002, the CONTAG leadership worked with the National Education Advisory Board (CNE) to pass legislation in support of *Educação do Campo*. The CNE is a body of twenty-four educational representatives, appointed by the federal government, charged with writing Brazil's national educational guidelines.[9] In the early 2000s, Edla Soarez, the former Secretary of Education of the municipality of Recife, Pernambuco, was a member of the CNE and a vocal ally of urban and rural social movements. The CONTAG leadership approached Edla and asked her to sponsor a new set of federal guidelines in support of *Educação do Campo*. Edla agreed and traveled all over the country to listen to rural groups about their educational experiences.

Edla made it a point to contact MST activists in each state, but these local MST leaders did not always show up. Edla suspected that they were more concerned with defending their own schools.[10] José Wilson, a CONTAG unionist, believed that MST activists did not participate because they did not have the necessary connections to help push through federal policy.[11] MST leader Rosali Caldart partially agreed: "We participated very little in writing the guidelines, the union movement was closer [to the process].... This is not because we decided not to participate but because this was not our world" (Marcos de Anhaia 2010). Consequently, although lots of rural populations are mentioned in the guidelines, including black communities, river people, and small farmers, the 2001 guidelines do not explicitly mention the residents of agrarian reform areas (i.e., settlers and campers). This would only change in a 2008 expansion of the guidelines.

On April 3, 2002, the National Education Advisory Board for Basic Education (CNE/CEB) approved a resolution supporting the "Operational Guidelines for a Basic Education in the Schools of the Countryside." Despite the MST's marginal role in this process, both MST and CONTAG leaders declared the new policy a victory. The guidelines stated that "populations of the countryside have the right to their own diverse forms of social organization, which are part of their identity ... [and therefore] schools of the countryside should be organized based on these local realities, conceptions of time, and knowledge of the students." The guidelines also mentioned the need to support an educational project that is connected to the "work of the students, social development, economic justice, and ecological sustainability."[12] The guidelines did not outline a single model; instead, they gave rural populations the explicit right to participate in deciding the organizational and pedagogical approaches of their schools.

A few months later, in November 2002, the same five organizations that had coordinated the first national conference—UNESCO, UNICEF, CNBB, the UnB, and the MST—hosted a national seminar to reflect on the new legislation. There were 372 participants from twenty-five states, with representatives from dozens of other social movements, universities, and subnational governments. This time CONTAG activists were present and had a prominent role in the conference deliberations. The timing was critical, as PT candidate Luis Inácio Lula da Silva had just won the presidential election. The final document of this seminar included a long list of educational demands for the President-elect. These demands included professional training for teachers, an increase in adult literacy programs, universal infant education, technical training for rural workers, textbooks, infrastructure, state seminars on *Educação do Campo*, a Secretary for *Educação do Campo* in the Ministry of Education, and the right for social movements and unions to participate in the co-governance of these educational programs. Legally, the seeds had been sown for *Educação do Campo* during the conflictive Cardoso administration; however, it would take the more left-leaning PT administration to put this new legislation into practice.

THE PT ERA: SOCIAL MOVEMENT PARTICIPATION AND CLASS COMPROMISE (2003–2010)

When President Lula took office in 2003, his administration represented a complex compromise between the "popular" (grassroots) movements that were the base of his party, and the economic and political elites with whom he had allied to be elected. Representative of this shift was Lula's "Letter to the Brazilian People," which he wrote several months before the 2002 election, committing to honoring an agreement with the International Monetary Fund (IMF) and maintaining a market-oriented macro-economic policy approach. Once Lula took office in 2003, one of his first initiatives was to cut back the public pension system for civil servants, which resulted in an exodus of left-leaning political groups from the PT and the founding of a new left party in 2004, the Socialist and Liberty Party (PSOL).[13] Then, in 2005, the big monthly payment (*mensalão*) scandal broke, revealing that PT leaders had been making payments to congressional representatives in exchange for political loyalty. This led to a new series of splits, with more prominent congressional representatives leaving the PT and joining the PSOL.

Thus, the PT that ascended to power in 2003 was a different PT than the one that had consolidated in the 1980s. Nonetheless, despite this conservative shift, Lula implemented many large-scale social programs, including the largest cash-transfer program in the world, *Bolsa Família*. By 2005 this program had reached more than 11 million families throughout the country and helped in reducing poverty by 15 percent (Ondetti 2008, 204). The Lula administration had the capacity to implement these redistributive programs due to the tremendous commodity boom during his two terms, which allowed for a steadily growing economy.[14] The PT administration also increased the institutionalization of social movement participation at the federal level. For example, as soon as Lula took office he created a Special Secretariat for Policies to Promote Racial Equality (SEPPIR), inviting leaders of the black movement to administer the new office (Paschel 2016). During Lula's first term in office, his administration organized twenty-nine national conferences and hundreds of state and municipal conferences to promote civil society debate on a variety of topics. Nevertheless, many activists criticized these efforts for having little effect on policy and fragmenting social movement demands (Goldfrank 2011b, 173).

As for the administration's agricultural policies, when Lula won the election in 2002, the rural social movements that had mobilized on his behalf assumed he would implement wide-scale agrarian reform. Consequently, just before Lula took office, thousands of families participated in new land occupations—organized by the MST and dozens of other groups.[15] However, while Lula publicly supported agrarian reform, in practice he continued many of Cardoso's market-based agrarian reform initiatives.[16] Thus, "without criminalizing the struggle for land and still counting on the support of the agrarian social movements and unions, the Lula government was able to operate in a type of 'accommodation' between constitutional agrarian reform and the loan programs for buying land that were supported by the World Bank" (Pereira and Sauer 2006, 198). Due to strong international prices, favorable exchange rates, and the PT's support, the agriculture industry boomed during Lula's first term (Ondetti 2008, 205).

Although the number of land occupations spiked during the first few years of Lula's administration, this number declined again as landless workers realized that the PT was not planning on implementing a wide-scale program of agrarian reform. In 2005 the MST organized the largest march in the movement's history, with 12,000 activists (including 130 children) walking 125 miles from Goiânia to Brasília. Following the march, the PT administration agreed to settle thousands of families; however, the majority of these families were settled on vacant lots in already established settlements or on public land. In other words, there was very little new expropriation of private land estates during Lula's first term in office (Ondetti 2008, 207). Despite their disappointment, MST leaders supported Lula in the 2006 election, fearing an even more hostile context if the right-leaning candidate became the new president. However, during Lula's second mandate (2007–2010), the administration settled even fewer families.[17] Figure 3.1 and 3.2 illustrate these trends, with more families participating in occupations after Lula took office (2003–2004), but the number of new families issued land rights only increasing during the last two years of his first mandate (2005–2006), and then decreasing thereafter.

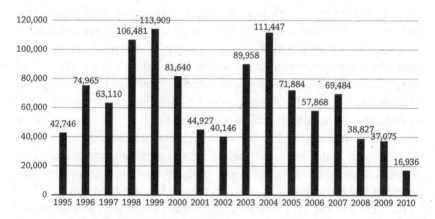

Figure 3.1 Number of Families in New Land Occupations, 1995–2010
Source: *DataLuta: Banco de Dados da Luta Pela Terra: Relatório Brasil 2016* (NERA 2017)

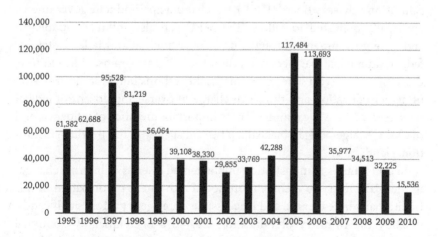

Figure 3.2 Number of New Families Issued Land Rights, 1995–2010
Source: *DataLuta: Banco de Dados da Luta Pela Terra: Relatório Brasil 2016* (NERA 2017)

Rather than implement large-scale agrarian reform, the PT's strategy to appease its rural constituents during this period was to invest more money in settlements. As described in Chapter 2, this strategy led to an increase in funding for many agrarian reform programs, including PRONERA. This surge in resources, and the administration's more participatory ethos, also led to a radical transformation of the historically impermeable Ministry of Education.

Institutionalizing *Educação do Campo* in the Ministry of Education

The Ministry of Education (MEC) is a large, hierarchical, and bureaucratic state agency, charged with modernizing the country's public education system. The MEC was created in 1930, when universal education first became a national goal. For thirty years, the provision of public education was centralized in this ministry, until the first National Education Law (LDB) was passed in 1961. This law devolved authority over the provision of public education to municipal and state governments. Although there was a partial recentralization of educational administration during the two decades of military dictatorship, the 1988 constitution decentralized educational governance once again, with state and municipal governments assuming the administration of the K–12 public school system. The most recent LDB, passed in 1996, reinforced this decentralized educational system.

Nonetheless, the MEC remains one of the most important educational authorities in the country. The MEC is charged with developing general policies and guidelines for education, in coordination with the National Education Advisory Board (CNE), which municipal and state governments are legally obligated to follow. The MEC can also influence municipal and state governments through conditional funding and federal–state or federal–municipal partnerships around specific programs. Furthermore, the MEC shares with state governments the responsibility for the provision of higher education and thus is in charge of overseeing dozens of federal universities across the country. These important methods of influence, and the MEC's large budget, make it a powerful agency in the Brazilian institutional landscape.

In 2004, Lula's administration implemented a series of internal changes in the MEC to try to include more social movement participation in this traditionally bureaucratic and inaccessible state agency. Most significantly, in 2004 the Ministry of Education created a Secretariat of Continual Education, Literacy, Diversity, and Inclusion (SECADI),[18] which included a Department of Education for Diversity and Citizenship.[19] The goal of SECADI, and more specifically the Department of Diversity, was to create educational programs that targeted populations facing educational challenges specifically due to their racial, ethnic, or geographical diversity, including indigenous populations, Afro-Brazilians, and communities located in the countryside.

Armênio Bello Schmidt became the director of the new Department of Education for Diversity and Citizenship.[20] Armênio was a teacher and long-time PT activist from Rio Grande do Sul. Armênio recalled the significance of the restructuring within the MEC: never before had there been an educational department that was charged with developing policies for the diversity of the Brazilian population. He said:

> There was no sector inside the Ministry that addressed diversity. Or in other words, those populations outside of the normal age in school, or illiterate populations . . . or blacks, who make up 50 percent of the population . . . there was a very strong prejudice against these populations and no one was addressing this issue. Or the question of the countryside, there was no space in the MEC that discussed the issues particular to education in the countryside.

In the Department of Education for Diversity and Citizenship, the administration created a specific office for *Educação do Campo*, directly drawing on the educational concept that the MST and other rural social movements had been promoting for the previous five years. As Armênio explained:

> There had been a discussion going on for several years, especially between the social movements of the countryside, the MST, CONTAG, and more than twenty other movements . . . that they needed an education that was specific to their communities. Not an uban education *in* the countryside, because they did not identify the curriculum and educational content in city schools. They wanted an education in the countryside for peasant populations.

As this statement illustrates, state officials in the MEC were aware of the major ideas underlining *Educação do Campo* and began to promote these ideas in their own discourse. Armênio told me that the social movements of the countryside had held several conferences in the late 1990s and then in 2002 the government passed the "Operational Guidelines for *Educação do Campo*," which became the legal justification for creating the office for *Educação do Campo* in 2004. Thus, this office was a direct response to the demands of rural social movements.

In addition to creating this office, the MEC established a permanent advisory board for *Educação do Campo*,[21] which could advise state officials on the process of implementing the federal *Educação do Campo* guidelines

(MEC 2004). The advisory board included representatives from all of the main social movements, NGOs, and university partners that had pushed for *Educação do Campo* over the previous five years. This advisory board worked directly with MEC officials to do this work. Thus, the antagonistic relationships between social movements and the MEC that had been common during Cardoso's administration appeared to have transformed, as CONTAG, the MST, and their allies were given an institutional space to co-govern rural education with state actors.

In August 2004, to inaugurate this new office, MEC officials helped to organize the Second National Conference for Education of the Countryside. Unlike the First National Conference in 1998, which the MST and four other organizations sponsored, the Second National Conference in 2004 had over thirty-eight groups that were the official organizers of the event. There were 1,100 participants, including members of social movements, unions, universities, and government agencies, and hundreds of school teachers. A total of thirty-nine groups signed the final document of the Second National Conference. The increase in participants was a result of the consolidation of the national movement for *Educação do Campo* over the previous five years, the inclusion of CONTAG—an organization perceived as more mainstream—in the coalition, the passing of a federal law to support these educational initiatives, and the PT's dedication to more inclusive and participatory state–society relations in the Ministry of Education.

Despite the plurality of voices present in the second conference, the MST and CONTAG continued to drive this process in a tenuous and contentious partnership. For example, as soon as the federal government created an office for *Educação do Campo*, both organizations demanded that the coordinator come out of their own ranks. Consequently, Professor Antonio Munarim, an academic at the Federal University of Santa Catarina not overtly associated with either movement, became the first coordinator of the MEC's office for *Educação do Campo*. As Antonio told the story, his name was suggested because he had extensive experience developing educational programs on MST and CONTAG settlements in the 1980s and 1990s; however, he was not considered a "member" of any one movement.[22] In fact, Antonio had not played any significant role in the national coalition for *Educação do Campo* in the late 1990s and early 2000s, precisely because he was finishing his dissertation. According to Antonio, the timing of his doctoral research was the major reason he was selected for the position—he had not been active enough for either movement to form an opinion about him!

In July 2004, the Secretary of SECADI, Ricardo Henrique, asked Antonio to go to Brasília and attend the Second National Conference for Education of the Countryside, where he would be announced as the coordinator.

Antonio laughed as he told the story: "Ricardo threw me into the scene to see if anyone would object, and if no one did, I would be picked." When Antonio arrived at the conference, he immediately ran into Rosali Caldart, a leader in the national MST education sector. Rosali exclaimed, "Professor Munarim, what are you doing here?" In response, he told Rosali that he had been tapped as the coordinator of the new office for *Educação do Campo*. Laughing, Rosali said that she had better not give him a hug yet, because if CONTAG activists saw him interacting with her, his name would be rejected from the nomination. On August 6, 2004, Antonio became the first coordinator of the office for *Educação do Campo*, representing an institutional compromise between CONTAG and the MST, mediated by the MEC officials.

The first actions that the new office for *Educação do Campo* took was to hold a series of seminars in every state of Brazil between 2005 and 2006. The goal of the seminars was to familiarize state and municipal governments with the *Educação do Campo* national guidelines that had been passed in 2002.[23] These seminars brought together all of the local organizations that had been participating in the national conferences for the previous five years, along with municipal and state government officials. Antonio said that these meetings were often intense, as Secretaries of Education from conservative political parties had never been put into the same room as MST leaders and other rural activists. Several meetings resulted in fighting, with government actors storming out of the meeting early. However, many seminars succeeded in creating regional state–society advisory boards, which offered local MST activists new paths of access to educational policymakers. Academics in universities throughout the country also began to establish research groups and academic programs in *Educação do Campo*. This happened organically, with the professors who were directly involved in the national coalition taking the lead to set up these programs at their universities. Thus, *Educação do Campo* quickly became an established field of academic study, with dozens of degree programs and research teams dedicated to this topic. The proposal for *Educação do Campo* was becoming hegemonic, not only supported by the MST and its allies but by different universities and subnational governments across the country.

"A Tiny Door That Opened to a Waiting Room": Hierarchy in the Ministry of Education

While the Second National Conference for Education of the Countryside in 2004, and the series of seminars that followed, represented the pinnacle of hope for the national *Educação do Campo* movement, frustration with this institutional process quickly followed. Although Armênio Schmidt had

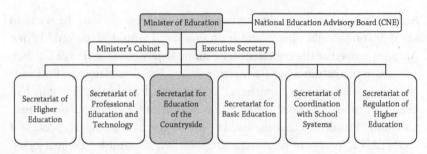

Figure 3.3 The MST's Proposal for Institutionalizing *Educação do Campo* (Education of the Countryside) in the Ministry of Education
Courtesy of author

described the creation of the Department of Diversity as a huge achievement, national MST leader Edgar Kolling recalled this development with anger. The MST had supported the creation of a "Secretariat of *Educação do Campo*" that reported directly to the Minister of Education. Instead, the office for *Educação do Campo* was located within a department, within a secretariat. Its placement deep within the hierarchy of the MEC meant that the decision-making power of the office for *Educação do Campo* was highly restricted. Figure 3.3 represents the MST's original proposal for restructuring the Ministry of Education, and Figure 3.4 was the actual organization of the MEC after 2004.

Indeed, from the beginning Antonio Munarim faced huge barriers convincing other officials in the Ministry of Education that his office had an important purpose. Although dozens of MEC officials worked directly with rural education, these other state actors were not concerned about adhering to the 2002 *Educação do Campo* guidelines. Antonio's inability to change the rest of the Ministry led to the increasing isolation of the office for *Educação do Campo*. He explained:

> We needed an organizational structure that was strong, with professionals who were competent, and this never happened. The contracting of more people never happened. . . . In that moment, the MEC showed what it really was, a heavy infrastructure. SECADI was an opening, a tiny door that opened to a waiting room, but it never let anyone in.

Antonio waited two years to be given some real power within the Ministry of Education, and eventually he decided to become more open about his critiques.

In August 2006, he wrote a letter to the members of the advisory board for *Educação do Campo* with a list of reasons why he believed that *Educação do Campo* was not moving forward:

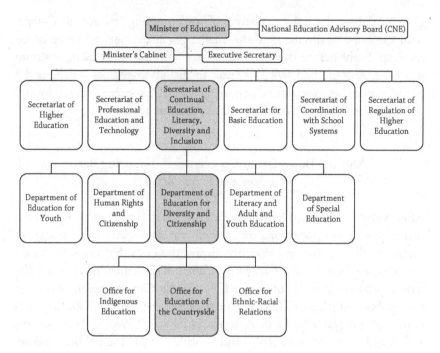

Figure 3.4 The Actual Institutionalization of *Educação do Campo* (Education of the Countryside) in the Ministry of Education
Courtesy of author

The creation of the advisory board for *Educação do Campo* signaled a strong commitment within the Ministry of Education for these proposals, and opened up the possibility of inviting civil society groups into these discussions. . . . The opposite has happened. Representatives from rural social movements have been the only effective presence in these meetings. . . . My impression is that the creation of the office for *Educação do Campo*, which at first seemed to be an advance, has ended up producing two undesirable consequences: first, the advisory board lost its role as an effective force within the MEC; and *second, the national movement for Educação do Campo demobilized* (emphasis added).[24]

In his letter, Antonio expressed frustration with the weak relationship between the advisory board for *Educação do Campo*, where civil society was participating, and the MEC government officials who had decision-making power. He claimed that the creation of the office for *Educação do Campo* actually weakened the national movement. The advisory board had been an attempt to transform the traditional relationship between the state and civil society. However, as Antonio wrote, the social movements often participated in this space without the participation of the MEC officials who had the power to implement their decisions. Antonio wrote this letter to generate debate about the challenges of implementing *Educação do Campo*, with the hope of discussing these challenges at the next advisory board meeting. Right before this meeting took place, in August 2006, Antonio was fired. Antonio had sent this letter to the advisory board without the permission of his supervisors. Bypassing the MEC's internal hierarchy and publicly criticizing the MEC's priorities were not permitted.

"Closing Down Other Experiences": Imposing Best Practices and *Escola Ativa*

After Antonio Munarim left the MEC, the office for *Educação do Campo* finally began to operationalize several national education programs. However, these programs were not always the ones that the activists on the advisory board for *Educação do Campo* had demanded. Rather, the largest program that the office for *Educação do Campo* implemented was the "global best practice" *Escuela Nueva*, one of the most well-known rural education programs in Latin America (McEwan 1998; Psacharopoulos, Rojas, and Velez 1993; C. Rojas and Castillo 1988). The political and economic circumstances that led to the choice of this program as the flagship *Educação do Campo* policy illustrate the difficult and often tenuous circumstances that social movements face pushing their agenda within the state sphere.

The Colombian government created *Escuela Nueva* in 1976, with the goal of improving the quality of education in small schools with multigrade classrooms. The centerpiece of *Escuela Nueva* was a series of self-instructional textbooks, which allowed students in multigrade classrooms to advance at their own pace. The program also promoted teachers as the facilitators of knowledge, peer tutoring, group work, "learning corners" (hands-on activities in different parts of the classroom), libraries "as a complement to the self-instructional textbooks" (Schiefelbein 1991, 21), a close relationship between the school and the community, and civic participation through student governments. The *Escuela Nueva* program was expanded to several thousand schools in Colombia in the late 1970s and early 1980s. Then, in 1986, the World Bank began financing the program, and it was quickly scaled up to 20,000 rural schools.[25]

In 1989, one of the founders of the program, Vicky Colbert, created the *Escuela Nueva* Foundation to continue promoting the program in Colombia and internationally. In the mid-1990s, *Escuela Nueva* began to receive international recognition as a series of studies were published that showed its positive effects on student achievement (McEwan 1998; Psacharopoulos et al. 1993; C. Rojas and Castillo 1988; Schiefelbein 1991). In 1996, the

Escuela Nueva Foundation hosted an international seminar, funded by the World Bank, bringing dozens of government officials from around the world to Colombia to learn about the program. Several officials from the Brazilian Ministry of Education were invited to the seminar. Impressed with the program, they decided to implement it in schools in the northeastern regions of Brazil, where multigrade classrooms were the most prevalent. In 1997, the first *Escuela Nueva* pilot project began in Brazil, funded through the World Bank and administered by the Maranhão state Decretary of Education. Soon after this pilot, the World Bank funded the expansion of *Escuela Nueva*, now known as *Escola Ativa* (Active School), to seven northeastern states, thirty-four municipalities, and 109 more schools. Then, in 1999, President Cardoso accepted a new World Bank loan, *Fundescola*, and with this new funding *Escola Ativa* expanded to nineteen states and several thousand schools over the next three years.

Despite the expansion of *Escola Ativa* between 1997 and 2002, the program was still largely unknown and peripheral within the Ministry of Education. Between 2002 and 2008, there was no significant program expansion, with *Escola Ativa* continuing to serve about 4,000 of the 50,000 multigrade schools in the country (MEC 2010, 13). In the early 2000s, Salomão Hage, a professor at the Federal University of Pará, was one of the few academics studying multigrade schools in Brazil. Salomão had mixed feelings about *Escola Ativa*: "During this period, *Escola Ativa* was a World Bank program that served 'priority zones' . . . this meant 10 percent of rural schools had everything, including teacher trainings, rich pedagogical materials. For the other 90 percent, it was just poverty."[26] Salomão thought *Escola Ativa* was important, as the only program for multigrade schools, but not a universal solution for rural education.

Meanwhile, in 2004, the PT administration created the Secretariat of Continual Education, Literacy, Diversity, and Inclusion (SECADI), with a specific office for *Educação do Campo*. The Director of Diversity, Armênio Schmidt, explained that he had to seek out programs and funding for the new office: "We had nothing, so we had to create programs and I had to find funding for them." At this time, *Escola Ativa* was still administered with funding from the World Bank program *Fundescola*. According to the head of the office for *Educação do Campo*, Antonio Munarim, there was an interest in transferring *Escola Ativa* to his office, given its focus on rural, multigrade schools; however, other state officials mobilized against transferring the significant resources supporting the program to an office that was controlled by social movements.

Nonetheless, Antonio and Armênio advocated for the transfer of *Escola Ativa* to SECADI, inviting several outside experts to discuss the program. One of those experts was Professor Salomão Hage, who by this time had become even more critical of *Escola Ativa*, due to his increasing proximity to social movements through PRONERA (see Chapter 2):

> Our involvement in PRONERA brought us closer to rural social movements . . . we began to learn about the history of struggle, of grassroots organizations, and *Escola Ativa* had nothing to do with this history. *Escola Ativa* was an island of excellence in the MEC, totally isolated from these movements . . . while PRONERA called us to engage with activism, to have a relationship to social movements, *Escola Ativa* brought us in contact with that idea of redemption and salvation.

As this statement suggests, despite the similarities between the MST's and *Escola Ativa*'s educational approaches—including student participation, community involvement, and active learning—the overall philosophy of each program was perceived differently by Brazilian social movements and allied professors. According to Salomão, while the MST saw education as a means of collective action, *Escola Ativa* approached education as helping poor populations. Salomão was invited twice to SECADI: "Both times I was clear that *Escola Ativa* was not the program for rural schools. I told this to everyone." Antonio explained that given this discontent, and the fact that other state officials were interested in controlling the funding that came with *Escola Ativa*, "it was not possible to transfer *Escola Ativa* to SECADI."

Then, in 2007, another change occurred: the World Bank stopped funding *Escola Ativa*. Antonio recalled, "When the World Bank funding stopped, the federal government had to finance the program. To our surprise, this led to the program's transfer to SECADI. It was a contradiction of contradictions." Although *Escola Ativa* had existed in relative anonymity for over a decade, once World Bank funding was cut it became a normal budget item of the federal government. At this moment, in 2007, the SECADI officials were still searching for a flagship program for the office for *Educação do Campo*; however, the MST's educational initiatives were too controversial to implement on a large scale. In this context, investing in *Escola Ativa*, a proven program from Colombia, made sense to both demonstrate the state's concern with rural education (the mandate of the office for *Educação do Campo*), while also investing in a safer program (that was not linked to a radical social movement). Funding *Escola Ativa* was part of the class compromise that characterized the PT era.

Activists from both the MST and CONTAG were furious about the imposition of *Escola Ativa* on the office they had mobilized to create. For them, this office was an institutional space for grassroots movements to implement *their* educational ideas, not a Colombian program sponsored by the World Bank. Despite these protests, the MEC continued to insist that *Escola Ativa* fit within the goals of *Educação do Campo*. Nonetheless, in order to appease the activists, Armênio opened up a call for other proposals to address the issue of multigrade schooling: "And what happened? They did not propose anything. Why? . . . Because their programs are good local solutions but not for scaling-up across Brazil." This last statement reveals the nature of the MEC: its legitimacy hinged on the ability to promote a universal educational policy. These state interests won out, and by 2010 *Escola Ativa* was one of the MEC's most expansive programs, implemented in twenty-seven states, 39,732 schools, and serving 1.3 million students (MEC 2010).

However, the MEC officials who supported *Escola Ativa* could not completely ignore the social movements' and unions' united disapproval, as these activists began publically mobilizing against the program. The MEC responded by allowing the advisory board to take part in a process of rewriting the *Escola Ativa* textbooks, which were based on the Colombian model of self-directed learning. Armênio recalled the extensive process of developing twenty-five new textbooks for *Escola Ativa*. The curriculum was also adapted into several regional versions, which were more sensitive to local realities. The result was a new hybrid curriculum, which included elements of both the Colombian program and the major philosophical underpinnings of *Educação do Campo*. For example, in 2010, the *Escola Ativa* teacher handbook discussed education as a process of social transformation and emphasized manual labor, cooperation, the cultivation of humanistic values, sustainable development, and participatory democracy (MEC 2010, 17–19). This language was very similar to the MST's own educational proposal. Thus, the hybrid form that *Escola Ativa* took represented both a process of imposition—of an external program into an office social movements had created—and a process of state concessions to these activists.[27]

Despite all of these changes and the hybrid forms that the *Escola Ativa* program took, the MST and other rural social movements continued to denounce the program. On April 18, 2011, these movements published a document critiquing *Escola Ativa*'s origins and pedagogical approach. For example, the movements claimed that the program had never been evaluated, had a theoretical approach based in pragmatism and constructivism (not critical theory), assumed that teaching was a neutral process that only required new techniques, and represented a top-down initiative that only superficially incorporated the concepts of *Educação do Campo* (FONEC 2011). Two months after this critique was published, *Escola Ativa* began making national news for a different reason: mathematical errors were found in one of the new textbooks. For weeks, national headlines critiqued the MEC: "MEC spends R$14 million to print 7 million textbooks that 'teach' $10 - 7 = 4$," "New Mess in the MEC."[28]

That same year, MEC officials began to discuss the end of *Escola Ativa*. In November 2011, the new head of the office for *Educação do Campo*, Viviane Fernandes, told me that *Escola Ativa* was being restructured because it "had already reached its goals, which had been teacher training and the distribution of didactic materials."[29] Although the broader objective of the *Escola Ativa* program had been a total restructuring of multigrade classrooms, Viviane suggested that *Escola Ativa* had only been created to train teachers and pass out textbooks. In contrast, André Lázaro, the Secretary of SECADI during the program's rapid expansion, blamed the program's termination on the conservative critiques of the textbook errors: "I think *Escola Ativa* was closed because of a lack of backbone. . . . When the textbook error was discovered, the program was denounced." Edson Anhaia, an ally of the MST who became the coordinator of the office for *Educação do Campo* in 2012, claimed that the social movements' critiques were responsible for the end of *Escola Ativa*: "During a national meeting, the movements declared, 'We no longer want *Escola Ativa*, we want another program that can attend to the specificities of the different regions in Brazil.' "[30] Finally, in August 2015 I asked Divina Lopes, the new coordinator of *Educação do Campo* who had worked in this office during the previous eight years, the same question. She had a different explanation: "We were sent a study from Professor Salomão Hage, who had done an evaluation of the program and found some problems . . . so, we decided to change the program."[31]

All of these explanations are clearly partial understandings of the contested political context that led to *Escola Ativa*'s termination. For example, Divina's claim that Salamão Hage's critique drove this process is unlikely, as he had been critiquing this program since the early 2000s. Similarly, the social movements had also critiqued *Escola Ativa* continually over the previous five years. Finally, while the errors in the textbooks were certainly embarrassing for the federal government, no one except Andre Lázaro, who took the brunt of the blame, claimed that they were the reason for the end of the program. Professor Salomão Hage himself offered one of the best explanations: "The universities, the social movements, the Right, everyone was critiquing the program, and the social movements published a document against the program, and the government began to say, 'Wow, I created a program. I scaled up and universalized a program that does not make anyone happy.' " From a Gramscian perspective, in which education is a state concession to civil society to maintain social stability, an educational program that was not in anyone's interest made absolutely no sense.

The rapid expansion and quick decline of *Escola Ativa* is representative of the tensions that develop when social movement goals are institutionalized under nominally progressive political regimes. On the one hand, these social movements were concerned with promoting their own educational initiatives, and they considered their co-governance of this process to be just as important as the programs themselves. Despite some of the similarities between *Escola Ativa* and the proposal for *Educação do Campo*, the MST and other rural movements refused to accept the imposition of an outside program into what they saw as "their" office. On the other hand, the state officials were searching out programs that were "proven" to be effective in improving rural education—the mandate of the office for *Educação do Campo*. Although social movement mobilization was the primary reason this office had been created, the MEC officials saw it as their responsibility to choose the appropriate programs. Social movements on the advisory board could offer advice, but the MEC officials had the final word. However, clearly the MEC officials did not have all of the power, as social movement mobilization forced them to significantly transform the *Escola Ativa* program and eventually led to its termination in 2012.[32]

"Losing Everything It Was Supposed to Be": Pitfalls of Rapid Expansion and the LEDOC

Another major program that the office for *Educação do Campo* sponsored was a baccalaureate-level teacher certification program that prepared people to teach high school in rural areas, known as LEDOC (*Licenciatura em Educação do Campo*, or Baccalaureate and Teaching Certification in Education of the Countryside).[33] In contrast to *Escola Ativa*, this program was based on one of the MST's own educational initiatives: the Pedagogy of Land program the movement had developed through PRONERA. The goal of the LEDOC program was to offer youth from rural areas access to higher education, and to train them to be high school teachers to teach in rural schools. The program would also introduce these students to the philosophical underpinnings of *Educação do Campo*.

The MEC officials allowed MST activists to help develop the LEDOC pilot program, given the movement's previous experience designing university degree programs through PRONERA. In 2006, the first LEDOC program was launched through an official partnership between the Ministry of Education, the University of Brasília (UnB), and the Educational Institute of Josué de Castro (IEJC) in Rio Grande do Sul—the MST's first independent educational institution founded in 1995 (see Chapter 1). Sixty students from rural regions across the country entered the first LEDOC cohort. A small group of UnB professors, many of whom were already involved in the national movement for *Educação do Campo*, were responsible for teaching in the program. The students in the LEDOC program were required to take all of the traditional UnB requirements for a degree in pedagogy, including courses on the history of the Brazilian school system and educational theory. The program's focus was on interdisciplinary training, rather than single-subject teaching credentials. This was important for rural schools for two reasons. First, one of basic principles of *Educação do Campo* is that the division of knowledge into disciplines is not appropriate for the countryside, where farmers must integrate different subject areas to survive. Second, the biggest challenge for offering secondary education in the countryside was finding qualified teachers; if rural schools required a different teacher for every discipline, there would not be enough teachers for these schools.

The four-year LEDOC program took place through the pedagogy of alternation, with study periods all at the IEJC. The fact that the first LEDOC program took place in one of the movement's own spaces—where the MST education sector had been implementing its pedagogical practices for over a decade—meant that the course adhered closely to the MST's educational approach. The MST educational leaders were daily participants, administers, and directors of the LEDOC program, even publishing a series of reflections on this first experience (Caldart, Fetzner, Rodrigues, and Freitas 2010). The MST activists incorporated pedagogies into the program that had been developed by the movement over the previous decade, including the organization of students into base nuclei; an emphasis on both manual and intellectual labor; a focus on agroecological training; and beginning each school day with *mística*. The students received a regular diploma from the University of Brasília; however, the MST was the dominant force in the day-to-day organization of the LEDOC pilot program.[34] The MST's prior experiences and educational expertise increased the MEC's institutional capacity to develop this program. Abers and Keck (2013) describe this as "practical authority," or the "kind of power-in-practice generated when particular actors (individuals or organization) develop capabilities and win recognition within a particular policy area, enabling them to influence the behavior of others" (2). This also illustrates how civil society can become important not only in processes of policy deliberation but also in helping to *mobilize the state's own capacity* to provide public goods (Abers and Keck 2009; Hochstetler and Keck 2007).

Even before the first year of the four-year pilot program was over, the MEC provided funding to three more universities to also offer LEDOC pilot programs.[35] Although the students studied through the pedagogy of alternation, this time the study periods would be on the universities' own campuses. These were all considered affirmative action programs, as only students living in rural regions could enroll. In 2007, a second cohort of students entered the University of Brasília LEDOC program but also took classes on the university campus. As LEDOC was implemented in each of these universities, activists in regional MST education collectives reached out to the LEDOC professors, explaining the origins and goals of the program. MST activists participated in the daily activities of the first few LEDOC cohorts; however, the movement's capacity to dedicate activists to oversee the LEDOC programs proved to be more difficult than at the IEJC, where a group of MST leaders was living and working at the school. Furthermore, even sympathetic university professors were finding it challenging to adhere to the original goals of the program.

After the first few pilot programs, the state officials in the Ministry of Education declared LEDOC a success and decided to expand the program as fast as possible. They were thinking of numbers, in particular, that over 150,000 teachers in rural areas lacked higher education. A few cohorts of sixty students were not going to solve this problem. The MEC's goal of resolving the issue of teacher training quickly and efficiently was a form of what James Scott (1998) calls "high modernism," or "a sweeping, rational engineering of all aspects of social life in order to improve the human condition" (88). In other words, as soon as the MEC officials tested the LEDOC pilot program and proved it was a successful model for addressing the lack of higher education and teacher training in the countryside, these officials immediately sought to replicate the model. Although the LEDOC pilot program had been based on the MST's pedagogical approach, which had developed through iterative experimentation and practice, the MEC's goal was to take this local experience and implement it at scale throughout the country.

Between 2008 and 2010, the MEC worked with dozens of universities to formalize LEDOC as a regular program offering. The MEC officials did not want to be responsible for running these programs; the officials wanted the universities to institutionalize the program into their own bureaucratic structures. The MEC provided funding for these universities to hire new faculty and staff, including resources for more than ten new tenure-track positions at each of these universities—in the area of *Educação do Campo*. By 2011, there were thirty-two universities that had LEDOC degree programs within their own institutional structure, with assigned staff, tenured professors, an official curriculum, and an annual application process—a tremendous transformation in the Brazilian higher education sphere. By 2015, forty-two universities had LEDOC programs and six hundred new faculty members had been hired to teach.[36] Map 3.1 illustrates the location of these LEDOC programs in 2015.

The rapid expansion of LEDOC across the country illustrates the MEC's capacity to quickly scale up programs and the agency's focus on quantifiable solutions to educational problems. In this case, the MEC had identified the lack of prepared teachers to work in rural high schools as the issue, and the solution was to create as many university teacher training programs as

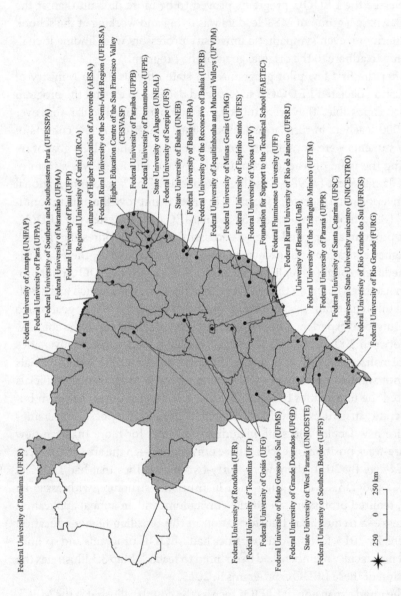

Federal University of Roraima (UFRR)

Federal University of Amapá (UNIFAP)
Federal University of Pará (UFPA)
Federal University of Southern and Southeastern Pará (UFESSPA)
Federal University of Maranhão (UFMA)
Federal University of Piauí (UFPI)
Regional University of Cariri (URCA)
Autarchy of Higher Education of Arcoverde (AESA)
Higher Education Centre of the San Francisco Valley (CESVASF)
Federal Rural University of the Semi-Arid Region (UFERSA)
Federal University of Paraíba (UFPB)
Federal University of Pernambuco (UFPE)
State University of Alagoas (UNEAL)
Federal University of Sergipe (UFS)
State University of Bahia (UNEB)
Federal University of Bahia (UFBA)
Federal University of the Reconcavo of Bahia (UFRB)
Federal University of Jequitinhonha and Mucuri Valleys (UFVJM)
Federal University of Minas Gerais (UFMG)
Federal University of Espírito Santo (UFES)
Federal University of Viçosa (UFV)
Foundation for Support to the Technical School (FAETEC)
Federal Fluminense University (UFF)
Federal Rural University of Rio de Janeiro (UFRRJ)
University of Brasília (UnB)
Federal University of the Triângulo Mineiro (UFTM)
Federal University of Paraná (UFPR)
Federal University of Santa Catarina (UFSC)
Midwestern State University unicentro (UNICENTRO)
Federal University of Rio Grande do Sul (UFRGS)
Federal University of Rio Grande (FURG)

Federal University of Rondônia (UFR)
Federal University of Tocantins (UFT)
Federal University of Goiás (UFG)
Federal University of Mato Grosso do Sul (UFMS)
Federal University of Grande Dourados (UFGD)
State University of West Paraná (UNIOESTE)
Federal University of Southern Border (UFFS)

250   0   250 km

Map 3.1 Location of Baccalaureate and Teaching Certification in Education of the Countryside (LEDOC) Programs in 2015

Source: Adapted from the Secretariat of Adult Education, Literacy, Diversity, and Inclusion (SECADI) in the Ministry of Education (MEC)

possible for rural students. The MST's participation in the first LEDOC program had been important, since the movement had experience developing PRONERA pedagogy programs. However, once the MEC decided that the pilot program had succeeded, the participation of social movements was no longer necessary. Again, this high modernist ideology, which promotes sweeping social programs to improve the human condition, denied the importance of local knowledge and participation. This is in direct contrast to PRONERA, where a local group of activists and professors had to adapt each program to their particular social and political context, and then propose this new program to state officials. In the case of LEDOC, in some universities there were allied professors who reached out to activists to participate in the LEDOC programs. In other cases, the LEDOC programs were institutionalized without any social movement participation.

Even where the MST had university allies, the movement did not always have the capacity to participate fully in the LEDOC programs—especially without the MEC's institutional support. The trajectory of the LEDOC program at the University of Brasília offers an important example of the challenges that emerge in the institutionalization of the program—even where there is a group of supportive professors participating. Luiz Antonio "Tonico" Pasquetti became a tenured professor in the University of Brasília LEDOC program.[37] Tonico had been an MST activist for over a decade and understood the history and purpose of *Educação do Campo*. In 2010, he explained to me that the LEDOC program drew on many of the MST's educational practices. Most significantly, the LEDOC professors promoted collective childcare (*cirandas*), class assemblies, and student self-governance. However, he continued, there were limitations to this collective process within a rigid university structure. For example, the students who entered the LEDOC program received individual fellowships for housing and food; although the professors encouraged students to contribute part of this fellowship money to the collective housing, the university did not make it a requirement. Students who had personal resources could add to their fellowship money to afford to live on their own or with other friends near campus. This was in direct contrast to PRONERA, where the program's funding went directly to support the collective housing of the students.

In 2010, MST educational leader Vanderlúcia Simplicio, who lived in Brasília, proclaimed that "LEDOC is expanding, but it is losing everything it was supposed to be." Vanderlúcia said that the MST's goal was never simply to provide more access to higher education for rural populations; if the movement had wanted more access, it would have fought for "quotas" (guaranteed slots in university programs for rural students). The movement's goal was to offer a different form of education that could train critically aware teachers who understood the history of exploitation in the countryside and were prepared to help students confront these injustices and construct a new socialist society. When I spoke with her in 2010, Vanderlúcia was helping to oversee the fifth cohort of the LEDOC degree program at the University of Brasília. Vanderlúcia explained that each year it was harder for her to ensure that the program adhered to the movement's original proposal. She believed part of the problem was that the students may come from the countryside, but many had no previous connection to any social movement. This meant that they were more resistant to the collective orientation of the program, such as the housing, collective studying, and shared chores. Vanderlúcia attempted to intervene, reminding students about the principles of *Educação do Campo*. Nevertheless, it was difficult, and she feared that the situation was even worse in universities where LEDOC was being implemented and there were no MST activists present.

The MST leadership's perspective on the LEDOC program is mixed. On the positive side, activists acknowledge that the mere existence of the LEDOC is a huge advance over the traditional bachelor's degree programs in pedagogy, which are urban-centric. Furthermore, the LEDOC is a form of affirmative action, specifically targeting populations living in the countryside. At the University of Brasília, many of the students who enroll in the LEDOC program are from *quilombos* (black rural communities, or maroon communities). When I spoke to Tonico in August 2015, he reflected, "I still have a lot of critiques of the program, but it is an important opportunity for rural youth. For example, 80 percent of the cohort is currently Afro-descendent—it is the blackest program in the university."[38] On the negative side, MST activists feel that they have lost their ability to actively co-govern these programs. When I spoke to Vanderlúcia in August 2015, she no longer helped to coordinate the LEDOC program. She still went to the university when the professors called her for an important meeting, but the MST was not involved in the day-to-day functioning of the program. Rosali Caldart, one of the major contributors to the pilot program, reflected, "The LEDOC proposal represents the MST's concern with all schools in rural areas, not just schools in MST communities." However, she continued, the process is more constrained than other programs that the MST supports.

The trajectory of the LEDOC program illustrates the ambiguities in defining social movement success. Unlike *Escola Ativa*, the LEDOC program was directly based in one of the MST's own educational initiatives, and the implementation of this program in more than forty universities was a huge achievement. However, the MST wanted to be both a protagonist in creating the program and a participant in the process of implementing the program as it expanded throughout the country. In part, the MST's interest in this form of co-governance of public services is linked to the movement's promotion of a direct, participatory democracy, where people take part in the decisions that affect their daily lives. The MST also wants to make sure that the LEDOC programs maintained the same political, economic, and social values as the movement itself. For the MST, success is measured by the extent to which a program helps the movement accumulate forces, to prefigure today the socialist world activists want to create in the future.

By these measures of movement success, the PRONERA university programs, in which the MST maintains a higher degree of control, might be considered more successful than the LEDOC programs. However, in terms of the scale of the MST's influence, the LEDOC programs are much more impressive. Despite the fact that many LEDOC programs have lost their radical roots, they still opened up space within the elite Brazilian public university system to rural populations who might never have had access to a quality higher education. Furthermore, the LEDOC programs are much more stable than PRONERA, as they have been institutionalized within more than forty universities and therefore are not at the whim of the federal government's support and funding. Finally, there are many MST activists, like Tonico, who have become university professors through the LEDOC program openings. Many of these activists continue to contribute to the movement, while being supported financially by their universities. I also met many young students living in settlements throughout the country who were studying to become teachers in LEDOC programs and were planning on returning to teach in their local schools. Therefore, in terms of both levels of educational access offered to marginalized communities and the MST's own internal capacity, the LEDOC program is clearly successful. Nonetheless, the program also illustrates that even when activists help to develop a pilot program, the scale of implementation that a large bureaucratic agency such as the Ministry of Education hopes to promote hinders civil society participation.

DILMA ROUSSEFF, AGRIBUSINESS, AND THE CONSOLIDATION OF CLASS COMPROMISE (2011–2014)

In 2010, in a tight presidential race, Lula's appointed successor, Dilma Rousseff, also of the PT, won the presidential election. Rousseff's administration represented the consolidation of the class compromise that began during Lula's previous two administrations, as well as an increasingly strong relationship between the PT and agribusiness sectors.

This influence of rural elites on contemporary Brazilian politics is part of a three-decade-long strategy that traces back to 1985, when a group of landowners created the Democratic Rural Union (UDR) with the goal of defending private property against land expropriations. Despite the widespread social mobilizations during this decade and the increasing number of land occupations, "the UDR showed that it had the strength to make its interests prevail" (Bruno 1997, 63). In 1993, agribusiness sectors founded the Brazilian Association of Agribusiness (ABAG), in order to "raise the consciousness of the nation about the importance of agribusiness" and to create "an institution representative of the common interests of all the agents of the agricultural production chain" (Bruno 1997, 36). The Brazilian Rural Confederation (CNA), originally founded in 1951, is also a powerful coalition that lobbies for policies that benefit large landowner and agribusiness interests. Between 1995 and 2006, the average representation of landowners and agribusinesses in Congress was 2,587 times greater than the representation of landless workers and small peasant farmers (Carter 2009, 62–63). Guilherme Costa Delgado (2009) writes that this "powerful political representation—the Rural Block—is structured in various political parties" and as of 2009 had "between one fourth and one third of all congressional representatives and senators voting in Congress" (108).

The Rural Block's congressional power resulted in a series of attacks against the MST during Lula's administrations, in the form of CPIs (congressional investigations) and CPMIs (mixed commissions, which is a joint inquiry of both houses of Congress). The first of these was the CPMI of land, launched in 2003 to investigate the MST's use of federal funds. Other investigations included the CPI of NGOs in 2009 and the CPMI of the MST in 2010, as well as several investigations carried out by the Brazilian Federal Court of Audits (TCU). Although none of these processes succeeded in condemning the movement, they did create more barriers to funding programs in areas of agrarian reform (e.g., see the discussion of the TCU investigation in Chapter 2).

Despite the PT administration's nominal support for agrarian reform, Lula incorporated agribusiness groups into his governing coalition during his first term and encouraged the investment of international capital in Brazilian agriculture. During this period there was a huge expansion of soybean, corn, and sugarcane production (Sauer and Leite 2012). By 2005, agriculture comprised 42 percent of Brazilian exports and was the principal source of income for the federal government to pay off foreign debt (Carter 2009, 68). The state had an important role in these developments; for example, between 2004 and 2011 the Brazilian National Development Bank (BNDES) increased its funding for agribusiness projects from 27.1 billion to 100 billion reais (MST 2013, 64).[39]

The continual growth and expansion of agribusinesses throughout the 2000s led the MST leadership to redefine the enemy of agrarian reform as transnational corporations such as Monsanto and Cargill, rather than the unproductive oligarchical landlords of the past. In the mid-2000s, the MST began organizing land occupations of some of these large industrial farms. The women in the movement played an important role in leading this more radical stance against agribusinesses. For example, on March 8, 2006, International Women's Day, two thousand women occupied the plantation of the corporation Aracruz Ceuloso, the world's biggest producer of eucalyptus pulp, and destroyed hundreds of eucalyptus seedlings (Wiebe 2006).[40] The movement defended the destruction of the seedlings and condemned the environmental and human harm caused by eucalyptus monoculture, including the deterioration of soil, drying up of rivers, and expulsion of family farmers from their lands. Nonetheless, these types of occupations of monoculture plantations significantly reduced support for the MST throughout Brazil.

When Dilma Rousseff took office in 2010, the contradictions between the federal government's nominal support for agrarian reform and its heavy investment in agribusiness intensified. According to a report published by the Pastoral Land Commission (CPT) in 2015, Rousseff's administration expropriated the least amount of land, recognized the fewest amount of indigenous and *quilombola* territories, and created the fewest extractive reserves, since the return to democracy in 1985.[41] Instead, Rousseff economics' policies focused on offering incentives for agribusiness and agroindustry, mining, and major infrastructure projects. Only slightly more than 40,000 families were settled during her first term, less than half of the number during Lula's previous mandate. Furthermore, many of those families were in the process of being settled before Rousseff took office. Figures 3.5 and 3.6 show the number of families participating in land occupations and the number of families settled during Lula's (2003–2010) and Rousseff's (2011–2016) administrations.[42] The figures illustrate a significant decline in families participating in land occupations during Rousseff's first and second terms, with an even sharper decline in the number of new families issued land rights. These number are related, as the fact that families were not receiving land rights made it difficult for the MST and other landless movements to convince people to participate in new land occupations.

Agribusiness Embraces *Educação do Campo*

When Dilma Rousseff became the president in January of 2011, the supporters of *Educação do Campo* were at a crossroads. On the one hand, there was no turning back; *Educação do Campo* was now the Ministry of Education's official approach to rural education. There were dozens of universities with *Educação do Campo* departments, hundreds of masters and doctoral students conducting research within this new disciplinary concentration, and several massive federal programs in the office for *Educação do*

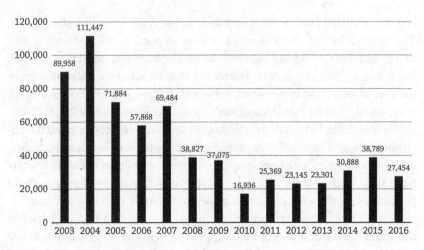

Figure 3.5 Number of Families in New Land Occupations, 2003–2016
Source: *DataLuta: Banco de Dados da Luta Pela Terra: Relatório Brasil 2016* (NERA 2017)

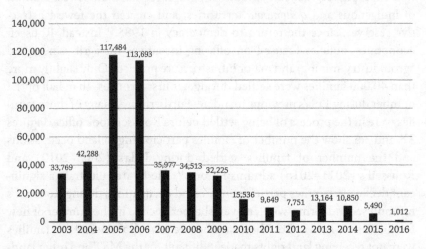

Figure 3.6 Number of New Families Issued Land Rights, 2003–2016
Source: *DataLuta: Banco de Dados da Luta Pela Terra: Relatório Brasil 2016* (NERA 2017)

Campo. On the other hand, the institutionalization of *Educação do Campo* in the MEC was a far cry from what the MST, the National Confederation of Agricultural Workers (CONTAG), and other civil society actors had wanted. For many, *Educação do Campo* was no longer linked to a socialist development model for the countryside. To the contrary, many of the new actors supporting *Educação do Campo* defended capitalist modes of production in the Brazilian countryside, including large agribusinesses, monoculture production, and the intensive use of pesticides.

On March 20, 2012, Dilma launched a new federal program, the National Program for Education of the Countryside (*ProNoCampo*). This was intended to be a huge, interministry program, expanding the politics of *Educação do Campo* beyond a single office in the Ministry of Education and integrating it into all of the ministries that deal with rural development. The program proposed to give 1.9 million rural students access to libraries and to transform the schedule in 10,000 schools into integral, or full, school days.[43] It would also provide 100,000 teachers with a college education specific for the countryside (through investment in the LEDOC program), construct 3,000 new rural schools, implement significant infrastructural improvements to 30,000 other schools, build 20,000 computer labs, increase access to technical training for rural youth, reverse the trend of rural school closings, and purchase 8,000 buses, bicycles, and boats to improve intrarural school transport.[44] Vanderlúcia declared *ProNoCampo* "marvelous on paper"; however, she worried about putting the program into practice.[45]

The most controversial development for *ProNoCampo* was the large role agricultural businesses played in these debates. Emblematic of this change was the combination of actors present at the table when President Rousseff announced the launching of *ProNoCampo* in March of 2012: Aloízio Mercadante, the new Minister of Education; José Wilson, a leader in CONTAG, who represented the "social movements of the countryside"; and Kátia Abreu, PMDB senator from the state of Tocantins and president of the National Confederation of Agriculture (CNA) between 2008 and 2011. Kátia was one of the biggest advocates of agribusiness in Brazil and was infamous among MST activists for her hatred of the movement. While many MST activists were also present in the audience that day, they were not given a chance to speak publically. The speeches were illustrative, first, of the tremendous success the movement for *Educação do Campo* has had transforming national consciousness, and second, of the contemporary conflicts over the meaning of *Educação do Campo*.

The speech of the new Minister of Education, Aloizio Mercadante, was representative of the legitimacy *Educação do Campo* had gained at the federal level: "We are sure that this program will contribute to the value placed on the populations of the countryside. Rapid urbanization is not the way forward. We need to value these populations, their stories and culture, and the huge contribution of rural workers to this country." Less than a decade before, statements such as these from prominent public officials were few and far between. Quality education was considered universal education, which did not differentiate between urban and rural populations. Now, in 2012, the Minister of Education was referring to a social debt the government of Brazil owed populations living in the countryside, and their right to an education that addressed their particular needs.

The speech of CONTAG representative José Wilson illustrated the critical role social movements have played in this process but also the tensions that still exist between movements. The fact that a range of social movements, including the MST, were allowed to attend a ceremony in which dozens of senators, congressional representatives, governors, mayors, Ministers, and the President herself were present, demonstrated both the degree of public credit given to these activists and the activists' willingness to be part of a public process in which they were no longer the principal protagonists. The choice of a CONTAG leader to represent these social movements, as opposed to an MST activist, demonstrated the decreasing amount of space the MST is allowed to occupy at the federal level. For the Brazilian government, CONTAG is a less radical organization with a long history of collaboration with the state. Allowing the MST to speak at such a prestigious ceremony would have been more controversial. José Wilson, however, allowed the MST to participate during his speech by pausing to permit Vanderlúcia to deliver the recently published *Dictionary of Educação do Campo* (Caldart, Pereira, Alentejano, and Frigotto 2012) to the President. Vanderlúcia performed a typical MST *mística*, reciting a poem about agrarian reform while proudly wearing an MST hat. At the end of the presentation, dozens of people in the audience stood up and sang a song about *Educação do Campo*, one of the many songs that MST activists had produced over the previous decade.

Finally, Kátia Abreu was invited to the podium, amid booing and hissing from many in the audience. After Dilma Rousseff assumed office in 2011, the President had formed a close relationship with Kátia Abreu, eventually nominating her as the Minister of Agriculture in 2014 (to the dismay of the MST). At this ceremony in 2012, Kátia was, for the first time, becoming a public advocate for *Educação do Campo*; however, her vision of this educational philosophy was not the same socialist vision the MST hoped to promote. Kátia began her speech, "There have been decades of abandonment of the countryside. . . . There are schools without Internet, without infrastructure; principals of schools absent, teachers earning much less than in the city." Kátia went on to say that for the past forty years, educational policies in the countryside have been focused on transporting students to urban areas. Thus, there have been no attempts to develop an education specific to the countryside. Up until this point, Kátia's speech could have been given by any one of the many MST activists in the audience. However, ideological differences over the future development model of the countryside quickly became evident. To more hissing, Kátia exclaimed, "Education is extremely important, so agribusiness can be stronger. . . . The youth of the countryside need to be skilled workers; whether as wage workers or as bosses, they need to advance more quickly." In this statement, Kátia claimed *Educação do Campo* as a proposal that supported agribusiness, the exact opposite as intended by its originators as an educational philosophy supporting small-scale, collective farming.

Six months after the public launching of *ProNoCampo* and the excitement and hope that accompanied this ceremony, the National Forum for Education of the Countryside (FONEC), a coalition of sixteen different social movements, labor confederations, and NGOs, as well as thirty-five institutions of higher education, wrote a lengthy report critiquing the entire program. These organizations had created FONEC in August 2010, as a response to the frustrations around the MEC's lack of support for *Educação do Campo*.[46] The movements had wanted a space of debate, independent of the Brazilian state, where they could discuss the future of *Educação do Campo* and the contradictions of its rapid growth over the previous decade.

The FONEC report argued that the rapid recognition for *Educação do Campo* in the late 1990s was a result of a grassroots struggle but also the historical moment: the traditional landlord class was in crisis and agribusinesses were not yet dominant in the countryside. It was during this brief historical conjuncture that the proposal for *Educação do Campo* gained momentum. However, less than a decade later, agribusinesses and transnational corporations were the dominant force in the Brazilian countryside. The article goes on to say that

> The recent investment in rural education by these dominant classes requires special reflection. This investment illustrates an interest in appropriating a discourse that defends the education of rural workers, in order to persuade (and confuse) society into believing that agribusiness is also interested in overcoming inequality.... This process of appropriation affirms that education has an important role in the maintenance of agribusiness. (FONEC 2012, 8)

According to FONEC's analysis, *Educação do Campo* was now being used to make workers believe that the owners of big industrial farms cared about issues of poverty, when in fact this supposed concern with poverty was diametrically opposed to agribusinesses' primary interest: the pursuit of profit. *Educação do Campo* has become hegemonic in the Gramscian sense of providing the moral leadership for a multiclass alliance that functions to support the dominant mode of production. Through the language of *Educação do Campo*, the agribusiness lobby was able to present its own interests as the interests of all.

Activist Reflections

The MST leadership was aware of the challenges they faced as more groups embraced the *Educação do Campo* proposal. Rosali Caldart explained:

The fact is that that *Educação do Campo*, in its original construction, came from the social movements. But now it exists in relation to the governments, to the universities . . . and these other groups are also going to dispute the meaning of *Educação do Campo*. This is because *Educação do Campo* is more than a project of education; it is a project of the countryside. Those that defend agribusinesses are going to have one vision of education, and those that defend peasant agriculture are going to have another vision.

As Rosali articulated, the concept of *Educação do Campo* no longer belonged to the social movements that first developed the proposal; now dozens of other organizations and groups were laying claim to these ideas. Comparing *Educação do Campo* to Freirean popular education, Rosali said that many contemporary popular education initiatives also have no real connection to Freire's *Pedagogy of the Oppressed* or social struggles. This is why some groups abandoned the term "popular education" because it was being deradicalized. For Rosali, the critical issue was not whether MST activists used the term *Educação do Campo*; what was important was that activists continued defending an educational project directly linked to their three goals of land reform, agrarian reform, and social transformation.

Salete Campigotto, one of the first MST activists involved in education in the early 1980s, also reflected on the pros and cons of the expansion of *Educação do Campo*. On the positive side, it was a huge advance from what existed before. Youth in the countryside were studying, even going to college, which many rural families never thought would be possible. "If you compare this to what we had when we started this movement . . . of course it is an advance!" However, for Salete, one of the negative sides was that people no longer had to fight for these benefits, which made them less connected to the movement. She also said:

What worries me a little is that *Educação do Campo* is turning into a fad and losing its primary objective. . . . I have lived in this region all my life, and I was a student at the University of Passo Fundo. And now, suddenly, I discovered that they have a course in *Educação do Campo*. I think they are using this name . . . but they are stripping the proposal we constructed of its original characteristics.

Similarly, Edgar Kolling discussed the benefits and drawbacks of expanding the coalition of allies fighting for *Educação do Campo*. "We realized that in calling for a broader movement there was a danger of creating something too 'light.'" However, Edgar also said that the creation of SECADI might not have been possible, without this broader coalition of allies. "[SECADI] has allowed the working class of the countryside to have a more active presence in the MEC . . . before the MEC would not even receive us . . . so this was an important advance. . . . We never thought we could create something so big." Nonetheless, there were challenges engaging in this now massive educational realm. "I think that we are a bit subsumed in all of this. We fought for public policies and when the government began to create these policies . . . we were swallowed up by these state initiatives." Edgar emphasized both the incredible gains of the national coalition for *Educação do Campo* and how these initiatives often consumed the MST's limited time and energy. Other actors in the *Educação do Campo* coalition also referred to these difficulties. Professor Bernardo Mançano Fernandes of the State University of São Paulo (UNESP) explained:

> *Educação do Campo* was born within the MST, but it no longer belongs to the MST. . . . There was one point that the MST was discussing whether the movement should continue fighting for *Educação do Campo*, since even the agrobusiness bloc has a program supporting *Educação do Campo*. I fought with the MST, and I argued that we have to maintain it. We cannot just give it up because others appropriated it. We are the originators of that name, and if we change the name of what we are fighting for, the new name will also be appropriated.

For Bernardo, the fact that *Educação do Campo* was in dispute illustrated the success that MST leaders have had transforming the debate about public education in Brazil, while also putting some limits on the movement's ability to co-govern these programs.

Finally, Elisa Urbano Ramos, a Pancararus indigenous woman who lives in an Indian reserve in the state of Pernambuco, was an active participant in the Pernambucan Committee for *Educação do Campo* in 2011.[47] She emphasized that *Educação do Campo* was necessary for all working-class populations in the countryside, including indigenous communities.[48] However, she said that the voices of the movements are often missing from the current debate. Elisa told a story about going to a local academic conference on *Educação do Campo*, where she was the only social movement leader present. She stood up and spoke, telling the participants that they should not forget the history of struggle when debating this proposal: "*Educação do Campo* was brought to us through conflicts, centuries of murder in the countryside. Blood was shed for these ideas to become legitimate." Although the current support for *Educação do Campo* is an advance, Elisa was disappointed that these histories of political struggle were often left out of the debates about *Educação do Campo*.

Together, these reflections from MST activists and other allies in the national coalition indicate both the impressive degree of institutionalization of *Educação do Campo* across the country and the fact that this educational program is often disconnected from its original intentions. Table 3.1 summarizes the conferences that took place, coalitions that formed,

Table 3.1 CONFERENCES, POLICIES, AND COALITIONS SUPPORTING *EDUCAÇÃO DO CAMPO* (EDUCATION OF THE COUNTRYSIDE), 1997–2012

		Date and Location	Purpose	Comments
Cardoso administration (PSDB, 1995–2002)	**CONFERENCE** National Meeting of Educators in Areas of Agrarian Reform (ENERA)	July 1997, University of Brasília	Discuss the MST's educational proposal for areas of agrarian reform	700 participants Coordinating organizations: MST, CNBB, UnB, UNESCO, UNICEF
	COALITION National Coalition for Education of the Countryside	August 1997, Brasília	Mobilize for an alternative educational proposal for all rural populations	Coordinating organizations: MST, CNBB, UnB, UNESCO, UNICEF
	CONFERENCE First National Conference for a Basic Education of the Countryside	July 1998, Luziânia, Brasília	Debate a new national proposal for Education of the Countryside for all rural populations	973 participants (19 universities, 22 grass-roots groups) Coordinator organizations: MST, CNBB, UnB, UNESCO, UNICEF
	PUBLIC POLICY National Guidelines for a Basic Education of the Countryside	April 12, 2001	Institutionalize Education of the Countryside as a right for all rural populations	Approved by National Education Advisory Board (CNE/CEB) Sponsor: Edla Soarez
	CONFERENCE National Seminar for Education of the Countryside	November 2002, University of Brasília	Reflect on the policies for Education of the Countryside and expand the national coalition	372 participants (movements, universities, teachers, government officials) from 25 states Coordinating organizations: MST, CNBB, UnB, UNESCO, UNICEF
Lula and Rousseff administrations (PT, 2003–2014)	**CONFERENCE** Second National Conference for Education of the Countryside	July 2004, Luziânia, Brasília	Debate Education of the Countryside and its institutionalization in the Ministry of Education	1,100 participants (movements, unions, universities, teachers, government officials); 39 groups sign the final conference document
	COALITION National Commission for Education of the Countryside	July 2004, Luziânia, Brasília	Establish a civil society–state commission to advise the Ministry of Education	Includes both state and civil society groups, coordinated by the Secretariat of Continual Education, Literacy, Diversity, and Inclusion (SECADI)

PUBLIC POLICY Expand National Education of the Countryside Guidelines	2008	Expand the 2001 guidelines, including references to families in agrarian reform settlements and camps	Approved by National Education Advisory Board (CNE/CEB)
COALITION Creation of National Forum for Education of the Countryside (FONEC)	August 2010, Brasília, CONTAG Headquarters	Support movements' and universities' autonomy from the state to discuss and promote Education of the Countryside	28 organizations (13 grassroots organizations and 15 universities) sign the declaration to support FONEC's creation
CONFERENCE Fourth National Seminar on PRONERA	November 2010 Brasília, Brazilian National Congress	Assess PRONERA's achievements and promote actions for its further expansion	667 participants (movements, unions, universities, teachers, students, and government officials)
PUBLIC POLICY Presidential Decree 7.352: National Policy on Education of the Countryside	November 2010	Legalize rural populations' right to an education based in their local reality; transforms PRONERA from a temporary program to a permanent public policy	With support of MEC, the MST, and CONTAG
PUBLIC POLICY National Program for *Educação do Campo* (*ProNoCampo*)	March 2012	An interministry policy for the tremendous expansion of Education of the Countryside programs and initiatives	Created by the federal government under the administration of Dilma Rousseff

and policies that passed, which transformed *Educação do Campo* into the Brazilian government's official approach to rural schooling.

CONCLUSION: A NATIONAL PROPOSAL FOR *EDUCAÇÃO DO CAMPO*

The MST first realized education's important role in the early 1980s, when it became clear that maintaining youth in the countryside and convincing them to fight for agrarian reform would require an intervention in the public educational sphere. MST educational leaders and their allies struggled to transform the conception of rural education from something backward, neglected, and destined to disappear into a new sphere of intervention that could produce sustainable, intellectual farming communities in the countryside. For the MST, this conception of rural education is explicitly tied to an alternative development model, which is centered on workers' ownership of their own means of production and different forms of collective agricultural practices. As Fernandes (2012) writes, "It is impossible to dissociate the origin of *Educação do Campo* from agrarian reform." The MST essentially created and then politicized what was until then a non-issue: rural education.

However, unlike the MST's initial educational practices, *Educação do Campo* is now a proposal for all populations in the Brazilian countryside. According to the *Dictionary of Educação do Campo* (Caldart et al. 2012), this educational proposal

(1) was created as part of rural workers' struggle for educational access;
(2) was solidified through the collective demands of communities for public policies that take into consideration the social needs of these communities;
(3) combines the struggle for education with the struggle for land, agrarian reform, the right to work, culture, and food sovereignty;
(4) attempts to respect the rich human diversity of the countryside;
(5) did not develop as an educational theory, but rather, a diverse range of educational practices to address the challenges of education in the countryside;
(6) is based on the notion that the state should provide the resources for public education but not control the educational process; and
(7) values teachers and students as the fundamental actors transforming their schools and thus promotes public policies and professional development programs to this end.

More broadly, the proposal for *Educação do Campo* embodies the recognition that the purpose of rural schooling is not to prepare students for an urban job market but, rather, to support the vibrancy of the diverse populations living in the countryside and contribute to the sustainable development of these rural communities. The concept of *Educação do Campo*—that populations of the countryside have the right to schools in their communities that are based in their local realities and support the sustainable development of those regions—has become part of the Brazilian government's official approach to rural education. This has created both opportunities and challenges for the MST. In particular, the institutionalization of *Educação do Campo* in the Ministry of Education expanded resources for rural education to an unprecedented level, but the MST lost much of its influence over the content and implementation of these programs. Furthermore, the fact that agribusinesses were trying to incorporate *Educação do Campo* into their own vision for the countryside illustrated how elite rural actors took advantage of new resources to establish willing consent for their own economic interests—a form of passive revolution (Gramsci 1971). There are multiple lessons these developments offer us about the outcomes of social movements engaging in the institutional sphere.

First, this chapter has illustrated the critical role of broad-based alliances for institutional transformation but also how these alliances shift the nature of political struggle. MST leaders established bilateral partnerships with multiple state agencies during the 1990s, to advance their own educational initiatives. These educational programs were primarily isolated in agrarian reform settlements and camps. The MST's reframing of its educational proposal as *Educação do Campo* was part of the movement's war of position to expand its educational proposal to the entire countryside and to create a new common sense about the importance of investing in rural education in Brazil. However, this new framing had deep implications for shifting the goals of that struggle. The most important ally in the *Educação do Campo* coalition became CONTAG, a movement of rural workers whose leaders were accustomed to promoting workers' rights through the legal realm. Both CONTAG and the MST transformed through their continual interactions, adapting to strategies and educational goals that were not part of their original intentions. Thus, framing is not only a tool activists use to mobilize more people but also a process that can redefine the meaning and content of mobilization (Steinberg 1999). These alliances between civil society organizations were a critical component of promoting system-wide institutional change, especially under a right-leaning federal government.

Second, this chapter has illustrated the risks of incorporating movement initiatives into existing institutions. As Piven and Cloward argued four decades ago, activists who work in institutional settings can create a demobilizing effect for their movements. This occurs because "political leaders, or elites allied with them, will try to quiet disturbances not only by dealing with immediate grievances, but by making efforts to channel the energies and angers of the protestors into more legitimate and less disruptive forms of political behavior" (Piven and Cloward 1977, 30). Foweraker (2001) makes a similar claim specifically about the MST, arguing that the MST has had a tendency to institutionalize, depend on state resources, and resemble an NGO more than a mobilized social movement (842). Several aspects of this chapter corroborate these arguments about the risks of activists working in the institutional realm: the office for *Educação do Campo* remains isolated within the MEC's hierarchical structure; a World Bank initiative originally developed in Colombia became the largest *Educação do Campo* program in the Ministry; and the mass implementation of LEDOC university programs has prevented sustained movement participation. State official Antonio Munarim even claimed that the advisory board for *Educação do Campo* demobilized the larger national movement. These examples all illustrate the barriers that activists face as they engage with state institutions. Furthermore, as *Educação do Campo* became supported by a multiclass alliance, it served as a form of consent for the very mode of economic production that the MST was trying to contest: large agribusinesses. This also aligns with Piven and Cloward, who argue that state concessions always "turn out to be compatible (or at least not incompatible) with the interests of the more powerful groups, most importantly with the interest of dominance economic groups" (35). In contrast to the education programs that the MST developed through PRONERA, this chapter has shown that movements can easily lose control of their proposals for institutional change, even under a sympathetic left-leaning administration. However, this decline in effective co-governance is not inevitable. Together, Chapters 2 and 3 also illustrate that the institutionalization of social movement goals can have widely different policy trajectories—depending on the nature of the agency in which these goals are institutionalized.

Nonetheless, a third point is that despite the perils of institutionalization, social movements can significantly shift national debates and policies concerning the provision of public goods in their communities. Piven and Cloward (1977) themselves assert that "What was won must be judged by what was possible" (xiii). The fact that the MST has been able to legitimize the idea that rural schools should have a differentiated educational approach than urban schools, and create dozens of educational programs specifically designated for rural populations, is significant. During the PT administration, the concept of *Educação do Campo* became hegemonic, which meant that certain public discourses—such as rural areas as "backward," urban schools as superior to rural schools, and education as a means to adapt rural youth to an urban job market—were no longer legitimate. The terrain of educational struggle was not the same as it was in the early 1990s. Agribusinesses could still contest the relationship between *Educação do Campo* and socialist models of rural development; however, these agribusiness interests could not contest the importance of expanding the access to and the quality of education in the countryside. This had not always been the case. Furthermore, there was a now a permanent space within more than forty Brazilian universities to study issues related to rural education, representing what Rojas (2007) refers to as a "counter center" that allows for oppositional consciousness within a state institution (21). Thus, the MST's ability to shift the debate surrounding rural education in Brazil has had real material implications for thousands of youth and adults living in the countryside.

In conclusion, despite the current disputes over the meaning of *Educação do Campo*, and the entrance of agribusiness groups into these debates, MST activists—through their interactions with other movements and state and university officials—have redefined the boundaries within which future policy decisions about public education will take place. Activists express genuine surprise at the degree of influence they have had in the educational realm but also ambivalence as to whether *Educação do Campo* will facilitate the economic and political changes they want in the countryside. To a large extent, the outcomes of this educational struggle in the Brazilian public school system have depended on the regional strategies of local MST activists living in diverse political and economic contexts, which will be discussed in Part Two.

PART TWO

Regional Cases of Contentious Co-Governance of Public Education

CHAPTER 4

Rio Grande do Sul

Political Regimes and Social Movement Co-Governance

It is not the school that changes society; it is society that changes and takes the school with it.
—Salete Campigotto, *local leader in MST Education Sector*

O ver the past two decades, MST leaders have been able to translate their social change vision into pedagogical practice through experiments in a wide range of educational institutions. In the early 1990s, movement activists began running literacy campaigns and offering high school education to teachers in their settlements and camps. In 1995, the MST founded its first independent school, the Educational Institute of Josué de Castro (IEJC), or ITERRA, which has offered high school and technical degrees to thousands of youth in areas of agrarian reform. In 1998, the federal government created the National Program for Education in Areas of Agrarian Reform (PRONERA), allowing the MST to partner with dozens of universities and provide rural families more educational access, from literacy courses to university programs. That same year, the MST reframed its pedagogical initiatives as an educational approach for all working-class populations in the countryside, *Educação do Campo*, and over the next decade the federal government passed policies and implemented programs supporting this approach. The MST also continued to found more of its own educational institutions during this period, from state-accredited high schools to institutes for technical training in agroecology.

Nonetheless, despite these gains, most students living in MST settlements and camps continue to receive their education through the traditional K–12 public school system. The Brazilian school system is decentralized, with twenty-seven state governments and 5,570 municipal governments administering schools across the country, each with relative autonomy.[1] This means that local MST education collectives have to convince hundreds of different subnational governments to let local activists co-govern the public schools. Even when schools are located on MST settlements, control over them is never given wholesale to the movement. Local MST leaders must continually negotiate, protest, and mobilize to implement their educational program in these institutions. The MST's capacity to lead this process of contentious co-governance varies radically across the country.

In this chapter, I analyze one of the first states where the MST began to participate in the contentious co-governance of the public school system, the southernmost state of Rio Grande do Sul (see Map I.1). In many ways, Rio Grande do Sul is an ideal case of state-movement cooperation, with a long history of mobilized social movements and progressive government administrations. Local MST leaders have been involved in the public educational realm since the early 1980s, as teachers and parents developing proposals for their local schools. The movement's first attempt to create a more systematic program for the transformation of the school system took place after the founding of the national MST education sector in 1987. Most significantly, in 1995 regional activists wrote a proposal for Itinerant Schools located in the occupied encampments. A combination of disruptive tactics and internal allies pressured the government to accept the Itinerant School proposal in 1996.

Then, when a sympathetic, left-leaning government took office in 1999, both these Itinerant Schools in the occupied camps and the movement's educational program for the schools on settlements flourished. Despite the fact that between 1999 and 2002, the federal government began cracking down on the MST's organizing and criminalizing land occupations (Ondetti 2008), in Rio Grande do Sul the governor shielded the MST from these attacks and advanced many of the movement's economic, political, and educational goals. Thus, the first part of this chapter is the story of an ideal case of movement-led institutional change, when three factors coalesced: a sympathetic political regime, a state with a high level of capacity for educational governance, and ample social movement infrastructure (top left corner of Table I.1 in the Introduction).

The second part of the chapter illustrates the fragility of these moments of state-movement cooperation and, more specifically, how a shift in the political regime can reverse institutional transformation. Although the MST education sector was able to participate in the contentious co-governance of the Itinerant Schools over three different political administrations, in 2006 an extremely conservative administration came to power and launched a frontal attack against all of the MST's organizing in the state. The Itinerant Schools were closed during this period, and the local activists in the settlement schools also found it harder to implement their educational initiatives. Although the MST leadership mobilized their movement base against these attacks, the movement could not prevent the reversal of many of their institutional gains (top center-right section of Table I.1 in the Introduction). Paradoxically, all of these attacks took place as the movement's educational proposal was receiving more recognition nationally, under a nominally sympathetic federal government, illustrating the different trajectories of institutional change at the local and federal levels. Above all, this chapter highlights the influence of a government's political leaning on a social movement's ability to participate in, co-govern, and transform state institutions.

Rio Grande do Sul is located in the far southern part of the country, bordering Uruguay and Argentina. The state has the fifth highest population in Brazil, with 10.7 million people as of 2010, 85 percent of whom are urban residents (IBGE 2011).[2] It is also the fourth richest state in Brazil, with strong agricultural and industrial sectors (IBGE 2011). According to a 2015 study, average monthly household income in Rio Grande do Sul was 1,435 *reais*[3] (about 530 US dollars in 2015[4]), the third highest per capita income in the country after Brasília and São Paulo, an indication of the state's relatively large middle- and upper-class populations.

During the nineteenth century, the federal government had encouraged a steady stream of European immigration (especially from Germany) to the southern Brazilian states. One of the government's goals was to whiten and populate the countryside by setting up European colonies in remote rural areas, where indigenous populations were living. With the decline of slavery and its abolition in 1888, there was another stream of European immigration to Brazil, primarily Italian and Portuguese. These waves of immigration transformed southern Brazil into one of the whitest parts of the country, especially in rural areas where the European farming colonies were established. In the 2010 census, 83.2 percent of Rio Grande do Sul's population identified as white, 5.6 percent black, 0.3 percent yellow, 10.6 percent mixed race (*pardo*), and 0.3 percent indigenous (IBGE 2010).[5] Residents of Rio Grande do Sul are known as cowboys (*gauchos*) due to the region's long history of family farming and cattle ranching.[6]

The state of Rio Grande do Sul is the birthplace of the MST: here, in the late 1970s, groups of landless workers organized the first occupations that led to the founding of the movement. As I described in Chapter 1, this was a very important historical moment when dozens of urban and rural social movements were mobilizing across the country, calling for an end to the dictatorship. In Rio Grande do Sul, these movement leaders were in constant communication and collaborated on a range of campaigns. There is also a long history of urban activism in the state's capital city of Porto Alegre, which led to the election of the city's first Workers' Party (PT) mayor, Olívio Dutra, in 1988. For the next sixteen years, the PT held on to mayoral power and implemented a range of participatory experiments that became internationally renowned.[7]

THE ITINERANT SCHOOL PROPOSAL: GOVERNOR ANTÔNIO BRITTO AND THE PMDB (1995–1998)

Throughout the late 1980s and 1990s, state-level politics in Rio Grande do Sul were dominated by the Brazilian Democratic Movement Party (PMDB). The PMDB is notorious in Brazil for the ambiguous political positions of its party members and their willingness to align with both progressive and conservative groups to maintain power.[8] In 1995, Antônio Britto of the PMDB was elected, in the midst of increasing social mobilizations, protests, and social movement activity throughout the state.

The MST was one of the many social movements that was expanding and gaining strength during this period. Between 1995 and 1999, there were over forty land occupations with 25,000 families, the largest number of families involved in occupations since the movement's founding in 1984 (NERA 2015).[9] Local educational activists in Rio Grande do Sul were also at the forefront of developing alternative educational practices in their camps and settlements, even before the establishment of a national MST education sector in 1987. As families occupying land were given land rights on new agrarian reform settlements, these activists helped parents organize protests to pressure the state or municipal government to build schools for their children. They also encouraged parents and other activists to form regional education collectives. These regional collectives studied the MST education publications (see Chapter 1) and discussed how to implement these pedagogical proposals in the settlement schools. Elizabete Witcel and Marli Zimmerman, two of these educational leaders, recalled visiting the camps frequently and encouraging families to set up educational initiatives for the children. Often, women who were hesitant to take on leadership positions in their camps became involved in these activities, which then became a gateway for them to take on more responsibility and leadership within the movement.

In 1994, the MST education sector in Rio Grande do Sul organized the first statewide Children and Youth Congress, with hundreds of students from all of the settlements and camps participating. The education sector organized pedagogical and political activities for the children, including designing signs about their right to education, learning songs about agrarian reform, and taking workshops on clowning to entertain crowds during protests. Over the next year, the MST education sector in Rio Grande do Sul also began to discuss the pressing issue of what to do with the children in the camps. As the families in the camps were constantly being evicted, there was little opportunity for the children to attend a regular public school. Educational activists set up makeshift schools for the camp's children; however, these schools were not recognized by the state. The MST education sector developed a proposal for Itinerant Schools: state-recognized public schools located within MST camps that would move with the occupying families through their various transitions, including evictions, marches, and new occupations. As Elizabete explained, "We began to discuss the idea of the school of the encampment, that the school should be where the kids are or, in other words, the school should be in movement with the movement of the parents and the struggle for land."

In October 1995, the movement held a Second Children and Youth Congress, with 110 children and youth and forty-five adults participating. This time the congress was organized with the explicit goal of studying the Brazilian Statute on Childhood and Adolescence, which the Brazilian Congress had passed on July 13, 1990. The children read the statute, and according to the MST leaders, this led to a consensus among the children that they were being denied their constitutional right to education, as they spent years out of school while occupying land. The MST education sector organized a march with the one hundred children to the state Department of Education, to present a proposal for establishing schools in their camps. The children shouted protest chants and sang songs about their right to education, and a group of children read out loud the Statute on Childhood and Adolescence (Camini 2009). Over the next year, the MST education sector continued to engage in a series of mobilizations to increase the political pressure on the government to provide an educational alternative for these children.

The movement also employed what Fox (1992, 2015) refers to as a "sandwich strategy": using someone inside of the state to actively facilitate the demands of outside activists. This person was Sister Alda Moura, a progressive nun and an educational bureaucrat inside of the Britto administration. Sister Alda had been a teacher previously, but she was also connected to social movements through liberation theology and her work with popular education in her local church.[10] In 1995, she ran into an old friend who was working in the Department of Education, who told her that they needed someone in their office who could be an intermediary with the social movements. The friend facilitated Sister Alda's hiring by the Department of Education, as a social movement liaison. The MST's disruptive mobilizations had convinced the government to hire someone who could more effectively interact with the movement.

As soon as Sister Alda began her new job, a collective of MST leaders invited her to a gathering of *sem terrinha* (little landless children). Alda listened to the children's concerns about their lack of educational access, the discrimination they faced in the local public schools, and their desire to have schools in their camps. Sister Alda agreed to help the MST write a proposal for Itinerant Schools in the occupied encampments. They wrote the proposal and presented it to the government, but a year passed and the Britto administration took no action.

In the fall of 1996, the MST organized another rally outside of the state Department of Education with hundreds of children—an occupation Sister Alda had known was planned for weeks. Sister Alda described the following scene that took place on the day of the occupation:

> I left a meeting at noon, knowing that the occupation would happen. I was very anxious. At this point the government was afraid of the MST, and when the MST arrived, I was called out to the front to talk to the MST leaders. There were lots of policeman and big ropes preventing the entrance of the children into the building. I told the Secretary of Education that she should ask a delegation of MST leaders to meet with her. *I told her that, but this was already the plan I had made with the MST* [emphasis added].

The MST was utilizing an insider-outsider strategy, both pressuring the state government through contentious protest and coordinating with a state official to facilitate the process of negotiation.[11] At the meeting it was decided that the movement leaders would have fifteen days to finalize their proposal for building schools in occupied encampments. Then, this proposal would go before the State Education Advisory Board.[12]

On November 19, 1996, the Advisory Board considered the MST's proposal for constructing Itinerant Schools in occupied camps. Elizabete described the events that occurred:

> On this day, we brought a few buses of kids from our camps to the State Education Advisory Board. . . . The children were outside the building pressuring the guards to enter. . . . Eventually it was agreed that the children could enter to listen to the debate about the Itinerant Schools. The Itinerant Schools were supposed to be the last point on the agenda, but as soon as the children came inside, the topic was put to the front of the agenda and it passed right away.

The MST brought eighty children to participate in the debate about the Itinerant Schools. Sister Alda believed that "under this pressure, the State Education Advisory Board was obligated to approve the proposal." Elizabete agreed that this political pressure was critical; however, she also insisted that "the proposal was good—it had clear arguments about how to organize schools in the camps and there was no way for the government to say no. It was a right of the children and it needed to be guaranteed." According to Elizabete's account, it was not only the MST's political pressure but also activists' ability to develop a well-written, high-quality proposal that convinced the government to support this educational initiative.

With the Advisory Board's approval, Governor Britto agreed to fund the Itinerant Schools as a two-year pedagogical experiment. The government provided resources for the construction of Itinerant Schools in two MST camps that had a high concentration of children. The families in the camps constructed these schools themselves, using the same wood frame and black plastic sheeting that they used to build the tents in their camps. The government provided resources for basic materials such as chairs, chalkboards, and textbooks, but the families in the camps had to set up the classrooms and decorate the schools. Each of the Itinerant Schools went from first through fourth grade, with a dozen or so students in each grade. The MST found their own activists who had teaching degrees to work in these schools, through temporary contracts. The MST education sector oversaw the construction of the Itinerant Schools, engaged the community in a collective discussion about their mission, and helped the teachers design the curriculum and plan their weekly lessons.

It was the combination of disruptive protest and the MST's insider-outsider strategy that convinced the government to allow the MST to build and co-govern the Itinerant Schools. Even after the proposal passed, this insider-outsider strategy continued to be central. Sister Alda remembered that many people in the Department of Education were still opposed to the schools and would purposefully delay the distribution of resources to them. She had to spend much of her time visiting camps and documenting the schools to change people's opinions within the Department of Education. The combination of external pressure and internal advocacy allowed the two Itinerant Schools to function, even under an unsupportive state government.

FULL GOVERNMENT SUPPORT: GOVERNOR OLÍVIO DUTRA AND THE PT (1999–2002)

In 1998, as a range of social movements continued to mobilize across the state, voters elected Olívio Dutra as Rio Grande do Sul's first PT governor. As Goldfrank (2011b) argues, Dutra was ideologically dedicated to participatory governance and—much more than other PT candidates across the country—he followed through on this position. In Rio Grande do Sul, the MST was aligned with Dutra and had mobilized to bring his party to power. Thus, unsurprisingly, the left-leaning administration immediately embraced the movement's educational ideas. The Secretary of Education under Dutra, Lucia Camini, explained the government's relationship to the MST:

> This was a very important political moment; we were growing so much in the state, and with such credibility that we conquered the government. . . . The people that were put in the Department of Education were leaders from the MST; they were people who had the experience of the movement. . . . There was a political decision not only to guarantee the Itinerant Schools but to encourage the MST's participation in settlement schools as well. . . . Olívio chose me for the Secretary of Education because the MST sent a letter to the governor recommending me. . . . He was a defender of their proposal.[13]

Lucia emphasized the blurring of the line between the government and the movement: Dutra's administration not only supported the MST financially but also placed MST leaders within its ranks. Lucia herself was a long-time activist in the state teachers union, and her sister Isabela Camini was an active member of the MST state education sector.

As the number of land occupations continued to grow during this period—with sixty occupations involving more than 20,000 families between 1998 and 2001—Governor Dutra provided the resources to build dozens of new Itinerant Schools. Lucia recalled that the structural frames of the Itinerant Schools were made out of wood, and that these frames were covered with thick black plastic that served as the walls and the roofs of the schools; however, Lucia thought this color was too gloomy for children. She searched across the state to find a lighter color of plastic that the MST activists could use for the Itinerant Schools. This type of government advocacy shows how the Department of Education was putting effort not just into policy or showy actions but also the mundane details of building and supporting the schools. The number of Itinerant Schools fluctuated during Dutra's administration, due to the ebb and flow of new occupations, camp evictions, and the transition of some camps into settlements. In 2002, Dutra's last year in office, there were sixteen Itinerant Schools in MST camps serving several thousand students studying in first through eighth grade (Camini 2009).

The government's support of these Itinerant Schools represented an ideal form of social movement co-governance of public education. The government provided the financial resources, bureaucratic apparatus, and basic curriculum for the schools. The families in the camps built the schools, chose the teachers, incorporated the MST's cultural practices into the schools, transformed the schools' organizational structure, and even had influence over much of the curriculum. To manage the administrative records for all of the children in the Itinerant Schools, a regular state public school—*Escola Nova Sociedade* (New Society School)—located on an MST settlement, became the official sponsor of these students. In official government records, all students studying in the Itinerant Schools were considered students at Nova Sociedade—even if studying in camps hundreds of miles away.

Teacher training was another area where coordination between the MST and the state government was critical. Sister Alda recalled that "The MST would choose the teachers, but we made sure that they were all studying. This was the big contribution of the government, the continual training for the teachers in the Itinerant Schools." The MST's proposal for the Itinerant Schools prioritized the recruitment of teachers from the camps themselves; however, there were not enough people in the camps with the appropriate degrees to work in the schools. To increase the level of education inside of the camps, the MST education collective began enrolling camp activists in the Educational Institute of Josué de Castro (IEJC), the independent high school that the MST had founded in 1995 (see Chapter 1). These activists enrolled in the MST's High School Degree and Teaching Certification Program (MAG), spending several months each year at the IEJC and then returning to their camps to teach in the Itinerant Schools as their community research project. In addition, the Dutra administration funded regional and statewide seminars for all of the teachers in the Itinerant Schools to attend. Thus, the Itinerant Schools served both to educate the children in the camps and to provide educational access to the adults.

The most distinctive characteristic of the Itinerant Schools was that they were legally permitted to move with the encamped families. Thus, the Itinerant Schools traveled with the camped families through these various evictions, with the teachers setting up makeshift classrooms with chairs and chalkboard wherever they went. If the MST organized a march, the Itinerant Schools would participate, with teachers using the march to study geography or biology. Marli recalled, "The teachers would help the children measure the kilometers they were walking, and they would analyze the different vegetation they saw." The Itinerant Schools became a national symbol of social movement co-governance and educational innovation.

During the Dutra administration, Marli and Elizabete passed the civil service exams that opened for new teachers and became part of the official state teaching network. Instead of assigning them to teach in the public schools, the Secretary of Education made Marli and Elizabete the official state coordinators of the Itinerant Schools. This meant that the state was now funding the MST leaders to travel to the different camps and administer the dozen Itinerant Schools across the state. Marli described this as "an interesting arrangement," since she was being paid to do the work she had previously done voluntarily as an MST activist. Her job included helping to build new Itinerant Schools when land occupations took place, teaching the schools' teachers about the MST's educational program, observing and offering advice to these teachers, and organizing state-wide educational seminars. Although Marli and Elizabete were responsible for these tasks as government employees, their primary allegiance continued to be to the MST.

Despite the close relations that developed between the MST and the Dutra administration, organizing the Itinerant Schools during this period was still not a simple task. Marli explained, "We did not get all of the money we needed for the schools to function, it was a very rough reality." Carlota Amado, a teacher in one of the Itinerant Schools, remembered that the teachers often received their salaries late or there would not be enough money for everyone, so they had to split their wages.[14] If state resources did not arrive, the MST had to rely on the encamped families to keep the schools functioning—in Gramscian terms, the consent of these families for the MST's alternative hegemonic project. The MST also had to continually revert to contentious protest. During one MST mobilization in Porto Alegre, encamped families from across the state occupied several government offices for seven months. The Itinerant Schools functioned during this entire period on the lawn outside of these offices—while still being funded by the state government. Thus, the state public school system essentially became a part of the mobilizing capacity of the movement.

GOVERNING SCHOOLS WITHOUT THE STATE: GOVERNOR GERMANO RIGOTTO AND THE PMDB (2003–2006)

In 2002, the PT lost gubernatorial power to another PMDB politician, Germano Rigotto. Although Sister Alda had worked in the state Department of Education for almost eight years, the new Secretary of Education asked her to leave the government. Sister Alda claimed that the Rigotto administration did not want a vocal supporter of the MST inside its ranks. Nevertheless, the administration decided to leave the MST's educational program—including the Itinerant Schools—largely in place. Elizabete and Marli continued to oversee the Itinerant Schools, as state employees. However, the administration stopped allocating resources for these schools.

Fernanda, an educational bureaucrat in charge of rural education during Rigotto's administration, explained the government's position concerning the Itinerant Schools: "We did not interfere at all in the pedagogy of the Itinerant Schools—the MST already had a lot of insightful publications about these schools, and we always respected their ability to drive this educational process." As Fernanda explained, the administrative and pedagogical aspects of the Itinerant Schools were the responsibility of the MST: "It was the MST that knew what they wanted in these schools. It was not our role to tell them what to do because the Itinerant School was a different type of school."[15] Several other government officials and MST leaders I spoke with confirmed this lack of action on the part of the Rigotto administration—an explicit attempt to avoid any political conflicts.

The governance of the Itinerant Schools became more difficult during this period, as financial resources for the schools shrank. Marli explained:

> When Rigotto became the governor, everything slowly began to get worse. The MST was called to present about the Itinerant Schools to the Department of Education. I presented about the Itinerant Schools and the resources they required. However, this administration was very slippery; they just listened and washed their hands of everything. They did not ignore us, but they did not do anything for us either.

Elizabete remembered dozens of reports that she had to write about the precariousness of the Itinerant Schools and the need for more resources to make the schools successful. Although the Itinerant Schools continued to be recognized as state public schools during this period, the state was not investing any resources in the schools.

This is when the MST's own capacity to govern the schools became even more critical. In order for the Itinerant Schools to continue functioning, the families in the encampments had to invest their resources and energy into the schools. Fortunately, by 2003, there was already a network of MST leaders who had teaching certificates and were familiar with the MST's educational project. These activist-teachers dedicated themselves to the Itinerant Schools, despite months at a time when they were not paid. When some amount of financial support did arrive, the MST education collective divided these resources among the dozen Itinerant Schools. The MST leadership also funded statewide seminars and teacher trainings, and Marli and Elizabete used their positions as state civil servants to coordinate these events. Thus, despite the decreased funding, the schools continued to function with the support of the MST's own movement infrastructure. Between 1996 and 2008, 4,601 students studied in the Itinerant Schools (Camini 2009).

PUBLIC SCHOOLS ON AGRARIAN
REFORM SETTLEMENTS

In addition to overseeing the Itinerant Schools, MST educational activists were also concerned about implementing the movement's educational program in the public schools on their settlements. During my five months of field research in Rio Grande do Sul in 2010 and 2011, I collected information about nine state public schools located on MST settlements, interviewing the teachers, principals, and government officials in charge of these schools.[16] Map 4.1 indicates the name and location of these schools in 2011 and the State Department of Education Regional Offices (CREs) responsible for administering each school.

Ivori Moraes, a member of the MST education collective in Rio Grande do Sul, said that the movement's plan in the mid-1990s was to focus on two issues: the Itinerant Schools and the public schools located on settlements. However, Ivori explained, as the work with the Itinerant Schools accelerated, activists lost their focus on the settlement schools. Although families continued demanding that public schools be built in their settlements, the collective emphasis among the MST leadership was on organizing support for the Itinerant Schools in camps. Nonetheless, in the settlements where MST activists were hired as teachers, they were able to implement some components of the movement's educational program.

When Olívio Dutra became the governor in 1999, the Department of Education created more openings for MST participation in the state public schools on settlements. First, between 1999 and 2002, Governor Dutra built dozens of new rural schools and expanded the physical structure of the public schools that already existed on MST settlements. This investment was in direct contrast to subsequent political administrations, which closed down hundreds of rural schools in order to prioritize the public schools in urban centers.[17] However, because MST communities were more mobilized than other rural communities, once the government built a school on an MST settlement it was not easily shut down. Of the nine schools on Map 4.1, six were either founded or had major expansions during the Dutra administration.

For example, Rosangela Nascimento, a teacher, MST activist, and ex-principal of the school Joceli Correa, explained that when the community first started discussing the need for a school, they had a debate about whether they should ask the municipality of Joía or the state government to build the school. "We decided we wanted a state school and not a municipal school, because we had a lot of conflicts with the municipal government." The negotiations with the State Department of Education

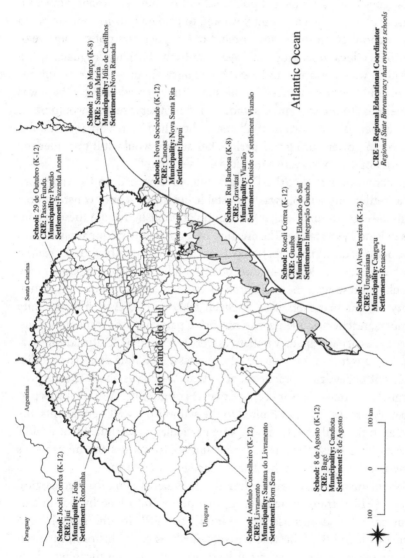

School: Joceli Corrêa (K-12)
CRE: Ijuí
Municipality: Jóia
Settlement: Rondinha

School: 29 de Outubro (K-12)
CRE: Passo Fundo
Municipality: Pontão
Settlement: Fazenda Anoni

School: 15 de Março (K-8)
CRE: Santa Maria
Municipality: Júlio de Castilhos
Settlement: Nova Ramada

School: Nova Sociedade (K-12)
CRE: Canoas
Municipality: Nova Santa Rita
Settlement: Itapuí

School: Rui Barbosa (K-8)
CRE: Gravataí
Municipality: Viamão
Settlement: Outside of settlement Viamão

School: Roseli Correa (K-12)
CRE: Guaíba
Municipality: Eldorado do Sul
Settlement: Integração Guacho

School: Oziel Alves Pereira (K-12)
CRE: Uruguaiana
Municipality: Canguçu
Settlement: Renascer

School: Antônio Conselheiro (K-12)
CRE: Livramento
Municipality: Santana do Livramento
Settlement: Bom Sera

School: 8 de Agosto (K-12)
CRE: Bagé
Municipality: Candiota
Settlement: 8 de Agosto

CRE = Regional Educational Coordinator
Regional State Bureaucracy that oversees schools

Atlantic Ocean

Rio Grande do Sul

Porto Alegre

Santa Catarina

Argentina

Paraguay

Uruguay

100   0   100 km

Map 4.1 Geographical Location of State Public Schools in Data Set in Rio Grande do Sul
Courtesy of Georgia Gabriela da Silva Sampaio

Regional Office (CRE) in Ijuí began in 1998, during the last few months of the Britto administration; however, it was only when Dutra took office in 1999 that the public school was approved for construction. Eliane Beatriz Muller, the principal of Oziel Alves Pereira, told a similar story. Her settlement was founded in 1999, and immediately afterward the municipality of Canguçu built a municipal public school on her settlement. However, Eliane explained, the community wanted to change it from a municipal to a state school, because the government of Canguçu was not supportive of the MST's educational program. "We went to the CRE in Uruguaiana, and we had to wait five hours to hear the response about whether or not our school could be administered by the state. They agreed because there was an openness to the settlements under Olívio; otherwise, this would never have happened."[18] According to Eliane, if there had been a different administration in power during this period, her school would still be under the authority of the conservative municipal government.

A second impact that the Dutra administration had on the trajectory of the settlement schools was the establishment of school constitutional assemblies (*constituinte escolar*). A pamphlet published about these assemblies in June 1999 states: "The creation of school constitutional assemblies is a process of direct participation of the school community with the *gaucho* society, in order to define the direction of public education in Rio Grande do Sul."[19] These were not one-time assemblies but four years of participatory forums that took place between 1999 and 2002 with community members, teachers, students, parents, principals, and government officials. These types of participatory initiatives were typical of the Dutra administration. There were several stages of this process, including collective studies of current pedagogical practices and extended debates about the purpose and goals of education for each particular community. Although this participatory process was not limited to the schools on MST settlements, the debates in the settlement schools were particularly dynamic, as local MST activists used these forums as opportunities to discuss the movement's pedagogical program and the struggle for agrarian reform.

School mission statements, referred to in Brazil as a Political-Pedagogical Project (PPP), transformed during this period into lengthy documents about educational purpose. For example, the PPP for the school Joceli Correa included the following parts: an analysis of the history of the settlement (starting with the initial land occupation); the meaning of the name of the school; the characteristics of the students; the characteristics of the teachers; the general objective of the school; the conception of education and schooling; a statement about pedagogy; a list of the different dimensions of human formation; and an explanation of the process of evaluation of the students, teachers, and the school as a whole. The PPP stated that the objective of the school was "To contribute to the construction of subjects with the capacity to analyze, reflect, and interact with the local and broader reality, while also learning through practice, preparing equally for manual and intellectual labor, and becoming a protagonist in the construction of the society that we desire."[20] Although this PPP was revised several times, the settlement families wrote the original version during the Dutra administration. One government official I spoke with expressed how impressed she was with the diversity of people that were invited to participate in these debates. For example, the service workers at the schools, the parent-advisory boards, and the students all participated.[21]

Despite these state-sanctioned spaces of debate and dialogue, a major theme in my interviews with government officials, teachers, and MST activists was that the Dutra administration did not have sufficient time to implement the many proposals that were discussed. For example, Rosangela from the school Joceli Correa said, "Olívio really needed another term, because we put all of this thought into how we wanted our school to function, and when it was time to put the talk into practice, the administration ended." Carmen from Santa do Livramento said that during this period they had dozens of people help to write a PPP, "but as soon as Olívio left, the new governments ignored the document." An interview with another government official confirmed the sentiment of these MST teacher-activists: "During Olívio's time, there were lots of meetings and attempts to change the schools . . . but these discussions never got implemented."[22] Nonetheless, in the public schools on MST settlements, the PPPs became the written justification for the implementation of the MST's educational program during the subsequent government administrations. Thus, the PPPs became tools that families on MST settlements used to make demands on the state, through contentious protest.

A third action that the Dutra administration took was to open two civil service exams to expand the official network of state teachers in 2000 and 2002. A group of MST activists took the exams and entered the school system as new school administrators and teachers. Once these activists became part of the official state teaching network, they could not be fired by any future administration. Of the sixteen teacher-activists I interviewed in the settlement schools, nine became teachers after passing one of these two public exams. This was critical, as no more civil service exams opened for the next decade. Together, these regional leaders convinced the other teachers in their schools to support the movement's educational program. This was also when Elizabete and Marli became state teachers, which allowed the government to hire them to oversee the Itinerant Schools. One coincidental factor that facilitated these MST activists' ability to pass the exams and enter the state school system was the timing of Governor Dutra's election, which coincided with the first Pedagogy of Land program at the University of Ijuí (see Chapter 2).

The story of MST activist Cleusa Reichenbach, who never became part of the official teaching network, illustrates why these public exams were so critical for the MST's continued participation in the settlement schools. Cleusa first began working in the settlement school Roseli Correa in the early 1990s. Initially she had a lot of freedom to implement the MST's educational proposal. "However, a rumor developed that the MST was teaching terrorism. The head of the CRE in Guaíba started to harass me . . . she wanted to fire me, but the community said no." Nonetheless, Cleusa's job security was uncertain as she was working through a contract. Eventually, the government was able to fire her with the justification that someone in the official network of teachers needed her position.[23] Government officials were not able to take similar actions against the MST activist-teachers who were part of this official state teaching network.

I asked dozens of MST activists in Rio Grande do Sul to express their opinion on the factors that facilitated the movement's contentious co-governance of the public school system. The overwhelmingly response was that a collective of dedicated teachers within the school was critical. This does not mean that all of the teachers in the schools have to be MST activists; most important was the presence of a small collective of teacher-activists who were familiar with the movement's educational program, and who could convince the other teachers about the merits of this approach. Here are several excerpts from the activists and teachers I interviewed in 2010 and 2011, emphasizing the importance of this collective leadership:

> Most important is a group of educators who maintain the proposal of the school and who helped to construct the school from the very beginning. If the group is not united, then the process is very hard. (Adilio, school principal, Joceli Correa)

> Teachers often work in several school, so it is hard to maintain a collective unity about one particular school. . . . That is why it is important for there to be teachers at the school that are connected to the MST's social struggle. They do not have to be MST activists, but they need some kind of link or connection. (Elizabete, teacher, Nova Sociedade)

> The intention of the teachers and community is critical. The willingness of the teachers to do something new. (Marli, school principal, Rui Barbosa)

> In the last instance, it is the teachers that are coordinating the daily activities in the classroom. That is why collectives of teacher in the schools who are supportive of the movements are so important. (Edgar Kolling, national MST education sector)

> Schools need to have educators who are activists. . . . If the teachers want to go beyond the daily routine of the classroom and do something new, they will do it. (Izabela Braga, state MST education sector, RS)[24]

According to these interviews, the presence of collectives of teacher-activists dedicated to the movement's pedagogical proposal was the essential ingredient for the MST's contentious co-governance of public education. These teachers did not all necessarily have to be MST activists, but they did have to support the MST's educational project in the countryside. In Gramscian terms, the general teaching body represented the civil society in areas of agrarian reform, more often than not reproducing traditional social relations in the countryside. However, a few dedicated MST activists, with a clear idea about how education could support new economic and social relations, could actively garner the consent of other teachers for this alterative educational project. Thus, the fact that small collectives of MST activists were able to become official state teachers during the Dutra administration shaped the future possibilities for transforming these public schools.

When Rigotto took office in 2003, his policy of nonconfrontation meant that these collectives of activists could continue implementing aspects of the MST's educational proposal. For example, Rosangela explained that when Rigotto took office, the PPP of their school was already constructed and could not be changed. "The new governor cannot just change a school's PPP; we were able to maintain our educational proposal during the Rigotto government." Cicero Marcolan, the school principal of Nova Sociedade in 2010, said that "When the PT was in power, there was more possibility of dialogue; there was more space for negotiation. When Rigotto entered, it was not as easy, but it was also not impossible." Cicero even told one story about the Rigotto administration's defense of his settlement school. The notoriously conservative magazine *Veja* published an article that critiqued the displaying of the MST's flag on the walls of the school. Cicero explained, "The Secretary of Education went on television and said that the school had the right to have the MST flag, because it was inside a settlement and the MST's struggle was part of its history." Therefore, at times, the Rigotto administration went beyond tolerance to openly supporting the MST's presence in the settlement schools.

REGIME CHANGE AND A FRONTAL ATTACK: GOVERNOR YEDA CRUSIUS AND THE PSDB (2007–2010)

In 2006, in a hotly contested election, Olívio Dutra of the PT and Germano Rigotto of the PMDB went head to head again, this time with a third candidate in the race. Over the previous four years, a group of right-leaning political leaders in Rio Grande do Sul—determined to prevent the PT from retaking power—began to organize within the Brazilian Social Democratic Party (PSDB). As discussed in previous chapters, the PSDB had a more coherent ideological position than the PMDB, generally dedicated to market-based economic policies and assuming a more confrontational and antagonistic relationship to social movements such as the MST. Yeda Crusius of the PSDB entered the 2006 race on an openly conservative plat-form, critiquing the access that the previous administrations had given to social movements. After a close first round of voting, Crusius beat Dutra in a run-off election.

Members of the Crusius administration were more than simply antago-nistic toward the movement; they were openly dedicated to weakening the MST's presence in the state. For example, Mariza Abreu, who became the Secretary of Education (2007–2009) under Governor Crusius, expressed disgust at the direction Rio Grande do Sul had moved over the previous decade. She said, "I refer to Rio Grande do Sul as the Socialist Soviet Bolshevik Republic of Workers."[25] Mariza's opposition to left-wing poli-tics in the state was consistent with her position on the MST. When I first asked Mariza about the Itinerant Schools on MST camps, she said, "Before you understand anything about the Itinerant Schools, you have to under-stand that the MST is a huge problem." Mariza claimed that the leaders of the movement only wanted to obtain political power and did not actually care about agrarian reform. She was critical of the dozen Itinerant Schools throughout the state, declaring that she had inherited this "awful situa-tion." She commented on multiple problems with the Itinerant Schools, in-cluding the MST's refusal to let representatives from the state Department of Education enter the camps. When the MST did let state officials in the camps, they found that the teachers on the payroll were never the ones teaching in the schools.

Nonetheless, Mariza Abreu could not simply close the Itinerant Schools; they had garnered too much attention nationally. Instead, she simply stopped meeting with the MST and drastically reduced the number of hours that Elizabete and Marli—the two MST leaders who had been hired by the state Department of Education to oversee the Itinerant Schools— could dedicate to this work. Elizabete and Marli were now required to spend part of their time working as teachers in their settlement schools. Marli said that during the entire Crusius administration Mariza only agreed to talk to the MST one time, because a member of Brazil's Chamber of Deputies had arranged for the meeting. Marli said, "Mariza treated us very badly. We were meeting to discuss ways to improve the Itinerant Schools, but Mariza ignored us. She said that the Itinerant Schools were no different than other schools and would get no more resources. It was a very hard and awful discussion."

The tensions between Governor Crusius and the MST went well beyond education. Throughout the four-year administration there were multiple conflicts, with dozens of camps disbanded and MST meetings broken up by the state military police. One of these occasions, in January 2008, was during a meeting of hundreds of MST leaders in the settlement Fazenda Annoni. As MST activist Roberto explained, "There had been a protest at a plantation before the statewide meeting. Dozens of state police arrived at the meeting because they said that a few objects had been stolen from the plantation. A conflict broke out with the police and several people were injured."[26] There were also violent interactions between the Crusius government and other social movements as well. In 2007 and 2008 alone, there were confrontations with the women's peasant movement, teachers unions, rural workers, city workers, and the movement of street people.[27] Crusius actively invested in the police force, increasing the salaries of the military police. Her administration quickly becoming infamous nationally for its criminalization of social movements.

Using the Law to End Participation: The Role of the Public Ministry

In 2008 Crusius's campaign against the MST received support from a powerful agency: the Public Ministry. The Brazilian Public Ministry functions at both the state and the federal level and is similar to a public prosecutor's office, with lawyers who can prosecute governments and state actors, either after a citizen complaint or if a lawyer in the agency decides to pursue a case on her or his own accord. Although Public Ministries are independent of the executive branch, state and federal governments can influence these agencies by appointing their heads, known as the Attorney General of Justice. In the case of a state Public Ministry, the governor chooses the Attorney General of Justice from a list of three people proposed by the ministry's lawyers, and then this appointment is approved by the state congress. Consequently, between 2007 and 2010, the Public Ministry in Rio Grande do Sul was closely aligned with the Crusius administration. In 2008, the Public Ministry executive council decided to open an investigation of the MST. This investigation eventually led to the closing of the Itinerant Schools.

Luis Felipe Tesheiner, one of the head lawyers for the investigation, explained that the Public Ministry had taken on this case because of multiple complaints by landowners about illegal activities initiated by MST activists across the countryside.[28] However, he said, "this case was unusual because it was the executive council of the Public Ministry that decided to take it on." This meant it was a top-down leadership decision from within the Public Ministry. The attorneys assigned to the case identified four locations in Rio Grande do Sul where there had been recent land conflicts.[29] "In one location there was a huge plantation that the MST had invaded, burning the farm equipment and killing the cattle . . . then they returned to their camps so no one could find them." Since the regular judicial system was not prosecuting the MST, it was necessary, he said, for the Public Ministry to do this on behalf of Brazilian citizens. Luis explained that the Public Ministry did not initially intend to investigate the Itinerant Schools. However, in the process of investigating the MST, the lawyers learned more about the Itinerant Schools and came to the conclusion that the schools were being funded with public money but were controlled by the movement. The Public Ministry began collecting more information about these schools, with the support of Secretary of Education Mariza Abreu.

Gilberto Thums, the lead attorney responsible for this investigation, explained to me how the Public Ministry began analyzing the Itinerant Schools:[30]

> We concluded that the Itinerant Schools must be closed because they served as an instrument of alienation for the kids . . .
>
> [RT: But how did this process of closing the schools begin?]
>
> There was an investigation into the situation of the MST in Rio Grande do Sul. But this investigation was not about the schools; it was about the movement in general, the violence in the countryside, the general violence in rural areas.
>
> [RT: And what was the role of the Department of Education?]
>
> There was agreement on the issue. We made contact with people in the Department of Education to find out if it was possible to close the schools. They said they no longer had control over these schools and they agreed that this was bad.

Thus, the closing of the Itinerant Schools was not initially because of an educational assessment of the schools; rather, it was the result of a more general investigation concerning the MST's presence in Rio Grande do Sul.

In contrast to Luis, who explained the case against the MST in a calm, detailed, and seemingly unbiased fashion, Gilberto was open about his ideological position against the MST. He went to great lengths to convince me of the MST's communist threat to society. In one part of our conversation, he discussed the MST's first independent school, the Educational Institute of Josué de Castro (IEJC) in Veranópolis. Although Gilberto did not even know the name of the school (mixing it up with the MST's Florestan Fernandes National School in São Paulo), he was convinced that guerrilla training was taking place there:

There is an MST school in the city of Veranópolis that you will never be able to visit. This is a school of guerrilla training. . . . It is very odd how this school functions, because it is not possible to visit. It is isolated and closed. . . . And this school, honestly, you have to know how to sing the national anthem of Cuba; it is very intentional teaching, directed, and there they learn techniques of guerrilla warfare.

[*RT: But when you say guerrilla techniques, you mean arms?*]

I do not know. We do not have this information. But certainly! Like what happened in Vietnam, everything used in Vietnam to attack American soldiers these people use here.

They learn these techniques to confront the police and learn how to invade a *fazenda* [plantation], and these schools continue functioning with public funding . . .

[*RT: Why doesn't the Public Ministry investigate the school in Veranópolis?*]

We would, but it is the jurisdiction of the federal Public Ministry and we are the state . . .

[*RT: Why doesn't the federal Public Ministry investigate?*]

They do not want to do this investigation, because the federal Public Ministry is also full of communists.

Gilberto assumed that I had never been to the school in Veranópolis, despite my explanation that I was a researcher studying the MST's educational initiatives. In fact, I had spent several weeks as a participant observer in this school, as I describe in Chapter 1. More important, for anyone with any degree of familiarity with the region, Gilberto's accusation that military training was taking place in the school was nonsensical. This school is not only located in the center of a relatively conservative middle-class city, but it is also attached to an elementary school. It is highly unlikely that MST activists could have used the school as a training center for guerrilla warfare without immediately drawing the attention of the community. Furthermore, the State Court of Accounts (TCU), a body that audits the spending of public money, had already prosecuted the IEJC for nineteen different cases of misuse of money—and the IEJC had been acquitted in all nineteen cases. It would seem that Gilberto's assertions about the MST were a deliberate attempt to delegitimize the movement; at best, he displayed striking ignorance about the movement as well as the schools.

This Public Ministry investigation resulted in a one-hundred-page report, published in June 2008, which analyzed the MST phenomenon. The report included a history of agrarian movements, the emergence and evolution of the MST, the international network of support for the movement, and an analysis of Rio Grande do Sul and the four municipalities that were the focus of the investigation. In the report, there was a section on the MST's educational program. In part, it stated that "The MST has implemented a parallel education system, over which public officials do not exercise power or control. The Ministry of Education does not even know where the schools under the governance of the movement are located. The state and municipal departments of education maintain the schools but have difficulties convincing teachers not linked to the MST to enter these schools." The report quoted one of the MST's own publications, which said students should "be dedicated to developing a class and revolutionary consciousness," arguing from this that the MST was imposing a "unitary ideology" on the children in these schools.[31]

The report made several concrete recommendations, which Crusius's government immediately helped to put into practice: increasing police security around MST settlements, evicting families from occupied camps, and closing the Itinerant Schools. Luis commented, "Yeda [Crusius] was important because she controls the police force. For the Public Ministry to act, we needed the support of the police." Similarly, Luis said that it was easy to shut down the Itinerant Schools, because Secretary of Education Mariza Abreu immediately agreed with the recommendation and took the necessary actions.

Although Mariza had always been critical of the Itinerant Schools, it would have been politically costly for the Department of Education to close the schools. As she explained, she welcomed the intervention of the Public Ministry:

The end of this contract with the Itinerant Schools was an initiative of the Public Ministry. Which I thought was great.

[RT: Why was it great?]

Because if we had made this decision, it would have been called into question, but because the Public Ministry made the decision it was considered more legitimate.

Because of the public recognition the Itinerant Schools had received over the previous decade, the PSDB government had to work with the Public Ministry to close down these schools. As the MST's lawyer in Rio Grande do Sul, Leonardo Kauer, commented, "The government did not have the guts to close these schools themselves." The Public Ministry also needed the state's support to put their recommendations into action. Luis referred to this as a "convergence of interests." Clearly, the attack against the Itinerant Schools was part of a larger attempt to weaken the MST's influence in the state or, in Gramscian terms, a frontal attack on the movement.

On November 28, 2008, representatives from the Public Ministry and the Department of Education signed a "Term of Commitment to Adjust Conduct" (*Termo de Compromisso de Ajustamento de Conduta*, or TAC), which mandated that the state government close down the schools.[32] For these government actors, closing the schools was necessary because they were contributing to the MST's political and economic goals, which at best were illegal and at worst terrorist. For the MST, the closing of the Itinerant Schools was part of a larger conservative attack on the movement throughout the state. The MST's decade-long, state-sanctioned co-governance of the Itinerant Schools was over.

"Closing Schools Is a Crime!": The MST Fights Back

Although conservative actors throughout Brazil praised the government's closing of the Itinerant Schools, these actions were widely criticized by the MST and the broader public. The MST's lawyer, Leonardo Kauer, said, "It was baloney, very stupid. They put together a false report that the schools were guerrilla training centers that were implementing a plan for a red revolution." The former Secretary of Education under Olívio Dutra, Lucia Camini, criticized the fact that the State Education Advisory Board was not consulted in the writing of this report, since the Advisory Board had approved the Itinerant Schools. The only educational official the Public Ministry lawyers interviewed for the report was Mariza Abreu. The MST leadership considered the report part of a larger national attack on the movement, what activists referred to as a "new moment of criminalization of social movements"—partially, a consequence of the PT's rise to power at the federal level (see Chapter 3). In July 2008, a month after the report was published, the MST along with nine human rights organizations sent a formal denunciation to the United Nations Human Rights Committee, condemning the Public Ministry's mischaracterization of the MST and its partisan alliance with the state government.[33]

The MST organized dozens of protests across the state to force Governor Crusius to reopen the Itinerant Schools, but the ideologically conservative administration, steadfast in its opposition to (one might say hatred of) both the PT and the MST, refused. Initially, however, the closing of the schools did not go smoothly. Many families living on MST camps continued to send their children to the Itinerant Schools, and the teachers continued to teach, even in the face of police intimidation, lack of school resources, and the cutting off of teachers' salaries.

In July 2009, eight months after the Public Ministry and the state government officially closed the Itinerant Schools, I visited one of the schools that was continuing to function.[34] The school was located in a camp near the settlement Fazenda Annoni, one of the oldest and largest agrarian reform settlements in Rio Grande do Sul. When I arrived, Alexandre, one of the teachers, was waiting to show me around. As we walked through the muddy encampment, Alexandre told me that there had been a lot of financial difficulties with the school ever since Crusius took office. The previous year all of the teachers had even gone on a hunger strike because they had not been paid for nine months. Nonetheless, the teachers continued working and were able to survive with the resources provided by the camped families, including some minimal money for food and the free housing.

Alexandre said that the official letter to close the Itinerant School, which had come on February 10, stated that the schools were inadequate and that the children would be sent elsewhere to receive a proper education. This was hypocritical, Alexandre said, because a lot of the stated inadequacies were because the governor had stopped funding the schools. He said, "After the schools were officially closed down, the police would arrive and go from tent to tent, trying to register the children and force them to transfer to the city schools. There were five or six parents from our camp that decided to send their children to the city school . . . however, the rest found ways to hide their children when the police came." Alexandre said that there was a team of eight teachers on the camp, most of whom were studying at the Educational Institute of Josué de Castro (IEJC)—the same school Gilberto Thums had misnamed. Alexandre started teaching at the Itinerant School two years previously, after he was invited to enter a High School Degree and Teaching Certification Program (MAG) at the IEJC. He spent several months a year studying and the rest of the year applying what he was learning in the Itinerant School.

In this camp, the Itinerant School only went up to fifth grade, because it lacked teachers with the necessary credentials to teach the higher grades. There were thirty-five to forty students in the school, but Alexandre admitted it was hard to keep track because students were often absent. "For example, today with the rain it is unlikely that a lot of students will come to school . . . it is very muddy and the children live in tents far away." At 1:30 PM, Alexandre and I headed to the Itinerant School for his afternoon class. The school's structure was very basic, made out of wood planks and thick black plastic. There were three rooms, one for kindergarten and first grade, one for second and third grade, and another, Alexandre's room, for fourth and fifth grade. When Alexandre was at the IEJC studying, another one of the teachers in the camp education collective would take on his teaching responsibilities. The students started arriving at the school one by one, some of them without shoes, walking through the mud. Alexandre said, "The way they are dressed they would never be accepted in the city school." Only one boy arrived for Alexandre's fourth- and fifth-grade class. This did not seem to disappoint Alexandre, who immediately started teaching, telling the boy in an excited voice about the math materials he had prepared. In another classroom, a teacher was working with three young children.[35]

Nine Itinerant Schools continued to function on MST camps in Rio Grande do Sul through 2009. Elizabete and Marli recorded everything that was taught and brought these reports to their State Department of Education Regional Office (CRE). However, the CRE was soon told by the Department of Education not to receive the MST activists. Lourdes, a state official in this office, explained, "The MST came to the CRE because they did not want the Itinerant Schools to close down. But we had to close them. . . . We notified the parents that their children had to go to other schools, but the classes still continued happening."[36] Cicero Marcolan, the principal of the settlement school that legally sponsored the Itinerant Schools, described these interactions: "The CRE tried to force us to enroll the students in other schools, but I refused because I did not believe in forcing parents to send their children to another school. The authorities issued a criminal charge against me, and nothing came of it, but it was a lot of pressure."

Through these scare tactics, the state government eventually convinced many parents to send their children to regular schools. Elizabete and Marli were also assigned full-time positions in settlement schools, which took them away from their work coordinating the Itinerant Schools. Slowly, the teachers on the camps also became involved in other activities, in order to make a living. In late November 2010, Izabela Braga, then the head of the MST statewide

Picture 4.1 An Itinerant School functioning in the state of Rio Grande do Sul even after the government mandated the closure of all Itinerant Schools. June 2009.
Courtesy of author

education sector, told me that "There are still some informal educational activities on the camps, but the Itinerant Schools are now closed." Governor Crusius had both the desire and the capacity to close the schools; she did so, even in the face of long-term resistance, through the systematic use of police raids, legal threats to parents, and administrative oversight. While the state's high capacity for educational governance had facilitated the implementation of the Itinerant School proposal between 1999 and 2002, this same capacity allowed the Crusius administration to close down the Itinerant Schools—in addition to hundreds of other rural schools across the state.

The eventual end of the Itinerant Schools did not mean that the MST stopped mobilizing around this issue. Throughout 2009 and 2010 there were dozens of protests concerning education in Rio Grande do Sul, with the theme "Closing a School Is a Crime!" These mobilizations were directed at both Crusius and the Public Ministry. I participated in one of these large protests in October 2010, during a statewide gathering of *sem terrinha* (little landless children), the sons and daughters of families living on settlements and camps. On October 13, 2010, hundreds of these children gathered in the center of Porto Alegre, outside the city's public market. We marched in two single-file lines through the streets, with a group of young MST activists drumming, playing music, and leading chants.

Eventually we reached our destination: the tall, glass building where the Public Ministry offices were located. We waited outside of the building for almost an hour, until two of the children were allowed to enter, accompanied by several MST activists. When the children came back outside, they announced that the Public Ministry had refused to make any promises to the movement about reopening the Itinerant Schools. The protest ended with one of the children reading a letter that had been written during the three-day *sem terrinha* gathering:

> We, the *Sem Terrinha* of the MST, come to the XIV State Gathering of *Sem Terrinha* with this theme: "To Close a School Is a Crime: *Sem Terrinha* in the Struggle for Education." We are here to demand from this government agency that it guarantees access to quality education, respecting our reality in the countryside. After thirteen years of the Itinerant Schools, the Governor Yeda, in 2008, with the Public Ministry, closed our Itinerant Schools, leaving more than six hundred children without a school. This is a crime! We demand that the government fulfill the law: to guarantee quality education for all children, whether in the countryside or the city, respecting their reality. . . . We are struggling for a piece of land for agrarian reform, and in this struggle the school has to be with us. . . . A right is a right! We do not accept no as an answer! Itinerant Schools Now!
>
> (Landless Workers Movement: For School, Land, and Dignity, Porto Alegre, October 13, 2010)

Picture 4.2 Educators and students from MST settlements and camps across the state protesting the closing of the Itinerant Schools. The banner reads, "To Close a School Is a Crime, Little Landless Children in the Struggle for Education." October 2010.
Courtesy of author

After this letter was read, we all stood and sang the MST anthem, and then the children were picked up in buses and returned to their homes on settlements and camps across the state.

These protests garnered national attention, leading a number of congressional representatives to denounce the Crusius administration. Although the negative publicity did not succeed in convincing the administration to reopen the Itinerant Schools, there were other repercussions for the actors involved. Gilberto, the head Public Ministry lawyer, admitted that the investigation of the MST had a personal cost for him: "I experienced a certain rejection from society . . . for example, I was giving a talk and the MST found out and organized a protest, and the chancellor of the university cancelled the talk because he did not want bad publicity." Luis Tesheiner also said that "The investigation was very hard on the agency." Four years of protest also weakened the PSDB in Rio Grande do Sul, as the party was constantly in the national spotlight, receiving negative publicity. In 2010, PT candidate Tarso Genro campaigned on the platform of ending the criminalization of social movements in the state and bringing back the Itinerant Schools; he beat Yeda Crusius in the first round of voting.

Public Schools on Settlements Face More Constraints

In addition to the Itinerant Schools, the PSDB government closed almost two hundred other rural schools between 2007 and 2010. The closing of these schools reflected an ideological position that the government took, which prioritized the construction of schools in urban areas.

Secretary of Education Mariza Abreu explained:

> The population is leaving rural areas. It is concentrating in the cities. . . . We need to open schools in cities where the population is growing . . . less schools in rural areas . . . this is the destiny of the world, to have 2 or 3 percent of the population in rural areas, with agribusiness, and the majority of the population in urban centers.

When I asked Mariza Abreu about the changes she implemented during her time as the Secretary of Education, she said her biggest accomplishment was transforming the "model of governance." Mariza said that the teachers' unions had always ruled the public schools, and that this created a bad environment for the students. "The logic of school administration always focuses on the teacher . . . my biggest change was to return control of the administration of these schools to the Department of Education." Mariza was open about her attempts to centralize decision-making power and take away the autonomy of the teachers. She embraced a series of educational policies that were becoming dominant globally, most notably, teacher merit pay, high-stakes testing, and standardized curriculum (Mundy et al. 2016; Sahlberg 2016). Although MST activists were able to maintain their positions as teachers and principals in many settlement schools during this period, this new educational paradigm was highly restrictive of any of the movement's educational innovations.

In 2010, at the very end of the Crusius administration, I talked to a handful of MST activists about their capacity to implement the movement's educational proposal in settlement schools during this period. Cicero, the principal of Nova Sociedade in 2010, described the situation as openly antagonistic: "The Department of Education refuses to address our school's needs. When we are short a teacher, it takes a long time for a new teacher to be assigned to our school because we are the last school the Department of Education wants to help." Carlota Amado, who works in the school Rui Barbosa, said that "Olívio came with the perspective that schools were about human formation. . . . Yeda has tried to transform schools into preparation for businesses." Carlota described the partnerships that the Department of Education established between her school and several local businesses. Although these partnerships were supposed to help the school financially, Carlota claimed that their primary function was to offer job training to the students. Elizabete described a more mundane issue: "Yeda [Crusius's administration] demands so much bureaucratic paper work that it is hard to have time for pedagogical issues. We are constantly behind in paper work."

Finally, Angelita da Silva described the new difficulties her school, Joceli Correa, faced offering alternative disciplines:

> Before, student self-governance and collective organization was considered an entire discipline, which worked really well because we had a lot of time to explain the base nuclei structure to the students ... in this new government we are no longer allowed to do this. Our names of disciplines have to match the official record of the state. We no longer have time to dedicate to teaching about student collectives. [37]

The principal of this school, Adilio Perin, also talked about the standardization of the curriculum and how this limited the school's autonomy to offer disciplines that aligned to the needs of the students in the countryside. Another teacher at this school, Rosangela, said that "Rigotto was not supportive, but Yeda is much worse. The government does not allow teachers to go to workshops, trainings; everything is more limited." Together, these interviews with MST activists and teachers working in public schools on settlements show the range of barriers to the MST's co-governance of the public schools during Crusius's administration: open antagonism, constraints in the school schedule, an increase in bureaucratic paperwork, more standardized tests, fewer professional development opportunities, less community–school partnerships, and a general trend towards preparing students for the urban job market.

In January 2011, the MST education collective in Rio Grande do Sul met at the Educational Institute of Josué de Castro to assess the status of the schools on their settlements.[38] Approximately twenty-five regional MST educational activists, including representatives from all of the schools on Map 4.1, were present at the meeting. Ivori Moraes began the meeting:

> I want to remember two important points for our state. The closing of the Itinerant School in February of 2009, now two years ago, and the closing of 175 other schools by the Yeda government. Mariza Abreu, under the perspective that urbanization is inevitable and a worldwide tendency, said it was important to close down these schools, that this it is a global logic. . . . We have to think about our schools in this new context.

Ivori's introductory analysis led into a daylong debate about how the MST would continue implementing the movement's educational proposal in their settlement schools, under these less than ideal conditions. The teachers spoke about the need for more statewide meetings and seminars on the MST's educational program. While these types of gatherings had been common during Dutra's and even Rigotto's administration, Yeda Crusius refused to pay for these seminars. The internal capacity of the MST education sector had suffered as a consequence.

In addition, between 1996 and 2010, the activists in the MST education sector had invested their energy primarily in organizing the Itinerant Schools, leaving participation in the settlement schools to local MST activists. This worked while there were supportive or at least tolerant state administrations in power, which offered these schools a high degree of autonomy. However, in the context of an antagonistic administration with a high capacity for educational governance, the ability for these MST activists to promote alternative educational practices decreased. As Rosali Caldart explained at the January 2011 meeting: "The MST education sector needs to coordinate the work that is happening in the settlement schools. . . . We want these schools to have autonomy from the state, but we do not want them to be autonomous from the movement." In contrast to the state's vision of public schooling as a universal public service for all Brazilian citizens, the MST leadership wants public schools to support the political and economic goals of the movement. However, in Rio Grande do Sul, the movement's ability to promote this form of institutional change was contingent on the ideological leaning of the political regime and, as the next section emphasizes, the movement's own internal capacity.

STATE SUPPORT WITH LOW MOBILIZATION: GOVERNOR TARSO GENRO AND THE PT (2011–2014)

When Tarso Genro of the PT became the new governor in 2011, one of the first actions he took was to announce that the Itinerant Schools would be reopened and to issue a statement against the closing of any more rural schools. However, it soon became clear that the Genro administration was driven by an anti-PSDB stance, rather than a concern with social movement participation. It was a different historical moment, and the party's dedication to participatory governance had waned over the previous decade (Goldfrank 2011b; Hunter 2011). Despite Governor Genro's nominal support of the MST's initiatives, the movement was not invited to participate in the government's administration.

I returned to Rio Grande do Sul in October 2011 to find out more about these changes. One of the first actions of the new administration was to create an *Educação do Campo* (Education of the Countryside) office in the Department of Education. In taking this action, Genro was following a national trend that began after the creation of an office for *Educação do Campo* in the Ministry of Education in 2004 (see Chapter 3), when dozens of state Departments of Education were encouraged to set up similar offices. The Crusius administration had refused to follow this policy. Governor Genro's policy in 2011 was an attempt to realign the state Department of Education with these national initiatives.

When I visited the state Department of Education in 2011, Nancy Perreira was the head of the office for *Educação do Camp*. Nancy was an advocate of liberation theology who had worked with the Pastoral Land Commission (CPT), a movement closely aligned with the MST (see Chapter 1).[39] Nancy said that when Genro took office, the MST leadership gave him a list of demands, such as new schools, teacher trainings, and other educational resources. Although Nancy said that it would be hard to respond to all of the MST's demands, she claimed that Genro was committed to working with the movement. Nancy gave me a document with a list of policy goals for the office for *Educação do Campo*. These included ending the closing of schools of the countryside; constructing new schools in and of the countryside; guaranteeing basic education in and of the countryside in infant, primary, and secondary education; and developing alternative pedagogies for schools of the countryside.[40] The Department of Education was working toward all of these goals. However, Nancy claimed that the most important victory thus far for the administration was finding a legal flaw in Public Ministry's investigation of the Itinerant Schools. She explained, "It is an important legal victory, even if we have not opened any Itinerant Schools yet."

The MST's perspective on these developments was quite different. MST educational leader Ivori Moraes spoke with me about the changes that had occurred during the first ten months of Genro's administration:

> The first thing to understand is that it was necessary for this government to reverse the educational policies of the previous government. They campaigned openly against the closing of the Itinerant Schools . . . so when Tarso [Genro] won, he publicly annulled the TAC [Term of Commitment to Adjust Conduct], saying it was illegal. . . . But the MST was not called to be part of this process. The TAC ended but the Itinerant Schools did not open. . . . It was a good media action for the Tarso administration, but in practice it changed nothing.

Ivori said that there were several good initiatives coming out of the state Department of Education, including the call to end the closing of rural schools throughout the state; however, social movements were not participating in this state decision making. Izabela Braga, the head of the MST state education sector in 2011, agreed: "The relationship with the government has been calm, but also very superficial. They think everything is perfect, but there is no way to go back to how it was: Yeda dismantled a lot."[41]

In 2011, the MST's local movement infrastructure in Rio Grande do Sul was also a lot weaker than it had been four years earlier. There were now very few occupied encampments in the state, each with only a handful of families. This meant that there were not even enough children living in the camps to merit opening a school. Four years of an antagonistic government had weakened the MST. In addition, the consolidation of agribusinesses throughout the state, the increasing cost of land, the federal government's refusal to implement agrarian reform, and the large federal cash-transfer program (*bolsa família*) all made it more difficult to organize land occupations. Importantly, there was also a contentious debate within the state leadership body that year about whether the movement's own strategic choices had resulted in the movement's decreased capacity for organizing large mobilizations. In particular, there was a group of activists who believed that it had indeed been the movement's emphasis on the institutional change— most significantly, the priority on promoting public poilcies that support agricultural cooperatives in settlements—that constrained the movement's more confrontational focus. This group of leaders left the movement in 2011, emphasizing in an open letter the trade-offs between the institutional concerns and the radical force of the movement.

Irrespective of the reason, the MST's reduced capacity to mobilize its base in Rio Grande do Sul in 2011 meant that the movement's ability to co-govern the public schools was not possible, even under a left-leaning government open to social movement participation.

CONCLUSION

In Rio Grande do Sul, between 1996 and 2006, the MST was largely successful in incorporating the movement's educational program into the state public school system, both through the Itinerant Schools on MST camps and the public schools on settlements. Initially, this was a result of two different factors: the movement's use of traditional social movement repertoires, such as protests, marches, and occupations, and internal allies within the state government. This combination of disruptive and institutional strategies convinced a centrist government to allow the MST to participate in the state public school system.

Then, in the late 1990s, increasingly high levels of social movement mobilization led to the election of a left-leaning PT administration. This war of maneuver, or direct attempt to transform the state, shifted the political opportunities for institutional change. This was a period when the lines between the movement and the government blurred, as MST activists quickly became embedded within the PT administration. These relationships allowed the MST to expand its Itinerant School proposal. The Dutra administration also facilitated the MST's long-term co-governance of the state public schools on MST settlements. The government constructed many of the schools currently located on settlements and invested in improving the infrastructure of other settlement schools throughout the state. The government also established a participatory process through which families could collectively define the educational goals of their schools, while also opening civil service exams that allowed a dozen MST activists to become part of the official state public school network. This ensured the long-term presence of small collectives of MST activist-teachers in the settlement schools.

During the four-year Dutra administration, MST activists succeeded in implementing many of the movement's curricular and organizational proposals in the state public school system on camps and settlements. The curricular proposals included adapting school curriculum to value rural life, moving beyond traditional disciplinary boundaries, encouraging students to engage in both manual and intellectual labor, including agroecological training and collective forms of work into the daily curriculum, and studying the history of agrarian reform. In terms of organizational proposals, activists transformed traditional hierarchies by forming student collectives and encouraging teachers to claim an equal voice in school leadership. When another centrist governor came to power in 2003, the new administration decided it was more politically savvy to allow the MST's initiatives to continue than to face the movement's contentious protests. Although the MST's educational initiatives were no longer financially supported, this tolerance meant that where the MST had a robust social movement infrastructure (Andrews 2004), activists were able to maintain the movement's educational program.

In 2007, a right-leaning government openly antagonistic to the MST's economic and political goals came to power and organized a frontal attack on the movement. The state government's high capacity for policy implementation, amplified by its partnership with the Public Ministry, was detrimental to the MST's strength throughout the state. The Public Ministry offered the state legitimacy, and the state offered the Public Ministry police and administrative support. The closing of the Itinerant Schools was only one of many actions the government took against the movement. Although this frontal attack resulted in national protests and negative publicity, the administration continued condemning the movement. Crusius was determined to end social movement participation in state institutions, and she utilized the state's capacities to effectively carry out this goal. A new PT governor was elected in 2010, but the damage had been done; after four years of a full-out attack on the movement, activists were no longer able to organize enough occupations to necessitate the reopening of the Itinerant Schools.[42]

In summary, the case of Rio Grande do Sul illustrates how political regimes directly affect social movements' ability to institutionalize their goals within the state apparatus. However, the effectiveness of a political regime is also related to its capacity for policy implementation. Essentially, a high capacity for implementing policy initiatives makes more coherent the programmatic (ideological) platform of the particular government in power. When a government is supportive of participatory governance, as was the case of Rio Grande do Sul between 1999 and 2002, the state's high level of capacity enhanced the coordination of government and civil society actors to create new participatory institutions. This aligns with scholars of participatory democracy, who argue that the bureaucratic capacity of the state and the state's know-how about institutional design facilitate civil society participation (Abers 2000; Baiocchi 2005; Cornwall and Schattan Coelho 2007; Heller 1999). This combination of high state capacity, a sympathetic government, and strong local social movement infrastructure produced an ideal context for state-movement cooperation. However, when the government is antagonistic to civil society participation, high state capacity can have the opposite effect, allowing the administration to more effectively block the demands of social movements to participate in the co-governance of public institutions.

In the next chapter, I examine a least likely case for the transformation of public schools: two municipalities in the northeastern state of Pernambuco, where clientelism and patronage are deeply embedded political practices. These cases offer a counterpoint to Rio Grande do Sul, showing that regime type is not always the determining factor in a social movement's contentious co-governance of public education.

CHAPTER 5

Pernambuco

Patronage, Leadership, and Educational Change

What we have today [in Santa Maria] is a result of a struggle since 1995. We did not win over the municipality from one day to the next. . . . We have struggled and we have won over all of our [school] principals—through a lot of work.

         —Adailto Cardoso, *local leader in MST Education Sector*

I attend to the needs of the evangelical church, the local soccer team, a guy who wants to go to the beach. Why not fund an MST youth gathering?

         —Ex-Mayor of Água Preta, *Eduardo Coutinho*

This chapter explores a least likely case for social movement co-governance: the pervasively clientelistic municipalities of rural Pernambuco. In contrast to Rio Grande do Sul, where local landless leaders began occupying land in the late 1970s, and which became the center of the movement's educational activities in the early 1990s, in Pernambuco MST activists only organized their first land occupation in 1989. The MST's engagement with public schooling in Pernambuco gained force in the late 1990s and early 2000s, as local MST activists had the opportunity to attend the movement's national conferences and courses and learn about the movement's educational approach. Thus, in contrast to Rio Grande do Sul where local MST leaders had to develop new educational practices, in Pernambuco activists drew on examples of how the movement had been implementing its educational program in other states for the previous two decades.

Also in contrast to Rio Grande do Sul, MST activists in Pernambuco have primarily engaged with municipal governments to promote their educational initiatives in public schools. This is because, in the late 1990s, there were no state-administered public schools located in agrarian reform settlements. Although the MST leadership in Pernambuco works with the state Department of Education to support particular educational programs, such as adult literacy campaigns, the schools in the settlements and camps are all under the jurisdiction of municipal governments. This means that the states the MST works with in Pernambuco—primarily poor municipal administrations, with low levels of capacity for policy implementation—are very different than the state government that the MST confronted in Rio Grande do Sul. One of most distinctive characteristics of the municipal governments in rural Pernambuco is the open system of political clientelism.

Political clientelism, or the dispensing of public resources in exchange for votes or other forms of political support (Burgwal 1995, 27), is a common practice throughout Brazil. In highlighting the role of clientelism in rural Pernambuco, I am not suggesting that elected officials in other states or levels of government do not engage in similar behavior. Nonetheless, during my eight months of research in Pernambuco, the degree to which clientelist practices defined the relationship between local citizens and politicians was much more evident than in my other research sites. In particular, in the public school system, the exchange of political support for job placement and promotion is a common, accepted, and semiopen everyday practice. This creates a situation where political divisions within and between schools define the educational experience for teachers, students, and community members.

Despite this seemingly unfavorable context, I argue that in rural Pernambuco there are many opportunities for the MST's participation in the municipal school system. In this context of local states with low levels of capacity for educational governance, the political orientation of the mayors is less relevant than the MST's own internal capacity for educational governance. In addition, if leaders maintain a strong relationship with their base (the hundreds of families living in areas of agrarian reform), as well as with the teachers working in the settlements, then municipal governments are often willing to support the movement's initiatives. Activists' ability to garner this consent for and belief in a particular social and economic project, what Gramsci refers to as "moral and intellectual leadership," is a continual process that involves a daily investment in relationship building and developing interventions that improve people's lives. A social movement's capacity to mobilize for a particular cause depends on this leadership.

In the case of the MST's educational struggle, this process of garnering consent takes place through teacher trainings, conferences, bachelor's degree programs, nonformal educational offerings, and other initiatives that teach activists and teachers about the movement's pedagogical and agrarian vision. These professional development offerings also increase the state's own capacity to provide a quality public education. This makes the state more willing to accept the movement's contentious co-governance of the public schools. Abers and Keck (2013), in their study of water basin councils, have referred to this as an individual's or organization's "practical authority," or their "problem-solving capabilities and recognition from key decision makers that allow them to influence public or private behaviors" (6). Hochstetler and Keck's (2007) study of environmental policies in Brazil also shows how actors inside and outside of the state are critical to coordinating actions throughout an entire policy process. Although social movement infrastructure has been a theme throughout the book, this chapter takes a closer look at why internal movement capacity differs across contexts, and how this affects the MST's ability to participate in the public sphere.

In the first case of Santa Maria da Boa Vista, the MST garnered the consent of diverse civil society actors, including families in the settlements, teachers, and state officials. I analyze the strategies that local MST activists used to engage these different groups, and how this civil society consent convinced multiple administrations to support the movement's educational initiatives (top right corner of Table I.1 in the Introduction). The second case of Água Preta illustrates what happens when social movement leaders lose the support of their base. I examine the MST's attempt to lead a process of educational change in Água Preta, where there are many opportunities for reform, but where families living in settlements rejected the MST's educational program (bottom right corner of Table I.1 in the Introduction). Together, these two cases illustrate both the opportunities available for social movement co-governance under seemingly unfavorable political regimes and the importance of the MST's investment in local infrastructure and collective leadership development to maintain its long march through the institutions.

THE MST'S ARRIVAL IN PERNAMBUCO

Pernambuco is located in the northeastern part of Brazil, the poorest region of the country, with a long history of state neglect. Although Pernambuco is one of the wealthier states in the region, in 2010 it still only contributed to 2.3 percent of the national GDP (IBGE 2011). In 2015, average monthly household income in Pernambuco was 822 reais (about 305 US dollars in 2015), the highest in the northeast but only a little more than half of Rio Grande do Sul. The population of the state was 8.8 million in 2010, with 80 percent urban residents. Also in 2010, 36.7 percent of the population identified as white, 55.3 percent mixed race (*pardo*), 6.5 percent black, 0.9 percent "yellow," and 0.6 percent indigenous (IBGE 2010).

Similarly to other parts of the north and northeast, the MST first began organizing in Pernambuco with the help of movement leaders from the south. Jaime Amorim, originally from Santa Catarina, was one of these activists who moved to Pernambuco in the late 1980s.[1] As Jaime explained, the MST decided to invest in organizing in Pernambuco because of the history of social struggle in the state, from slave revolts to peasant leagues. Furthermore, in 1986 the socialist labor leader Miguel Arraes won the governorship. Given the presence of a seemingly sympathetic state government, in 1989 the MST leadership decided to organize their first land occupation in Pernambuco, near the capital city of Recife. However, the MST miscalculated Governor Arraes's sympathy for the movement. Arraes deployed police forces to evict the camp, accusing the MST of dividing the workers in the countryside. Arraes felt that the most pressing issue was not agrarian reform but organizing the salaried rural workers. Jaime said, "our camp was decimated, so we had to move the families to the side of a highway near the capital city to regain our forces." At the end of 1989, the movement agreed to the government's offer to accept land in a far-off region in the interior of the state. Jaime explained, "We accepted the proposal so the movement could continue existing."

It was only in 1992 that the MST "took back their movement in Pernambuco," as Jamie described it, organizing several large land occupations in the sugarcane region where production had declined, including in the municipality of Água Preta. From this point on, the movement consolidated across the state, with leaders organizing successful land occupations in several other sugarcane regions. Then, in 1995, MST activists began leading land occupations in the semiarid (*sertão*) region, organizing two thousand families to occupy a plantation in Santa Maria da Boa Vista. During the late 1990s, the movement expanded rapidly in both the semiarid and sugarcane region. By 2011, the movement had a total of 202 settlements across Pernambuco, with 14,100 families, and more than 10,000 families still living in camps waiting for land rights. Map 5.1 highlights the locations of Santa Maria da Boa Vista and Água Preta, the municipalities with the highest concentration of MST settlements in Pernambuco and the foci of this chapter.[2]

EDUCATION AND CLIENTELIST POLITICS IN SANTA MARIA DA BOA VISTA

Santa Maria da Boa Vista is a municipality in the western part of Pernambuco, located alongside the vast river São Francisco, which separates the state

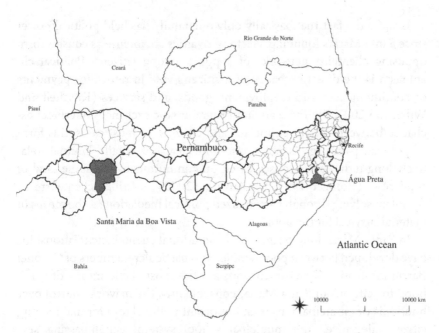

Map 5.1 Locations of Santa Maria da Boa Vista and Água Preta
Courtesy of Georgia Gabriela da Silva Sampaio

from Bahia. Santa Maria is located in the *sertão*, a semiarid region with limited irrigation, making small-scale and subsistence farming extremely difficult. Although the third largest municipality in Pernambuco (3,000 km²), Santa Maria contains a population of only 39,435 people with 38 percent urban residents (IBGE 2011).[3] Santa Maria has a much higher concentration of Afro-Brazilians than the rest of Pernambuco, especially in the rural interior where many people are descendants of runaway slave communities (*quilombos*).[4]

Ever since its founding in 1872, Santa Maria has been controlled by a system of *coronelismo*, a "form of chieftainship or leadership by big men, the heads of large, extended households," who rule over rural areas as the dominant authority (Scheper-Hughes 1992, 87). All of the mayors in Santa Maria over the past century have been part of this lineage—relatives of Florêncio de Barros Filho, known as Coronel Barrinho. While most of the citizens of Santa Maria are black, the Barrinhos are white, direct descendants of the Portuguese. Coronel Barrinho was born in 1894, and he and his wife Judith Sampio Gomes had ten children. Between 1920 and 1960, Coronel Barrinho was the mayor of Santa Maria multiple times, with other close relatives assuming office between his terms and during the decade of the 1970s. For most of the 1980s, Coronel Barrinho's son Noé Barros was the mayor.[5] Since 1996, all of the mayors have been the nephews of Coronel Barrinho.

Despite the fact that basically only one family has held political power since Santa Maria's founding, electoral rivalries are intense as cousins form opposing clientelist networks of support among citizens. Political clientelism is the direct exchange of a citizen's vote in return for payments or continuing access to employment, goods, and services (Kitschelt and Wilkinson 2007, 2). These are not programmatic exchanges but direct exchange between certain politicians and citizens. In most cases, this form of political patronage is not a one-time deal but entails "mutual, relatively long-term compromises based on commitments and some kind of solidarity" (Roniger 1994, 5). Auyero (2000) describes clientelism as "problem solving through personalized political mediation . . . the means of material survival for the poor."

In Santa Maria, long-term, multigenerational clientelistic relationships have developed between poor families and particular members of Coronel Barrinho's family. Government jobs are the most stable means of livelihood for citizens in Santa Maria; consequently, the mayor's control over hundreds of municipal jobs is an important political tool for maintaining citizen allegiance. The municipal school system, encompassing seventy schools serving around six thousand students,[6] is part and parcel of this clientelist system. Each time a new cousin takes power, all of the municipality's seventy school principals are fired and replaced with seventy political supporters.[7] Teachers who are civil servants and cannot be fired are also affected, as their political loyalty determines the schools where they will teach, some of which require a several-hour commute. It is hard to exaggerate the turmoil this causes for the schools, with principals and teachers transferred every four years and deep partisan divides and resentment developing between school personnel and among community members. During these periods of transition, the education of thousands of students is put on hold.

First MST Land Occupations (1995–1996)

The MST's first land occupation in Santa Maria took place in 1995. Several large fruit plantations went out of business, leaving hundreds of people unemployed and large tracts of land lying fallow. The MST statewide leadership organized an occupation of one of these areas, with two thousand families from the region. This occupation resulted in the creation of the settlement Harvest (*Safra*). Since there was only enough land to settle 220 of the families, the other families went on to occupy more plantations in the region, resulting in the creation of more and more agrarian reform settlements over the next decade. By 2011, Santa Maria had fifteen settlements with 1,824 families. Most of these settlements are located on one road known informally as the Highway of Agrarian Reform (Map 5.2).

Founding an MST Education Collective

After the initial land occupations in the mid-1990s, the MST began struggling for public services, such as roads, agricultural assistance, and, of course, public schools. Statewide MST leaders organized activists in the settlements and camps into regional leadership collectives, based on different thematic concerns (e.g., agriculture, education), to make these demands on the government. Teresneide Varjão was one of the original members of the MST education collective in Santa Maria. Teresneide was living across the São Francisco River, in Curaça, Bahia (see Map 5.2), when the first MST land occupation took place in 1995. As she recounted, she visited the occupation and "fell in love with the community."[8] Unlike the majority of people living in the camp, Teresneide had completed eighth grade. The families asked her to teach the children in the camp how to read and write. Teresneide began traveling to the camp on a daily basis to lead these nonformal educational activities.

Soon after, MST statewide educational leader Rubneuza Leandro approached Teresneide and three other women involved in similar educational initiatives, asking if they would form an MST education collective in the region. They agreed, and with Rubneuza's support, the members of the newly formed education collective began to study the MST's national educational publications and organize pedagogical activities in all of the camps in the region, based on these publications. During this early period there were no schools or teachers in any of the MST's settlements or camps. The four activists organized protests in front of the municipal Department of Education to demand schools in their communities. Mayor Gualberto Almeida (1993–1996), a rich landowner and the first and only person to oust the Barrinho family, agreed to send one teacher to work in Safra. The classes took place in the previous landowner's home. The women in the education collective frequently visited and talked to the teacher about the MST's educational approach.

In 1998, fourteen-year-old Erivan Hilário also joined this education collective; less than twenty years later, Erivan would become one of the two national coordinators of the MST education sector.[9] Erivan came from a very poor Afro-Brazilian family, one of twelve children, and his parents always struggled to survive. In 1995, when Erivan was eleven, his parents participated in the first land occupation in the region. The following year Erivan's family received land to live on a new settlement that had been created, settlement Vitória II. Erivan was scared to move there, because he had seen a news reporter say bad things about the MST. However, in January 1998, Erivan moved to the settlement with his family.[10] The following is Erivan's own account of what happened (written in third person):

> When he went to the settlement, people were still living in tents made out of black plastic. Erivan was shocked at the conditions in the camp, which were different than anything he had experienced. Everything was new for him. He saw that the way the people talked and worked with each other and showed unity; he watched the children in the settlement sing songs about land and struggle. He saw that the children in the settlement were considered people who had the right to participate in the discussions in the camps and the general assemblies. . . . When Erivan went to the settlement, something new was born inside of him, a feeling of struggle.[11]

One day, Teresneide visited Erivan's settlement and asked if anyone was willing to teach adults in the region how to read and write. Erivan immediately volunteered. He attended two MST seminars, where he learned about Paulo Freire's literacy method: a local seminar in the neighboring municipality and a national seminar on adult education in Recife, the capital city of Pernambuco. This was the farthest Erivan had ever been from Santa Maria.

Erivan began to teach adults in a nearby settlement how to read and write. Erivan also continued studying, but the closest school to the settlement was located across the São Francisco River, in the city of Curaçá, Bahia. Every morning Erivan woke up with the other children in the settlement Vitória II, worked a few hours in the fields, and then walked thirty minutes to the river's edge and took a boat to Bahia to attend his afternoon seventh-grade class (see Map 5.2). When classes ended at 5:30 PM, Erivan took the boat back over the river but he would get off at a port earlier than his friends, in the nearby community of Barro Alto. There, he taught literacy classes to adults from 7 to 9 PM, and then waited for a bus that took him back to his settlement. In these literacy classes Erivan tried to implement the Freirean educational methods that he had learned in the MST seminars.

In 1999, the national MST education sector organized the first ever High School Degree and Teaching Certification Program (MAG program, see Chapter 1) in northeastern Brazil, with funding from the National Program for Education in Areas of Agrarian Reform (PRONERA, see Chapter 2). The statewide MST leadership in Pernambuco wanted all of the members of the regional education collectives who did not yet have a high school degree to enroll. The MAG program was offered by an agricultural high school run by the Federal University of Paraíba (UFPB), in João Pessoa, the capital city of Paraíba, a ten-hour drive from Santa Maria. The three-year program was organized through the pedagogy of alternation—a combination of intensive study periods and community research (see Chapters 1 and 2). Teresneide and Erivan enrolled in the program, spending January, February, and July in Paraíba. The UFPB professors taught the classes each day, which included all of the traditional high school course offerings, such as math, science, and literature. A collective of MST activists known as the CPP (Political-Pedagogical Collective, see Chapter 2) lived with the students during the study periods and oversaw the program. The CPP made sure that the program adhered to the MST's educational approach by integrating practices such as student self-governance, collective work, the daily performance of *mística*, and participation in local political struggles. Erivan described the course "as a dream . . . It initiated my activism. I learned to love teaching and I learned that I wanted to be a teacher, but not just any type of teacher." The MST educational leaders in the CPP assigned Erivan and Teresneide a strategic task to complete during their community research period: to implement the movement's educational proposal in the Santa Maria da Boa Vista public school system. Table 5.1 outlines the political transitions in Santa Maria da Boa Vista between 1995 and 2012, and the MST's educational victories during each of these periods, described in detail in the following sections.

Table 5.1 POLITICAL TRANSITIONS AND MST EDUCATIONAL ADVANCES IN SANTA MARIA DA BOA VISTA, 1995–2012

Years	Mayor	Developments in the MST's Educational Proposal
1919–1993	Florêncio de Barros Filho, known as Coronel Barrinho, with his various relatives in power between his many mandates	
1993–1996	Gualberto Almeida (PMDB)	First MST land occupation in 1995; first teacher sent to work in a settlement
1997–2000	Leandro Duarte (PFL)	More occupations, several schools built in settlements; mayor sends teachers to MST regional and statewide teacher trainings
2001–2004	Rogerio Junior Gomes (PSB)	MST education collective officially co-governs eleven schools serving MST settlements; two MST activists hired by the mayor for this task
2005–2008	Leandro Duarte (PFL/DEM)	*Educação do Campo* office created and MST co-governance of municipal public education expands to sixty more schools
2009–2012	Leandro Duarte (DEM) and Jetro Gomes (PSB)	*Educação do Campo* and MST co-governance supported under both administrations, with several municipal conferences and programs

Building Schools on Settlements: Mayor Leandro Duarte and the PFL (1997–2000)

Two years after the MST's first land occupation in Santa Maria, in 1997, Leandro Duarte became mayor. Leandro, the nephew of Noe Barros (the son of Coronel Barrinho), was affiliated with the conservative political party PFL (Liberal Front Party).[12] By this time, several agrarian reform settlements had been created in Santa Maria, but none of them had public schools (which is why Erivan had to study in Bahia). Teresneide, Erivan, and the other members of a small but dedicated education collective began to put pressure on the Duarte administration to build schools in MST camps and settlements. According to Leandro, he was willing to attend to these demands because the cost of construction was minimal and it improved his reputation. He explained:

> After being elected I started to have a better relationship with the MST, and we began to improve the schools. I constructed schools in all of the settlements. . . . In one settlement, I turned the old master house of the *fazenda* into a school. I always took the opportunity to build a school, even if there was not the proper structure.
>
> [*RT: Did you take these actions because of the MST's political pressure?*]
>
> No, it was not that; this was very much my choice.[13]

Teresneide had a different view of these developments: she said that the schools were only built after families in the settlements took to the streets and engaged in contentious protest. Sometimes the families would construct a makeshift school themselves and then simply demand that a teacher be assigned to the school. These contrasting accounts are comparable to the state–society dynamics highlighted in other studies of clientelism (e.g., Burgwal 1995), in which politicians and settlers disagree over the meaning of exchange: politicians stress their goodwill, while the poor highlight their own collective action.

In 2011, when I carried out most of my field research in Santa Maria, there were eleven municipal public schools (first through eighth grade) located in or next to MST settlements—almost all of them constructed during Leandro's first administration. Ten of these municipal schools were built along the Highway of Agrarian Reform, and the eleventh was located in another part of the municipality in the settlement Luis Gonzaga. During this period, the MST also worked with a twelfth municipal public school, Gabriel Percico, that served the workers of the large plantation Fazenda Milano, located on this same road as the settlements. Map 5.2 illustrates the location of these twelve municipal public schools.

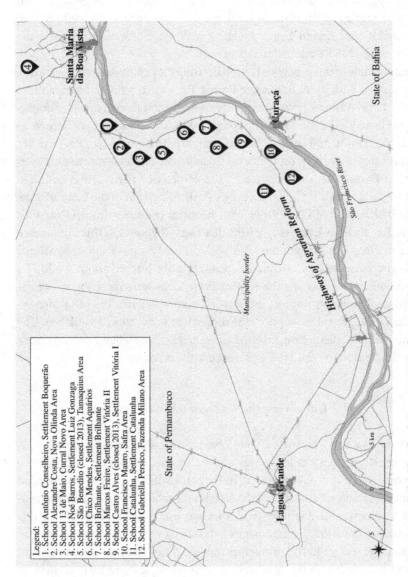

Legend:
1. School António Conselheiro, Settlement Boquerão
2. School Alexandre Costa, Nova Olinda Area
3. School 13 de Maio, Curral Novo Area
4. School Noé Barros, Settlement Luiz Gonzaga
5. School São Benedito (closed 2013), Tamaquius Area
6. School Chico Mendes, Settlement Aquários
7. School Brilhante, Settlement Brilhante
8. School Marcos Freire, Settlement Vitória II
9. School Castro Alves (closed 2013), Settlement Vitória I
10. School Francisco Mauro, Safra Area
11. School Catalunha, Settlement Catalunha
12. School Gabriella Persico, Fazenda Milano Area

State of Pernambuco

State of Bahia

Santa Maria da Boa Vista

Curaçá

Lagoa Grande

São Francisco River

Highway of Agrarian Reform

Municipality border

0   5 km

Map 5.2 Municipal Public Schools Serving MST Settlements in Santa Maria da Boa Vista in 2011
Courtesy of Georgia Gabriela da Silva Sampaio

The impressive expansion of educational infrastructure on agrarian re-form settlements in Santa Maria was not sufficient for the movement. The MST leadership also wanted to transform the pedagogical approach in these schools. Teresneide and Erivan had a clear vision of what this educa-tional approach should look like, as they were living it through their high school program in Paraíba. To implement these practices in Santa Maria, Teresneide and Erivan began meeting with state officials to discuss the merits of the MST's educational proposal.

An example of this process is the relationship they cultivated with Leandro's Secretary of Education, Bernadete Barros. Bernadete, who had grown up in Santa Maria and knew Erivan since he was an infant, was open to this dialogue. She explained, "The MST's methodology was acknowledging they were from a different reality and that we had to recognize this reality. . . . I agreed, we cannot force something on them. . . . I participated in their meetings. I even went to Brasília for a conference."[14] The conference Bernadete mentioned was the First National Conference for a Basic Education of the Countryside, organized by the MST in 1998 with financial resources from UNESCO, UNICEF, and the University of Brasília (see Chapter 3). This conference was a key moment that put the MST's educational proposal into the national spotlight. Bernadete's participation meant that she learned about the MST's educational goals and saw the respect these ideas were receiving at the na-tional level. This was not lost on Mayor Leandro Duarte. The MST also or-ganized local protests to support the movement's educational initiatives. The combination of disruption, internal allies, and public recognition convinced Leandro to sanction the MST's presence in the schools.

Garnering the Consent of Teachers

Once Erivan and Teresneide were given permission to visit the schools, their most pressing challenge was convincing the teachers to support the movement's educational proposal. Initially, the MST leadership had wanted to put their own allies inside of the settlement schools. However, since mu-nicipal jobs were in high demand, this was not possible. Faced with this constraint, the MST leaders began interacting on a daily basis with the teachers who were in the municipal public school system. Teresneide and Erivan reflected with the teachers on their pedagogy and invited them to attend MST educational seminars. This work was initially difficult, because most of the teachers were from the city and their only knowledge of the MST was through the mass media's portrayal of the movement as a violent group of outlaws. Nonetheless, many teachers began to appreciate this sup-port. One teacher, Josilene Alves Cardoso, explained:

The relationship and opinion I had of the MST was a feeling of fear. . . . Occupying land for me was robbing land . . . but I was invited in 1997 to a MST camp to teach. . . . I was very much welcomed. They asked me not just to teach there but to live there. . . . I moved to the MST camp. I could do my work and not pay rent. I went with my entire family.[15]

Initially fearful of the movement, Josilene decided to move to an MST camp herself, teaching as well as participating in the agrarian reform struggle. Over the next decade, Josilene became an active member of the MST education collective in Santa Maria.

Teresneide and Erivan also slowly learned that in order to transform the public schools in Santa Maria they could not openly discuss party politics. This would simply alienate the different groups that had a stake in the public school system—teachers, principals, parents, and community members—who were all deeply beholden to different politicians in oppositional clientelist networks. Instead, the MST activists organized what Gramsci refers to as a "war of position," engaging with teachers' complicated and contradictory understanding of the world (their common sense), and convincing them of the importance of an alternative educational approach in the countryside. If teachers appeared sympathetic, the MST activists would invite them to attend one of the movement's statewide teacher trainings generally held in the MST's main political training school (*escola da formação*) in Pernambuco, in the city of Caruaru, the Paulo Freire Training Center. As another teacher, Graça, explained, "My vision was similar to everyone, I was scared and thought that this was an invasion. . . . In 1997, I went to an MST teacher training in Caruaru; I began to understand the movement in another way, my vision expanded. . . . I am connected to the MST and always participating."[16]

Through these statewide teacher trainings and activists' daily presence in the settlement schools, the MST succeeded in garnering the consent of many teachers for their educational project. However, this process was never finished. Every time a new mayor was elected, seventy principals were fired and all of the teachers were transferred based on their political allegiance. As Teresneide described, "The difficult issue is that we were always re-initiating our work. We would joke every time the teachers changed, 'we are in re-re-re, we are always in re-start.'"

Social Movement Co-Governance: Mayor Rogerio Junior Gomes and the PSB (2001–2004)

Right before the 1999 mayoral election, Leandro, who was still part of the conservative PFL party, had a fight with his vice-mayor and cousin, Maria

Graciliano. Maria decided to join the more left-leaning Brazilian Sociality Party (PSB), and she convinced another cousin, Rogerio Junior Gomes, to join the party and run for mayor. Despite Leandro's relative openness to the MST between 1997 and 2000, the MST supported Rogerio in the next election because of his affiliation with the PSB.[17] During the 1999 election year, Leandro cut off all dialogue with the MST and ended the educational initiatives that he had previously supported. This increased the animosity between the MST and Leandro, culminating in what became known as the famous "bean incident" in which Erivan threw a sack of beans onto Leandro's feet, a sign of disrespect for local authority.

Rogerio succeeded in defeating Leandro, and after he took office, the MST was rewarded with complete freedom to participate in the govern-ance of the eleven schools located on MST settlements. Rogerio even allowed MST leaders to choose the principals—from among his political supporters. In addition, two MST leaders were hired to oversee the daily functioning of these schools. The new Secretary of Education, Osmilda Brandão, explained, "We had two people from the MST that worked for the Department of Education. But they did not come to our office; they did the work that they had to do in the community."[18] These two MST leaders organized monthly meetings with the eleven principals in the settlement schools and met regularly with a collective of teachers in each school to help with lesson planning. MST activists had already been organizing these types of educational activities, but now they had the official support of the government. Rogerio explained why he endorsed the MST's educational program:

> After I was elected, the MST became part of the administration; they helped to run the government. They began to make a lot of suggestions about education, and we invited them to participate. . . . It was very practical. The MST education collective had already been working in the municipality for a long time.[19]

When Rogerio became mayor, dozens of teachers in the municipality, both his allies and adversaries, were advocates of the MST's educational goals. In addition, local MST activists had proven their "practical authority" (Abers and Keck 2013) in educational policy, or their ability to help the municipal government develop and implement effective policies. This civil society support and practical contribution to state capacity building—in addition to the MST's political support—convinced Rogerio to hire MST activists to co-govern the settlements schools, thus directly funding the movement's activism in the region.

Within this context, the activists in the regional education collective began implementing a range of curricular and organizational initiatives that supported their struggle for agrarian reform. They promoted participatory democracy, created teacher and principal collectives, incorporated Freirean-inspired generative themes into the school curriculum, and encouraged students to do community research projects. They also integrated manual labor, agroecology, and MST cultural practices into the daily school routine. Every morning the children would perform *místicas*, using a combination of poetry and music to valorize agrarian reform and their right to education. The children then hoisted the Brazilian, Pernambucan, Santa Maria da Boa Vista, and MST flags, each day singing a different anthem: national, state, municipal, or MST.

MST Participation Deepens: Mayor Leandro Duarte's Return (2005–2011)

In the 2004 mayoral election, Leandro beat Rogerio, winning a second, nonconsecutive term. Erivan, who had thrown the beans on Leandro his previous term, went to meet the mayor in his office. To his surprise, Leandro said that the MST could continue helping to oversee the eleven schools in their settlements. Leandro later told me that his four years out of office allowed him to "think, mature, and act more calmly." He had learned a vital lesson from the previous election about the importance of avoiding political conflict, and consequently, when he took office again in 2005, he agreed to let the MST participate in the co-governance of the municipal public schools. Rogerio also commented on this support: "Leandro is not stupid. He saw that working with the MST was offering some results for the schools. He saw that this work needed to be done, and he did not want to hurt his political relationships."

Leandro even allowed the MST to choose the principals of their eleven settlement schools, but like Rogerio, he required that they be his political supporters. Luckily for the MST, all of the teachers who had been sent to work in the MST's schools during Rogerio's administration had been sent there as punishment because they were Leandro's allies. These teachers had spent the previous four years attending MST teacher trainings and participating in MST-led teacher collectives. For example, Elizângela Maria Gomes da Silva was transferred to the far-off settlement school Catalunha (see Map 5.2) because of her family's allegiance to Leandro. When she first arrived, she was scared that the activists would be unfriendly toward her. However, as she attended MST teacher trainings and learned about the movement's educational program, she became excited to work with the MST education collective. When Leandro became the mayor, the MST selected her to be the principal of the settlement school. Elizangela explained:

I am no longer a teacher who just comes, teaches, and leaves. I have a very strong connection with the MST. And I see myself as a type of activist (*militante*). I am part of the
fight. . . . I am in Leandro's party, but today Leandro has a strong connection with the
MST, he lets teachers go to MST meetings and teacher trainings. . . . I know I am in this
position as a principal for a while, but this position is not mine. I was chosen because
I am a teacher and support Leandro, but also because I am linked to the MST; I wear an
MST shirt.[20]

Elizangela identified as an MST activist, while still being Leandro's political ally and confidant. Allowing for these multiple identities was critical: if
the MST had tried to convince teachers to switch their political allegiance,
the movement would have created enemies. As the MST interacted with the
teachers and talked to them about the movement's educational vision, these
teachers became "organic intellectuals" (Gramsci 1971, 5), in turn teaching
their students, colleagues, and the rest of the community about the struggle
for agrarian reform. Auzenir dos Santos, a school principal in 2011 also
aligned with Leandro, explained this process: "There are no teachers who
resist the MST's pedagogy. There was a teacher who arrived and had never
worked with the MST, and we talked to her and explained how the pedagogy works. We explained to her the goals of the movement."[21] Of course,
not all teachers are as strong advocates of the MST's educational proposal;
however, given the municipality's official support of the movement's educational program, none of these teachers refused to follow these practices.

During this period, Leandro continued to hire two MST leaders to co-
govern the eleven settlement schools. Again, he could easily find teachers
within his clientelist network to take on this task. One of those dedicated
activists was Rivanildo Adones, whose family members had been Leandro's
long-time supporters. In 2001, Rivanildo passed a teaching exam and became part of the municipal teaching network; however, since Rogerio was
the mayor and he supported Leandro, he was sent to a far-off school in an
MST settlement as punishment. Rivanildo said, "I was surprised when
I arrived. I did not accept that we had to learn the MST anthem, the protest
songs. . . . In the beginning, I used to complain."[22] But gradually he began to
appreciate the MST's pedagogical support. In 2002, to his surprise, he was
invited by the MST leadership to enroll in a bachelor's degree program in
the Pedagogy of Land at the Federal University of Rio Grande do Norte.
Rivanildo jumped at the offer to receive a college education, since he only
had a high school degree. "I became enchanted—this program really affected me. I wanted to be part of the MST, part of constructing a pedagogy
for the countryside."

In 2008, Jetro Gomes, who like his sister was affiliated with the left-leaning
PSB, ran against Leandro. In this election the MST did not openly campaign

Picture 5.1 A teacher in front of a municipal public school in Santa Maria da Boa Vista, Pernambuco, located in the MST settlement Catalunha. The teacher is wearing her official municipal teacher uniform, which incorporates the MST's flag. May 2011.
Courtesy of author

for either political candidate, as the movement had come to realize that gambling with party politics was not actually the most productive way to implement their educational goals—especially when both candidates were from the same family. After Leandro was elected for a second term, the MST demanded the creation of an office for *Educação do Campo* (Education of the Countryside) within the municipal Department of Education. By this time, in 2009, *Educação do Campo* was a well-known educational initiative across the country (see Chapter 3). Santa Maria would be the first municipality in Pernambuco with an office for *Educação do Campo*, which would bring the town national prestige. Leandro agreed to create the office, but he demanded that it provide services to all of the rural schools in the municipality, another sixty or so schools. Rivanildo was hired as the head of this new department. Reflecting on this political appointment, Rivanildo said, "It helped the MST that I had supported Leandro because then Leandro was more open to them."

In July 2009, I attended the first municipal conference for *Educação do Campo*, funded by Leandro's administration. All of the teachers that worked for the municipality were required to attend. The MST education collective organized the event, inviting national MST leaders and other proponents of *Educação do Campo* to speak to the hundreds of teachers. The invited speakers included Edla Soarez, who wrote the *Educação do Campo* Federal Guidelines that were passed in 2001 (see Chapter 3); Ademar Bogo, a prominent MST national leader and poet; and Rubneuza Leandro, the head of the MST state education sector in Pernambuco. For three days the teachers of Santa Maria listened to the speakers, who lectured about capitalist exploitation, socialist alternatives, and the philosophical underpinnings of *Educação do Campo*.

In April 2011, still during Leandro's third term, I attended a meeting of the "collective of school principals"—one of the MST's most important institutional spaces for supporting educational change in Santa Maria. This meeting was sponsored by Leandro's administration, but two MST activists were leading the meeting, hired by the municipality for this task. All of the principals of the eleven settlement schools were required to attend, and their transportation and food were paid for by the municipal government. The meeting took place in the municipal school São Benedito. To start off the meeting, the students at the school presented a *mística*, with music and poetry about living in the countryside. Each of the principals had to present a "diagnostic" of his or her school—an analysis of the advances and challenges of implementing the MST's educational program. Then, the two MST leaders coordinating the meeting discussed the upcoming Third Seminar for *Educação do Campo* and how the principals could prepare their teachers for the seminar. Finally, the whole group planned for some upcoming activities: a week of contentious protest to promote agrarian reform, the decoration of the schools and settlements, the settlement schools' participation in the city's anniversary celebration, and community meetings to debate the schools' Pedagogical-Political Projects (PPPs, School Mission Statements). The meeting that day was both an educational meeting, helping to plan the educational work of the schools, and an organizing meeting, planning the MST's activities and events for the upcoming year.

I heard a range of perspectives about why Leandro, part of an extremely right-leaning political party, supported the MST's educational program. Návia Silva, a principal in the opposition party, said, "If Leandro did not embrace this proposal, he would have been hurt in the elections because the MST would go out en masse against him."[23] In contrast, Rivanildo claimed that "Leandro thought the MST's educational work was interesting. He ended up agreeing with the people in the movement that it was a good proposal." The view of Kátia Medrado, one of the Secretaries of Education during Leandro's second term, fell somewhere in the middle: "People critique the MST, but it is not possible to ignore the movement, it is very strong. . . . We maintained a peaceful coexistence. . . . Leandro never felt threatened by the MST's educational philosophy, because his concern was to serve the citizens of the municipality."[24]

In May 2011, I asked Leandro himself why he endorsed the MST's educational proposal, given its overtly Marxist character. He responded:

> The movement has its goals of agrarian reform . . . invasion,[25] production, and resistance. But after some time the MST realized the settlement was already created and they could not invade more; they had to develop the settlements, not just in agriculture but also in education. . . . It was our responsibility to offer people education, so we brought together these interests. . . . I always work with the MST's intellectual leaders. I invite them here to offer lectures to our teachers.
>
> [RT: I know a lot of the MST's intellectual leaders, and they are all Marxists. Why are you financing these lectures when they do not support you during elections, and you are in a right-wing party?]
>
> I think it is an evolution on our part. I do not agree with the Marxist line, the more radical line of seeing the world. But also I cannot ignore the MST when the settlements have a relationship with the movement. I do not want to create conflict.

As many of the interviewees indicated, a principal goal for Leandro was maintaining and expanding his network of supporters. If letting the MST participate in the school system avoided conflicts, he supported these initiatives. In Gramscian terms, this was a concession that Leandro had to offer the movement, given the MST's force in the settlements and among the teachers. The MST activists' ability to implement their educational goals in more than sixty public schools increased their ability to win over more allies for the agrarian reform struggle—by extending their "war of position" to new parts of the municipality.

The MST statewide education sector invested in leadership development in Santa Maria throughout the 2000s, both for youth living in the settlements and sympathetic teachers. One of the movement's strategies was to offer Pedagogy of Land bachelor's degree programs in the region, through PRONERA. I met dozens of teachers and young activists in Santa Maria who obtained college degrees through these MST–university partnerships. As Sydney Carvalho, the Secretary of Education in Santa Maria under Jetro Gomes, explained, "The MST became a model. They were very well connected and organized. They have been able to get university programs offered to the people in our town. The government of Santa Maria has never been able to convince a university to offer a college program in our region."[26] As Sydney suggested, the MST had more capacity than the municipal government itself to deliver higher educational access to Santa Maria citizens. The teachers and youth who enrolled in these programs quickly became closer to the movement.

When I was in Santa Maria in 2011, the head of the regional education collective was Adailto Cardoso.[27] Adailto grew up in a small Afro-descendent (*quilombo*) community, located between two large MST settlements. Adailto became active in the movement in the mid-2000s, after he graduated high school and the MST education collective invited him to enroll in a Pedagogy of Land baccalaureate program at the University of Pernambuco, in the neighboring city of Petrolina. Although he entered the program merely to earn a university degree, through this four-year program he learned about the MST's struggle and began to identify with the movement. Along with several other women in this program, he became active in the regional education collective. As activists such as Teresneide and Erivan took on statewide and national movement tasks, Adailto and this new generation of activists became the leaders of the regional MST education collective in Santa Maria.

Family Feuds: Leandro and Jetro Vie for Power (2009–2011)

Between 2009 and 2011, there was an ongoing court battle between Leandro Duarte and his cousin Jetro Gomes, resulting in four political transitions in three years. The municipality suffered as a result, with hundreds of principals fired and teachers transferred every time Jetro or Leandro assumed office. When I spoke with the teachers and principals in the schools, everyone was openly critical of these transitions. However, while in most public schools in Santa Maria the transitions caused turmoil, in the eleven schools on MST settlements the tensions were less acute. As Auzenir explained, "The principals changing caused a lot of conflict in other schools. . . . In our school there was no conflict; we try to separate out politics from the school. . . . The MST helped a lot, trying to focus us on coordinating *Educação do Campo*." Interestingly, despite the overtly political orientation of schools on MST settlements—with the movement's anthem sung each day, courses on the history of agrarian reform, and student participation in protests each year—the teachers at these schools consider themselves above politics, in this case understood as party politics.

When Jetro finally won the court battle in 2011, he fired all of the principals of the seventy schools and transferred the teachers. However, Jetro continued to support the MST's educational program, funding the municipality's third seminar for *Educação do Campo*. Adailto summarized for me the nature of the MST's educational struggle in Santa Maria:

Our hardest challenge was to win over the municipality of Santa Maria da Boa Vista; it was a process of struggle. What we have today is a result of a struggle since 1995. We did not win over the municipality from one day to the next. . . . The people we work with are very affected by this political party question; it is hereditary, an issue that comes from our roots and is part of the culture of the municipality. . . . But we have struggled and we have won over all of our [school] principals—through a lot of work. And the government might have the right to say a certain person cannot be principal because they did not vote for their party, but we have our own autonomy to not accept just anyone that voted for that party to enter our areas. We have to reach a consensus.

The MST's attempt to implement their educational goals in Santa Maria is not simple; it involves a complex compromise with local political officials. Adailto refers to the political party question as something hereditary in the municipality, part of the culture. Even for a dedicated MST leader, "clientelist politics is taken for granted; it is normal (and normalized) politics" (Auyero 2000, 179). Nonetheless, through a slow and continual war of position that garnered the consent of a range of civil society groups for the movement's educational program, local activists were able to convince oppositional mayors to support their contentious co-governance of the public school system.[28]

EDUCATION AND LEADERSHIP—BASE DIVIDES
IN ÁGUA PRETA

Água Preta is a municipality located in the eastern end of the state of Pernambuco, a two-hour drive from the capital city of Recife. Água Preta is 350 miles east of Santa Maria da Boa Vista and although it is only a sixth of its geographical area, their populations are similar in size, with Água Preta containing 33,095 residents in 2010, 43.7 percent classified as rural (IBGE 2011). A different world than the semiarid *sertão*, Água Preta (Black Water) is in the heart of the southern sugarcane region southern forest (*mata sul*), with a long history of forced and semiforced labor. There has never been a small-farming tradition in the *mata sul*, as large sugarcane plantations have always dominated the economy in the region. On the bus from Recife to Água Preta for the first time, I was taken aback by the miles of sugarcane that lined the highway for the last thirty minutes of the drive. The same extreme wet seasons that allow sugarcane to thrive in the *mata sul* also bring frequent flooding. The large river that runs through the center of Água Preta flooded in 2010, destroying hundreds of houses.

In Água Preta everyone plants sugarcane; however, it is the owners of the sugarcane factories (*usinas*) that wield power.[29] Sugarcane production dates back to the era of Portuguese colonialism, when labor-intensive sugarcane mills (*engenhos*) that relied on slave labor were common. This system of milling sugar on each individual plantation only changed in the late 1880s, with the end of the slavery and the rise of the *usinas*, which had the capacity to both process and distil huge amounts of sugarcane.[30] During the dictatorship, between 1964 and 1984, there was much more government assistance to large-scale sugarcane producers in the northeast of Brazil and a concentration in land ownership due to technological modernization. This led to a boom in sugarcane production. However, by the late 1980s the sugarcane industry was in crisis, which was exactly when that the MST began to organize.[31]

In the early 1990s, the MST convinced hundreds of struggling sugarcane workers to occupy unproductive plantations throughout the region. These occupations succeeded in pressuring the federal government to redistribute much of this land to the occupying families. Less than a decade later, there were dozens of agrarian reform settlements in the *mata sul*, with the majority in Água Preta. With the encouragement of the MST leadership, and the help of government loans, many of the families living on these settlements began to diversify their crops with fruits and other produce. The MST leadership encouraged families to invest in bananas and coconuts, which they thought would have a good market return in the region. The leadership even obtained funding for a small candy-processing factory, which turned bananas into sweets that could be sold for higher prices (Wolford 2010b). The dozens of agrarian reform settlements in Água Preta, and the alternative economic practices that developed in the late 1990s, made the municipality an MST stronghold in Pernambuco.

The Partisan Politics of the Sugarcane Region

Although Água Preta and Santa Maria da Boa Vista have very different agrarian histories, the clientelistic relationships between politicians and citizens are uncannily similar. I learned this first-hand when I went to the home of Mayor Eduardo Coutinho (1997–2004, 2009–2012), in July 2011. As we turned into Eduardo's driveway, after miles on almost-impassable muddy roads, we saw a group of people waiting outside of his gate. I was escorted to Eduardo's office, and he asked me to take a seat and wait while he "attended to the people outside." The first person who entered was a woman who said her son was sick, and she asked Eduardo if he could help. Eduardo told his assistant to give her 50 *reais* (in 2011 about 30 US dollars). Eduardo said to the woman, "It is only a little, but it is from the heart, so you can buy some groceries." After the woman left, two men came inside. The first told

Eduardo he had walked barefoot for four hours to ask for his help. The other said he needed money for his family. Eduardo told his assistant to give each of them 30 *reais*. After they left, he turned to me and said, "I know that it should not happen this way, but I have to help people when I can."[32] The citizens of Água Preta rely on Eduardo, the mayor and a major patron in the city, for material survival.

In contrast to Santa Maria, the electoral struggle in Água Preta is not within one family but, rather, between several different powerful families. Eudo Magalhães was the mayor of Água Preta from 1989 to 1992, at that time a member of the Democratic Workers' Party (PDT). In 1992, Eudo was not allowed to run due to rules about consecutive term limits, so he supported the candidacy of his nephew César Magalhães. With his uncle's support, César beat their family's political rival, Eduardo Coutinho, the grandson of one of the largest landowners in the state. During this period, rural union advocate and former governor of Pernambuco Miguel Arraes, of the Brazilian Socialist Party (PSB), was extremely popular in this region. Although Eduardo's family was historically associated with the Brazilian military party (ARENA, which became the PFL in 1985), Eduardo decided to enter the PSB in 1995. As he put it, "The problem is that the sugarcane region is more linked to the left, so this is where everyone was leaning."[33] In other words, Eduardo joined the PSB due to a general left-leaning political turn in the region.

In 1996, César stepped down so his uncle Eudo could run against Eduardo again. The bitter election ended in Eduardo's victory and a temporary ban on Eudo's participation in politics for alleged involvement in several assassinations linked to drug trafficking.[34] Unable to run for mayor in the next election, Eudo supported Paulo Barreto, a local businessman. Paulo explained, "My father was always linked to Eduardo's father, but when Eudo said he would support us, we became his allies."[35] Running on the PMDB (Brazilian Democratic Movement Party) ticket, Paulo lost to Eduardo in 2000, then beat him four years later in 2004; he then lost again in 2008 while running as a member of the more left-leaning Republican Party (PR). The reason Paulo switched parties, he explained, is "because of the legacy of Miguel Arraes and the PSB in the region, and Lula's popularity, which was making everyone vote for the left." Despite these political calculations, Paulo lost the mayoral election in 2012 and Eduardo was elected for a third term.

None of the mayors I spoke with, except Eduardo, claimed that his party defined who he was as a politician. Paulo explained, "Left and right wing does not mean anything [in Água Preta]. What exists are individuals; no one votes for the parties." Eudo's nephew César, who was the youngest mayor ever elected in Pernambuco, also went into detail about this political

Table 5.2 POLITICAL TRANSITIONS IN ÁGUA PRETA, 1988–2012

Years	Mayor (Party)	Comments	Secretaries of Education
1988–1992	Eudo Magalhães (PDT)	Previously PFL, later PR	Maria Celha Negeira de Goiás
1993–1996	César Magalhães (PDT)	Eudo's nephew; twenty-one years old when elected	Sebastião Sales; Ines Senna
1997–2004	Eduardo Coutinho (PSB)	Left the PFL to join the PMDB and in 1995 the PSB. Family owns largest sugarcane plantation in the region and is historically linked to the PFL	Julieta Pontual; Rosana Lopes de Melo
2005–2008	Paulo Barreto (PMDB)	Wins with the support of Eudo Magalhães. During this term Paulo Barreto switches to the PR, due to the dominance of the "left" in the region	Ines Senna
2009–2012	Eduardo Coutinho (PSB)	Third, nonconsecutive term	Albertina Maria de Melo Tenório

culture: "To be sincere, in the rural interior the dispute for power is much more personal than it is political. It is about fights between people much more than about ideologies."[36] César claimed that Eduardo only joined a left party because "my family occupied the political space on the right." Eduardo, on the other hand, claimed to be "different" than the rest of his family and genuinely support the PSB. Table 5.2 summarizes these electoral shifts in Água Preta and the names of the municipal Secretaries of Education during each government administration.[37]

Mayors' Reluctant Support for the MST

By the mid-2000s there were over thirty agrarian reform settlements in Água Preta—organized by both the MST and other rural social movements. I spoke to all of the mayors of Água Preta since 1988, who all expressed support of the idea of agrarian reform. However, they were also critical of the fact, they claimed, that once families received land they did not always grow food and often sold their land. For example, Eudo said, "The MST and agrarian reform should exist . . . however, there are people who are part of these invasions who have nothing to do with the countryside, and they get land so they can sell it." Nevertheless, Eudo assured me that while he was in office he tried to respond to all of the MST's demands: "The MST came to ask for transport and money, and I would help them ... it was just to make them happy, to avoid conflict." Paulo Barreto, who was in a right-leaning party when he was elected in 2004, explained, "There were no conflicts between us ... whenever MST leaders came to ask for anything we attended to their needs, for example, offering them transportation for an event."

Eduardo Coutinho had the most complex relationship with the MST. He was part of the PSB, a left-leaning party that was aligned with the MST at the state level. Eduardo also frequently funded MST events; however, when I spoke with Eduardo, he did not express complete sympathy for agrarian reform or the MST. He said that if land was unproductive, then it should be redistributed, but he was openly critical of recent MST occupations of productive land. Eduardo claimed that his financial support of the MST did not necessarily mean that he agreed with the movement: "I have always had a good dialogue with the MST. Why shouldn't I support a meeting of MST youth? I attend to the needs of the evangelical church, the local soccer team, a guy who wants to go to the beach, why not fund an MST youth gathering?" Clearly, Eduardo understood his relationship with the MST as similar to his other clientelistic bonds in the municipality. When I asked him why the opposition candidate, Paulo, also supported the MST, he responded, "In order to minimize conflict with the MST. It is the philosophy of 'Good Neighbors.'" These interviews illustrated the mayors' same general orientation toward the MST: they sought to avoid conflict, supporting the MST in some ways and keeping most of their major criticisms to themselves.

The MST's Educational Struggle in Água Preta (1995–1999)

Almost all of Água Preta's thirty agrarian reform settlements are in areas that the local people still refer to as sugar mills (*engenhos*) despite the fact that the mills themselves are no longer functioning. In the early 1900s, many of the owners of these sugarcane plantations had set up schools for the children of their employees. However, when workers started to be displaced by technological innovations and moved to the city centers, the plantation owners transferred the responsibility for these schools over to the municipal government. Consequently, in this region (unlike Santa Maria), when the MST began to occupy land, many of the properties already had functioning schools. During the late 1990s and early 2000s, local MST activists were able to convince the mayors of Água Preta to let the movement participate in the governance of the schools. This was not immediate but, rather, a gradual process of garnering the consent of each new set of mayors, secretaries of education, and teachers in the municipality for the MST's educational program.

Founding an MST Education Collective in the Mata Sul

Mauricéia Lima is one of the founders of the MST education collective in the *mata sul*. In 1995, she graduated from a local high school, which she described as "basically having a doctorate in this region." That year her brother-in-law took part in an MST land occupation in Água Preta, and he reached out to her to visit the camp and teach the young children living there how to read and write. Mauricéia went and, in her words, became "enchanted" by the organization of the camp. A few weeks later, statewide MST leader Jaime Amorim visited the camp. He saw Mauricéia's work and asked her to come to Caruaru to visit the MST's state headquarters for a week. Mauricéia ended up staying for four months, learning about the movement's educational program. After four months, activists in the MST state education sector asked Mauricéia to return to Água Preta to found a regional education collective.

What did founding an MST education collective mean? In Água Preta during this period there were dozens of MST activists focused on organizing land occupations, coordinating the camps, and setting up alternative agricultural initiatives in the settlements. However, there was not yet a collective of MST leaders thinking about how to provide educational access to the members of the movement. Mauricéia said that by 1996 there were fourteen settlements in the *mata sul*, with five public schools. Mauricéia's job was to "find out about the schools, what the teachers were like, and the conflicts." Her assessment of the teachers was that they were scared of the movement and had a lot of negative stereotypes: "They thought MST activists were a bunch of thieves and they would call the children [in the settlement schools] thieves also." She reached out to the teachers and tried to show them another side of the movement. She also visited the occupied camps, searching for people who could help her in this educational work.

In 1998, UNESCO partnered with the MST to organize literacy courses for ten thousand adults in eighteen different states in Brazil, with resources from the Ministry of Education. Unintentionally, this national literacy program strengthened the MST education collective in Água Preta. Mauricéia found dozens of youth in the municipality who wanted to earn incomes as literacy trainers, and who quickly became dedicated MST activists through this program. Elienai da Silva and Flavinha Tereza were two young women living in the region, who became members of the MST education sector through this literacy program.[38] In 1997, Elienai was seventeen and had just separated from her abusive husband. She moved back in with her father, who lived on an agrarian reform settlement. Mauricéia reached out to dozens of local leaders like Elienai's father, asking if anyone was interested in being part of an adult education program. Elienai's father suggested that Elienai join the program; as she was unemployed with no income, she agreed. In January 1998, Elienai was sent to a statewide meeting in Caruaru to prepare for this literacy program. She remembered "falling in love" with the MST during this meeting: "I had never seen *mística*. I fell in love with the MST through *mística*. I was captivated. I saw that the MST was fighting to help poor people without opportunities and who were living in misery."

Flavinha had her first contact with the MST several months later.[39] Flavinha was from the city center of Ribeirão, a municipality in the *mata sul* thirty minutes from Água Preta. She did not know anything about the MST, but she had a friend who had met Mauricéia and told her about the possibility of being paid as a literacy trainer. That same month of January 1998, the MST was planning a National Meeting of Adult and Youth Educators (ENEJA) in the city of Recife, Pernambuco, with eight hundred participants. This conference would be an opportunity to discuss the MST's educational approach with all of the literacy teachers in the program. Flavinha attended the conference and quickly became friends with Elienai. Over the next few months, Elienai and Flavinha taught in the adult education program and through this process became dedicated MST activists. The MST statewide education sector invested in the schooling of these local MST leaders, enrolling them in the movement's high school and bachelor's degree programs. Through these formal education programs, Elienai and Flavinha deepened their knowledge of the MST's educational program and their dedication to promoting these practices in the *mata sul*.

Collaborating with Educational Officials in Água Preta

During the late 1990s and early 2000s, as more land occupations took place in the sugarcane region, additional schools were constructed in agrarian reform settlements. Together, the activists in the regional MST education collective managed to visit all of these schools, talking to the teachers about the movement's pedagogical approach and encouraging them to attend MST seminars. Between 1998 and 2005, the two Secretaries of Education were Ines Senna and Julieta Pontual (see Table 5.2). Both Ines and Juliana were initially skeptical of the MST. Ines said, "I never had any contact with an MST activist. I thought they were terrorists, ignorant. But after becoming Secretary of Education I began having contact with them and I changed. I thought they were marvelous . . . there was nothing they asked for that I did not give to them."[40] According to Ines, she allowed local MST activists to visit the schools and organize community–school gatherings.

She even gave teachers time off to attend MST teacher trainings. Ines was supportive of these activities because they improved the quality of education in Água Preta.

Julieta also spoke positively about the movement. She had attended an education event herself in the MST's Paulo Freire Training Center in Caruaru and was impressed with its organization. In particular, she emphasized the dedication and seriousness of Rubneuza, the head of the MST education sector in Pernambuco. "Rubneuza and other MST activists were already working in the municipality when I arrived . . . I always supported them. I let them sleep in the schools when there was an event in the settlements. . . . I became very good friends with Rubneuza."[41] Rubneuza confirmed this support, saying, "There were never any conflicts with the government during this period. Julieta was there as the Secretary of Education and she was very open." However, other MST activists described the situation slightly differently. For example, Flavinha said, "The Secretaries of Education do not fight with us; they pretend to be sympathizers, allowing teachers to go to our gatherings, but in private they tell the teachers, 'You do not have to go if you do not want to.'" While the Secretaries of Education claimed to embrace the MST's educational approach, activists insisted that the officials were simply tolerant of the initiatives. Regardless of these contrasting perspectives, it is evident that the MST activists had at least some degree of political opening throughout this period.

Winning Over Teachers

Although teachers in Água Preta were initially skeptical of the movement, there were a few who became passionate activists. Brasilina Barbosa da Silva had been working in her school for years before the area was occupied and turned into an agrarian reform settlement. Her parents were renting a house near the old sugar mill when the MST occupation took place, and because of this, her family had the right to a plot of land in the settlement with the other families. Although Brasilina was initially scared of the MST, she "began to make friends and get to know the movement's leaders."[42] Brasilina was soon invited to an MST teacher training that transformed her perspective, as she began to understand the movement's pedagogical proposal and participate in its educational struggle. Similarly, Sonia Lopes dos Santos had been teaching in the same school for twenty-three years when I talked to her in 2011. In the late 1990s, the MST had occupied the land surrounding her school. She explained, "The MST activists came to have a conversation with us in the school. They said, now this community is going to be a landless (*sem terra*) community, and they put a MST flag up in the school."[43] Although Sonia worried about what would happen, over time, as activists kept visiting her school and offering their support, she became sympathetic to the MST's educational program. She began to attend MST teacher trainings and learn about the struggle for *Educação do Campo*.

Finally, Norma Maria Azevedo da Silva was another teacher in Água Preta who became an open advocate of the MST's educational project. She recalled her first MST event, a gathering of children living in settlements and camps (*sem terrinha*) from across the state:

> We brought sixty kids from our region and there were three thousand children at the gathering. . . . What impressed me the most was the march on the last day. We walked to the government's palace, and there were emergency vehicles and cold water waiting for us. It was very well organized . . . in the end three children were allowed to talk to the governor and give him their educational demands.[44]

Norma was impressed with both the organization of the march and the power the MST had to pressure the governor to meet with the children. In 2009, Norma was appointed to a new job in the municipal Department of Education as one of four "rural coordinators," taking on the responsibilities of a principal for a dozen small, multigrade rural schools. She continued to be an open advocate of the MST within the government. These political openings and the persistence of the MST education sector was slowly shifting the perspective of the municipal teaching body toward the movement. As in Santa Maria, it seemed likely that the MST's contentious co-governance of the municipal public schools would continue to move forward in this region.

Losing Moral and Intellectual Leadership (2000–2011)

Between the late 1990s and the early 2000s, the relationship between the MST regional leadership in the *mata sul* and the families living in the settlements transformed. In 1999, international sugarcane prices began to rise, after a decade of decline, due to lower levels of production in India and Cuba. In 2001, there was also a drought in the sugarcane region of São Paulo, resulting in more demand for sugarcane from the northeast. Then, in 2003, President Lula took office and increased investment in ethanol production through subsidies to sugarcane producers. Sugarcane thus became even more valuable as a source of ethanol. Consequently, by 2003, the sugarcane prices in Brazil had shot up and people all over the Pernambucan *mata sul* began growing sugarcane again. This included the families on agrarian reform settlements. The owners of the sugarcane factories promised these families an immediate cash return on their crops, which was more persuasive than the MST's economic initiatives (Wolford 2010b).[45]

Conflicts immediately emerged between the MST leadership and these settlement families. As Wolford (2010b) describes, this divide was part of a larger cultural struggle about what it meant to live on an agrarian reform settlement. During the previous years, the MST had convinced many sugarcane workers living in settlements to diversify their crops, through a lot of cultural and political work that attempted to associate sugarcane production with exploitation and diversified agroecological farming with being a good agrarian reform citizen. However, when sugarcane prices skyrocketed, many of the MST's economic initiatives were abandoned. Historically dominant cultural understandings of agricultural production as a means for economic survival reemerged. As Flavinha explained, "In Água Preta the sugarcane culture is very strong . . . people plant sugarcane because the harvest allows for a reliable family income."

Deep divisions grew between families who saw sugar as the most viable means of economic survival and the MST leadership who tried to convince the farmers that this form of economic production was exploitative. Wolford (2010b) writes that "production decisions became a political battlefield. MST leaders argued that planting bananas and subsistence crops signified a higher political consciousness, and the settlers came to equate planting sugarcane with going against the movement's wishes" (181). Families left the movement because "sugarcane had been presented and come to be seen as antithetical to MST politics" (188). The growing divide between the MST leadership and its base also signaled to the movement that continuing to invest in these settlements would be futile. When I talked to statewide MST leaders in 2011, they expressed a sense of pessimism about the region. Jaime said, "The sugarcane region is our oldest region, but the development of activists there is very hard." Rubneuza expressed this opinion even more strongly: "The profile of the people in the area reflects the culture of sugar mills. There is no social organization in the population, only oligarchies . . . people are afraid of political participation. There is a culture of violence."

The MST leadership continued to invest energy in maintaining the movement's political relationships in Água Preta, but the activists gradually began to distance themselves from the settlements.[46] As local MST activist Alex Santos described, "The MST leadership has relationships with the mayors and we can get money for gatherings from them. But we no longer discuss agrarian reform with the families in the settlements." Alex believed that this increasing divide between the leadership and the base of the movement would also have repercussions for their political relationships, because "politicians like Eduardo Coutinho only care about the MST if the families are aligned with the leadership." Eduardo himself alluded to this reality: "I still have a relationship with the MST, but the MST has lost a lot of society's support." Although in 2011 Eduardo was still supporting the MST financially, he had certainly noticed the lack of moral and intellectual leadership the MST activists had in the settlements.

Community Resistance to the MST's Educational Program

When Eduardo Coutinho took office in 2009, he appointed Albertinha Tenório as his Secretary of Education. Albertinha, like Eduardo's previous Secretary of Education, was open to the MST's educational proposal.[47] In 2009, Albertinha agreed to host a seminar on *Educação do Campo* in the municipality, organized by the regional MST education collective. As Flavinha described, "In 2009 our relationship with the municipality matured and we had a seminar on *Educação do Campo*, paid for by the government of Água Preta." During this seminar, the two keynote speakers were Rubneuza Leandro, MST statewide leader, and Edla Soarez, the writer and sponsor of the *Educação do Campo* federal guidelines. Albertinha said she was enthusiastic about the opportunity to host the seminar and she raved about the importance of a visit from Edla, who was also the president of the National Union of Municipal Secretaries of Education (UNDIME). It is unlikely that such a prestigious visitor would have come to Água Preta without the MST's political maneuvering. All of the teachers in the municipal school system were required to attend the seminar and learn about *Educação do Campo*. This increased recognition for the movement as an educational authority.

Despite these political openings, in 2009 local MST leaders were encountering resistance to their educational program from the families living in the agrarian reform settlements. Albertinha alluded to these difficulties:

> When I became the Secretary of Education, the MST came to talk to me about the schools in the countryside.... We try to give the MST whatever they want.... However, something I realized is that even though we are open to this, it is often the community that does not want the MST in the schools.... One time the parents came here to say they did not want a certain teacher in their school because she was teaching the children to be *sem terra* [landless].

Albertinha claimed to be an advocate of the MST's educational proposal; however, she was also cautious about her support when she observed the parents in the settlements rejecting these ideas.

The teacher that Albertinha said the parents complained about was Elienai, one of the original members of the MST regional education collective. In 2009, Elienai took a civil service exam and became part of the official municipal teaching network. As she was a well-known MST activist, Albertinha assigned her to a school in an agrarian reform settlement. Elienai, with permission from the government, began to incorporate some of the MST's educational practices into her classroom: forming student collectives, teaching songs about *Educação do Campo*, and discussing the history of agrarian reform. However, after a few weeks the parents began to criticize Elienai and her teaching method as bringing "the movement" into the school. Although many of these families had previously supported the MST, it had been years since the MST leadership had visited their community. This had produced a rejection of all activities associated with the movement. Maria Jose da Silva, the rural coordinator overseeing the school, explained:

> When I went to Elienai's school, the parents told me that she was teaching the "movement," and it was polemic. We had to meet with Elienai, and we had to tell her to follow the municipal educational proposal . . . for me Elienai was forming critical citizens who know their rights, but for [the parents], she was creating troublemakers.[48]

Maria Jose claimed to admire the MST's educational program; however, she said the government could no longer allow Elienai to use these pedagogies because of the lack of parental support.

Elienai was open about the difficulties that the MST was facing in the region. She explained that over time the MST had become more absent from the settlements and that this had affected the movement's ability to implement its educational program. She added:

> Another issue that I see is that, right now, if we had a teacher in a settlement school that we did not like, we could not change this, because we no longer have the support of our base. With the help of the base we could have a protest in the city, but we do not have this support. Today, if we wanted to have a protest about municipal education in Àgua Preta, bringing people to the streets would be difficult.

With few activists, little money, a pessimistic outlook about organizing, and too many other activities, the MST's local support—described by Gramsci as a movement's moral and intellectual leadership—was disappearing. According to Elienai, there were settlements in Água Preta that MST activists had not visited for several years.

In the public schools, these lost opportunities were evident. When I visited Água Preta in 2011, teachers who had previously supported the MST did not express resentment but a longing for the movement's presence. For example, Brasilina said, "The MST has to be more present; they have to talk to people and open their eyes because when the MST is not here in the schools, no one participates . . . I feel alone. A collective of people needs to support my work." Brasilina explained that in contrast to the period between 2000 and 2005, the majority of the teachers in her school have not had any contact with the MST. When I interviewed Sonia, I asked her what aspects of the MST's pedagogical proposal she was implementing in her school. She simply responded, "There needs to be more MST participation, the teachers need more support." Sonia was finding it difficult to implement any of the MST's educational ideas on her own. Thus, even the teachers that the MST previously won over, teachers who already attended dozens of MST teacher trainings, felt unable to support the MST's educational program without the movement's collective leadership. Even if they were able, in 2011 it was unclear if the families in these settlements would permit them to do so.

CONCLUSION

In Santa Maria da Boa Vista, between 1997 and 2012, MST activists never transformed the clientelistic political regime. The same family maintained power, using the school system to distribute government jobs to loyal citizens. Nonetheless, during this period the MST education collective worked with all of these mayors—who were part of oppositional clientelistic networks—and obtained resources for supporting their educational program in the municipal public school system. Rather than attempt to take power through electoral politics, the MST engaged in a Gramscian war of position, garnering the consent of multiple actors in the municipality for their educational and agrarian vision. Through this process, the MST education collective expanded to include many teachers who began to identify as MST activists. Despite the fact that public schools continued to function to maintain the power of the same elite family, these schools were also spaces that promoted the MST's alternative hegemonic project.

In Água Preta, the same clientelistic political relationships and the low level of capacity for educational governance also offered the MST countless opportunities to participate in the public school system. Even in 2009, when local MST activists were facing increasing difficulties in the region, the municipal Department of Education was willing to host a seminar about the MST's educational approach. However, in the settlements themselves the MST did not have enough moral and intellectual leadership to capitalize on these openings. This was not a problem specific to the MST education sector; it was representative of a general disconnect between the MST leadership and the families living in agrarian reform settlements. Despite the government's willingness to work with MST activists, it was the divide between the movement's base and the leadership, and the subsequent decline in local social movement infrastructure, that obstructed the MST's co-governance of the public schools.

There are two major lessons from this chapter, which build on the previous case study of Rio Grande do Sul. The first lesson is that government ideology does not determine social movement outcomes; to the contrary, it is possible for social movements to implement their goals within state institutions even in least likely contexts, such as conservative and clientelistic political regimes. The case of Santa Maria, where one family has maintained political power for most of the history of the municipality, should have been an impossible location for activists to promote their educational program. Nonetheless, the municipal government in Santa Maria is also not as competent as the state government in Rio Grande do Sul. This offered opportunities for activists to participate in educational governance. Abers and Keck (2013) describe a similar process of noninstitutional actors gaining both capabilities and recognition, or "practical authority," to influence the behavior of state actors (19). Although in this case I am describing a large and contentious social movement, not individual actors, the MST's participation in schools followed a similar process. The prestige that the MST's educational proposal brought to the municipality, the professional development opportunities and educational access the movement offered citizens, and activists' daily problem solving in the schools contributed to the state's capacity to offer a higher quality of education. Despite the MST's incorporation of practices in the schools that questioned the power of local elites, these short-term benefits for the state and the recognition the movement was receiving nationally were more important than the long-term effects of this consciousness-raising process.

A second lesson is that the MST's promotion of this institutional change is always contingent on activists' ability to garner the consent of diverse civil society actors. The first group that local MST leaders had to win over in Santa Maria and Água Preta were the teachers, and the movement did this both by educating the teachers about the movement's pedagogical approach and helping teachers in their daily tasks in the schools. Thus, moral and intellectual leadership is not simply ideological; it is about resolving people's daily problems and integrating them into alternative social practices. The principal and teacher collectives that the MST organized in the schools illustrated the benefits of collectivity, rather than individualism. Similarly, the teacher trainings and the high school and university programs the movement offered allowed the teachers to prefigure the MST's educational vision in practice. Importantly, in Santa Maria the families in the settlements were also allied with the MST leadership, and they supported the movement's work in the schools.

In contrast, in Água Preta, there was a growing rift between the MST leadership and the settlement families, due to the different visions of how to engage in economic production in the region. This led to a decline of social movement infrastructure, and more specifically, a decrease in resources, organization, and local collective leadership. Consequently, although state officials and teachers in Água Preta were open to the MST's educational program, the settlement families rejected this proposal. Importantly, these chapters illustrate that movements can participate in the contentious co-governance of state institutions under a diversity of political and economic contexts, but only with robust, collective leadership.

In the final empirical chapter, I analyze one of the MST's most impressive examples of social movement co-governance: a network of high schools built in settlements in Ceará in 2010 and 2011. This chapter shows how the national context, while not determining of regional trajectories, directly influences local relations between activists and state actors. Chapter 6 will also illustrate the evolution of the MST's educational program, what these practices look like in the contemporary context, and how the contentious relationship between movement activists and state actors continues to characterize these initiatives.

CHAPTER 6

Ceará

The Influence of National Advocacy
on Regional Trajectories

Here is the thing: the state government was never open to Educação do Campo, but the Ministry of Education was, and it had the resources to be used to this end.

—Susana, *official in the Ceará state Department of Education*

The knowledge we have accumulated in this struggle for Educação do Campo is how to construct socialism. We have no doubt that our project is socialist. We have to plant the seeds and the fertilizer and cultivate this objective now so socialism can flourish one day. Just because we live in a capitalist world does not mean we cannot dream with socialism.

—Maria de Jesus Santos, *national leader in MST Education Sector*

By 2010, the MST education sector had been engaging with the Brazilian public school system for almost three decades. At the national level, the most important educational program the movement developed was the National Program for Education in Areas of Agrarian Reform (PRONERA), created in 1998, which funds adult education, high school, and university degree programs for citizens living in areas of agrarian reform. Also in 1998, the MST began discussing a proposal for all working-class populations in the countryside, what became known as *Educação do Campo* (Education of the Countryside). In 2001, the government approved national educational guidelines supporting *Educação do Campo*, and in 2004, the Workers' Party (PT) administration established an office for *Educação do Campo* in the Ministry of Education.

It is impossible to understand the MST's regional educational struggles without taking into consideration this broader context. Partially, this is because all of the MST activists that became protagonists implementing the movement's educational program in their schools have taken part in at least one of these national initiatives. Thus, the educational access that the MST leadership won at the national level directly increased the strength of regional MST education collectives. Furthermore, MST activists in different states across Brazil learned from each other's experiences during this thirty-year period, refining how they were implementing the movement's educational ideas in their own context. The MST leadership accumulated so much knowledge about education, and had so many inroads within the multiple levels and institutions of the state, that they transformed the terrain of educational struggle.

In Brazil, subnational governments do not act in isolation from the federal government; to the contrary, the state consists precisely of this complex relationship between municipal, state, and federal governments, and the different institutions and agencies under their administration. By the late 2000s, the MST's gains at the national level were having a "boomerang effect" on states and municipalities, convincing otherwise unsympathetic subnational governments to embrace the MST's educational goals. Keck and Sikkink (1998) coined the term "boomerang effect" in their study of transnational activist networks. The boomerang effect is when domestic actors, unable to influence their governments, seek out international allies to put pressure on national public officials to respond to local demands. A similar process took place in the case of Ceará, on a domestic scale. The national coalition for *Educação do Campo*, which included social movements as well as university and government allies, put pressure on the state of Ceará to respond to the demands of local MST activists. This network offered both information about *Educação do Campo*, and resources for its implementation. The MST leadership in Ceará strategically used this national advocacy to make demands on their state government.

Ceará is the perfect case to analyze the MST's educational struggle in this contemporary context, as the movement's most important educational victory took place relatively recently with the opening of a network of four high schools on MST settlements in 2010 and 2011. These high schools have the official recognition of the state government as *escolas do campo* (schools of the countryside), with the right to a differentiated pedagogical approach constructed in partnership with the families in the settlements and local communities. These *escolas do campo* are among the largest and most well-structured schools of any MST settlement in the country. The MST state education sector co-governs the *escolas do campo*, implementing many of the movement's historical educational practices, as well as developing new initiatives, including three new high school disciplines. The MST also organizes teacher trainings each year in the *escolas do campo*, in coordination with the state government.

The Ceará *escolas do campo* are one of the most important examples of the MST's contentious co-governance of public education. I draw on the case of Ceará to make three arguments about the MST's educational struggle in this contemporary context. First, we can only understand the MST's regional outcomes if we analyze how the federal context, in particular, how the national coalition for *Educação do Campo* influences states' local educational trajectories. As Hart (2002) writes, this type of relational comparison analyzes regional cases "in relation to one another and to a larger whole . . . it is through clarifying how these relations are produced and changed in practice that close study of a particular part can illuminate the whole" (14). Ceará sheds light on how the MST's previous educational victories are currently influencing regional trajectories, and how these local interventions contribute to the national movement. Second, and related to this point, I argue that the MST's educational interventions in Ceará represent a thirty-year accumulation of the MST's educational practices. Thus, the institutionalization of the MST's educational goals in the *escolas do campo* sheds light on how the MST's pedagogical program has evolved since the early 1980s. Finally, even in this open context, with multiple opportunities for social movement participation, the MST's relationship to the state continues to be a form of contentious co-governance with both collaboration and tension characterizing these connections. This raises important questions about *who* has the right to represent the interests of the poor.

THE MST'S AGRARIAN REFORM STRUGGLE IN CEARÁ

The state of Ceará is located in the northeastern part of the country, bordering western Pernambuco to the south. Ceará is one of the top tourist destinations in Brazil due to its long, pristine coastline; however, most of the state is encompassed by the semiarid *sertão*, with the same difficult living conditions as Santa Maria da Boa Vista. Poverty and death have been constant threats for the *sertanejo* population in Ceará. Between 1978 and 1983, during a five-year period of extreme drought, thousands of rural people were forced to leave their communities and migrate to the capital city of Fortaleza. In the late 1980s, Ceará had one of the highest concentrations of landownership in Brazil, with powerful landholding families (*coronéis*) dominating politics throughout the state. In 2015, Ceará's average monthly household income was the third lowest in Brazil, a mere 680 *reais* (about 250 US dollars in 2015). In the 2010 census the population of Ceará was 8.5 million, 75 percent of which was urban (IBGE 2011).[1] Of this population, 61.9 percent identified as mixed race (*pardo*), 32 percent white, 4.7 percent black, 1.2 percent "yellow," and 0.2 percent indigenous (IBGE 2010).

The MST's first occupation in Ceará occurred in 1989, the same year as in Pernambuco, also with the help of several MST leaders from southern Brazil. These activists organized 450 families to occupy land in the middle of the *sertão*, in the municipality of Madalena (see Map 6.1). Nine days after this land occupation started, the federal government gave land rights to these families and established the first agrarian reform settlement in the state, Settlement 25 de Maio (May 25). A few months later, MST leaders organized eight hundred more families to occupy another large land estate in the nearby municipality of Canindé. Unlike the first occupation, this time the police arrived and evicted the families. These families went on to occupy several other properties in the region, eventually pressuring the federal government to create dozens of agrarian reform settlements. These initial victories were critical to the MST's rapid expansion in Ceará throughout the 1990s (Morissawa 2001, 187). In 2011, the MST worked in approximately two hundred agrarian reform settlements throughout the state, with thousands of people still living in occupied encampments, waiting for land rights.

Building an Education Collective: Maria de Jesus's Story

Maria de Jesus Santos, the head of the MST state education sector in Ceará in 2011, remembered the MST's initial land occupations. During the late 1980s, Maria de Jesus was living in the poor rural municipality of Canindé, in the community Ipuera dos Gomes, in the semiarid *sertão*. She had always enjoyed being a student, and her dream was to complete eighth grade. However, the school in her community only went up to fourth grade. Maria de Jesus finished fourth grade when she was nine, but she continued going to school and repeating the same lessons for the next five years, in order "to not be sitting around doing nothing." In 1987, when she was fifteen years old, a local priest invited her to a one-year course on liberation theology at the Institute of Catechesis São Francisco. This course emphasized poor people's liberation from economic and political oppression and transformed Maria de Jesus's perspective on poverty and inequality. When she went back to her community the next year, she became involved in political organizing in the region. She also became a teacher in her local school, although she was still sixteen years old and only had a fourth-grade education. That year, the municipality opened up a middle school in her community; Maria de Jesus taught in the mornings at the elementary school and studied in the afternoons in the middle school. She was involved in her local CEB (base ecclesial community, a church study group also inspired by liberation theology, described in Chapter 1), took a leadership role in her teachers union, and later that year helped to found a PT chapter in Canindé.

Several MST leaders visited Maria de Jesus's community in 1989, explaining that they were organizing people to participate in the first land occupation in Ceará. Maria de Jesus did not participate in this first occupation, but when a second land occupation happened several months later in a nearby town, she went to visit the camp. She became involved in organizing educational activities in the camp, and soon after, she was invited to participate in a meeting for educators in areas of agrarian reform, which took place in 1991 in Fortaleza. National MST educational leaders Edgar Kolling and Rosali Caldart participated in this meeting. Maria de Jesus remembered, "When I learned about the Pedagogy of the MST, I fell in love. I had dreamed about finding this movement—it was addressing everything I was angry about. I knew that people were not poor because God wanted them to be poor." Maria de Jesus began to connect her passion for education and social justice to the agrarian reform struggle. Soon after, she participated in an MST land occupation and quickly became a prominent leader in the movement.

Over the next decade, Maria de Jesus had the opportunity to learn more about the MST's pedagogical approach. First, she was invited to enroll in one of the MST's High School Degree and Teaching Certification Programs (MAG programs) in the city of Braga, in Rio Grande do Sul (see Chapter 1). Through the pedagogy of alternation, Maria de Jesus spent several months in Braga studying and then several months in her community in teaching internships. Then, in 1998, she enrolled in the MST's first Pedagogy of Land baccalaureate program at the University of Ijuí (see Chapter 2). Shortly afterward, Maria de Jesus enrolled in a PRONERA graduate program on *Educação do Campo* at the Federal University of Santa Catarina. She also participated in all of the MST's national educational conferences in Brasília during this period, including the First National Meeting of Educators in Areas of Agrarian Reform (ENERA) in 1997 and the first and second National Conference for Education of the Countryside in 1998 and 2004 (Table 3.1 in Chapter 3).

Maria de Jesus played a central role in helping to establish an MST education sector in Ceará. The education sector organized dozens of activities during the late 1990s and early 2000s, including literacy campaigns, adult education programs in primary education, teacher trainings, and statewide gatherings of *sem terrinha* (little landless children). As in Pernambuco, the literacy campaigns were critical not only to reduce the rate of illiteracy in the settlements but also to integrate more youth and women into the movement by offering them jobs as literacy agents. The Ceará education sector also drew on the experiences in Rio Grande do Sul, and in the mid-2000s, activists organized six simultaneous cohorts of the MAG program, funded through PRONERA. The programs took place in different parts of the state in partnership with six state universities. The education sector also sponsored several PRONERA bachelor's degree programs in the Pedagogy of Land, Journalism, Agronomy, and Social Work.

In a number of municipalities, MST educational activists developed close relationships with local authorities and implemented some aspects of the movement's pedagogical program in the municipal public schools. For example, in the municipality of Caucaia, the municipal Department of Education hired an MST activist to oversee the settlement schools in the region. In another municipality, the MST successfully fought for access to preschool for the families living in camps and settlements. However, as MST activist Joel Gomes explained, most municipalities were antagonistic toward the movement and blocked activists' participation. According to Joel, these developments "depended on the local correlation of forces."[2]

In summary, by the mid-2000s, the MST's educational struggle in Ceará already had a long history, with activists establishing programs and implementing alternative pedagogical practices in the areas of adult education, preschool, primary and secondary schooling, and higher education. However, at this point, almost all of these programs were either funded through the federal government or were in partnership with local municipalities. There were still no schools located on MST settlements that fell under the jurisdiction of the state Department of Education. The right-leaning Brazilian Social Democratic Party (PSDB) had been in power in Ceará continually since 1991. Consequently, the officials in the state Department of Education had a traditional orientation toward rural schooling, assuming that it was only necessary to invest in new schools in urban centers. This only began to change in 2006, when the national coalition for *Educação do Campo* intervened.

FEDERAL INTERVENTIONS: GOVERNOR LÚCIO ALCÂNTARA AND THE PSDB (2003–2006)

In 2003, Lúcio Alcântara of the PSDB became the governor of Ceará, narrowly being the PT candidate by a mere three thousand votes, thus continuing a decade of conservative dominance in the state. Nevertheless, unlike the other PSDB administrations, Governor Alcântara's governing alliance was politically weak and vulnerable. As his Secretary of Education Sofia Lerche (2003–2005) described, the 2002 election marked the year that the PT arrived in national politics, with the election of Lula as well as dozens of PT congressional representatives. This represented people's desire for change across the country.[3] Sofia described, "In Ceará, this change almost happened, but didn't. It was a close race. Governor Alcântara represented the end of an era."

Therefore, Governor Alcântara had a weak political mandate. In addition, when he took office, Ceará was in a dire financial situation, with outstanding debt to the World Bank and other international organizations. In the educational sphere, the state government also had minimal resources, partially due to the devolution of primary education to the municipal level over the previous decade. Although the federal government had created a program in 1998 that redistributed funding to subnational governments overseeing elementary schools, the expansion of this program to middle and high schools would only take place in 2007.[4] This funding arrangement was difficult for poor, state governments in charge of secondary education. As Sofia remembered, "We only had enough money to pay our teachers' salaries, nothing else."

At the same time at the national level, the proposal for *Educação do Campo* was consolidating, with a diverse coalition of activists, unionists, professors, and state officials advocating for this alternative educational approach. One of the goals of this national coalition was to convince state governments to embrace *Educação do Campo*. In 2005, the Ministry of Education (MEC) reached out to the Alcântara administration to host a state seminar on *Educação do Campo*. Despite the political dispute between the PSDB and PT at the national level, the state Department of Education was open to this proposal as a means to invest in the underfunded rural school system. Furthermore, according to Secretary of Education Sofia Lerche, "The Ceará government liked to be part of national programs. We were always searching out partnerships with the MEC; it did not matter that we were in an opposition party to the PT."

Susana, who had been working in the Ceará state Department of Education since the mid-1970s, became the point person for these *Educação do Campo* initiatives.[5] Although she was born in the capital of Fortaleza and identified as "completely urban," Susana had a wide range of experiences working in agrarian reform settlements, as a government official in the state Department of Education. As Susana explained, "When the Ministry of Education asked us to organize a seminar on the *Educação do Campo* federal guidelines, the state Secretary of Education called on me to do this because I already had a history with the settlements . . . I was asked to organize a seminar for 350 people." Susana invited representatives from the State Department of Education Regional Offices (CREDEs), municipal secretaries of education, the universities, and dozens of organizations that worked in the countryside, including the MST and the rural union federation FETREACE, an affiliate of the National Confederation of Agricultural Workers (CONTAG). Although the state Department of Education was in charge of contacting these participants, it was the national coalition for *Educação do Campo* that provided the support to organize the state seminar, offering information, local contacts, and financial resources.

During the four-day seminar, participants read and discussed the *Educação do Campo* Federal Guidelines and planned their implementation. Members of the MST statewide education sector, including Maria de Jesus, were invited to speak on panels about the history and philosophy of *Educação do Campo*. This first seminar led to the creation of the Ceará Committee for *Educação do Campo*, which included a combination of government, university, and civil society representatives. The MST educational leaders in Ceará were already actively promoting these ideas in their state, and they became the most prominent and vocal members of the committee. Slowly, the conception of rural education began to shift in the state Department of Education—at least among the government officials involved in these initiatives. For example, the state Department of Education published a document after the first seminar that stated: "*Educação do Campo* is a political and pedagogical conception that is intended to create a more dynamic link between human beings and the production of their social conditions in the countryside."[6] In just a few years, the state government went from disregarding rural education to openly linking education of the countryside to an alternative development model.

Why did Governor Alcântara support these initiatives? According to Susana, it was the federal government and the national coalition for *Educação do Campo* that influenced the educational debate in Ceará. Again, this is similar to what Keck and Sikkink (1998) refer to as the "boomerang effect," in which "networks provide [local activists] access, leverage, and information (and often money) they could not expect to have on their own" (13). Given the Ceará state's low level of capacity for educational governance, particularly in far-off rural regions, the government could not simply ignore this advocacy and funding. Maria de Jesus agreed with this assessment when I asked her why the Alcântara administration supported these initiatives. "It was the pressure from the MEC, because the MEC has a lot of power over the states . . . The state cannot go against the federal system."

Over the next two years, the Ceará Department of Education, with financial support from the Ministry of Education, organized more seminars and events to push forward Educação do Campo. In January 2005, the Ceará Department of Education organized a second state seminar on

Educação do Campo. A year later, in March 2006, the Department organized a third state seminar on *Educação do Campo*. In December 2006, the Department organized a teacher training program for hundreds of teachers from rural areas. The teachers spent five days studying the theoretical foundations of *Educação do Campo*, analyzing the relationship between *Educação do Campo* and issues of gender and race, and discussing the possibilities for incorporating *Educação do Campo* into the curriculum.[7] Local MST activists used the seminar to talk about their own experiences implementing this educational program, and also made new demands on the state to support these educational initiatives.

THE SAO PAULO COUNTEREXAMPLE: STATE CAPACITY TO REJECT FEDERAL TRENDS

It is important to note that the influence of this national advocacy was not homogenous across the country. In other words, while Maria de Jesus is correct that the Ministry of Education has a lot of power over the states, the degree of power depends on states' own capacity for educational governance. São Paulo is the richest and most populous state in the country, and as in Ceará, the PSDB has dominated politics in São Paulo since the early 1990s.[8] However, in contrast to Ceará, the PSDB party members in São Paulo are the most important adversaries of the PT at the federal level. For example, Governors Geraldo Alckmin (2001–2006; 2011–2018) and José Serra (2007–2010) ran as presidential candidates against the PT in 2002, 2006, and 2010. During these campaigns, both Alckmin and Serra were publicly critical of the cozy relationship between the MST and the federal government. [9] In terms of education, when I interviewed two former state Secretaries of Education in São Paulo, Roserly Neubauer da Silva (1995–2001) and Maria Helena Castro (2007–2009), a major theme was the need to standardize curriculum throughout the state, not diversify schools.[10] For example, Maria Helena dismissed the idea that rural schooling should have any type of differentiated pedagogy, and she insisted that rural schools in São Paulo followed the same curriculum as schools in urban centers.

In 2006, MEC officials in the office for *Educação do Campo* tried to organize a seminar in São Paulo to discuss the federal *Educação do Campo* guidelines. Although the MEC had organized these seminars in every state of Brazil, the São Paulo state government refused to host a seminar. The director of the Department of Diversity in the MEC at this time, Armênio Schmidt, explained: "The PSDB was in power and the state Department of Education thought that they did not need a seminar, because they said that São Paulo no longer had any countryside." Antonio Munarim, the MEC official who reached out to the PSDB government, went into more detail about the state's rejection of *Educação do Campo*. He had contacted the Secretary of Education during that period, Gabriel Chalita, multiple times, but was never able to speak with him. Then, he saw Chalita at a national education gathering: "I talked to Chalita and I told him that I was having problems being put in contact with him. I told him that we were having *Educação do Campo* seminars in every state, and we wanted to have one in São Paulo . . . Chalita claimed that he supported the idea." Chalita gave Antonio the name of a state contact, but again, this person never responded to Antonio's requests. "They never told us no, especially in written responses, but they found a way to make sure that the seminar did not happen."[11]

São Paulo's refusal to host an *Educação do Campo* seminar was likely a product of several factors. Unlike other, poorer states, the government of São Paulo did not need the financial and administrative support of the federal government, nor were they as easily influenced by the national coalition for *Educação do Campo*. The PSDB leadership in São Paulo was the biggest opponent to the PT at the federal level, and therefore, PSDB government officials tended to reject opportunities for collaboration. The government officials in São Paulo also rejected *Educação do Campo* because they viewed São Paulo as a modern and urban state. As Maria Helena Castro said, "In São Paulo there is very little tradition with rural education. There has been an intense process of urbanization, and rural schools are like urban schools." Despite the fact that São Paulo had a large agricultural industry, and was the state with one of the highest number of land occupations, officials considered it completely urbanized.[12]

Most important, the São Paulo administration had the capacity to follow through on these ideological positions. In other words, for the wealthy state of São Paulo, the MEC's financial incentives were insignificant and state officials could refuse to implement all *Educação do Campo* initiatives. However, for the poor northeastern state of Ceará, the MEC's arrival drew a lot of interest and was seen as an opportunity to channel resources into the rural school system. Thus, in Ceará, *Educação do Campo* programs flourished between 2005 and 2006, with the support of the federal government. In São Paulo, none of these educational initiatives were implemented. This comparison aligns with the overall argument in this book that social movement co-governance is more difficult under the purview of states with right-leaning administrations and a high-capacity for policy implementation (top center-right section of Table I.1 in the Introduction).[13]

CONSTRUCTING HIGH SCHOOLS ON MST
SETTLEMENTS: CID GOMES AND THE PSB
(2007–2014)

In January 2007, Cid Gomes, a member of the left-leaning Brazilian Socialist Party (PSB), became the governor of Ceará. Both Cid Gomes and his brother Ciro Gomes (ex-Governor of Ceará, 1991–1994) had been members of the PSDB; however, they left this party in the mid-1990s and in 2006 they joined the PSB, which was allied with the PT nationally. For many MST activists I spoke with, despite this new party affiliation, Gomes still represented politics as usual. For example, although MST leader Erivando Barbosa admitted that Gomes was more likeable than previous governors, he doubted Gomes's genuine support for agrarian reform.[14] Given these doubts, when Gomes reached out to the MST state leadership for support during his gubernatorial campaign, the movement refused to endorse his candidacy.[15]

Nonetheless, despite this skepticism, when Cid Gomes took office in 2007, he was much more open to the MST than any previous governor. Gomes's openness to the movement was most likely a combination of opportunism—not wanting to create political enemies—and the fact that his party was allied with the PT, which was supportive of the MST at the federal level. Consequently, the election of Gomes meant more political opportunities to discuss the MST's proposal for implementing *Educação do Campo*. However, in an unfortunate twist of fate, this was also the moment that the MEC withdrew much of its financial support. Susana, the state official responsible for *Educação do Campo*, explained:

> In the Lúcio [Alcântara] period the Ministry of Education was behind us and always gave us resources. If they wanted us to implement something, we would implement it . . . Lúcio supported us, always cautiously, but he would do it because the Ministry of Education was there. . . . I had much more support from Lúcio than I did during Cid Gomes's administration.

Susana said that while she continued to be the point person for *Educação do Campo*, resources were becoming scarce. The members of the Committee for *Educação do Campo* stopped showing up to the meetings, as there was no money to implement the committee's proposals. Despite the election of a government with a more supportive orientation toward the MST, the state's *Educação do Campo* initiatives could not move forward without the MEC's organizational and financial support. Maria de Jesus, for her part, had always been skeptical of these state-led initiatives, including the Committee for *Educação do Campo*. She said, "The problem with committees and advisory boards is that their major role is sharing information and public relations; it is only the struggle that wins victories in the end."

With this perspective in mind, after Cid Gomes took office in 2007, the MST leadership organized dozens of protests—including a twelve-day occupation of the capitol building in March 2007—with a list of demands for the new PSB governor. Among these demands was the construction of sixty-four public schools on MST settlements, including ten high schools. At that time, there was not a single high school on any MST settlement in Ceará, which meant that students living in settlements had to move to nearby cities or spend hours commuting each day to continue studying. Constructing high schools on settlements was a high priority for the education sector in Ceará, in order to keep youth connected and engaged in the movement. When the MST presented their demands to the governor in 2007, he agreed to construct ten new settlement schools, four of them high schools. However, although Governor Gomes made this promise to the movement, the construction of these schools never moved forward because the state Department of Education claimed that there was no funding to build these schools. Meanwhile, the unfunded Committee for *Educação do Campo* existed only in name.

In 2008, the MEC established a new program for funding the construction of high schools throughout Brazil, which created yet another political opportunity for local MST activists to promote *Educação do Campo* in Ceará. The state Department of Education submitted a request to the MEC for the construction of dozens of new high schools, and the MEC approved the construction of eleven schools. The MST leadership immediately increased its pressure on the government to build these schools on agrarian reform settlements, and Governor Gomes eventually agreed to build four high schools on MST settlements.[16]

I asked dozens of state officials and MST activists why Cid Gomes conceded to building these schools. People emphasized different reasons. For example, MST leader Neidinha Lopes said, "It was not the Governor being nice that got us the schools. We won the schools through struggle, the communities in the settlements mobilized to demand these schools."[17] MST activist Erivando emphasized the federal government's intervention: "Let me tell you a very important detail about these schools. They were constructed with federal resources. The state only gave us a small part of that allotment . . . the governor was able to fit our demands within the resources that the federal government offered." Finally, one state official who was also a movement ally, Ana Edith, believed that Gomes agreed to the construction of the four schools to "neutralize any political resistance." She offered a detailed explanation:

The MST would never agree to an ideological alliance with Cid Gomes's government. But, yes, the movement wants the financial support of the government to meet its educational demands, because the movement understands that this advances the struggle of rural workers. Cid and Ciro [Cid Gomes's brother] have a similar interest in the movement... they know that the MST is never going to walk shoulder to shoulder with them, nor will they ever walk shoulder to shoulder with the MST during a land occupation. But they do not want the MST as an enemy, because they need to win votes in the interior of the state.[18]

According to this latter account, both Governor Gomes and the MST leadership were using each other to push forward their political goals, in what scholars have referred to as a class compromise (Heller 1999; Przeworski 1986).

Several points cut across these interviews. The first is that after Cid Gomes came to power, the MST engaged in contentious political action to make demands on the state—despite Gomes's membership in a more left-leaning political party. A second point is that Cid Gomes's government was more open to having a relationship with the movement, whether for genuine ideological reasons or for strategic political calculations. Third and finally, the Gomes administration only acted on its promises once the state government received support from the Ministry of Education. Thus, similarly to the previous right-leaning administration, the state's support for *Educação do Campo* only concretized after the federal government increased Ceará's capacity for educational governance, this time by investing in school infrastructure. This combination of factors began a new chapter in the MST's educational struggle in Ceará: the movement's contentious co-governance of public high schools on agrarian reform settlements.

ESCOLAS DO CAMPO: INSTITUTIONALIZING THE MST'S EDUCATIONAL PROGRAM

Choosing the Location of Four New High Schools

After the MST leadership won the right to build four new high schools in their agrarian reform settlements, a process of negotiation began about where these schools would be located. As the schools were already a concession, Governor Gomes agreed to let the MST decide the location of the schools. Simone Ramos, an MST leader who became the principal of a school in the coastal settlement of Maceió, explained the movement's internal decision-making process:[19]

After we won these four schools the question became, where will the schools be built? Since there were so many settlements that needed educational access we established some criteria: the schools had to be built in the oldest settlements that were the most densely populated, to attend to the largest number of youth. Another criterion was that the settlements had to have a long history of participating in the agrarian reform struggle.

As Simone explained, the MST leaders thought it was only fair for the schools to be located in the oldest settlements, and also where there was a high student demand. However, another criterion was the settlement's history of participation in the MST's agrarian reform struggle, or in other words, the degree of local support for the movement. This latter point illustrates the dual purpose of the high schools. On the one hand, the schools would offer educational access to youth who would otherwise have to travel to far-off cities to study. On the other hand, the MST wanted the schools to be part of its "social movement infrastructure" (Andrews 2004) contributing to the organization, leadership, and resource base of the movement. This would require the support of the communities surrounding the school.

The first settlement that the MST selected was 25 de Maio, in the semi-arid *sertão* region of the state, created after the first MST land occupation in Ceará in 1989. This was an important symbolic choice, as the first MST agrarian reform settlement, but also pragmatic. As Sandra Alves, the MST leader who became the principal of this school, explained, "There were students from this community that would leave their houses at 4 AM to attend high school, and they would only get home at 5 PM. It was a huge burden. Many youth dropped out of school."[20] The community decided to name the school João dos Santos Oliveira, or João Sem Terra (Landless João) High School, to honor an MST activist that had been part of the initial land occupation in 1989 and had participated in the movement his entire life, dying in 2008 at the age of sixty-nine.

The second location the MST leadership chose was the settlement Lagoa do Mineiro. This was another one of the oldest settlements in the states, located on the coast in the northern part of Ceará. The families in this region began fighting for this land in 1984, well before the MST arrived in the state. It was the Pastoral Land Commission (CPT) that initially helped the families occupy this area, eventually leading to the establishment of a settlement in 1986. When the MST leadership organized its first land occupation of 25 de Maio in 1989, families in the Lagoa do Mineiro settlement supported the occupation. The families eventually decided to join the MST and integrate their settlement into the movement's organizational structure. Ivaniza Martins, who was part of the original CPT-led land occupation in 1984, became the principal of the new high school. Ivaniza said that the community named the school Francisco Araújo Barros to honor a man who was assassinated by a gunman during the first occupation.[21] Although the families identified as part of the MST, they also continued to honor their own history of struggle.

Another settlement in the *sertão* region where the MST leadership chose to build a school was Santana. This settlement is even more remotely located than 25 de Maio, with the closest town an hour drive away on a bumpy dirt road. According to Rita Francisco dos Santos, who became the principal of this school, there were already some classrooms in the settlement that were considered "annexes" of schools in the city.[22] A group of teachers living in the settlement were working in these classrooms. In other words, there was both demand in the settlement for an independent school and local teachers living in the community. Rita explained that they named the new high school after the Marxist sociologist Florestan Fernandes, "due to the fact that he was a great defender of education, an important sociologist that inspired us to fight for this alternative educational proposal." Rita recited her favorite quote from Florestan Fernandes: "If we have a revolution in the school, people will create the revolution in the streets.'" The choice of Florestan Fernandes as the name of the school illustrated the hope the MST had for the high school to be connected to a process of social transformation.

Finally, the MST leadership chose one more coastal settlement to build a school, Maceió, a few hours south of Lagoa do Mineiro. This settlement was surrounded by a dozen other non-MST communities, whose youth also needed secondary school access. According to Simone Ramos, who became the principal of this school, the families in this settlement had participated en masse in the 2007 mobilizations to demand the four settlements schools. As for the name of the school, Simone explained: "The community chose the name Nazaré Flor. Nazaré was a leader in the community who died the year we won the right to construct this school. She was a popular educator, a poet, without any academic training." As in the other three settlements, the families in Maceió chose a name for their school that was connected to their settlement's history and the struggle for educational justice. Map 6.1 shows the location of the four settlements where these high schools were constructed, two settlements in the semiarid *sertão* and two in the coastal region.

Once the MST leadership determined the location of the four schools, each of them was put under the jurisdiction of a State Department of Education Regional Office (CREDE), the local government bodies responsible for overseeing state schools. This meant that the point of movement-state contact shifted to a more local level. This initially caused conflict, as the CREDE officials knew very little about the MST or the movement's educational proposal. For example, the state official who was overseeing the

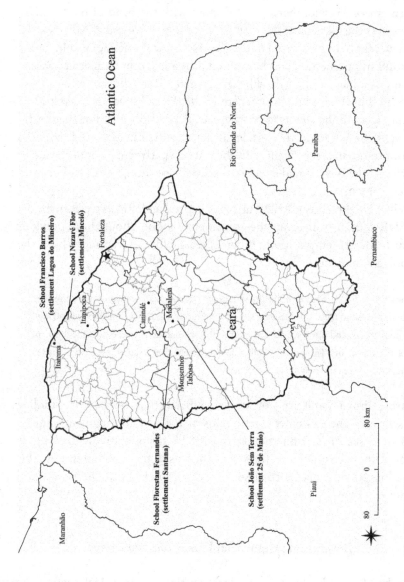

Map 6.1 High Schools Built on MST Settlements in Ceará, 2009–2010
Courtesy of Georgia Gabriela da Silva Sampaio

high school in the settlement 25 de Maio, Laura, told me that everyone was shocked when they built such a beautiful school in an MST settlement.[23] "When I went there with a colleague, he was so impressed with the structure of the school that he said, 'You see, only a president like Lula would do this, create such a pretty thing in a poor *sertão* region like this.'" In the settlement of Maceió, there was a dispute with the head of the CREDE, Pedro, over the location of the school. According to Simone, "Pedro wanted the new school to be located in the city. He knew the school would have a beautiful infrastructure, and he wanted it in a location with easier access. There was a huge conflict, and he threatened, 'This school is not going to be located in the middle of nowhere (*mata*, literally, woods).'" The MST families went to the streets to protest Pedro's position, claiming that he did not want the school in the settlement because he saw the countryside as inferior to urban areas. Eventually, the state Department of Education told Pedro that the MST could decide the school's location, as this had been an agreement with the governor.

When I visited this CREDE in 2011, Pedro had left. I asked Beatriz, the CREDE official overseeing the settlement school, about these previous conflicts. Beatriz emphasized a different reason for not wanting to build the school in a settlement:

> Initially we had wanted to build the school in another area because we were thinking about the entire region. There were lots of communities in the region who needed high school access, and if the school was built in the settlement, it would be difficult to enroll these students. These other families do not agree with the settlement school . . . they think it will prepare their kids to be farmers.[24]

Beatriz claimed that it was not the state officials that were against building the school in the settlement; rather, it was the neighboring communities who were skeptical. Nonetheless, the MST's negotiations with the governor were more influential than the concerns of these communities. This had a long-term effect for the region, because once built, schools are hard to move.

Designating High Schools as *Escolas do Campo*

After the MST leadership chose the location of the four new high schools, the next step was to negotiate with the state about the type of pedagogical proposal that the schools would adopt. The MST education sector demanded that the schools adhere to the national *Educação do Campo* guidelines. Neidinha remembered, "We realized that a beautiful building was not enough. We needed another form of organizing the schools." There were already some people in the state Department of Education who were familiar with the *Educação do Campo* proposal, such as Susana. However, by 2009, Susana had very little support to promote this educational program. Furthermore, most state officials did not have clarity about the difference between *Educação do Campo* and rural education. Mariana, one of these state official, recounted, "We invited the MST to the Department of Education, and they explained that having a school located in the countryside is not the same as having a school of the countryside . . . they offered to visit the CREDEs throughout Ceará and have this discussion with all of the regional state officials."[25] The MST state education sector took on the responsibility of dialoguing with government actors about the meaning and purpose of *Educação do Campo*.

The MST demanded that the state Department of Education create an office that could oversee the high schools with the intention of implementing the *Educação do Campo* federal guidelines. The Secretary of Education, under pressure from the Governor to negotiate with the MST, agreed to this demand, creating a new office for *Educação do Campo* that would oversee the four schools. Eventually, the MST state education sector also obtained permission to have the four new high schools designated as *escolas do campo* (schools of the countryside). This designation meant that the schools were legally recognized as different from urban schools, with the right to a curricular and organizational approach more appropriate to the reality of local families.

This agreement to designate the four high schools as *escolas do campo* became a formal institutional arrangement. Multiple government policies were passed, which both promoted the idea of *Educação do Campo* and the inclusion of the MST in the process of co-governing these four schools. For example, on the Ceará state Department of Education website, the following was written:

> The state Department of Education . . . recognizes the struggle of social movements and unions of the countryside to guarantee access to a quality high school education for the populations of the countryside. We support this through the construction of new high schools in rural regions and in settlements. . . . These schools are denominated as *escolas do campo* due to their pedagogical proposal to connect the curriculum to the social, economic, and cultural reality of these populations. The goal is for schools to reflect about the identity and culture of peasant communities. The actions that are being developed in these schools take place through a continual dialogue with the school principals, teachers, other school staff, *and with the MST education sector* [emphasis added].[26]

This excerpt from the website illustrates not only the degree to which the state embraced the proposal for *Educação do Campo* but, moreover, the process of co-governance established with the MST education sector. This opening in Ceará was a consequence of a more left-leaning political context but also the federal government's multiple interventions and resources supporting *Educação do Campo* over the previous years. (Given this increased state capacity and left-leaning government, during this period Ceará had the combination of characteristics in the top left corner of Table I.1 in the Introduction). Local MST leaders' own accumulated knowledge and experience implementing their educational proposal also allowed them to take advantage of these openings. Over the next five years, MST educational activists dedicated themselves to the contentious co-governance of the four *escolas do campo*.

Infrastructure

All four *escolas do campo* were built with the same design. When I visited my first *escola do campo* in September 2011, Francisco Barros High School, on the northern coastal settlement of Lagoa do Mineiro, I was shocked at the school's infrastructure. It was by far the largest and best equipped rural public school that I had seen in my year of field research. There were five brand-new brick buildings, with bright red roofs, spread out around a large outdoor area surrounded by a tall fence. The school had a total of twelve classrooms, spaciously located across the five buildings. There was a computer room equipped with new computers and a science laboratory with technical equipment. The school also had a gym area, with a basketball court, soccer nets, and a mini outdoor amphitheater. In the middle of the five buildings, there was an open space where students could sit and socialize and a kitchen where school staff cooked snacks each day for the students. The MST's presence was obvious throughout Francisco Barros High School, with pictures of MST protests and marches, signs denouncing agribusiness, and posters encouraging agroecology. In front of the school, the MST flag hung from the flagpole, next to the Brazilian and Ceará flags.

I visited all four *escolas do campo*, located in MST settlements in remote locations across the state. All of the schools had the same infrastructure, resembling mini-college campuses, with posters about agrarian reform hung throughout the hallways and classrooms. According to state officials, these four schools are among the most well structured in the state, in both rural and urban regions. For example, Beatriz, the CREDE official in charge of Nazaré Flor High School, told me, "This is a model school. It has all of the infrastructure needed for the world today. Science laboratories, computer rooms, video rooms, classrooms for the student government, a covered gym, amphitheater, a library . . . of the forty schools I oversee, this is the most beautiful." The construction of these four modern high schools valorized the MST's settlements as spaces of the future, not simply the past.

Picture 6.1 One of the four new high schools built on MST settlements in Ceará in 2009 and 2010 and officially designated as *escolas do campo* (schools of the countryside), November 2011.
Courtesy of author

School Mission Statements (Pedagogical-Political Projects)

Even before the *escolas do campo* opened, the MST education sector began organizing a series of debates in the local communities about the goals of the schools. These debates were the basis for writing the schools' Pedagogical-Political Projects (PPPs)—school mission statements. Although school administrators usually submit PPPs that are boilerplate statements of bureaucratic requirements, the MST used the construction of the PPPs as an opportunity to engage the community in a collective discussion about educational purpose. Maria de Jesus described the process as long and tedious: "We formed education collectives in all of the settlements, and we did grassroots work to make sure everyone was involved in the discussion. We had debates about the PPPs and we discussed how we were going to write them." Cilene, a teacher in the settlement Maceió, also described this process: "When it was decided that the high school would be constructed here, the work of creating the PPP began."[27] Cilene said that they organized discussion groups in different parts of the settlement, asking people what type of school they wanted for their community. She asserted proudly, "Even before this school had its first brick, it existed in people's minds."

Sandra, who became the principal of João Sem Terra High School, described in more detail the writing of the PPP. First, they created an education collective inside the settlement, which included both long-time MST leaders and local community members. Sandra remembered that the process of constructing education collectives in the settlements actually served to strengthen the MST's statewide leadership, as more people were integrated into the movement's organizational structure. The MST education collective also brought university professors to the settlement to discuss different educational theories with the families, and they invited national MST educational leaders to lecture on the history and purpose of *Educação do Campo*. Sandra said that writing their PPP required a lot of studying and also systematizing—summarizing and synthesizing dozens of contributions. Sandra commented: "We already have one hundred pages . . . but we are not done the PPP. We will never think of it is as finished, we need to keep studying."

The government officials in the CREDEs also commented on this process. CREDE official Camila compared the writing of the PPP at the Francisco Barros High School to the other schools she oversaw. "We recently met with the teachers and parents in all of our schools to explain the process of creating a PPP. The *escolas do campo* did not participate—the teachers and parents were much more organized and already in the middle of this process . . . their PPP is almost finished."[28] While in most schools the writing of the PPP is a top-down state initiative, in the *escolas do campo* the writing of the PPP became a community-wide, participatory process.

In 2011, each of the PPPs was structured slightly differently, but they all had four major components: (1) *marco referencial* (referential framework, a statement of the social function of the school and the vision and values of the school); (3) *marco situacional* (situational framework, a collective analysis of the historical, political, economic, and social context of the region and settlement); (3) *marco conceitual* (conceptual framework, the theoretical orientation of the process of learning and social transformation; and (4) *marco operacional* (operational framework, the organization of the school to achieve these goals, including the curriculum, school governance, and the other concrete aspects of how the school functions).

Cilene said that in her opinion the most powerful part of writing the PPP was discussing the situational framework. She described how this process occurred in her settlement:

> The situational framework means telling the entire history of the settlement . . . and this was the most beautiful thing, hearing people's depositions of their histories. We integrated the memories they told into the PPP. The beautiful histories of the women in this region . . . who pushed forward the struggle for land. Through this process we rescued the history of the settlement.

For Cilene, writing the PPP was not only a process of learning and reflecting about education but also recording the oral histories of the settlement itself. "The school is inside the history of the settlement, and the settlement is inside the history of the school," she reflected. However, the PPPs did not just recount these histories; they also connected these histories to educational purpose. For example, in the PPP for João Sem Terra High School, the section on the conceptual framework discussed an "alternative development model for the countryside based in peasant agriculture ... manual labor as a central educational process ... social struggle and culture as part of human formation." These themes of sustainable development, manual labor, social struggle, and culture, are four of the most important components of the MST's educational program.

Finally, the PPPs also drew on legal frameworks to justify the implementation of *Educação do Campo*. The following is from the PPP of Florestan Fernandes High School:

> This PPP is new and innovative, and has the goal of putting into practice the *Educação do Campo* federal guidelines. . . . Our school is part of a public policy for affirmative action, which promotes social inclusion. . . . It is an educational proposal that supports the political, cultural, and economic interests of peasant farmers, investing in the knowledge and technologies that will help the social and economic development of populations in the countryside. . . . The goal is to promote a dialogue between teachers in different disciplines and overcome the fragmentation of knowledge.

As this PPP illustrates, the mission of the Florestan Fernandes High School is explicitly linked to an alternative development project for the countryside. There are continual references to the *Educação do Campo* national guidelines, which provided the legal justification for having a school with a different organizational and curricular structure. The PPP also states that Florestan Fernandes High School is part of an affirmative action policy, which promotes the social inclusion of rural populations. Among the pedagogical approaches listed are interdisciplinary learning and basing the curriculum in the reality of the local communities. The settlement communities, in coordination with the MST education sector, wrote these documents well before the *escolas do campo* opened in 2010 and 2011. The PPPs, which were all between fifty and one hundred pages, set the groundwork for the MST's educational interventions in the years to come.[29]

Selection of Principals, Staff, and Teachers

Another task the MST education sector had to think about before the *escolas do campo* opened was who would become the principals and pedagogical coordinators (similar to a vice principal) of the schools. For the MST leadership, it was important for these school administrators to know about the movement's pedagogical proposal. However, their selection also had to follow a bureaucratic process in which the positions were announced online and anyone could apply. The MST decided on a creative solution to this dilemma: they asked to help write the online job description. Although they could not require applicants to be MST leaders, the movement did convince the government to require applicants to have a bachelor's degree in the Pedagogy of Land. According to MST leader Erivando, "this decision was not made by Cid [Gomes]. It was decided by the Secretary of Education, with the help of the office for *Educação do Campo* . . . we won over the people in the office and then they pushed forward this demand. They found a gap in the law that allowed them to create a special application process." The MST's constant presence inside of the state Department of Education, dialoguing with state officials about the movement's educational program, was finally paying off as these officials became internal advocates for the movement.

This special application process was a strategic way for the MST education sector to ensure that their own activists would be hired for these positions. Over the previous decade, the MST had offered dozens of Pedagogy of Land degree programs throughout Brazil, and two had taken place in Ceará. These degree programs were critical in forming a collective of activist-teachers in Ceará who understood the MST's educational approach. For example, Joel, who became the pedagogical coordinator of Francisco Barros High School, graduated from one of these Pedagogy of Land programs. He reflected, "The program was important because you were able to live the movement's proposal in practice." Joel described the collective organization of his cohort, "which allowed us to experience an educational process that does not exist in any other part of the university . . . the base nuclei, student self-governance . . . it allowed us to practice an extraordinary form of cooperation." Cilene, who become the pedagogical coordinator of Nazaré Flor High School, was in this same cohort and also emphasized the importance of the Pedagogy of Land program. She told me that:

> It was crucial for us to understand what the movement wanted. . . . The movement talked about *Educação do Campo*, but we had never lived through a real experience. We just kept dreaming about it. What is it like? How do we promote *Educação do Campo*? The Pedagogy of Land program helped us understand, because we lived *Educação do Campo* in practice.

The selection process the Department of Education established for the *escolas do campo* ensured that only teachers who had graduated from these transformative degree programs, which I described in Chapters 1 and 2 as "real [educational] utopias" (E. O. Wright 2010), were able to apply to be the principals and pedagogical coordinators of the four *escolas do campo.* Simone, the principal of Nazaré Flor High School, explained this application process: "There was an open call for candidates for the school administrator positions, and Cilene and I were chosen. There was not a requirement that we had to be part of the MST, but we had to have studied the Pedagogy of the MST." Beatriz, the CREDE official overseeing Nazaré Flor High School, elaborated on this story:

> The one requirement for the school was that the principal had to have a Pedagogy of Land degree. The government accepted this proposal because the principals *should* have knowledge about these rural areas . . . Simone is part of the MST, but she is also the principal. She applied for the position and had the required Pedagogy of Land degree. She was very enthusiastic. She has a good profile to be the principal.

Although it was the MST state education sector that decided Simone and Cilene should apply for their positions, Beatriz saw the state as leading the selection process. In 2011, all four principals and pedagogical coordinators of the *escolas do campo* were leaders in the MST education sector.

Another hiring decision concerned the staff that would work in the schools, for example, the janitors, cooks, and security guards. At first the local CREDEs wanted to assign people from outside the settlements to take these positions. However, for the settlement families the new high schools were an important form of employment and income. The families demanded that the state assign support staff for the *escolas do campo* from the settlement, in order to increase the social benefit of the school. In the settlement Maceió, the families even decided that only people who had been dedicated to social struggle should be offered these jobs, which meant that the support staff ended up being activists who were close to the movement.

These social justice and residence criteria were harder to apply to the teachers, who generally had to be selected from the already existing statewide teaching network. Furthermore, the *escolas do campo* needed teachers specialized in every discipline, and there were not enough activists with this training. Therefore, in most of the *escolas do campo*, the applicants for the teacher positions were people from nearby cities with no connection to the movement. Nonetheless, the education collective in each settlement still played an important role in the selection process, which at least ensured that the teachers hired were not openly antagonistic to the movement. Camila, the CREDE official overseeing Lagoa do Mineiro High School, emphasized this participation: "Generally because of the lack of teachers in the region, it is Ivaniza (principal of Lagoa do Mineiro) that enters in contact with teacher candidates, and then they come here and do an interview." Camila also explained that although the teacher candidates were not required to have a Pedagogy of Land degree, they did have to be familiar with the national guidelines for *Educação do Campo*. This meant that, at the very least, teachers who wanted positions in the *escolas do campo* had to read these guidelines before their interview. Other criteria included familiarity with the national high school guidelines, communication skills, ability to manage a classroom, and competence of the curricular content.

Nevertheless, the majority of the teachers who were hired to work in the *escolas do campo* were still unfamiliar with the movement's educational program. Therefore, much like in Santa Maria da Boa Vista, local MST educational activists had to engage in a slow process of garnering moral and intellectual leadership among these teachers, through seminars, teacher trainings, and a constant presence in the schools. One method that the MST education sector developed was annual, week-long "Pedagogical Seminars for the High Schools of the Countryside in MST Agrarian Reform Areas."[30] These seminars were co-organized by the state Department of Education and the MST education sector and brought together all of the teachers and administrators of the four *escolas do campo*. The MST education sector also provided support the rest of the year through visits to the schools, helping teachers organize the student collectives, incorporate interdisciplinary themes into their teaching, and integrate manual labor and agroecology into the daily school routine. Although some teachers initially critiqued these practices, the fact that the state Department of Education officially supported the movement's co-governance of the schools minimized resistance.

Cultural Practices and Student Self-Governance

Two of the most important practices that the MST education sector implemented in the *escolas do campo* were cultural practices and student self-governance. The cultural practices, which took the form of student-led performances known as *místicas*, were the most visible aspect of the MST's pedagogical proposal. One morning, at Florestan Fernandes High School, I observed the students perform a *mística* that involved dancing, singing, and the displaying of various aspects of peasant culture, including local agricultural produce, straw hats, farming tools, and books. The *mística* ended with all of the children singing a song about *Educação do Campo*:

> I want a school of the countryside
> that has to do with my life, with
> loving people who are organized
> and running it collectively.

I want a school of the countryside
that not only teaches equations
but that has a basic principle:
manual labor and collective work.

I want a school of the countryside
that does not have gates
that does not have walls
where we can all learn
that we are the builders of the future.

Another sign of the MST's pedagogies in these schools was the organizational structure, which included student self-governance through base nuclei (NBs). In Florestan Fernandes High School when I visited the classrooms, each student NB presented itself as a collective, shouting a chant about agrarian reform. Throughout the day, the student NBs had different tasks they had to complete, including cleaning the classrooms and taking care of the school garden. Rita, the principal, explained that organizing students into collectives was easy because their settlement was already organized collectively. Therefore, the students had personal experiences participating in their parents' NBs. Thus, there was a dynamic relationship between the school's and the community's organizational structures.

Nevertheless, in 2011, not all of the high schools (or settlements) were as advanced in their implementation of the MST's cultural and organizational practices. When I asked Cilene, the pedagogical coordinator of Nazaré Flor High School, which of the MST's pedagogies were present in her school, she responded, "We have *mística*, but it is happening at a slow pace. We need more workshops to teach the students about what *mística* is . . . there are also base nuclei but there are a lot of limitations and insufficient time to work with all of the students." Unlike the settlement Santana, the settlement of Maceió where Nazaré Flor High School is located was not organized collectively. As MST leader and teacher Nonata Sousa explained, there had been conflicts in the settlement between the MST and a local nongovernmental organization, and the collective leadership structure had fallen apart.[31] Consequently, it was more difficult for the teachers at Nazaré Flor to implement the MST's pedagogies, because students did not have the experience of performing *místicas* and observing their parents collectively govern their settlement. Cilene, the pedagogical coordinator, also described the difficulties implementing the MST's pedagogies in the school: "These practices are happening, but with limits . . . We have work teams, student collectives, interdisciplinary themes, all of this exists on paper. But we need more time for their implementation."

School leaders in Francisco Barros High School were experiencing many of the same difficulties as in Nazaré Flor. One of the reasons for these challenges was that the school's enrollment came from dozens of different local communities, not just the MST settlement. Joel Gomes, the pedagogical coordinator, explained, "We work with twenty-three different communities, indigenous, fishermen, landless . . . our challenge is to work with these different populations . . . it is difficult, we have to find curricular themes that make sense for all of these groups." Although students were organized into NBs, Joel admitted, "They do not understand these groups yet. In some grades, they are functioning, and in other grades, we need more work."

Transforming the Curriculum

Finally, in 2011, one of the MST's main educational goals was to transform the traditional high school curriculum in the *escolas do campo*. Article 26 of the Brazilian Law of Basic Educational Guidelines (LDB) states that every school has the right to implement a diversified part of the curriculum that is sensitive to regional characteristics, in addition to following the national curricular standards.[32] However, there are very few schools in Brazil that have developed additional subjects. In 2011, the MST education sector, drawing on the LDB, proposed adding three disciplines to the curriculum: Organization of Work and Production Techniques; Projects, Studies, and Research; and Communal Social Practices. Each of these disciplines represented a core component of the movement's educational program.

The Organization of Work and Production Techniques was primarily a way for the students to practice agroecological farming methods. When I visited the *escolas do campo* in 2011, all of the schools already had experimental farms—fields cleared near the schools for the students to practice farming. Nohemy Ibanez, the state official who was put in charge of the *escolas do campo* in the state Department of Education, spoke enthusiastically about these farms: "The idea of the farms is that they can be a laboratory for the students to develop new production practices and technologies, like soil correction, and to illustrate to themselves and to their families that it is possible to produce from an agroecology perspective, more sustainably."[33] In many of the *escolas do campo*, students were already working in the experimental farms after the school day was over. However, the MST hoped that by turning this into a formal discipline the students could engage in this agroecological farming more systematically, with a qualified teacher and the intentional incorporation of collective labor practices.

The second discipline that the MST proposed was Projects, Studies, and Research, which would allow students to develop their own research projects and engage in primary data collection in their community. For example, I was told that the students could analyze the most common agricultural practices in the settlement, or local gender relations. This additional discipline was inspired from the movement's experiences with the pedagogy of alternation in the high school and university degree programs. In this model, students study intensively for a few months and then return home to put this knowledge into practice through community research projects. In the case of the *escolas do campo*, this emphasis on putting theory into practice would be an ongoing initiative throughout the entire school year.

Finally, the class on Communal Social Practices would be an opportunity for students to practice and refine their participation in the governance of their school. The MST's vision was for the students to govern the *escolas do campo* collectively, through student NBs, class coordinating collectives, and school-wide coordinating bodies. However, in 2011, this was still difficult to implement in practice. By creating a discipline focused on communal social practices, students would have time to meet in their NBs or participate in a general assembly about hiring a new teacher. This class would also offer the students an opportunity to study the theorists that inspired the MST's educational approach, such as Paulo Freire, Anton Makarenko, and Moisey Pistrak (see Chapter 1).

Together, these three new disciplinary offerings in agricultural production, research, and social practices would create the structural changes necessary for the MST activists to prefigure the major components of their educational vision in the rigid state school system. To incorporate these new disciplines, the MST proposed the transitioning of the *escolas do campo* to full school days.[34] Maria de Jesus explained this proposal:

> We want these themes of work, research, social practices to be part of the curriculum, and for all of them to be related to peasant agricultural practices . . . we want experimental gardens in each of the schools to teach youth about the land, to have them grow food and create youth cooperatives . . . but these practices are impossible if students do not have a full school day.

In 2011, the state officials responsible for overseeing the *escolas do campo* talked to me about this demand, describing the difficulties of making such a huge change to a public school. Letícia said, "Full school days are one of the MST's biggest demands and they want us to respond yes or no. But we had to say maybe. Because we have to analyze what this would mean, the consequences of shifting to full school days." The concerns of these state Department of Education officials included the cost, whether the extra disciplines would take away from the more traditional academic offerings, and how the teachers would develop the new curriculum. Nonetheless, the MST state leadership had both the law on their side and a national advocacy network of activists, professors, and state officials who supported their proposal. In 2012, the MST won the right to transition the four *escolas do campo* to full school days and to incorporate three new disciplines into the curriculum. This structural shift in the state school system, a transformation that is notoriously difficult in public education (Tyack and Tobin 1994; Binder 2002), represented an accumulation of the MST's educational interventions over the previous three decades—since the first public school was built in an MST settlement in 1982.

CONTENTIOUS CO-GOVERNANCE AND THE CEARÁ STATE

The MST education sector's active involvement in the construction, planning, and oversight of the *escolas do campo* in Ceará has created relationships of both cooperation and conflict with state officials, what I call a form of contentious co-governance. In terms of cooperation, I refer to the state's embrace of the movement's educational proposal and the official partnership that exists between the state Department of Education and the MST education sector. Nohemy Ibanez, the head of the Department of Diversity that oversees the *escolas do campo*, talked enthusiastically about *Educação do Campo*: "Today *Educação do Campo* is offering another conception of education that contributes to the sustainable development of the countryside, ensuring that people are no longer migrating to the cities." I asked Nohemy about the MST's participation in the public schools. She quickly listed four of the movement's contributions: developing a strategy of mobilization to achieve their objectives; fighting for public schools and school mission statements that attend to the needs of the communities; politicizing the teachers and principals so they are more comfortable making demands on authorities; and increasing a general political consciousness of rural communities' right to an education different than in urban areas. Nohemy clearly supported *Educação do Campo*—and at least some aspects of the MST's involvement.

Other state officials, who had less familiarity with the MST, also expressed the belief that *Educação do Campo* was a necessary policy. In 2011, Helena and Letícia had only worked in the office for *Educação do Campo* for a year.[35] Helena said, "When I first heard the phrase *Educação do Campo*, I did not understand its difference with rural schools . . . but

Educação do Campo is different; it is a different conception of a school, with a different curriculum and form of administration." Letícia had a similar shift in perspective, saying, "Not all rural schools are schools of the countryside . . . the difference is the curriculum, the types of disciplines, and the school's organization, which cannot be the same as an urban school." Helena and Letícia talked excitedly to me about the proposal to develop new disciplines for the *escolas do campo*, which would connect the school curriculum to the lives of the families engaged in agricultural production. Helena explained, "The *Educação do Campo* proposal is not about professional development. It is about sustainable agricultural production." Again, despite the fact that Helena and Letícia had no connection to the MST before they were assigned to this office, they were already articulating the core aspects of the MST's educational program—most important, its connection to an alternative form of rural development.

Beatriz, the CREDE official overseeing Nazaré Flor High School, also made a distinction between rural schools and *escolas do campo*. She said, "At first it was difficult, but now I understand and defend [the MST's] right to participate . . . living with them and seeing their project, their school philosophy, how they care about the students. They are convincing . . . Rural education is a school in a rural area, but *escolas do campo* are different. They are an alternative project and philosophy." Beatriz described *escolas do campo* as an alternative "project and philosophy," or in other words, an education system intentionally organized to prefigure different social and economic practices. Beatriz certainly did not come to these conclusions by herself. It was through her participation in meetings and seminars with MST activists that she was sensitized to these ideas, and eventually took them on as her own. Similarly, even though CREDE official Camila only began her position earlier that year, she also expressed a basic understanding of *Educação do Campo*. "We have one *escola do campo* and three rural schools. I think the difference is that the *escola do campo*, the one in the settlement, is trying to preserve local culture and prepare students to work with the land . . . to develop the countryside." When I pushed these CREDE officials a bit, asking why these schools should be different than other rural schools, both of them cited Article 26 of the National Educational Law (LDB), which states that communities have the right to adapt their curriculum to local social, economic, and cultural characteristics and customs.

This broad-based acceptance does not mean that the state officials agreed with everything that the MST education sector was doing in the schools. All of the officials I spoke with about the MST also expressed some degree of hesitation about the movement's involvement. For example, CREDE official Camila said, "*Educação do Campo* is necessary because of the diversity of the people in the countryside." However, she admitted, "We are also running a risk. We run the risk of having too much diversity . . . University programs only for people in the settlements, this is discrimination." In my conversations with CREDE official Laura during her visit to João Sem Terra High School, she was generally enthusiastic about the school. However, at one point after a coffee break, Laura said in a whisper, "Sometimes I wonder if all of the students' parents really identify with the struggle, if they really want all of this ideology . . . maybe they want to leave the countryside."[36] Beatriz, the CREDE official overseeing Nazaré Flor High School, stated her support of the MST while also expressing the concern that "Sometimes the principals obey the MST more than the state, and I have to tell them 'Look, the schools belongs to state, not to the MST . . . the state pays for the schools.'" She also commented to me that she thought the MST was a "bit radical, but thank God we are managing to work together." This latter statement expresses perfectly the contentious partnership that developed between state officials and MST activists, which could erupt in conflict at any moment.

The most concrete expression of these government doubts came from Nohemy herself. The Secretary of Education chose Nohemy as the Director of the Department for Diversity because of her history of activism in rural areas and her many experiences working in MST settlements. Nohemy even lived in the settlement Lagoa do Mineiro for nine months, helping with a women's community development project. However, despite her general support of the MST, some of her doubts about the movement's participation emerged during our interview:

> We try to have a dialogue with the MST. But we also believe that the schools are not the property of the MST. The schools are for the people who live in these communities. The schools are a tool of the community, and the MST is welcome to participate, but there are limits to their appropriation of the schools; these are not schools of the MST . . . We realize the principals and some of the teachers are MST leaders . . . and the MST has been very influential in the writing of the PPPs, but *we need the community to take ownership of the schools. Not just the MST education sector* . . . For example, the MST is always saying that they spent two years discussing the PPPs. Maybe people have been involved, but not everyone participated . . . The MST has demands for the governor, but we need to go through a process. We need to have more time to discuss the curriculum; to create something that is sustainable once the MST leaves [emphasis added].

I interviewed Nohemy for over an hour, and during most of the interview she expressed her support of the MST and the implementation of *Educação do Campo* in Ceará. However, at moments, Nohemy also acknowledged these doubts. Like the other state officials, Nohemy wanted to be clear that the *escolas do campo* were state schools, not the MST's schools.

She acknowledged that many of the principals and teachers in the schools were MST leaders, and even referred to one pedagogical coordinator as an "organic intellectual in the community." However, Nohemy questioned whether the process of writing the school PPPs was actually as participatory as the MST leadership claimed. Most important, Nohemy repeatedly made a distinction between the MST and what she referred to as the community. She said, "The schools are a tool of the community, and the MST is welcome to participate." For Nohemy, the families living in the settlement and the MST leadership are not one and the same.

Nohemy's distinction between the MST and the community is telling, because while the MST claims to represent these agrarian reform settlements, there is often a divide between the movement's leadership and the settlement families. The MST's legitimacy in the eyes of the state clearly depends on the movement's ability to garner the allegiance of these families. If the movement is not able to do so, the state will tend to draw a distinction between the movement and the communities, and potentially put limits on the MST's participation. For now, the MST education sector in Ceará has convinced enough families in the settlements and surrounding areas to support their educational program. However, maintaining this consent—the MST's moral and intellectual leadership—will require a constant and continual process of grassroots organizing.

The MST leaders, for their part, are also skeptical of the state. The MST education activists defend their right to participate in the public schools based on their understanding of the state's role in society. Maria de Jesus explained, "The MST does not want to replace the state. The state and the movement have to work together in a process of popular participation, each group with its own responsibility. We all have a job. But one thing I do not accept is to be simply a beneficiary of a program. We have agency and we want to be part of the process." Maria de Jesus insisted that the state had a responsibility to provide certain services, such as public education. However, she did not want to simply receive these services. She said that citizens had the right to participate in constructing and implementing government programs. At one MST education meeting, I heard Maria de Jesus exclaim in frustration, "A lot of people want *Educação do Campo*, but they want it without the MST."

This statement, of course, conveys the fundamental tension in the movement's educational program: the MST leadership does not simply want access to public schooling; they want to participate in the co-governance of these state institutions. The MST wants schools to be part of their movement infrastructure, organically connected to and supporting the struggle for agrarian reform. Government officials might support most of these initiatives, and even allow the MST to participate directly in the co-governance of the schools; however, for the state the schools are a universal public good, not a tool in the movement's struggle. The MST can counter this critique by claiming that it is not the movement but, rather, the families that the schools are serving who are leading this educational process. As Erivando said to me, "The school should not belong to the principals, or the administrators, or the governor—it should belong to the people." Of course, "the people" the MST leadership imagines governing these public schools are those aligned with the movement's political and economic goals.

CONCLUSION

In 2014, the PT won the gubernatorial race in Ceará in an alliance with the previous PSB governor Cid Gomes. In 2015, the Ceará state Department of Education agreed to construct four additional high schools in MST settlements. Two of these schools, located in the municipalities of Canindé and Santana do Acaraú, opened in 2016. The other two, in the municipalities of Mombaça and Ocara, opened in January 2017. These schools are all considered part of the network of *escolas do campo*, with the right to a diversified curriculum and organizational practices appropriate for rural populations. In 2016, the MST education sector was already initiating discussions with the communities who would attend these schools about their school mission statements. Also in 2016, the Ceará state Department of Education passed its Plan for Education, which included as one of its goals preserving communities' right to *Educação do Campo*. In January 2017, the MST statewide education sector organized its seventh "Pedagogical Seminar for the High Schools of the Countryside in MST Agrarian Reform Areas." This seminar brought together all of the principals and teachers from the old and new *escolas do campo* to analyze the current educational and agrarian context, evaluate the implementation of the PPPs in the schools, and strengthen the school's agroecological initiatives.[37] The MST's participation in the *escolas do campo* in Ceará is a dynamic process that continues to progress, with government support, despite the many barriers, constraints, and state officials' frequent skepticism of this process.

Several lessons can be drawn from this contemporary example of social movement co-governance in Ceará. First, the MST's ability to demand these schools was at least partially a result of the recognition *Educação do Campo* had already gained at the federal level. Two key moments of intervention were critical: the introduction of the concept of *Educação do Campo* to state government officials in 2006, under a right-leaning administration, and the federal government's construction of more new high schools in 2009, with a more left-leaning state government in power. The national coalition for *Educação do Campo* initiated the first discussions about this educational program in 2006 and helped to bring together a diverse group of government officials and social movement and union leaders to discuss these ideas. When the coalition withdrew its support for these initiatives, it seemed as though *Educação do Campo* would slowly disappear—despite a new left-leaning governor in office. It took another federal intervention, the funding of a dozen new high schools in the state, for *Educação do Campo* to re-enter the debate. Drawing on Keck and Sikkink, I have referred to this as the "boomerang effect," as local activists in Ceará reached out to national allies to put pressure on their state and municipal governments to concede to their educational demands. Although the federal government was the most visible actor, the national advocacy network for *Educação do Campo* included other movement, union, and university allies. However, as the counterexample of São Paulo illustrates, the boomerang effect's degree of influence directly depends on the subnational state's capacity to reject these national trends.

A second lesson is that the MST's capacity to govern the *escolas do campo* in Ceará was a consequence of the movement's accumulation of more than three decades of experience implementing alternative educational practices in the Brazilian countryside. In other words, it was not simply the federal interventions but the MST's "practical authority" (Abers and Keck 2013) and ability to capitalize on these opportunities that facilitated the movement's participation in the four new high schools. The MST education sector in Ceará had a clear sense of what type of educational proposal they wanted to develop, because they had learned from the countless experiences that had taken place in other states over the previous decade. The MST leadership convinced multiple state actors of the importance of implementing this educational program, both citing laws and illustrating the effectiveness of the proposal in practice.

Finally, a third lesson is that, despite this favorable context—a left-leaning government, local social movement infrastructure, and outside support that increased the state's capacity for educational governance (top left corner of Table 1.1 in Chapter 1)—social movement co-governance is always a process full of tensions and conflict. Although there has been a gradual acceptance of *Educação do Campo* among many state actors in Ceará, there are also reservations about the MST's involvement. The *escolas do campo* have become a part of the MST's movement infrastructure, integrating youth, parents, and teachers into the agrarian reform struggle. State officials generally defend the MST's participation, citing national laws and educational guidelines as justification for the movement's participation.

Nonetheless, the MST leadership's high degree of influence over these schools is also uncomfortable for government officials, who see themselves as the guardians of these institutions and responsible for ensuring that they serve all Brazilian citizens. I refer to social movement's participation in state institutions as a form of contentious co-governance, which simultaneously promotes universal participation and particular political, economic, and social goals. The MST leadership's only way of overcoming this tension is garnering the consent of families and teachers inside and outside of the settlements for their agrarian reform struggle. This organic relationship between the movement leadership and its base is the most important factor influencing activists' ability to institutionalize and prefigure their economic, political, and social goals within state institutions. In the Conclusion, I revisit the different lessons that emerged from the MST's national educational struggle and these regional case studies to suggest some broader lessons for understanding effective social movement strategy, education, and social change in the twenty-first century.

Conclusion

Social Movement Strategy, Education, and Social Change in the Twenty-First Century

The first step in emancipating oneself from political and social slavery is that of freeing the mind. I put forward this new idea: popular schooling should be placed under the control of the great workers' unions. The problem of education is the most important class problem.

—Antonio Gramsci, *Avanti* (1916)[1]

On September 20, 2015, twelve hundred teachers working in public schools located in MST settlements and camps across the country traveled to the capital city of Brasília, to participate in the Second National Meeting of Educators in Areas of Agrarian Reform (ENERA). Hundreds of the teachers who arrived for the event were long-time MST collaborators and self-identified MST activists. Other teachers at the conference had only recently started working in areas of agrarian reform, and this would be their first time learning about the movement's educational approach. Also participating in the conference were dozens of dedicated, full-time MST educational leaders who had been implementing the movement's educational program in public schools in areas of agrarian reform for the previous three decades. The first ENERA, held in July 1997, had marked the MST's entrance into the national debate on rural schooling. Now, eighteen years later, the goal of the second ENERA was to discuss the current status of the MST's pedagogical initiatives and ways to advance the movement's educational program in the current political moment.

On the first day of the national meeting, the teachers and MST activists gathered outside of the auditorium. Members of the MST's culture collective played music and led dances, keeping everyone energized as they waited for the event to begin. The MST education collective had decorated the halls of the conference center with symbols that represented the rural countryside (straw hats, rope, seeds, agricultural produce, machetes, decorative fabrics) and social struggle (pictures of land occupations, anti-agribusiness posters, MST flags). Inside the auditorium ten-foot-high pictures of the movement's "intellectuals" (*pensadores*) hung from the walls, including Antonio Gramsci, Frida Kahlo, Nadezhda Krupskaya, Lenin, Rosa Luxemburg, Anton Makarenko, José Martí, Karl Marx, Moisey Pistrak, Milton Santos, and Zumbi. There was a section in the front of the auditorium reserved for two dozen government guests who would participate in the morning's event, including several heads of ministries.

Once everyone was seated, an elaborate forty-minute cultural performance began—a typical MST *mística*. Tractors (built out of cardboard) identified as Monsanto and the Federal Court of Audits (TCU) attempted to plow down rural farmers. A swarm of people wearing black followed, carrying signs that said Agribusiness (*Agronegócio*), Pesticides (*Agrotóxico*), Monoculture (*Monocultura*), and Education for All (*Todas Pela Educação*), a coalition of mostly private-sector actors increasingly involved in defining the educational agenda in Brazil.[2] Then, dozens of people in straw hats and farm clothing came running into the auditorium, pressuring these enemies off the stage. An MST leader read a poem about the 1871 Paris Commune. A dozen other activists dressed as oil workers joined the farmers, bringing with them a large hammer and sickle that symbolized working-class solidarity between the MST and the oil workers on strike across Brazil. The government officials in the audience watched politely. After the presentation, everyone was asked to stand up for the singing of the MST's anthem. The government officials stood silently, as the teachers and activists sung proudly around them.

More than an hour later, after each of the invited government guests had a chance to speak—almost all of them emphasizing the importance of agrarian reform and *Educação do Campo*—one of the best-known MST national leaders, famous for his rousing talks, came to the front: João Pedro Stédile. João Pedro spoke about why the struggle for agrarian reform required, in addition to land, dignified housing, the production of healthy food, and of course, people's control over knowledge. He exhorted the crowd: "The working class needs to organize its class project, and in order to do this we have to organize in all spaces of social life." Pointing to the picture of Lenin, he continued, "Some people have interpreted Lenin incorrectly. They think we can just take the presidential palace and then have power. But there is nowhere in Brazil with less power than the presidential palace!" The crowd laughed at the remark, all too appropriate as thousands of people across the country were calling for President Rousseff's impeachment and it seemed likely that she would soon be pushed out of office. Then João Pedro pointed to the picture of Gramsci in the back of the auditorium. "We prefer to follow Gramsci, who says that the people have to create their own social projects and contest power in all spaces of social life, the school, the land, the senate, and the presidential palace. We are here this week to discuss how to continue one single chapter of our struggle, the conquest of knowledge and education." João Pedro turned to address the government officials: "These are our friends here. I am not here to curse you, because today you are on our team. We will curse you on Wednesday! Wednesday you can fear us because we are going to Brasília!" The teachers started cheering, as João Pedro listed all of the buildings they were going to occupy, and the state officials they would denounce, two days later.

The Second National Meeting of Educators in Areas of Agrarian Reform, which took place thirty-one years after the movement's founding, represents one instance of the MST's attempt to transform public schooling in diverse regions of Brazil, by integrating teachers into the movement's educational struggle. As João Pedro emphasized, these educational initiatives

Picture 7.1 Educators and activists at the Second National Meeting of Educators in Areas of Agrarian Reform (ENERA). A picture of one of the MST's intellectual inspirations, Antonio Gramsci, is hanging in the back. September 2015.
Courtesy of Celeiro de Memoria

comprise a single chapter of the MST's broader fight for land, agrarian reform, and social transformation. João Pedro's reference to Gramsci helps to shed light on the MST's political strategy for achieving these goals: rather than wait to take state power to transform society sometime in the future, MST activists are attempting to prefigure, in the present, the forms of economic production, political participation, social relations, cultural activities, and pedagogical approaches that the movement supports. The MST engages in these prefigurative politics with, in, through, and outside of the state. This long march through the institutions requires both negotiation with a myriad group of political actors and open political contestation.

It is only possible to understand the MST's educational demands in the context of this broader Gramscian strategy, to integrate as many people as possible into a new social project in the Brazilian countryside. However, it is also necessary to update and extend Gramsci, and show how his theories can be applied to contemporary movements. I have emphasized three major lessons that emerge from the MST's thirty-year attempt to transform Brazilian education: that social movements can increase their internal capacity by participating in state institutions; the importance of simultaneously engaging in multiple movement strategies, including disruption, persuasion, negotiation, and co-governance; and that the government's political orientation, the state's capacity for educational governance, and social movements' internal infrastructure directly influence the possibilities for institutional change. In the rest of this chapter, I revisit these three central claims and offer several more lessons about social movement strategies and the role of education in social change in the twenty-first century.

STRATEGIC SOCIAL MOVEMENTS: CONTENTIOUS CO-GOVERNANCE AND PREFIGURATION

The thesis that social movements engaging in the institutional sphere are destined to demobilize and decline, an argument often attributed to Piven and Cloward (1977) and Michels (1915), is still a powerful trope both among social movement scholars and activists. As I summarized in the Introduction, many scholars have taken a more nuanced position on this question, discussing the effectiveness of activists' "dual strategy" (Alvarez 1990) of working both within and outside of the state, or combining non-institutional and institutional politics (Andrews 2004; Banaszak 2010; Meyer and Tarrow 1997). These studies push us beyond the concept of social movement co-optation and, instead, "'unpack' the State and examine its multiple institutional and ideological instances" (Alvarez 1990, 272) that allow social movements to make meaningful impacts on diverse state institutions. More recently, Alvarez and colleagues (2017) have pushed for a new perspective on civil society, which focuses on both the civic and the uncivic actions of diverse movements—the permitted and the unpermitted.

Nonetheless, the question of how social movements should engage the state continues to vex movement activists and researchers. For example, many people celebrate the Zapatista Army of National Liberation's (EZLN) strategy in Mexico for choosing the exact opposite path as the MST: rejecting all government resources and building counterinstitutions completely outside of the realm of the state.[3] In the US Occupy movement, the question of whether to make concrete demands on state actors, or to reject state power and build an alternative social world within the boundaries of Zuccotti Park, divided the movement (Smucker 2017). The Chilean student movement, which led huge mobilizations in 2006 and 2011, has factionalized over debates on the role of government negotiations and electoral politics (Larrabure and Torchia 2015). In Brazil itself, the MST's close relationship to the Workers' Party (PT) and willingness to accept government funding is highly critiqued by leaders of multiple left political tendencies and parties. To many leftist organizers in Brazil, the MST has indeed been co-opted—exchanging its capacity to mobilize large, contentious protests for the crumbs of the neoliberal state. Forty years after Piven and Cloward published their polemic against the institutionalization of social movements, the debates that it sparked have only intensified, and they continue to represent a central dilemma facing twenty-first-century social movements.

I have tried to reframe the process of institutionalizing social movement goals as not just a means to an end but, rather, as a form of co-governance. When social movement leaders engage in the contentious co-governance of state institutions—or perhaps more appropriately, the occupation of those institutions—they are testing the validity of their theories by trying them out on the ground. This form of prefiguration or praxis leads to new perspectives, ideas, practices, and strategic actions. For example, when social movement leaders help to develop, implement, and oversee state service delivery, they are experimenting with ways to transform those public goods to adhere to alternative social and political ideals. This includes the creation of alternative media outlets, agricultural production processes, public health centers, and schools—all of which increase activists' technical and political capacity for co-governance.

This argument also offers a new perspective on a long-standing debate among scholars and activists about prefigurative politics.[4] In this discussion, it is often assumed that the prefiguration of social and political values is a process that can only take place outside of formal institutions, in an autonomous movement sphere not corrupted by state power. In contrast, I have shown that social movements can also prefigure radical goals within state institutions, and although this will always be a contradictory process, the institutional expression of activists' political projects is a powerful way of obtaining needed resources, building local leadership, and increasing organizational capacity. However, the key point is that social movements engaging in institutions must continue to be movements. The MST has participated in the state sphere for three decades, without demobilizing, by combining disruption, persuasion, negotiation, and co-governance. This latter process has involved continual conflict and tension between MST leaders and state actors, a process I have termed *contentious co-governance*.

Experimentation, Accumulation of Learning, and Real Educational Utopias

The real puzzle of this book is explaining how MST activists made such tremendous gains in the institutional sphere, while maintaining their autonomy as an independent movement. A key lesson is that transforming state institutions is an iterative process of experimentation and cumulative learning. This book began by describing activists' first trials with alternative educational approaches in the 1980s, and then it traced how the movement's educational initiatives transformed Brazil's approach to rural education over the next three decades. Local MST activists began to experiment with alternative educational approaches immediately after the movement's first land occupations took place, drawing on the theories that were available and the everyday practices of their communities. Then, in order to continue offering educational access to movement activists, the MST leadership sought out partnerships with governments to organize high school degree and teaching certification programs. In the late 1990s, the MST expanded these high school programs to other states, while also establishing baccalaureate and graduate degree programs in dozens of subject areas through the National Program of Education in Areas of Agrarian Reform (PRONERA).

Two decades later, these PRONERA programs are still reserved for students living in areas of agrarian reform and are offered separately from the regular university programs. The MST has been a major participant co-governing these programs. However, the MST's approach to implementing its educational proposal in the university sphere has been a process of trial and error, as activists had to learn how to navigate the conflicts that arose when their vision of justice clashed with the university's own vision. The MST has also helped to establish a handful of other educational institutions that offer high school and university degrees with an emphasis on agroecology, thus linking the movement's educational program to its goal of promoting agroecology and food sovereignty in settlements.[5]

By establishing institutional arrangements in which activists have almost full autonomy to structure students' educational experience, the movement has experimented with the implementation of a range of educational practices. Since the first high school programs in the 1990s, thousands of MST activists have experienced these real educational utopias, living the MST's pedagogical approach for several years at a time. As these programs expanded across the country, they integrated more educational activists into the movement, while equipping them with the necessary degrees to become teachers and principals. Thus, the process of experimenting with new educational practices, accumulating learning through trial and error, and establishing real educational utopias has played a critical role in activists' ability to transform local public schools.

Strategic Allies and Multiple Access Points

A second lesson that comes out of this long-march view of social movements (Paschel 2016) is the importance of finding strategic allies and multiple access points within the state when promoting an alternative social vision. In the early 1990s, in a period of intense conflict between social movements and the federal government, several international organizations, including UNESCO and UNICEF, began to partner with the MST and directly fund the movement's literacy programs, bypassing the federal government. The movement organized these programs through partnerships with dozens of different universities, which allowed local activists to develop close relationships with hundreds of university professors. The MST's ability to demand a national program for education in areas of agrarian reform in 1997 depended on the advocacy of these university faculty, who navigated the politics of their institutions to garner support for this initiative—and then used their institutions' prestige to make a case for the new program to the federal government. The following year, in 1998, these same allies pushed the MST to articulate its proposal for a broader rural population— *Educação do Campo*. This reframing was key in bringing new actors into this struggle, most prominently, the rural union movement.

As I argued in Chapter 3, this alliance between the MST and the rural union movement initially appeared improbable, as these organizations had antagonistic social and economic visions and conflicting relationships to political parties and institutional politics. Nonetheless, this coalition was critical in convincing the federal government to embrace an education proposal for the entire Brazilian countryside, even before the PT took office in 2003. Then, under the PT, the government reorganized the Ministry of Education to institutionalize the participation of these rural social movements in policymaking. Thus, while the MST developed its pedagogical approach through experimentation in local settlements, rolling out this pedagogy on a large scale required garnering the consent of other social and political groups. Throughout this process, the participation of university professors offered these movements legitimacy and institutional support.

Not All Institutions Are Created Equal

A third lesson is that the institutions of the state vary widely in their capacity, autonomy, and bureaucratic culture, and these differences sway movement strategies and outcomes—suggesting the need to reconstruct the Piven and Cloward and Michels thesis. In some contexts, as Piven and Cloward would predict, the process of institutionalizing social movement goals leads to social movement decline and deradicalization. In other cases, the institutionalization of these goals can fortify a social movement's organizational capacity and resources, and buttress ongoing mobilization. Thus, the concept of co-optation is not useful in capturing the diverse trajectories that social movements have inside of state institutions.

The cases of the National Institute of Colonization and Agrarian Reform (INCRA) and the Ministry of Education (MEC), elaborated in Chapters 2 and 3, elucidate this finding. INCRA is underfunded, decentralized, and relatively neglected in national politics, while the MEC is well funded, centralized, and highly visible in policy debates. Between 1998 and 2005, MST activists institutionalized aspects of their educational proposal in both of these federal agencies (through the National Program for Education in Areas of Agrarian Reform [PRONERA] and the *Educação do Campo* office), with different impacts. In the case of INCRA, the MST has been able to maintain real and meaningful participation in the development of all PRONERA programs. However, the fact that PRONERA has allowed for so much social movement participation has also meant that the program has been more open to attacks by conservative actors. In the MEC, the *Educação do Campo* office has been able to implement some major rural education initiatives, including programs for adult education, infrastructure, multigrade schooling, and perhaps most significantly, a massive university program to train teachers to work in the countryside. Although MST activists did not support all of these initiatives, in many cases they had the opportunity to participate in the initial designs of these programs. However, when the MEC began to implement these programs on a mass scale, the MST's participation and oversight was no longer viable. Furthermore, by 2012, agribusiness interests began to embrace the call for *Educação do Campo*, succeeding in capturing funds that supported their own vision of educational purpose—training workers for industrial agricultural jobs. This comparison suggests that movement outcomes can be diverse, even when the same proposal is promoted by the same movement during the same historical moment—depending on the institution that is targeted. For the MST's internal capacity, it was better to engage in the weaker and less prominent institution; however, for implementing widespread policy reform, the more powerful institution had a larger impact.

In assessing these impacts, I argue along with other social movement scholars that it is more helpful to think in terms of outcomes rather than success or failure. As Andrews (2004) writes, "The concept of 'outcomes' or equivalent terms such as 'consequences' or 'impact' provides greater flexibility because scholars can assess the influence of the movement in many different domains of activity and examine intended and unintended impacts of the movement" (17). According to the MST leadership, PRONERA has been one of the movement's most important state programs, offering educational access to families in settlements and camps with activists' direct oversight. Thus, the MST's measure of educational success centers on the level of independence the movement has to govern an educational program, the degree to which activists can implement their pedagogical goals, and the extent to which this process strengthens the movement by integrating new members and increasing the intellectual and technical capacity of activists.

Nonetheless, while the MST has significant control over PRONERA, the scale of these programs pales in comparison to the MEC's *Educação do Campo* programs. For example, the baccalaureate and teaching certification degree is an affirmative action program that has become a permanent offering at forty universities, allowing more rural students than ever before to enter the elite public university system. Similarly, *Escola Ativa*, which the MST vehemently critiqued, has offered significant resources to the most precarious rural schools with multigrade classrooms. Although these MEC programs do not increase the MST's internal capacity as directly as PRONERA, they still provide immense resources to hundreds of rural communities across the Brazilian countryside—and the fact is that these programs would not exist if the MST had not pressured the state to invest in rural education. In sum, the MST's engagement with the MEC has resulted in greater resources and more expansive policy, at least in the short term. However, the fact that PRONERA directly increases the MST's internal capacity suggests that this latter program might prove more important for the movement's ability to maintain pressure on the government, to implement more structural and radical reforms over the long haul.

Partisan Allegiances Are a Double-Edged Sword

Finally, another lesson in this book is that movement outcomes vary across regions and time, especially in a federal system such as Brazil. The three factors I identified—the political orientation of the government, state capacity, and social movement infrastructure—are all emphasized in different strands of literature; however, no one has proposed this particular analytical scheme for understanding movement outcomes. Government ideology, of course, echoes much of the literature on political opportunities; nonetheless, I have shown that ideological alignment is only important in certain contexts, where the state has a high capacity for governance. When state capacity is low, activists can create their own opportunities in a sense, by illustrating the practical benefits of working with the movement—through both protest and the movement's own capacities for implementing policy goals. This latter point—that civil society can increase the capacity of the state to achieve its goals—echoes an important finding in the literature on participatory democracy (e.g., Abers and Keck 2013), but it is not discussed in the social movement literature. Finally, I have also highlighted the importance of what Andrews (2004) calls social movement infrastructure, which includes a movement's internal resources, organization, and leadership, in exploiting different opportunities in the political realm. I have built on this concept by suggesting the particular influence of collective leadership, which is not a series of individual characteristics but a movement's moral and intellectual leadership in civil society. In the Introduction, I presented a table illustrating the interaction of these factors (Table I.1). In this chapter, Table C.1 replicates Table I.1, indicating how the five regional cases explored in this book map onto this analytical framework.

First, the case of Rio Grande do Sul illustrates the temporary benefits of social movements aligning with leftist governments (top left corner of Table C.1). In this state, between 1996 and 2006, the combination of protest and internal allies helped MST activists obtain permission for the construction of Itinerant Schools in their occupied camps. Then, when a supportive and left-leaning governor took office in 1998, this educational experiment became an official state program and the Itinerant Schools received much more support. By 2006, the Itinerant Schools in Rio Grande do Sul had become a nationally celebrated educational experiment, famous for the participation of social movement leaders in their co-governance. Nonetheless, the political shifts in Rio Grande do Sul immediately following this period illustrate that partisan allegiances can also work against a movement (top center-right section of Table C.1). In 2007, an administration openly antagonistic to the MST came to power and sought to weaken the movement by

Table C.1 BARRIERS AND CATALYSTS TO THE MST'S CONTENTIOUS
CO-GOVERNANCE OF PUBLIC EDUCATION: REGIONAL CASES

		Political Orientation of the Government			
		Left-leaning		Right-leaning	
Social Movement Infrastructure	**High**	Best context *Rio Grande do Sul* (1999-2001) Ceará (2009-2014)	Many opportunities	Difficult context *Rio Grande do Sul* (2007-2010) São Paulo	Many opportunities *Santa Maria da Boa Vista, PE*
	Low	Difficult context *Rio Grande do Sul* (2011)	Difficult context	Difficult context	Difficult context *Água Preta, PE*
		High	**Low**	**High**	**Low**
		State Capacity for Educational Governance			

closing the Itinerant Schools. The state government's ability to shut down the Itinerant Schools was enhanced by the Public Ministry, who issued a legal order to close the schools. This whole period, when repression against the movement was much greater than ever before, led to a decline in the number of occupations and, consequently, the number of children living in the MST's camps. Although the left-leaning administration that took power in 2011 annulled the legal order that had closed the Itinerant Schools, there were no longer enough children in the camps to merit their reopening (bottom left corner of Table C.1). Importantly, during this period a group of MST leaders left the movement, declaring that the movement's institutional focus had led to its lack of capacity to organize the same widespread and massive land occupations of previous eras.

The cases of Santa Maria da Boa Vista and Água Preta, in Pernambuco, show the many opportunities that exist for social movement participation under right-leaning administrations in low-capacity state contexts—as long as social movements invest in local movement infrastructure and, most important, collective leadership. In Santa Maria, there were more steady opportunities for social movement co-governance over a fifteen-year period than in Rio Grande do Sul. The municipality's low level of capacity for educational governance facilitated the teachers', principals', and bureaucrats' openness to the MST's involvement in education (top right corner of Table C.1). Likewise, in Água Preta, in the late 1990s, a clientelistic political culture similar to Santa Maria provided an opening for the MST to engage the municipal government and begin to transform the public school system. However, by the mid-2000s, the MST itself was in crisis in this region, partially due to the resurgence of the sugar industry.

Unable to surmount the challenges of the shifting political economy, the base of the movement increasingly distanced from the leadership. Despite the many opportunities for MST–state collaboration, this divide between the MST leadership and the families in the settlements makes Água Preta a difficult location for contentious co-governance (bottom right corner of Table C.1).

The case of Ceará reveals how social movement outcomes at the federal level can impact state trajectories. Following Keck and Sikkink (1998), I have referred to this as a national version of the "boomerang effect" (12): local activists bypassing their municipal or state governments and reaching out to national allies to gain leverage, information, and resources to pressure their subnational governments to implement policy reforms. In Ceará, the federal government's interventions introduced *Educação do Campo* (Education of the Countryside) to state officials. Then, in 2009, the federal government intervened again, offering Ceará the financial and administrative resources needed to construct a dozen new public high schools—thus increasing the governing capacity of a left-leaning government (top left corner of Table C.1). The MST leadership demanded that four of these schools be built on the movement's own agrarian reform settlements, designated as *escolas do campo*. The MST leadership in Ceará drew on the movement's thirty years of accumulated experience in the educational sphere to make this demand. These *escolas do campo* are now one of the most impressive examples of the MST's co-governance of public education in the country, allowing the movement to prefigure in the everyday school routine its social, political, and economic vision.

Finally, although I only briefly mention São Paulo in Chapter 6, this case reinforces the point that partisan politics is a double-edged sword. In São Paulo, twenty years of a high-capacity, right-leaning state government—antagonistic to the MST and to the PT's initiatives at the federal level—has prevented the MST's educational program from moving forward (top center-right section of Table C.1). Thus, despite the dozens of well-resourced schools on MST settlements throughout the state, and the high number of land occupations over the past two decades, the movement's pedagogical practices are basically absent.

What do these regional cases add up to? Again, one of the major findings of this comparative case study is that context matters, but not in ways that are anticipated by the literature. Studies on social movement outcomes suggest that like-minded politicians are key to gaining policy influence (Amenta et al. 2010). In contrast, I show that movements can gain influence under a variety of political regimes. In fact, aligning with a leftist government might not be the most strategic choice for the long-term sustainability of institutional change. A key variable influencing activists' ability to implement their ideas is the state's capacity for policy implementation and local governance. In those cases where the reach of the state is limited, movements have much more power—what Abers and Keck (2013) call "practical authority"—to influence policy and participate in the co-governance of public services. This builds on the participatory democracy literature as it shows how movements—even those with political projects inherently in contradiction to the Brazilian state (Dagnino 2001)—can momentarily overcome these differences and work together, thus mobilizing the state's own capacity to deliver public goods.

Politics Is Often Insurmountable; Collective Leadership Is Not

The most important take-home point from the regional case studies, however, is that a social movement's own internal infrastructure—in particular, local, collective leadership—is the most critical factor influencing outcomes. Collective leadership is difficult to build, as allegiance to the movement has to be continually (re)produced through multiple forms of grassroots work with families living in areas of agrarian reform. Drawing on Gramsci, I see this process as activists' attempt to gain moral and intellectual leadership in the countryside for an alternative hegemonic project. In this sense, the activists who are involved in the everyday struggle of promoting the movement's goals are similar to a Gramscian political party, or what Tuğal (2009) refers to as "the sphere where society organizes to shape state policies but also to define the nature of the state and political unity" (25). Political parties are the link between civil society and the state, or between civil society and an alternative hegemonic project. The MST leadership is clearly fulfilling this role, as activists attempt to link rural populations to an imagined political body—the MST—and help to constitute people's everyday experiences with politics. This process is always in competition with other organizations attempting to gain "moral and intellectual leadership" among the rural poor.

There are three major social actors that participate in the MST's educational struggle: the MST leadership, or activists who identify as part of the movement and participate in the regional, statewide, and national leadership bodies; the families living in agrarian reform settlements and occupied camps, who have different degrees of allegiance to the movement; and teachers, university faculty, education officials, and other actors that are connected to schools in areas of agrarian reform. However, when the MST succeeds in leading a process of participatory co-governance in public schools, the divisions between these three layers of social actors disappear, as activists, teachers, principals, parents, students—and sometimes even state officials—come together to implement the movement's pedagogical proposal. When the MST fails to develop local leadership in an agrarian reform settlement, however, teachers and families perceive themselves as separate from the movement and are sometimes even hostile to MST activists. This makes it difficult to participate in the public schools, as state actors begin to (correctly) see the MST leadership as separate from the agrarian reform communities that the state is supposed to serve.

The case of the MST's thirty-year struggle for agrarian reform shows that organizing a mass-based political movement requires, above all else, maintaining strong relationships between the leaders of the movement and the base of people that it claims to represent. This does not mean simply inviting people to a meeting and assuming that politically superior ideas will convince them to participate. Organizing a movement involves an intense process of relationship building, engaging with people's stories, histories, and common-sense understandings of the world, and attempting to garner their consent for and belief in an alternative economic and political project. These are not one-time discussions but, rather, relationships that have to be built over and over again throughout the life span of a movement. If movement leaders neglect this task of relationship building, the result is an ever-increasing divide between the movement's full-time participants and its base—and consequently, an inability to promote institutional change.

Real Tradeoffs and Real Gains

Finally, although this book argues that social movement activists can advance their goals and build their movements by strategically engaging state institutions, this "long-march" strategy is not without tradeoffs. Developing new curriculum and strategically placing activists in schools consumes time, energy, and resources that could be used for other activities, namely contentious actions. This, of course, is the exact concern that Piven and Cloward (1977) and many other scholars and activists have highlighted (e.g., Offe and Weisenthal 1980; Przeworksi 1986). Nonetheless, throughout the 1980s, Brazilian social movements and political parties made institutional transformation a central part of their political and economic goals. Brazilian political strategist Juarez Guimarães (1990) described this as the "tweezer strategy," in which the arm of a movement that occupies institutional spaces is counterbalanced by a second arm, which focuses on building grassroots, popular power. In other words, rather than the institutional struggle implying a tradeoff, the goal was to contest the institutional realm in order to promote initiatives that could directly serve, over time, to build a socialist hegemony. Of course, many left-wing activists' critique of the PT and other social movements in the 1990s was that there was an imbalance between taking institutional power and building popular power. As MST leader Gilmar Mauro (2017) described this period, "The institutional dispute and space became the strong arm, and the social movements were the weak arm."

In this book I have argued that the gross imbalance between an institutional and a grassroots strategy is not inevitable. To the contrary, the MST's educational programs and other institutional initiatives have been in the direct service of the movement's growth, sustainability, and ongoing mobilization. There are still class compromises that take place, sometimes as explicitly as a conservative mayor devolving authority over the school system to placate the MST leadership. The result is an immediate tradeoff, as MST leaders are forced to dedicate their energy to the enormous task of overseeing dozens of day-to-day, mundane, school activities—while the mayor maintains political power. Nonetheless, what the MST activists gain is not simply an improvement in workers' immediate conditions.[6] Rather, activists are now able to practice implementing their socialist ideals with students and teachers, with significant resources and infrastructure. This directly contributes to the movement's long-term goal of transforming society through the partial prefiguration, in the current context, of socialist relations and practices. While the PT's institutional struggle improved workers' conditions without necessarily building the conditions for socialism, the MST's institutional strategy has directly contributed to training and educating a new generation of movement activists.

RETHINKING EDUCATION: SCHOOLS AS A POWERFUL SPHERE FOR MOVEMENTS TO EXERCISE INFLUENCE

In addition to these broad insights about social movement strategy, this study also suggests that among the diverse state institutions that affect people's daily lives, public education is particularly important for social movements to garner influence. As Marxist theorist Althusser (1971) suggested more than four decades ago, the educational system is one of the most important ideological state apparatuses of contemporary society, an institution that plays a critical role in helping to cultivate the societal values of meritocracy, competition, and expertise, and helping to integrate people into the capitalist economy. Nevertheless, the MST's success in implementing educational practices in public schools that support alternative modes of production illustrates that public schools are not necessarily destined to be institutions of social reproduction. Although Althusser (1971), Bowles and Gintis (1976), and Bourdieu and Passeron (1990) provide a powerful framework for analyzing the correspondence between schools and capitalism, their theories do not offer language for understanding resistance. Similarly, the social movement literature does not offer a framework for analyzing how activists can utilize schools as spaces of grassroots leadership development and mobilization.

This study has shown that schools, which monopolize the waking hours of most youth and many adults, are important institutions where movements can begin to prefigure, in the current world, the social practices that they hope to build in the future. While the MST leadership promotes these types of social, economic, and political practices in other movement spaces—such as meetings or agricultural cooperatives—public schools are unique institutions that bring together students and parents who might not otherwise engage with the movement. If the MST does *not* dispute public education, the teachers assigned to work in these schools will have little knowledge about the movement and will almost certainly reproduce the urban bias in the Brazilian school system, encouraging students to leave the countryside for jobs in the cities. Movement leaders can engage in nonformal consciousness-raising activities, but this will only go so far if youth are spending the whole day in school learning a totally separate consciousness. On the other hand, if activists can obtain permission to co-govern these schools, they can promote the idea that the countryside is a vibrant place for young people. Through the mentorship of the MST leadership and the movement's many teacher training programs, the educators in these schools—often previously unconnected to the movement—become Gramscian organic intellectuals, promoting socialism, food sovereignty, and collectivity in schools.

This, of course, touches on the key question of educational purpose. As Carnoy and Levin (1985) argue, there is a contradiction within school systems between the goal of training the future workforce and promoting a more democratic and equal society. They write, "there are two major forces that mold the agenda of the schools: one presses for an education that will provide opportunity, mobility, equality, democratic participation, and the expansion of rights; the other presses for an education that will provide appropriately trained workers with the required skills, attitudes, and behavior for efficient production and capital accumulation" (230). The MST is in fact pushing for a third vision, the expansion of rights and democratic participation for all students, but also the integration of students into production processes that are explicitly anti-capitalist. In other words, the MST's goal is to train the next generation of students for a socialist society that may never exist. Is this at the expense of students' integration into the current economic system? Some families certainly resist the MST's educational program because they perceive the movement's influence as taking away from the aspects of schooling that result in individual career advancement. Nonetheless, many of the students who have graduated from these MST-inspired educational programs go on to become teachers, lawyers, accountants, agricultural technicians, doctors, and more, even if they leave the movement. Thus, although there is a real and constant tension between the strategic use of public education for a particular social vision and the universal goal of education for career advancement, it is probable that the MST's educational interventions have served both ends for rural populations.

Gender, Social Prestige, and Technical Skills

What are the exact mechanisms through which occupying public schooling, rather than simply investing in informal or nonformal educational practices, contributes to a movement's social movement infrastructure? As I argue throughout the book, and particularly in Chapter 2, the MST's formal education programs have helped to build the movement by integrating students and teachers into regional leadership bodies, providing activists with degrees that elicit societal respect, and allowing movement leaders to prefigure their social and economic values in institutional settings. Many of the youth who have become dedicated MST activists over the past two decades entered their first MST education program not as activists but, rather, as members of poor communities without any other educational access. Through both the MST's high school and higher education programs, such students learned about the movement's political goals, economic initiatives, and organizational structure. These youth were also constantly involved in discussions about the MST's political strategy and were asked to take on coordinating tasks within the movement's thematic sectors. For the participants in these courses who were already active in the MST, the three- or four-year programs were opportunities to collaborate and strategize about the future of the movement. The programs brought activists who were involved in organizing in their local communities in contact with other activists from around the country, helping to build relationships of friendship and solidarity.

The education sector has also been a point of entry (*porta da entrada*, as it is frequently called within the movement) for women and gay leaders. Although the MST encourages entire families, including women and children, to occupy land, in the camps it has traditionally been the heterosexual men who take on leadership roles. Nationally, the MST implemented a quota system in the mid-2000s to guarantee equal gender representation in all of the movement's decision-making bodies (Peschanski 2007). Yet the movement's education collectives have always been majority women, and also with a much larger number of gay men than other movement sectors. As these activists are given movement tasks to complete, such as organizing a childcare center or negotiating with the governments to construct a school, they gain more confidence in their abilities as community organizers and leaders.[7] They circumvent the unequal gender relations that might have prevented their participation in other movement sectors and eventually demand to take on more prestigious leadership roles. Many women I spoke with who held leadership positions in the national directorate or the agricultural production sector began their activism as educators in camps and settlements. By making what is often considered women's work a central part of the movement's struggle, the MST has provided a pathway for more women and gay men to participate in the movement. This not only diversified the activist composition of the movement; it also led to these activists' engagement with new spheres of social struggle, such as gender equality and gay rights.

Finally, the public education system is also a means to obtain the many technical skills that movements need for co-governance. Dagnino (2001) argues that the accumulation of technical skills is one of the most challenging barriers to civil society participation in the state sphere. The MST leadership perceived this issue in the late 1980s, when they realized that local activists did not have the appropriate degrees to be teachers in their own schools. In the early 1990s the MST began promoting teacher training programs to fill this technical need, while also experimenting with the movement's educational approach. Since then, the movement has promoted high school and university degree programs in cooperative management, public health, social work, law, veterinary studies, agronomy, and many other areas. Instead of relying on outside experts, the movement has produced its own organic intellectuals who have the technical skills to integrate into concrete professional tasks. Although the MST leadership could have also promoted this technical training in nonformal educational programs, the professional degree itself is an important tool in the MST's ability to participate in contentious co-governance, enhancing activists' power to negotiate with elite actors and engage state institutions. Consequently, the MST's advancement in the educational sphere is not only a goal but also a means for the movement's successful long march through dozens of other state institutions.

Social Movement-Led Education Reform Versus the Global Education Reform Movement

The MST has had tremendous influence on the Brazilian public school system over the past thirty years. However, it is important to emphasize that the MST is only one of the many social movements in Latin America that has made education a core demand. For example, in Brazil, "the focus on access to quality education was one of the most consistent demands of diverse black movement organizations throughout the twentieth century" (Johnson and Heringer 2015, 2). During the 1980s, black leaders visited schools to advocate for the inclusion of Afro-Brazilian history in the curriculum, produced dozens of educational documents that supported this inclusion, and pressured the government to pass policies that addressed racial inequality in schools (Amilcar Pereira 2015). Upon taking office in 2003, the first law that Lula passed mandated the teaching of Afro-Brazilian history in all public schools. While in 2002 only three universities had affirmative action policies, by 2011 there were 115 public higher education institutions that had implemented affirmative action, and in 2012, the federal government made affirmative action a requirement in all federal universities (Heringer 2015, 120). Indigenous groups in Brazil also fought for the right to govern their own schools in the 1980s and 1990s. In 1996, the federal government passed a national law guaranteeing indigenous communities' right to a differentiated education—an explicit concession to this movement (Sobrinho, de Souza, and Bettiol 2017). While schools in indigenous territories continue to be part of the public education system, communities appoint their own teachers who teach in their local language and incorporate the histories of their nations into the curriculum. However, similarly to the MST, the implementation of these indigenous educational rights varies widely across the country.

In the broader Latin American context, perhaps the most well-known example of social movements' contentious co-governance of public education is in Ecuador. In 1988 the Confederation of Indigenous Nationalities in Ecuador (CONAIE) won the right to administer a new bilingual intercultural education program for thirteen indigenous nationalities, which meant that indigenous leaders coordinated teacher trainings and curriculum development, created standard orthography for indigenous languages, and oversaw the regional implementation of the program (Oviedo and Wildemeersch 2008). In Argentina, the workers who occupied factories in the late 1990s established secondary schools in many of these factories, for themselves and the local community. The government recognized these schools as part of the state school system; however, the leaders of the factory occupation movement were able to shape the curriculum and pedagogy in these schools to value working-class culture (Jaramillo, McLaren, and Lázaro 2011). In other parts of Latin America, teachers unions have been the principal protagonists demanding teachers' and communities' right to participate in educational governance. A primary example is the democratic teacher movement (la CNTE) in the southern region of Mexico, a dissident union group within the official Mexican teachers union

(Cook 1996). In 2010, in the state of Oaxaca, these dissident teachers won the right to implement their own "Plan for the Transformation of Oaxacan Education," which included community-centered cultural programs, infrastructure projects, teacher training, and an alternative evaluation system.[8] Also in Mexico, rural teacher colleges, known as normal schools (*escuelas normales*), have promoted radical educational training for decades, through the influence of different left-leaning political organizations. This was undoubtedly the reason for the kidnapping and murder of the forty-three students studying in an *escuela normal* in Ayotzinapa in 2014, although as of the this writing the case remains officially unresolved.

In the United States, perhaps on a smaller scale, there are also examples of low-income communities demanding and winning control over their educational services. For example, black female activists in Mississippi administered the Head Start childcare services that were part of the Great Society programs in the mid-1960s (Sanders 2016). A few years later, black communities in New York City briefly won the right to control the hiring practices of their public schools (Perlstein 2004). In the higher educational sphere, the Chicano, Black, and other Third World Liberation movements succeeded in reconfiguring public education through the establishment of Black Studies and Ethnic Studies programs (Rojas 2007). In Tucson, Arizona, Latinx activists have won access to ethnic studies programs at the high school level, despite multiple conservative attacks. In Chicago, in the late 1980s, poor communities insisted on the establishment of local school councils to have more voice in educational governance (Fung 2001). In other regions community organizing groups such as the Industrial Areas Foundation, the Association of Community Organizations for Reform Now (ACORN), and the Ella Baker Center for Human Rights have incorporated educational campaigns as a central part of their larger social justice struggles (Mediratta, Shah, and McAlister 2009; Shirley 1997).

Thus, across the Americas, grassroots movements have engaged in both contentious actions and political negotiation to transform their school systems and take part in educational co-governance. In many cases, as in the case of Mexican normal schools, these struggles have resulted in violence and death, illustrating the high stakes of these educational conflicts. However, these movements and unions are not the only actors attempting to influence public education. Recently, scholars have written about a global education reform movement (GERM) (Mundy et al. 2016; Sahlberg 2016), which comprises a diverse array of public and private-sector actors attempting to improve schooling by increasing competition, choice, privatization, and a range of teacher accountability mechanisms, such as performance pay, scripted curriculum, and high-stakes standardized testing. Reformers who are part of this movement highlight the variable quality of teaching as the principal barrier to improving student learning (e.g., see Bruns and Luque 2014). The first steps in improving teacher quality are standardizing the curriculum, aligning teacher training with national standards, and rewarding (or punishing) teachers based on both their knowledge of the material and ability to help students perform this knowledge on exams. These reformers point to teacher movements, in particular unions, as the biggest barriers to educational progress (Grindle 2004; Moe and Wiborg 2017).

In this new world of standards and accountability, alternative visions of educational purpose have no place. The global education reform movement has been particularly influential in Brazil over the past decade, as a network of corporate foundations promoting "accountability" coalesced (Avelar and Ball 2019; Martins and Krawczyk 2016). Unsurprisingly, it is in São Paulo, where this reform movement has been the strongest, that the MST has had the least success participating in the public schools. During the 2015 Second National Meeting of Educators in Areas of Agrarian Reform (ENERA), the MST highlighted the corporate influence over Brazilian education as the most direct contemporary challenge to their educational vision. The increasing influence of the global education reform movement in Latin America suggests that conflicts over who has the right to define educational purpose are likely to intensify in the coming years. Therefore, documenting the educational visions of grassroots social movements, the many pedagogical innovations they have created, and how they have attempted to reorganize and reinvent schooling is a more important task than ever.

LOOKING FORWARD

This book rejects the assumption that social movements' engagement in the institutional sphere necessarily leads to their demobilization and decline. Rather, I have argued that activists' involvement in the contentious co-governance of state institutions can help to build their movements' internal leadership capacity, organizational structure, and resource base. This does not mean that social movement leaders should stop organizing contentious actions; rather, it is by combining the strategic occupation of state institutions with contentious political actions that movements can effectively pursue their goals over several decades. Undoubtedly, the political context directly conditions movements' ability to engage in contentious co-governance; however, in almost all democratic political systems, there are multiple access points through which activists can enter the state. Educational institutions are a particularly strategic sphere for movements to garner influence. The most important factors influencing the effectiveness of this strategy are leaders maintaining a close connection to the base of people they claim to represent and a clear vision of the long-term purpose and goals of institutional change. If all of these pieces align, then social movements can effectively occupy diverse state institutions and begin to prefigure their social, political, and economic goals, whether those goals are food sovereignty, racial justice, gender equity, or socialism. It is only through this praxis—implementing theories in practice and allowing the tensions, contradictions, challenges, and possibilities of that process to inform and reform those theories—that we can begin to build the world we hope to inhabit in the future.

Epilogue

What Is Left of the Brazilian Left?

On Sunday, October 21, 2018, a week before Brazil's election, the ultra-right presidential front-runner, Jair Bolsonaro, addressed thousands of his supporters who had packed Avenida Paulista, the cultural and financial heart of São Paulo. The former army captain spoke to the crowd via a live video link from the patio of his home in Rio de Janeiro, where he was recovering from a near fatal assassination attempt. His tone was serene and jovial, but his words were full of blood, as he vowed to purge the country of his political opponents. "Either they go overseas or they go to jail," he said. The sea of yellow-and-green-clad supporters erupted in cheers and chants. He continued, "These red outlaws will be banished from our homeland. It will be a cleanup the likes of which has never been seen in Brazilian history." After promising to jail his electoral opponent, Fernando Haddad, he called out the MST "crooks," whom he said would be classified as terrorists. Bolsonaro had made similar threats many times during his campaign, warning "the MST scumbags that we're going to give guns to agribusiness, we're going to give guns to the rural producer, because the welcome mat for a land invader is a bullet."[1] He ended his speech promising, "We are the majority. We are the true Brazil. Together with the Brazilian people we will build a new nation . . . We do not want socialism."[2]

A week later, the worst fears of the Brazilian left became a reality. Bolsonaro handily won the presidential election, cruising to a ten-point victory over Haddad. Just months before, Bolsonaro had been seen as a fringe candidate, known primarily for his exuberant endorsement of dictatorship, torture, and assassination; virulent misogyny, homophobia, and racism; loathing of the poor; and catastrophic environmental policies. Among his most infamous statements, he once told a female congressional colleague, who had denounced the use of rape against political prisoners during the military dictatorship, that she was not "worth raping; she is very ugly."[3] His stunning election marked a political U-turn for Brazil, where the previous four presidential elections had been won by the leftist Worker's Party (PT), which had overseen historic gains for poor, black, indigenous, and LGBTQ Brazilians. Bolsonaro's election is part of a larger trend across Latin America: the crashing of the pink tide, that is, the fall from power of most left and left-of-center governments in the region. His election is also part of a global trend of the rise of right-wing populism. The dynamics of this far-right resurgence are different in every country, as are its effects on grassroots social movements. Nonetheless, the MST, as one of the world's largest and most influential social movements, is an important indicator of the future state of the popular left, in Latin America and globally.

This epilogue explores how the Brazilian left wound up in this position and the future prospects for the MST in the current political moment. Bolsonaro's rise to power is a serious setback for the movement; nonetheless, the core argument of this book still holds: the MST's thirty-five-year strategic engagement with the Brazilian state significantly expanded its internal capacity, including its organizational structure, resource base, and collective leadership, and the movement is unlikely to disappear in the near future. This long march through the institutions was only possible because activists engaged in contentious political mobilization, while also prefiguring their social and economic vision within a variety of state spheres and under a diversity of political regimes. I will argue that even in this new political context activists will be able to defend many, if not all, of their institutional gains, and I explain why those advances are likely to help the movement withstand, if not fully deflect, this far-right resurgence.

ECONOMIC CRISIS AND THE RESURGENCE OF THE FAR RIGHT

What were the economic and political developments that led to this shift out of the era of class compromise and social movement participation, to the current era of economic crisis, authoritarian right-wing resurgence, and ultra-austerity? In 2011, a decade of tremendous economic growth—a central factor for the PT's continued popularity—began to slow. Over the next three years, in an attempt to reignite the economy, Rousseff lowered interest rates, increased investment in industrial production, subsidized energy costs, spent money on highway and railway infrastructure, and

implemented a series of other measures aimed at promoting national production (Singer 2015). However, in the context of a global commodity bust,
the Brazilian economy's reliance on primary exports (and in particular, the
government's bet that oil prices would remain high enough to make drilling
in pre-salt offshore wells profitable) made economic revival impossible. The
PT's golden decade had been dependent on the commodity boom, which
stimulated expansion of the internal market, and the party had not been
perceptive enough to realize it was living on borrowed time. Other factors,
ranging from industrialists' refusal to cooperate with Rousseff's economic
plan to government ineptitude and the public revelation of political corruption, also prevented economic takeoff. More than a decade of relative
labor peace came to an end; the year 2013 saw 2,050 strikes, a 134 percent
increase from 2012 (Braga 2016).[4]

Meanwhile, in June 2013, Brazil took the world by surprise as millions
of people around the country flooded into the streets, seemingly following
the path of the recent global unrest that had been characterized as spontaneous, horizontal, and leaderless—from the Arab Spring and the Gezi Park
protests in Turkey, to the indignant (*indignado*) anti-austerity protests in
Spain and Occupy Wall Street in the United States.[5] The original provoca-
tion for the Brazilian demonstrations was the police crackdown on a series
of small protests that had taken place in early June 2013, organized by the
Free Fare Movement (MPL), against recent bus fare hikes. As images of
batons and tear gas used on the protesters went viral, more people piled into
the streets, with 100,000 people marching through the city of São Paulo
within days. The demands of these protesters were diverse, from free public
transportation, to a condemnation of World Cup spending, to a call for political reforms. Many of the demonstrators were young and middle class, fed
up with the false promises of a "pragmatic left" economic approach, which
had attempted to combine redistributive policies for the poor with economic incentives for the rich.[6] For the 42 million members of "Brazil's new
middle class" (Neri 2015), educational access had increased but without
the expected economic opportunities (Braga 2012, 2014). However, this
potentially progressive critique was soon hijacked by a conservative countermovement that attempted to redirect anger toward PT corruption. The
powerful media establishment, initially critical of the protests, increasingly embraced them, reframing mass mobilization as reflecting an anti-
government ethos. Even though the June 2013 protests quickly tapered off,
the mobilizations inaugurated a new moment in Brazilian politics.

It was in this context that the MST organized its Sixth National Congress
in February 2014 (described in the Introduction), with more than 15,000
people participating, to discuss the future of the movement's struggle
for land, agrarian reform, and social transformation. On the third day of

this event, thousands of activists surrounded the presidential palace, demanding a meeting with Rousseff. A conflict broke out, with the police lobbing tear gas canisters into the crowd, several angry MST leaders fighting back against the police force, and hundreds of activists running to find areas free of the conflict. These protests reflected the movement's increasingly contentious relationship with the PT, and its vocal denunciation of the federal government's embrace of agribusiness over the previous decade. Nonetheless, later that year when Brazil was beset by a closely contested electoral battle between the incumbent president and the explicitly anti-MST candidate Aécio Neves of the Brazilian Social Democratic Party (PSDB), the MST came out in support of the PT. In the end, Rousseff triumphed by 3 percent (3.5 million votes), with the help of movements such as the MST that had begrudgingly mobilized on her behalf. However, when Brazil fell into a full-blown economic recession in early 2015, Rousseff repaid these movements by resorting to orthodox austerity policies (and policy advisors), enraging and further dividing the left.

Several months before these elections, in March 2014, an investigation known as Operation Car Wash (*Lava Jato*) had also started making national news, with accusations that government officials in the state oil company, Petrobras, had been accepting bribes in return for awarding contracts to construction firms at inflated prices. During the course of 2015, dozens of PT party members were implicated in this scandal, accused of money laundering and bribery.[7] Although politicians from other political parties were also involved, the scandal fed into a growing wave of anti-PT mobilizations. On March 15, 2015, half a million people marched through the city of São Paulo.[8] On April 12 and August 16, hundreds of thousands of protesters again took to the streets. While the nominal reason for these mobilizations was the *Lava Jato* scandal, some protesters chanted Cold War–era anti-communist slogans, held signs declaring *Chega de Doutrinação Marxista, Basta de Paulo Freire* (Enough Marxist Indoctrination, No More Paulo Freire), and even called for a military coup.

The powerful Brazilian media establishment worked hard to frame these protests as civil society versus the corrupt PT, and international media also largely portrayed the mobilizations as the Brazilian population's united outcry against the party. However, the Brazilian population was far from unified in its opposition to the PT. On August 20, 2015, the MST joined with the Central Union of Workers, National Union of Students (UNE), and the Communist Party of Brazil (PCdoB) to mobilize against austerity and in defense of Rousseff, reclaiming the June 2013 protests as a popular mobilization for more, not fewer, social rights (Singer 2013). On September 5, thousands of delegates from these organizations came together to found a national coalition, the Brazil Popular Front (*Frente Brasil*

Popular), "to defend the rights and aspirations of the Brazilian people, to defend democracy and an alternative economic model, and to defend national sovereignty and regional economic integration [in Latin America]."[9] Then, on October 8, 2015, another coalition of leftist groups, including the powerful homeless movement (*Movimento dos Trabalhadores Sem Teto*, MTST), launched the People Without Fear Front (*Frente Povo Sem Medo*). The formation of two separate coalitions reflected the deep divide within the Brazilian left about the PT's legacy, and more specifically, a disagreement about whether the strategy of disputing power within elite institutions had come at the expense of an independent and mobilized working class.[10] Despite the MST's contentious relationship with the PT and critiques of Rousseff's economic policies, the movement still believed that the party represented the most viable left leadership for Brazil. As I have emphasized, this is not simply because the conditions of working-class people improved during the PT administration; more important, the public programs that the MST pushed forward through the PT administration helped activists build concrete socialist experiments, or real utopias. Resentment towards the MST for supporting the PT was evident on September 22, 2015, when protesters confronted MST leader João Pedro Stédile upon his arrival at the Fortaleza airport, chanting, "*Ô MST, vai para Cuba com o PT!*" (MST, Go to Cuba with the PT!).

During the first half of 2016, these ideological battles came to a climax. Conservative leaders and upper- and middle-class citizens continued to call for Rousseff's impeachment, citing political corruption as the primary reason. Rousseff was also losing support among millions of working-class people, as indicated by her plummeting approval ratings. At the same time, the organized left—active and often full-time participants in movements, unions, and left-leaning political parties, which only includes a fraction of working-class sectors—was mobilizing against what they saw as an attempt to unseat an elected government by any means possible in order to implement conservative reforms. Even among this organized left contingent, complete unity was not possible, as some groups also called for Rousseff's ousting, citing the PT's treasons to the working class, from Lula's public pension cuts to Rousseff's austerity policies.

In the end, the small and fractured left was not able to save the PT. On May 12, 2016, after thirteen years of PT rule, the Brazilian Congress voted for Rousseff to step down from office to face impeachment charges.[11] Although there was not any evidence implicating Rousseff in the *Lava Jato* corruption scandals, she was charged with fiscal peddling: delaying fiscal obligations and manipulating budget transfers in order to mask public debt.[12] Vice President Michel Temer of the Brazilian Democratic Movement Party (PMDB) became the interim president, immediately firing all of the heads of the ministries and establishing an all-white, all-male cabinet.[13] Ironically, it was the PT's acceptance of an alliance with the PMDB, informally during Lula's first mandate and then formally during his second mandate, which set up the possibility for the PMDB to strategically break this alliance in 2016 in order to seize power.[14] On August 31, 2016, after a four-day hearing, the Brazilian senate voted to impeach Rousseff, in an overwhelming 61-to-20 vote.

The political right justified the impeachment as a critical step in establishing order and prosperity in the country, blaming the economic downturn on the PT's corruption, misinformed policies, and inability to govern. There is certainly truth to some of these arguments, as multiple PT leaders have been found guilty of corruption, and it seems unlikely that the party leadership did not know about the enormous graft schemes in Petrobras. Rousseff also implemented a series of economic reforms during her first term that did not succeed in revitalizing the economy. On the other hand, the political left argued that this coup was driven by a cadre of corrupt senators who sought to shield themselves from investigation in the name of fighting corruption, and were trying to implement a right-wing agenda that had been defeated in the ballot box in election after election. Underlying the specific dynamics of the collapse of what had been considered a consolidated democracy is a set of basic structural problems. Brazil's reliance on an export-based economy makes it incredibly vulnerable to commodity booms and busts, and international competition; furthermore, the expansion of the internal market had been dependent on widespread credit, which led to a cycle of debt and decreased spending. Inequality throughout the country also facilitated the continued political power of traditional elites, entrenching a reactionary form of decentralization that made programmatic party politics almost impossible, especially at the local level. The coalition party system, which rewards corruption, payoffs, and opportunistic alliances, has its roots in this economic inequality and facilitated the removal of a sitting president on flimsy pretenses.

Although Lula and Rousseff had already embraced many conservative economic policies, Temer's presidency still represented a fundamental break with the PT's social and economic program. In a renewed alliance with the PSDB,[15] Temer pushed forward a series of far-reaching and radical neoliberal policy reforms, with the hope of reviving the economy and increasing international financial investment. The most important of these initiatives were a freeze on public spending for public education and health for twenty years (described by the United Nations as the "most socially regressive austerity package in the world"[16]); a change in workers' rights legislation to allow contracts to trump workers' rights laws, a law that makes the outsourcing of workers easier for employers; and most polemically, a major retrenchment of the public pension system (more extreme than the PT's previous cuts). There has been widespread outrage against these reforms. In 2017, the two left coalitions capitalized on this popular anger to organize several national protests, marches, and two general strikes—the first of their kind in two decades. However, despite these protests and the corruption allegations against Temer himself, the interim government pushed forward all of its policy initiatives except the pension reform. Decades of workers' rights legislation seemed to be coming apart at the seams.

To be sure, the real prize was the October 2018 presidential elections. Despite facing a corruption conviction, Lula declared his candidacy early on, promising to reverse Temer's economic policies and return the country to an era of industrial growth and wealth redistribution. He quickly garnered widespread support throughout the country as he traveled to dozens of cities in a national caravan, promising a new era of prosperity. These hopes were put on hold in April 2018, when Brazil's top court upheld Lula's conviction of corruption and money laundering, charges many believed rested on flimsy evidence.[17] The court ruled that his twelve-year prison sentence would begin immediately, despite his intention to continue appealing the case. In a picture that went viral globally, thousands of workers surrounded the ex-president in the manufacturing district of São Paulo where he had begun his union career, as he surrendered to the police. The MST immediately set up a permanent encampment outside of Lula's prison in Curitiba, Paraná, and helped lead the national campaign *Lula Livre!* (Free Lula!).

In September 2018, the courts officially barred Lula from running for office. The PT's strategy for electing their backup candidate, former Minister of Education and São Paulo mayor Fernando Haddad, was to promote Haddad as "Lula's choice" and thus to channel Lula's supporters to Haddad. Unfortunately, in Brazil political figures are often bigger than their parties, and Haddad had a serious uphill battle to win Lula's base of support. The other leftist in the race, the charismatic leader of the homeless movement, Guilherme Boulos, the candidate of the Socialism and Liberty Party (PSOL), had less than 1 percent of the vote. Meanwhile, the new front-runner in the presidential race was not Geraldo Alckmin from the economically conservative PSDB or Henrique Meirelles from the chameleon PMDB,[18] but rather, right-wing populist Jair Bolsonaro from a small obscure party, the PSL (Social Liberal Party). Bolsonaro's support of torture and dictatorship, violent misogyny, and disdain for queer, black, and indigenous Brazilians has led critics to call him a neo-fascist.[19] Nonetheless his tough-on-crime, tough-on-communism, and anti-PT rhetoric resonated during a period of record-high rates of crime and a deep recession. Furthermore, Bolsonaro had deep roots in the ever-more-powerful Pentecostal and neo-Pentecostal communities.[20] Bolsonaro mobilized support through social media, which allowed for the dissemination of propaganda through rapidly pro-liferating questionable news outlets, rather than through traditional TV campaigns or party machinery.[21] A month before the election, events took a violent turn when a man stabbed Bolsonaro during a rally. Despite losing 40 percent of his blood, Bolsonaro recovered over the next few weeks and his popularity continued to grow.[22]

On Sunday, October 7, 2018, Bolsonaro outperformed predictions, win-ning 46 percent of the vote, in a presidential race with thirteen candidates. Haddad won 29.3 percent of the votes, which put him in a two-way runoff race with Bolsonaro. The fear of fascism had an immediate mobilizing effect on the left, with even the most radical left parties campaigning for Haddad's election in an unprecedented unity.[23] A frantic three weeks unfolded, with social movement, labor, and party activists attempting to flip votes in urban peripheries throughout the country, one of the most massive grassroots organizing drives in the country's history. However, these organizing efforts were too little, too late.

CONSEQUENCES OF FAR-RIGHT RESURGENCE FOR THE MST AND CONTENTIOUS CO-GOVERNANCE

At the Brazilian Studies Association conference in April 2016, Tianna Paschel, a sociologist and scholar of the Brazilian and Colombian Black movements, posed the following question to the society: what is left of the Latin American left? Her question was a response not only to the Brazilian context but also to the wave of right-leaning electoral victories and conservative protests over the previous year, from the election of Mauricio Macri in Argentina to the landslide victory of the Chavez opposition in Venezuela in December 2015. However, Paschel's question was also about whether this decline of the left's electoral and governing power in Latin America meant that the hundreds of grassroots movements that had emerged over the previous decades and brought those administrations to power, from indigenous movements to the Black, homeless, waste pickers, LGBTQ, and landless movements across the continent, were also declining in significance, strength, and influence.

As I have suggested, the MST is a good indciator of the overall state of the Latin American left under these new political developments. It is im-portant not to be overly optimistic about the prospects for this grassroots movement. As I have argued, an antagonistic government in power in a high-capacity state context *is* one of the biggest threats to social movements' ability to sustain institutional gains. Even before Bolsonaro's victory, over

the previous two years the center-right Temer administration had seriously undermined workers' rights and cut back government spending and
public services. Temer also implemented a series of strategies to weaken
the MST. Some of these strategies were coercive attempts to repress the
movement, including spying, disbanding land occupations, and arresting
MST leaders. The conservative climate also emboldened local government
officials and militias to take similar actions against local activists. These
conflicts often ended in violence, and unsurprisingly, in 2016 there were
more lethal repressions of rural activists than in any year since 2003, with
sixty-one people dying in land conflicts.[24] The number of assassinations in
the Brazilian countryside continued to rise the following year. A Global
Witness report published in July 2018 declared Brazil the most dangerous
country in the world "for land and environmental defenders, with agribusiness the industry most linked to killings."[25]

Another government strategy was to cut the funding that supported the
MST's alternative economic initiatives. Immediately after taking his interim position as president, in May 2016, Temer terminated the Ministry
of Agrarian Development (MDA), the institutional host of the National
Institute of Colonization and Agrarian Reform (INCRA). He folded the
MDA into a Secretary of Family Agriculture and Agrarian Development,
now overseen by the Presidential office itself, which significantly decreased
INCRA's institutional autonomy. This shift came along with the freezing
of dozens of INCRA's national programs and the cutting of significant resources. The future of the MST's most important educational program,
PRONERA (National Program for Education in Areas of Agrarian Reform),
is uncertain. In 2016, the federal government halted all of PRONERA's op-
erations and delayed scheduling a meeting with the program's civil society
advisory board for more than a year. Between 2015 and 2017, PRONERA
saw its budget cut by 90 percent, which has meant no funding for new
courses and uncertainty about whether courses started during the previous
administration will be completed. The new Minister of Education, José
Mendonça Filho, imposed new leadership and draconian budget cuts on
the Secretariat of Continual Education, Literacy, Diversity, and Inclusion
(SECADI) and the *Educação do Campo* office. Although many of the same
civil servants still work in the *Educação do Campo* office, when I spoke with
them in 2016 it was unclear if the office's diversity programs would continue.
To the contrary, the Ministry of Education began to put its political weight
behind an initiative for a standardized, common core curriculum (known
as the Base Nacional Curricular Comum, BNCC), a proposal supported by
conservative foundations in Brazil and abroad. During 2016 and 2017, the
Minister also began to lend support to "School Without Political Parties"
(*Escola Sem Partido*), a movement that has emerged advocating for the

banning of discussions of gender or sexual orientation and proposing to sanction teachers that discuss politics, broadly defined, in schools.

Finally, the most detrimental action Temer took was to push for policies that regularize families living in settlements, issuing them land titles so they no longer qualify for loans or other special programs designated for areas of agrarian reform. By transitioning families from the status of settled to landowners, the state effectively rids itself of any social obligations it has to this sector of the Brazilian population. This process has the potential to slowly erode the movement, as areas of agrarian reform will have to adapt to the dominant economic model in the countryside. Politically, this strategy also has the benefit of not being reversible by a future administration. In 2017, the MST led a campaign against the proposed policy, visiting settlements and asking families to sign a petition to demand concession of use rights. This would allow families to live on the land if they are producing on it and also transfer these use rights to their children—but not have the rights to sell this land. As I observed in April 2017, during a visit to an MST settlement in Paraná, while many families support the MST's proposal, others want individual land rights and reject the MST's position. Activists' power to intervene in these regions will certainly decline if settlements cease to exist as public territories. Leaders also fear that land speculators will take advantage of the privatization of settlements and buy up large swaths of these areas, thus increasing the concentration of land ownership that spurred the rise of the movement in the first place.

When Bolsonaro assumes the presidency on January 1, 2019, these political attacks against the MST will intensify, as will police and paramilitary violence. As already mentioned, Bolsonaro has declared his intention to arm landowners, promising that acts of violence against rural movements will be treated with impunity. Other forms of intimidation and persecution are also likely. Immediately after Bolsonaro's election, conservative senators reintroduced a bill that characterizes certain forms of activism and protest as terrorism, including many of the MST's mobilizing tactics.[26] As of this writing, the outcome is unknown, but if passed, this bill is certain to increase the risk of arrest, torture, and assassination for MST leaders.

In the educational realm, Bolsonaro's election has given renewed energy to the "School Without Political Parties" movement. The day after the election, a newly-elected state deputy in Santa Catarina launched a campaign on Facebook telling her followers to report any "indoctrinator teachers" who critiqued Bolsonaro's victory. She provided a WhatsApp number for students to "film or record any party-political or ideological expressions that humiliate or offend your freedom of faith and consciousness."[27] Another attack on free expression occurred in the days leading up to the election, when military police invaded several federal universities, demanding the removal of all political banners and posters, including statements against fascism.[28] In both cases, the court systems quickly declared these actions a violation of freedom of expression, suggesting some hope that Brazilian judicial institutions will defend against the worst of human rights abuses. Additionally, Bolsonaro's administration promises to continue Temer's politics of austerity,[29] with pension reform still a primary goal, as well as cutting any and all previous funding sources that went to agrarian reform regions.

REASONS FOR CAUTIOUS OPTIMISM?

Despite the significant threats of the current political moment, there are reasons for some cautious optimism. First, the definitive end of political diplomacy in Brazil has distinct advantages, with the potential of generating a surge in MST-led occupations and protests. After all, the MST is still a movement born of a repressive military dictatorship, when leaders succeeded in organizing massive land occupations, despite dangers and uncertainty. Brazil, the "country of the future," is quickly becoming a country of the past with a return to familiar political and economic strategies. It was precisely in the era of Fernando Henrique Cardoso (1995–2002), when there was an increase in violent repression against the movement, that the MST had its broadest support and won the most land redistribution. Thus, we would expect not a collapse of the MST, but a return to some old (but not that old) repertoires of collective action and engagement with the state. Furthermore, there are still tens of thousands of families occupying land across the country. Although it is unlikely that the new government will offer land rights to these families, disbanding all of the camps will require vast political and military capacity, and would likely provoke massive countermobilizations. As I finish writing this epilogue in November 2018, the courts have approved the eviction of 450 families in the state of Minas Gerais from an area that they have been occupying for twenty years—a worrying harbinger of what lies ahead. Yet calls for international solidarity also immediately followed, with hundreds of international allies writing emails to the judges, condemning the eviction.[30] This international solidarity is unlikely to stop the eviction, but it illustrates the huge political costs Brazil might incur from attempting to evict other encamped families across the country. Thus, the strategy of continuing to engage in land occupations and to set up occupied encampments could prove effective even under a right-wing authoritarian administration.

As Peter Evans (2008) has written, "every system of domination generates its own distinctive set of opportunities for challenge and transformation"

(298). With the PT out of power, the MST no longer has to engage in a delicate political dance with the federal government; it can mobilize against the new administration and openly contest its legitimacy. The unveiling of the function of the capitalist state also creates opportunities for strategic alliances and solidarity. The PT's rise to power fractured the Brazilian left; after Temer's election, for the first time in more than two decades, the majority of these left groups came together with a common slogan, "Out With Temer!" (*Fora Temer!*) and coordinated their organizing efforts through two large popular fronts. To be sure, these mobilizations failed to achieve their goals, but this does not mean that united left fronts will always fail in the future. After the first round of voting, these left groups came together again to mobilize for Haddad's election, despite different levels of support for the PT's previous administrations. This level of coordination among the organized left has not been seen since the PT's own founding in the 1980s, also a period of military dictatorship when there was a similar unifying rallying call for a return to democracy.

These national political developments have local consequences. In 2016, in Santa Maria da Boa Vista, Pernambuco (see Chapter 5), local MST leaders abandoned two decades of nonpartisan politics and led a PT mayoral campaign to oust the family that had held power for the previous century, winning despite all odds.[31] This was particularly impressive, given that as a result of the 2016 elections, the PT had gone from holding power in 652 municipalities across the country to only 254.[32] As local MST leader Adailto explained to me, "We took the municipal election as an opportunity to organize a campaign against the coup, to denounce the coup and the loss of workers' rights." Thus, it was the MST's national commitment to condemn the coup that led to these local realignments. Many teachers working in the settlements broke with their previous political loyalties and supported the MST's candidates, illustrating the long-term consequences of the movement's contentious co-governance of the municipal school system. Furthermore, by 2016 there was a generation of youth in Santa Maria also influenced by the MST through their public schools, who had been taught to be critical of municipal politics.

The agrarian reform youth are the second reason for optimism. Today's MST is a movement of young people who grew up in settlements and camps, obtained education through the movement's formal educational programs, and participated in MST activities and events. Through these experiences and the practice of direct, popular democracy within their schools and settlements, these youth have become "political subjects" (Paschel 2016) who defend their right to participate in the political process. While many MST youth have migrated to cities, thousands remain on the settlements and could prove critical to the long-term relevance of the movement. Thus, the MST's current potential for renewal is a consequence of its deliberate, thirty-five-year strategy of investing in local leadership development. Youth's influence is also likely to be relevant for the broader population as well. In the lead-up to and aftermath of Rousseff's impeachment, there has been a surge of protests, some drawing hundreds of thousands of participants. Some of these protesters are weathered veterans of the dictatorship resistance, but a core component is youth. Many of these youth are not affiliated with any organization, but their participation represents the potential of building a new mass movement.

During the 2018 election campaigns, there was also a huge mobilization of women across the country, with their rallying call "*Ele não, ele nunca!*" (Not him, never him!). The weekend before the election, hundreds of thousands of women from different political parties and ideological leanings came together to protest Bolsonaro's misogynistic rhetoric and policies, in what has been called the biggest protest of women in the country's history.[33] In a postelection interview, MST leader Stédile announced the MST's intention to return to *trabalho de base* (grassroots organizing) in poor neighborhoods throughout the country.[34] Stédile admitted that if the MST and other left groups had had the patience to go door to door in the urban peripheries for the previous six months, listening to people and talking with them, instead of only engaging in these organizing efforts the last three weeks of the election, there could have been a different election result. Stédile agreed with Brazilian rapper Mano Brown, who criticized the PT the week before the election for failing to seek out and talk with voters beyond its party base. Bolsonaro's revanchist agenda will inflict devastating hardships on the working class generally, and particularly on women, black, brown, indigenous, and queer people. Nonetheless, such hardships also offer an opportunity for the MST and other movements to mobilize these populations through sustained, grassroots organizing in poor neighborhoods. Austerity policies like pension reform might make particularly useful targets for building broad cross-class solidarity.

Third and finally, the MST is now engaging in this contentious political struggle with a new arsenal of material, ideological, and sociopolitical resources, which I have argued are a product of the movement's long march through the institutions. Over the past three decades, the MST has helped redistribute land to hundreds of thousands of families, and the communities and relationships that have formed through this process cannot easily be destroyed. Furthermore, the MST's force has always been defined by its ability to garner the moral and intellectual leadership of settlement families. Now is no different. MST leaders will continue to engage in this work—even if settlements are privatized—by helping to integrate families into alternative economic enterprises, inviting them to new educational programs, and organizing events that discuss and celebrate the movement's accomplishments. Clearly, the MST has not succeeded in its goal of making small-scale agricultural production, agroecology, and collective work practices the hegemonic mode of production in the Brazilian countryside. During the thirteen years of PT rule, there was a resurgence of agribusiness, an increase in the influence of international capital, and a renewed emphasis on a primary export model.[35] The MST's institutional gains in the sphere of agriculture were miniscule compared to the gains of agribusiness. Therefore, critics on the left are partially correct to characterize this period as a Gramscian "passive revolution," or the absorption of revolutionary movements into existing systems.

Nonetheless, even the small number of successful experiments in alternative agricultural production on MST settlements, which have remained bastions of anti-capitalism, have a transformative effect. Federal support for these initiatives, ranging from subsidized loans to programs that support the purchasing of food from family farmers, was critical to the success of these economic experiments. This federal support is already beginning to end, and Bolsonaro will likely cut off these programs permanently. However, unless the administration takes a truly fascist and authoritarian turn, the federal government does not have the power to abolish the already viable cooperatives on MST settlements, which are now essential parts of local economies. These cooperatives will continue to serve as important bases of mobilization, offering examples of economic alternatives to Brazilian citizens and serving as a source of financial support for the movement.

As Stédile said at the National Meeting of Educators in Areas of Agrarian Reform in September 2015, power in Brazil is not the sole property of the presidential palace in Brasília. In many ways, the MST's thirty-year war of position within Brazilian civil society and in state institutions has been preparation for the current political moment. The MST leadership is inextricably woven into a complex fabric of political relationships throughout the country, and it has developed meaningful connections with thousands of state and institutional actors. The state–society relations that have been established at these subnational levels and within diverse Brazilian agencies—relationships that often supersede ideological and party divides—will continue, even under a far-right federal government. The October 2018 election results highlighted this point, as twelve governors allied with the MST won their elections, mostly in the north and northeast of the country. Haddad himself also won many more votes in the northeast of the country than Bolsonaro, again illustrating the geographical divide in Brazil and the likelihood of the northeast representing a stronghold for social movements' institutional struggles. The PT still holds more representatives in Congress than does any other party, and even in the conservative stronghold of the state of Rio de Janeiro, the leftist PSOL party elected four black women, three to the state assembly and one to the National Congress, a partial reckoning of justice after the March 2018 assassination of Marielle Franco, a black, queer, female, socialist member of the Rio de Janeiro city council. The Bolsonaro administration is entering a political terrain of extreme polarization, which will rely much more on coercion than consent, in contrast to the relatively stable hegemonic administrations of the past.

The MST's educational struggle offers one of the best examples of why the movement's institutional gains cannot easily be reversed. Over thirty years, the MST has been able to win access to 2,000 schools with over 8,000 teachers attending to 250,000 students. State and municipal governments administer almost all of these schools, and in many cases, they collaborate with the MST in educational co-governance. Even in the midst of Brazil's rightward lurch in 2016 and 2017, dozens of new schools opened on MST settlements, including four new high schools in Ceará (*escolas do campo*, see Chapter 6). In addition, the MST leadership has helped to develop programs for adult literacy, primary and secondary schooling, high school, and bachelor's and graduate degrees with over eighty different educational institutions. Although federal support was initially critical for funding these programs, many of the university professors who became committed activists through their involvement will continue to work with the MST, independently of the federal government. The MST-inspired baccalaureate program for training teachers to work in the countryside (Chapter 3) was institutionalized in more than forty federal universities, resulting in the hiring of hundreds of new faculty. In June 2016, a month after Rousseff stepped down from office, the MST organized a seminar on agroecology and education for science and math teachers, funded by the Federal University of the Southern Frontier.[36] Dozens of other university-sponsored seminars and events supporting *Educação do Campo* and the MST's educational initiatives were rolled out in 2017 and 2018.

As some opportunities for participation are cut off, other possibilities for institutionalizing the MST's goals will undoubtedly open. As I have argued throughout this book, new opportunities for contentious co-governance are likely to emerge in contexts where the movement's leadership has the strong support of its base, and where the capacity of the state itself is enhanced by activists' involvement in local governance. Bolsonaro rapidly mobilized millions of supporters through social media at a moment of economic crisis, but it remains to be seen if he can sustain this support over time. The MST, in contrast, has conducted decades of grassroots consciousness raising about the consequences of neoliberal capitalism, an educational strategy that has ensured strong, sustained support for the MST in many regions, which activists can draw on to continue demanding institutional gains under sympathetic local and state administrations. Even in more closed and authoritarian contexts, MST leaders may continue making inroads if they engage in enough contentious protest that state concessions become a desirable solution to public unrest.

The MST's struggle has always moved forward under contradictory and conflictive relations with the Brazilian state. Activists began experimenting with alternative educational pedagogies in a period of movement ascendance and participatory experimentation across Brazil. Throughout the 1990s, the movement found countless allies and state configurations to institutionalize their educational ideas—partially because the mobilizations of the 1980s had transformed Brazilian society. Although conservative actors blocked the most radical reforms, many left-leaning actors also gained power within the state. The MST won some of its most important concessions in the 1990s, as a result of violent conflicts and in partnership with national and international allies. Lula's victory in 2002 shifted the terrain by creating more openings at the national level, but it did not ultimately change the MST's strategy of finding different access points within the state for promoting institutional change and social movement co-governance in different forms and varying levels of intensity across the country. The Brazilian participatory context produced the MST, but the MST also strategically used this participatory context to support the movement. Now, in the context of an anti-participatory and authoritarian federal government, MST leaders have to defend their previous gains through mobilizations and protests, find new institutional arrangements at subnational levels to support their political project, and perhaps most important, use the accumulated fruits of their thirty-year war of position to sustain the many movement activities that do not require a formal political-institutional expression. Now is the test: we are going to see the true strength and limits of the MST's long march through the institutions. All eyes should be on Brazil, as the evolving state–society dynamics in this country will almost certainly influence the rest of Latin America.

November 2018

First National Meeting of Educators in Areas of Agrarian Reform, July 1997—Manifesto of Educators of Agrarian Reform to the Brazilian People

In Brazil, we have arrived at a historical crossroads. On the one hand, there is the neoliberal project, which will destroy the nation and increase social exclusion. On the other hand, there is a possibility of the organization of a countermovement and the construction of a new social project. We need to take a position as the working-class population. For these reasons we have written this manifesto.

1. We are educators of children, youth, and adults of camps and settlements in all of Brazil, and we fight for Agrarian Reform and social transformation;
2. We manifest our profound indignation regarding the misery and injustice that is destroying our country. We share the dream of constructing a new development project for Brazil, a project that belongs to the Brazilian people;
3. We understand that education alone does not resolve the problems of the people, but it is a fundamental element in the process of social transformation;
4. We struggle for social justice! In education this means the guarantee of public education for everyone, free and of a high quality, from preschool education to university access;

5. We consider the end of illiteracy not only to be a responsibility of the state, but also a question of honor. For this reason, we are dedicated to literacy training;

6. We demand, as educational workers, respect, professional value, and dignified conditions for our work. We want the right to think about and participate in the decisions concerning our schools;

7. We want schools that are concerned with the major questions of our time, and that help to strengthen our social struggle and create solutions to the specific problems of each community in the country;

8. We defend a pedagogy that is concerned with all human dimensions. We are dedicated to creating an educational environment based on democratic participation and related to the culture and history of our people;

9. We believe that education can awaken the dreams of our youth, can cultivate solidarity, hope, and the desire to always learn and teach and transform the world;

10. We understand that in order to participate in the construction of a new school, we, the educators, need to construct collective pedagogies with political clarity, technical competence, and humanist and socialist values;

11. We struggle for public schools in all camps and settlements in areas of agrarian reform and we defend the right these school communities have to participate in the landless struggle;

12. We strive for a school identity specific to rural life, as a pedagogical-political project that will strengthen new forms of development in the countryside. This development will be based on social justice, agrarian cooperation, respect for the environment, and the valuing of landless peasant culture;

13. We renew, in front of everyone, our political and pedagogical dedication to the causes of the people, and especially to the struggle for Agrarian Reform. We continue to keep alive the hope and honor of our country, our principles, our dreams;

14. We join with all people and organizations that have dreams and projects for social change, because together we can create a new education in our country; an education based in the new society that we have already begun to construct.

MST Agrarian Reform: A Struggle for Everyone
First National Meeting of Educators in Areas of Agrarian Reform
We pay honor to the educators Paulo Freire and Ché Guevara, Brasilia,
July 28–30, 1997

Curriculum of the University of Ijuí Pedagogy of Land Program (1998–2001)

Course Names	Type	Credits	Total Hours	Class Hours	Activity Hours
First Semester (Jan/Feb 1998)					
Philosophy I	General	4	60	40	20
Study of Brazilian Problems	General	4	60	40	20
Sociology	General	3	45	30	15
Methodology of Research I	General	4	60	45	15
Introduction to Science	General	2	30	20	10
Applied Biology	General	4	60	45	15
Math	General	5	75	60	15
Physics	General	2	30	20	10
Chemistry	General	2	30	20	10
Introduction to Social Studies	General	5	75	60	15
Second Semester (July 1998)					
Political Economy	General	4	60	40	20
Portuguese	General	6	90	50	40
Methodology of Research II	General	4	60	40	20
Philosophy II	General	4	60	40	20
Cartography	Social Studies	4	60	30	30
Contemporary Society I	Social Studies	4	60	40	20
Contemporary Society II	Social Studies	4	60	40	20
Philosophy of Education	General	4	60	40	20
Sociology of Education	General	4	60	40	20
Science: Module 1	Science	14	210	110	100
Mathematics I	Math	4	60	45	15
Geometric Design	Math	4	60	45	15
Brazilian Culture	Portuguese	5	75	45	30

Course Names	Type	Credits	Total Hours	Class Hours	Activity Hours
Literature and Literary Text I	Portuguese	7	105	75	30
Third Semester (Jan/Feb 1999)					
Contemporary Society III	Social Studies	4	60	45	15
Contemporary Society IV	Social Studies	4	60	45	15
Contemporary Society V	Portuguese	4	60	45	15
Reading and Textual Production II	Portuguese	6	90	75	15
Approach to Literacy Text	Portuguese	6	90	60	30
History of Education	General	4	60	45	15
Structure and Function of Basic Education	General	4	60	45	15
Education Planning	General	4	60	30	30
Practices of Teaching I	General	3	45	15	30
Method of Research III	General	4	60	45	15
Basic Physics	Science	4	60	45	15
Basic Chemistry I	Science	4	60	45	15
Basic Biology I	Science	4	60	45	15
Geometry	Math	4	60	45	15
Functions I	Math	6	90	60	30
Trigonometry	Math	3	45	30	15
Fourth Semester (July 1999)					
Introduction to Historical Study	Social Studies	4	60	45	15
Introduction to Geographical Study	Social Studies	4	60	45	15
Literary History and Brazilian History	Portuguese	5	75	60	15
Linguistic Studies I	Portuguese	7	105	75	30
Developmental Psychology	General	4	60	45	15
Anthropology	General	3	45	30	15
Movement and Learning	General	3	45	30	15
Practices of Teaching II	General	3	45	15	30
Methodology of Research IV	General	3	45	15	30
Science: Module II	Science	13	195	135	60
Functions II	Math	4	60	45	15
Methods of Research in Math Education I	Math	4	60	45	15
Analytical Geometry	Math	4	60	45	15
Mathematic Computation I		3	45	45	0
Fifth Semester (Jan/Feb 2000)					
Methodology and Research in History and Geography I	Social Studies	4	60	45	15
Methodology and Research in History and Geography II	Social Studies	4	60	45	15
Methodology of Teaching	Social Studies	6	90	60	30
Study of Linguistics II	Portuguese	7	105	75	30

Course Names	Type	Credits	Total Hours	Class Hours	Activity Hours
Infant and Youth Literature	Portuguese	5	75	45	30
Methodology of Teaching Portuguese and Literature	Portuguese	4	60	30	30
Methodology of Research V	General	3	30	15	15
Psychology of Learning	General	4	75	45	30
Practices of Teaching III	General	3	30	15	15
Didactics	General	4	60	45	15
Fundamentals of Methodology of Teaching in Basic Education	General	4	60	45	15
Basic Biology II	Science	4	60	45	15
Basic Physics II	Science	4	60	45	15
Basic Chemistry II	Science	4	60	45	15
Spatial Geometry	Math	4	60	45	15
Introduction to Calculus	Math	4	60	45	15
Methods of Research in Math Education II	Math	4	60	45	15
Statistics	General	4	60	45	15
Sixth Semester (July 2000)					
Teaching Art	General	4	60	45	15
Population and Society	Social Studies	5	75	45	30
Nature and Society	Social Studies	6	90	60	30
Culture and Society	Social Studies	5	75	45	30
Linguistic Studies III	Portuguese	6	90	60	30
Reading and Textual Studies	Portuguese	6	90	60	30
Principles and Methods of Administration in Education	General	4	60	45	15
Process of Literacy	General	4	60	45	15
Practices of Teaching IV	General	3	45	15	30
Method of Research in Education	General	4	60	30	30
Method of Research in Math Education III	Math	4	60	45	15
Linear Algebra	Math	5	75	50	25
Commercial Mathematics and Finance	Math	4	60	30	30
Mathematical Computation II	Math	3	45	45	0
Science: Module III	Science	13	195	135	60
Seventh Semester (Jan/Feb 2001)					
Practice of Teaching (Supervised Internship in Teaching History and Geography)	Social Studies	5	75	30	45
Practice of Teaching (Supervised Internship in Teaching Mathematics)	Math	4	60	30	30
Practice of Teaching (Supervised Internship in Teaching Science)	Science	4	60	30	30

Course Names	Type	Credits	Total Hours	Class Hours	Activity Hours
Practice of Teaching (Supervised Internship in Portuguese Language)	Portuguese	4	60	30	30
Practice of Teaching (Supervised Internship in Elementary Education)	General	4	60	30	30
Principles and Methods of Supervision and School Administration	General	4	60	45	15
Final Thesis	General	4	60	15	45

Each student chooses one concentration in either Math, Portuguese, Sciene, or Social Studies

APPENDIX C

Curriculum of the UNESP PRONERA Geography Program (2007–2011)

Discipline	Credits	Total Hours	Classroom Hours	Community Activity Hours	Classroom Activity Hours
First Semester (First Period, 2007)					
Geographical Thought	4	60	40	20	—
Geography of Brasil	4	60	40	20	—
Human Geography	4	60	40	5	15
Introduction to Research in Geography	4	60	40	20	—
Applied Statistics in Geography	4	60	40	20	—
Second Semester (Second Period, 2007)					
Contemporary History	4	60	40	20	—
Sociology	4	60	40	20	—
Economy	4	60	40	20	—
Physical Geography	4	60	40	5	15
History of Education and Education of the Countryside	4	60	40	20	—
Third Semester (First Period, 2008)					
Climatology	4	60	40	5	15
Cartography	4	60	40	20	—
Geo-cartography	4	60	40	5	15
Structure and Functioning of Primary and Secondary Education	4	60	40	20	—
Practice in Teaching Geography I: Analysis of the Public School	4	60	40	20	—
Field Research: Territorial Dynamic	5	75	75	—	—

Discipline	Credits	Total Hours	Classroom Hours	Community Activity Hours	Classroom Activity Hours
Methodology in Geography	4	60	40	20	0
Fourth Semester (Second Period, 2008)					
Economic Geography	4	60	40	5	15
Region and Regionalization	4	60	40	5	15
Educational Psychology	4	60	40	20	—
Practice in Teaching Geography II: Psychological Aspects of Development and School Learning	4	60	40	20	—
Fifth Semester (First Period, 2009)					
Geomorphology	4	60	40	5	15
Geology	4	60	40	20	—
Urban Geography	4	60	40	5	15
Research in Geography	4	60	40	5	15
Practice in Teaching Geography III: Planning, Execution, and Evaluation of the Learning Process	7	105	55	50	—
Project of Disciplinary Integration I	6	90	—	—	90
Territorial Rural Development and Production Alternatives for the Brazilian Countryside	6	90	72	18	—
Sixth Semester (Second Period, 2009)					
Geopolitics of Global Space	4	60	40	—	20
Rural Geography	4	60	40	5	15
Cultural Anthropology	4	60	40	20	—
Didactics	4	60	40	20	—
Seventh Semester (First Period, 2010)					
Natural Resources	4	60	40	5	15
Geo-processes	4	60	40	20	—
Regional Geography of Brazil	4	60	40	—	20
Geography of Social Movements	4	60	40	20	—
Project of Disciplinary Integration II	6	90	—	—	90
Practice in Teaching Geography IV: Supervised Internship	12	180	40	140	0
Eighth Semester (Second Period, 2010)					
Bio-geography	4	60	40	5	15

Discipline	Credits	Total Hours	Classroom Hours	Community Activity Hours	Classroom Activity Hours
Territorial Planning	4	60	40	20	—
Public Polices and Agrarian Rights	4	60	40	20	—
Rural Work	5	75	75	—	—
Ninth Semester (First Period, 2011)					
Applied Climatology	4	60	40	20	—
Applied Geomorphology	4	60	40	20	—
Photogrammetry and Remote Sensing	4	60	40	20	—
Analysis of Landscape	4	60	40	20	—
Management of Natural Resources and Studies of Environmental Impacts	4	60	40	20	—
New Approaches to Geography	4	60	40	20	—
Tenth Semester (Second Period, 2011)					
Urban Space*	4	60	40	20	—
Rural Space*	4	60	40	20	—
Supervised Internship	12	180	40	140	—
Regional Planning	4	60	40	20	—
TOTAL	231	3,465	2,077	988	400

*Students choose only one of these two disciplines.

APPENDIX D

Fourth National Seminar on PRONERA, November 2010—Final Document "Commitments for the Consolidation of PRONERA"

The 667 participants of the Fourth National Seminar on the National Program for Education in Areas of Agrarian Reform—PRONERA—support the following manifesto. These participants include the president of ANDIFES [National Association of Presidents of Federal Education Institutions], deans, parliamentarians, teachers, program coordinators, encamped and settled families, students, representatives of social movements, trade unions, nongovernmental organizations, officials from INCRA and various agencies, partners of eighty-seven different PRONERA programs, and representatives of more than 15,000 people directly involved in the implementation of these programs. These participants met in Nereu Ramos Auditorium, in the House of Deputies, in Brasília, on November 3–5, 2010, following the election of the first woman president in Brazil.

1. PRONERA

Over the past twelve years, social movements and trade unions have led the struggle for *Educação do Campo* nationally and have created PRONERA, one of the most important agrarian reform programs promoting social justice in education.

Thanks to PRONERA's participatory, mobilizing, and innovative structure, the program has succeeded in enrolling 400,000 people in literacy, undergraduate, and graduate education programs. These students are youth
and adults from areas of agrarian reform in every Brazilian state.

PRONERA is an *Educação do Campo* program that has involved hundreds of professors from federal and state universities, agro-technical
schools, federal institutes, family-farm schools, and educational institutes.
These educational institutions have offered PRONERA programs through
institutional partnerships with the government, and their involvement has
guaranteed a higher level of educational access to working-class people in the
countryside. It has also provided workers and rural residents of agrarian reform settlements with learning materials, transportation, accommodations,
and meals throughout study.

PRONERA is a public policy that has opened the doors of educational
institutions to workers. PRONERA has allowed workers to access literacy
and basic education, as well as undergraduate and graduate programs in different subjects. This educational access has increased the expertise needed
for the economic and social development of the settlements, as well as the
environmental, cultural, and political development of encamped families.

PRONERA has trasnferred *Educação do Campo* inside the universities
and federal institutes. PRONERA transformed the dream of thousands of
families living in the countryside, to have better schools and quality education for their children, into a reality. The educational access that PRONERA
provides is different from other programs. Through the pedagogy of alternation, with periods for studying and then periods in the community,
the students' learning is shaped by the reality, culture, and struggles of the
populations living in the countryside. PRONERA has ensured that youth
and adults can access education without abandoning their rural communities, which strengthens the struggle for agrarian reform.

In addition to these youth, adults, and families from settlements, other
people benefited from this program, including college students enrolled in
regular university programs, interns, coordinators, and fellows who have
had the opportunity to interact with PRONERA students and visit the
settlements.

The academy has become more connected to the countryside, through
the presence of youth from settlements on their campuses, through the
students' research projects, and through the new academic disciplines that
have been created. The PRONERA students' desire for more education has
also led them to enter graduate programs within these universities.

The projects developed by PRONERA have also expanded the
university's scope, stimulating research and enriching the academic training
of the students, and expanding the educational sphere with the creation of

new curricular components and university programs. This has greatly contributed to the continued training of university faculty through reflection and practice, fostering a process of knowledge construction in different subject areas.

PRONERA has stimulated the production and dissemination of knowledge, the creation of research groups, and the establishment of centers for the study of *Educação do Campo*. It has also fostered the creation of events and publications that have inserted agrarian reform and *Educação do Campo* into the agenda of higher education institutions. It has increased the participation of the state and society in the economic, social, environmental, and political development of the countryside.

PRONERA was built by many hands and through concrete practices on the ground, both in the countryside and in the academy. PRONERA's partnership with the National Research Council (the CNPq) has offered research grants and technological support to students and teachers in PRONERA programs (secondary, undergraduate, and graduate programs). This support has ensured a better quality of planning, implementation, and mentoring.

All this became possible due to the commitment of the social movements and trade unions of the countryside. These organizations, which represent rural workers of the countryside, have raised the level of education of the rural population and thus transformed the countryside. An important part of this process has been the participation of professors committed to educating working-class populations of the countryside through a liberatory teaching practice.

2. CONSIDERATIONS

The achievements listed above were not easily accomplished. A program with these multiple dimensions and high levels of participation has a widely recognized social value. However, this program and the social rights of the rural population have been challenged by capitalist interests.

The main challenge we confront is how to ensure that PRONERA has autonomy in its management, planning, and institutionalization. The recent restrictions on the program are an affront to this autonomy. These restrictions prohibit the payment of the university faculty, technicians, engineers, and public officials who work in PRONERA programs, as well as prohibiting student fellowships. It is necessary for Congress to pass a law that authorizes INCRA's full autonomy over the management of PRONERA, including its planning, implementation, evaluation, and ensuring that everyone involves has the appropriate working conditions.

Another challenge for PRONERA is the Federal Court of Audits' (TCU) judgment 2653/08, that INCRA can no longer establish institutional partnerships with educational institutions to implement new programs. The court judgment requires PRONERA to establish new programs through contracts, which requires an open bidding process. It is necessary to legalize institutional partnerships, as the most appropriate instrument for the implementation of public policies in education that involve mutual interest and cooperation.

The TCU judgment denies the right of social movements and trade unions to participate in the planning, implementation, and evaluation of PRONERA. This decision goes against constitutional principles, in particular, universities' right to autonomy. It also goes against the Law of Basic Educational Guidelines, which in Article 1 declares social movements to be educators, together with the family, work, and society.

The limits created by the court judgment have constrained the creation of new PRONERA programs, including in literacy, adult education, high school, and higher education. There are currently more than fifty approved PRONERA programs that will only be implemented if the TCU judgment is reversed. These are programs that will be implemented in partnership with federal and state universities, family agricultural schools, and state and municipal departments of education. If implemented, these programs will enroll 5,000 people and would raise the general schooling level of the Brazilian populations living in the countryside.

3. PROPOSITIONS

1. The immediate rescinding of TCU judgment 2653/08, thus allowing INCRA to partner with educational institutions, and the recognition of the necessity of social movement participation in PRONERA;
2. The Congress's approval of a specific law that authorizes the payment of scholarships to students, professors, and public officials who work in PRONERA;
3. The implementation of the Presidential Decree that declares PRONERA and *Educação do Campo* public policies; an expansion of PRONERA's budget to meet educational demand in areas of agrarian reform;
4. Investment in the construction of elementary, middle, and high schools in agrarian reform settlements, based on local architectural norms. Improvement of existing school infrastructure, in partnership with the Ministry of Education and state and municipal secretaries of education, and the prevention of further closures of schools of the countryside;

5. An expanded participation of universities, Federal Institutes, Family Centers of Training Based on Alternation (CEFFAS), and technical schools;

6. An increase in the amount of PRONERA programs offered at all educational levels;

7. The expansion of PRONERA's connection to other programs with similar development projects for agrarian reform settlements, such as PRONATER and TERRASOL, developed by the MDA/INCRA, as well as other government programs and other ministries, especially MEC, MCT (CNPq), MDS, Ministry of Culture, MTE, MMA, and MS;

8. The promotion of exchanges with other international programs, especially in Latin America, Africa, and Asia, that also promote education for populations of the countryside;

9. An increase in the publication of pedagogical materials that are produced collectively, through local communities' reflection, recording, and systematization of their experiences;

10. The deepening of academic and scientific research on *Educação do Campo* and incentives to increase the training of researchers of the countryside;

11. The strengthening and the expansion of partnerships with CNPq, MCT, CAPES, and other foundations that can foster research and technical support for PRONERA projects;

12. The creation of research centers and universities dedicated to agrarian issues and *Educação do Campo*;

13. The establishment of mechanisms for including graduates from PRONERA high school and higher education programs into development projects in areas of agrarian reform;

14. The creation of a PRONERA website, containing a database of all the technical and scientific research produced through PRONERA;

15. The establishment of an INCRA internal regulation that ensures the right of settled people to access professional education and pursue a career without having to leave areas of agrarian reform;

16. The creation of professional development programs for the professors, teachers, scholars, and technicians who work in PRONERA programs.

Brasília, November 5, 2010

APPENDIX E

Second National Meeting of Educators in Areas of Agrarian Reform, September 2015—Manifesto of Educators of Agrarian Reform

We are educators of children, youth, adults, and the elderly living in occupied encampments and agrarian reform settlements throughout Brazil. We are connected to the MST, an organization of peasant workers that for thirty-one years has struggled for land, agrarian reform, and social transformation in Brazil. In February 2014, the MST held its Sixth National Congress and reaffirmed its historic commitment to the People's Agrarian Reform and the democratization of land ownership. We engage in this struggle through a discussion with civil society about the agricultural development project we defend in Brazil and around the world.

Since the founding of our organization we have prioritized the struggle for a high-quality and universal public education, from infant education to university schooling. We believe that educational access is the key to integrating families in settlements and camps into a new social project in the countryside and to struggle for social transformation. We have sought to collectively build a set of educational practices that support the construction of an emancipatory social project, carried out by working-class populations.

As participants of the Second National Meeting of Educators in Areas of Agrarian Reform, we have partnered with other working-class organizations to produce the following analysis of the current political and economic context:

1. We live in a capitalist society increasingly unequal, which produces wealth for a few and misery for many. Global capitalism is now led by financial capitalists and large transnational private companies, which dominate and control the production and movement of commodities around the world. In this context, everything becomes a form of profit: food production, health, education, and leisure. More and more frequently, public spaces are also subordinated to the interests of elite capitalist classes, endangering human life and nature;

2. Since the main objective of these companies is to make a profit, workers' living conditions and hard-won social rights are always in danger. Currently in Brazil many of our economic and social gains are being reversed, and access to public transportation, housing, employment, health care, and quality public education is becoming more difficult;

3. This economic model is the same one that organizes agricultural production as a capitalist business, known as agribusiness. Agribusinesses make profit through the private appropriation of natural resources, water, minerals, and biodiversity. These agribusinesses are based on monoculture food production, which allows for large-scale production but destroys biodiversity. This model of food production needs artificial inputs that disrupt the reproductive processes of nature. The advance of agribusiness is supported by laws and maintained by public funding that guarantee its expansion through the expropriation of the land and territories that belong to peasants, indigenous populations, *quilombolas* . . . In Brazil, the absence of agrarian reform is indicative of the governments' misguided faith in this agribusiness model, which has serious repercussions that are being discussed globally;

4. We believe that it is possible to promote an alternative form of agriculture development, by making the production of healthy food for the entire population the primary objective of agricultural production. There are many agricultural practices that already exist that produce food while respecting human health and nature. However, the scaling-up of these agricultural practices will require further scientific and political research that recovers farmers' and peasants' historical knowledge. The people who decide how to use our public resources are not investing in this type of research;

5. It is this same perverse logic that turns everything into a source of profit, which has also led companies to begin intervening in education. The owners of these companies have always seen education as a means of training workers for the capitalist job market, but now they also want to make education a branch of their business and they seek to take control over the political and pedagogical organization of schools;

6. Large corporate groups are increasingly intervening in educational policy, writing policy proposals that governments accept due to the proposals' false pretense of improving the quality of public education. In reality, these policy proposals represent an accelerated process of commodification of education at all levels. First, they seek to demonstrate that public education is in crisis, that students do not learn, that teachers do not know how to teach, and that the educational system does not work. Then, they present as the solution that schools should start to operate according to the management logics of capitalist enterprises. This means setting measurable goals, the external control of the educational process, the loss of the teacher's autonomy in the classroom, accountability for individual student learning, and curricula that are determined by large-scale evaluations. The owners of these companies argue that, in order to increase the efficiency of this educational model, the companies themselves should undertake the management of schools and receive public funds for this task. In Brazil these large corporate groups are organized in the *Todas Pela Educação* (Education For All) movement;

7. There are also many workers, educators, students, and communities that are trying to transform and improve public education, but for a different purpose. We believe it is necessary to transform public schools, in order to support the full development of students and their long-term emancipatory human formation. Currently, there are innovative educational practices that are being developed for this purpose;

8. There are two educational projects that are currently in dispute in Brazil, but on unequal grounds. The state is more and more siding with the corporate educational reformers (similarly to the state's decision to support agribusiness). Therefore, the public schools are now facing a serious risk. They are becoming less public, less democratic, less inclusive, and more instrumental. Increasingly, working-class populations have less autonomy to develop their own educational practices;

9. In Brazil, the right to universal education has not yet been achieved. The history of slavery, land concentration, and agricultural exports in Brazil explains why we have not yet guaranteed educational access for all workers, and why there are 14 million young people and adults who are still illiterate. The history of unequal economic relations is responsible for the current educational inequalities in the countryside;

10. Despite the historical struggles of populations living in the countryside for educational access, 20.8 percent of the rural population is still illiterate and on average rural people only have 4.4 years of schooling. The populations of the countryside have the largest number of children out of school, the lowest rates of infant education, the most precarious school infrastructure, the worst teacher working conditions, the most

temporary-employment contracts, and the largest number of teachers who work without the required educational degree;

11. The capitalist model of agriculture, which pushes families to leave their rural communities, is attempting to privatize education and also accelerate the closure of public schools in the countryside. This makes it more difficult to provide all levels of educational access in the countryside, which denies rural populations the right to study in the communities where they live and work. Between 2003 and 2014, more than 37,000 schools in the countryside were closed. The government's policy of transporting children in rural areas to urban schools pushes these children to drop out of school, due to the time they have to spend travelling on bad roads and the precarious means of transportation;

12. Schools in the countryside that are resisting the corporate educational reform logic are suffering an increasingly strong onslaught of propaganda from agribusiness companies. These companies send brochures to these rural schools and develop educational programs for the students and teachers in the countryside that represent their own class interest. These initiatives also support the attempt to privatize public schooling.

Given this current reality and honoring our history, we have written a manifesto of our current commitments of struggle:

1. To keep fighting for a just, democratic and egalitarian society, without the exploitation of labor and nature, with agrarian reform, and a development project that supports our health, culture, and a quality education for all workers;

2. To fight against any kind of neoliberal reform that reduces the rights of workers and compromises the democracy and the sovereignty of our country;

3. To combat the agribusiness model, which represents disease, death, and the destruction of nature and of the populations living in the countryside, especially indigenous people and *quilombolas*. To resist the agribusinesses' offensive in our schools in the countryside, and their attempt to subordinate teachers and students to a destructive logic with false speeches about educational innovation;

4. To build the People's Agrarian Reform, which involves land distribution for populations who live and work on the land, and the advancement of an agricultural model based on peasant farming practices and with the main objective being the production of healthy and environmentally sustainable food for the whole society;

5. To promote agroecology as a technological approach to farming and to invest in the production of knowledge and an agricultural system based on the principles of biodiversity and food sovereignty;

6. To fight against the privatization of public education, in all of its forms, and defend the right to public education from kindergarten to university schooling. To struggle against the corporate educational reformers represented by the "Education For All" movement, which seeks to subordinate schools to the requirements of the market, eliminate the multiple dimensions of education, reduce the time for learning, and promote an unhealthy competition between students and teachers that increases social exclusion;

7. To defend the allocation of public funding exclusively for public education;

8. To fight against the capitalist cultural industry that promotes a consumerist and individualistic lifestyle;

9. To continue denouncing the closing of schools in the countryside and asserting that "To Close a School Is a Crime!" To fight against the educational inequality in our country and for the construction of more public schools in the countryside that have adequate infrastructure and are adapted to the realities of local communities;

10. To demand more literacy programs and educational access for young people and adults, and to demand an increase in levels of schooling for the entire Brazilian population;

11. To defend for all working-class populations in the countryside and the city the right to an emancipatory education that aims to promote the development of the human being in all dimensions of life. The goal is to expand the worldview of a new generation and allow youth to experience new forms of social relations based on values of justice, solidarity, collective work, and internationalism;

12. To continue promoting schools that are linked to the lives of the students, which integrate socially productive work practices, political struggle, collective organization, culture, and history as organizational principles of the schools. To promote these practices through the participation of the communities and the self-governance of the students and teachers in the schools;

13. To fight against all forms of violence, ethnic and racial stereotypes, homophobia, and gender discrimination;

14. To participate in teachers' struggles, who are currently demanding better working conditions, professional respect, and adequate training and continual professional development;

15. To continue fighting for the Pedagogy of the Movement, Education of the Countryside, and Socialist Pedagogies for all working-class populations;

We pay our tribute to Florestan Fernandes, a great leader in the struggle for education and for public schooling in Brazil, who dedicated his life to the service of working-class people. His legacy keeps inspiring our organization: we will not let ourselves be co-opted; we will not let ourselves be crushed. We will always fight!

We call on our comrades to work together to overcome the contradictions of this historical moment by collectively struggling towards the changes necessary to construct a future socialist society.

Fight, Build the People's Agrarian Reform!
Luziânia, Goiás, September 21–25, 2015

GLOSSARY OF PORTUGUESE TERMS

auto-gestão Self-governance (e.g., students' self-governance of schools).

ciranda Childcare center (based on the MST's pedagogical approach).

Educação do Campo "Education of the Countryside," the right for schools in the countryside to have an educational approach that supports the local realities and sustainability of diverse rural communities.

engenho Sugarcane mill.

Escola Ativa "Active School," program for multigrade rural schools; first created in Colombia in the1970s as *Escuela Nueva* (New School).

escolas do campo "Schools of the countryside"; in Ceará, high schools that are legally differentiated from urban schools.

escolas da formaçao Political training schools, or schools for "human formation."

fazenda Large plantation or land estate.

frente de massa "Front of the masses," grassroots organizing, the MST's direct action thematic sector.

mata sul "Southern forest," the southern sugarcane region of Pernambuco.

mística Cultural-political performance involving song, dance, poetry, and other artistic expressions that reflect on aspects of social struggle.

núcleo de base (NB) Base nucleus or base group, a small collective of families or students that form the organizational structure of camps and settlements and schools.

pedagogia da alternância "Pedagogy of alternation," the organization of the school calendar with several months of study and several months of community research projects.

Pedagogia da Terra "Pedagogy of Land," the name of the baccalaureate programs in pedagogy the MST helped to create in partnership with dozens of universities.

quilombos Maroon communities, populations that are descendants of runaway slave communities or have social practices that evolved out of this history.

sem terrinha "Little landless children," identity that MST leaders cultivate among children living in areas of agrarian reform.

sertão semi-arid region of northeastern Brazil

NOTES

INTRODUCTION

1. Municipal governments are similar to the county level in the United States, sometimes encompassing several towns or cities, with a mayor and a municipal council that oversee that level of government.

2. For extensive histories of the MST's emergence and expansion, see Branford and Rocha (2002), Carter (2015), Fernandes (1996), Ondetti (2008) Wolford (2010), and Wright and Wolford (2003).

3. The number of families who receive land through MST occupations is difficult to calculate because over one hundred organizations lead land occupations, and the government does not register these organizations when assigning families' land rights. The MST claims that the movement helped 350,000 families receive land rights between 1984 and the early 2000s (A. Wright and Wolford 2003), with tens of thousands of families still occupying land. Carter and Carvalho (2015) estimate that 134,440 families were settled through MST land occupations by 2006. This latter estimate draws on data from the MST (2007) and the State University of São Paulo (DATALUTA 2008). In addition, the other groups that lead land occupations in Brazil are also often influenced by the MST (Sauer and Welch 2015), suggesting the MST's indirect influence in even more occupations.

4. Brazil has a total of twenty-seven federal units: twenty-six states, and one federal district (Brasília).

5. These 250 delegates represented grassroots organizations from twenty-seven different countries. I participated in this congress as a translator for the US delegation.

6. Rosali Caldart (2004), one of the MST's most important educational leaders, describes the movement's educational proposal as having five components (*matrizes*, literally, matrixes), which all contribute to the movement's political and economic vision: collective organization, work, culture, history, and struggle.

7. Informal conversation with Edson Anhaia, June 16, 2014.

8. This is similar to Santurino Borras's (2001) point that "societal actors attempt to influence and transform state actors, but in the process are themselves transformed—and vice versa" (548).

9. Tianna Paschel (2016) also uses this framing in her study of black movements in Colombia and Brazil.

10. Anthony Pahnke (2018) makes a similar argument in his recent book, *Brazil's Long Revolution: Radical Achievements of the Landless Workers Movement*.

11. This is similar to Jonathan Fox's (1992) concept of a "sandwich strategy," whereby "an objective alliance between entrepreneurial reformists and autonomous social movements can offset the power of entrenched authoritarian elites" (8). Likewise, Doowon Suh (2011) emphasizes the blurred line that often exists between the polity and a social movement, and the fact that activists can work simultaneously with and against state actors in

achieving their goals (464). Suh calls for a "revisiting or stretching" of the "conventional conceptualizations of social movements" as outside of formal politics.

12. In later writings, Alvarez (1999, 2009) focuses on how the increase in feminist NGOs has affected this dual strategy. She vacillates on the issue, arguing that in the late 1990s, overall, the rise in NGOs has inhibited this dual strategy as NGOs now primarily function as the administrators of state programs (Alvarez 1999). A decade later, she shifts to defending NGOs as critical to sustaining the feminist field through their constant engagement with "movement work" (Alvarez 2009). In this later article, Alvarez (2009) concludes, "There is, in short, no 21st century Iron Law of NGO-ization" (182).

13. The idea of class compromise is also elaborated by Przeworski (1986), who critiques both instrumental and autonomist theories of the state. Instead, he argues that the state is an expression of a class compromise that is in the interest of both capitalists and workers.

14. The term *prefiguration* had been discussed prior to Boggs's article, in both religious texts and in communist party debates. However, Boggs helped develop the contemporary understanding of what is today referred to as prefigurative politics. For more background and perspectives on prefigurative politics, see Breines (1980, 1989) and Raekstad (2017).

15. Following Andrews (2004), I draw on the concept of outcomes, rather than "success" or "failure."

16. For this critique, see Andrews (2004, 38) and McAdam and Boudet (2012, 25).

17. Bansaszak (2010) has written about how these differences between organizational units within the state directly influence social movement outcomes. She writes, "A movement-state intersection is likely to appear with different probabilities at different locations within the state and the location of a movement-state intersection within the state will affect the movement's ability to alter state policy" (18).

18. Skocpol (1985) identifies stable administrative-military control of territories, loyal and skilled officials, and financial resources as some of the historical underpinnings of state capacity.

19. Taylor (1989) refers to this same internal infrastructure as social movement's "abeyance structures."

20. "Common sense" does not refer to something "obvious" or "intuitive"; it is people's contradictory and complex understandings of the world. Gramsci wrote that within everyone's "common sense" beliefs, which are highly influenced by the dominant ideology, there is a kernel of "good sense": an accurate interpretation of the real nature of class relations.

21. In this definition of cognitive liberation, McAdam (1999) writes that "Movement emergence implies a transformation of consciousness within a significant segment of the aggrieved population. Before collective protest can get under way, people must collectively define their situations as unjust and subject to change through group action" (51). Shifts in the economic and political context can also contribute to cognitive liberation, but I am focusing here on the role of activists' organizing efforts in this process.

22. A similar combination of facilitating factors has been identified in studies of participatory democracy. Facilitating factors include committed bureaucrats and officials, bureaucratic-legal capacities of the state, enabling policies and legal frameworks, a mobilized civil society, and a history of mobilization (Abers 2000; Baiocchi 2005; Coelho 2007; Cornwall and Schattan Coelho 2007; Heller 1999; Ostrom 1996).

23. Note that in Portuguese the last part of the word *conscientização* means "action," an important linguistic emphasis that is not translatable into English, which highlights the need to connect consciousness to action.

24. Critical pedagogy in the United States grew out of scholars' engagement with Freire's work (Darder, Baltodano, and Torres 2003; Giroux 2001; hooks 1994; Macedo 2006; McLaren 2003).

25. More specifically, in this latter book, Apple (2013) analyzes several historical figures that theorize education and social change, including Freire, George Count, W. E. B. Du Bois, and Carter G. Woodson.

26. Similarly, church-based study groups (CEBs) recruited many people to participate in social movements who initially joined the CEBs only for religious reasons.

27. Marxist feminists have used the term "reproductive labor" to describe domestic work such as childcare, cleaning, and cooking (e.g., Bhattacharya 2017) . These jobs, typically unpaid and carried out by women, enable the reproduction of waged labor (Boydston 1990; Hartmann 1976; Secombe 1974). More recently, scholars have analyzed forms of paid reproductive labor in the public sphere, including primary and secondary education, which also reproduce the next generation of waged laborers (Duffy 2007; Laslett and Brenner 1989).

28. The first national seminar on LGBT issues within the MST took place in 2015. However, there had been regional initiatives before this national seminar, including an LGBT wing of an MST march in the state of Bahia in 2013 and a seminar about sexual diversity in Ceará in 2011. In 2018, the MST's LGBT collective won the right to have a representative in the MST national directorate (see Fig. 1.6).

29. All quotes or information in the book from Maria de Jesus Santos are from an interview on September 5, 2011, unless noted.

30. Often, MST leaders who are appointed to these professional positions will give part of their salary to the movement, as a form of economic solidarity.

31. Boggs (1977) describes prefigurative politics in contrast to more top-down forms of leadership, writing, "The dilemma persists: how to combine prefiguration with the instrumental concerns of political effectiveness" (383). In this book, I argue that activists engaging the state and prefiguring a future world they hope to create are complementary goals.

32. McAdam and Boudet (2012) have critiqued "selecting on the dependent variable." Although I am choosing previous movement activity as a baseline requirement for my cases, my case selection is intended to highlight different movement outcomes and not select only cases of movement success.

33. Students in primary and secondary school were not the focus of the study. However, I constantly interacted with these students throughout my field research.

34. In Brazil, the MST faces constant external critiques and leaders are understandably skeptical of outside scholarship on the movement. Dozens of people who have researched the MST have either left without offering anything in return (not even their publications) or, worse, only emphasized negative aspects of the movement and provided fodder for conservative critics (Navarro 2009, 2010). Furthermore, hosting researchers takes time, energy, and financial resources away from the MST's other tasks.

35. In 2012, after I returned from the field, I joined the national coordinating collective of the Friends of the MST, the official solidarity organization of the MST in the United States.

CHAPTER 1

1. Ondetti (2008) offers a good account of how the landless movement has been shaped by the broader political environment. In addition, see Fernandes (2000), Branford and Rocha (2002), Fernandes and Stédile (2002), Wright and Wolford (2003), and Wolford (2010), all of which are book-length accounts of the MST.

2. *Grilagem* is the practice of putting a false land deed into a cabinet with a few crickets (*grilo* means cricket). After a few weeks the cricket waste makes the document appear old and thus helps to "prove" ownership of the land.

3. For a more detailed discussion of the history of slavery in Brazil, see Bergad (2007), Graden (2006), and Klein and Luna (2009).

4. This concentrated economic and political power among milk and coffee producers in the states of São Paulo and Minas Gerais became known as the "café com leite" (coffee with milk) political bloc; see Skidmore (2010) for more on this period.

5. The Brazilian Communist Party (PCB) was founded in 1922.

6. The Movement of Landless Farmers (MASTERS) was active in southern Brazil and supported by populist governor Leonel Brizola (Ondetti 2008, 11).

7. These were literacy programs that Paulo Freire developed in the 1950s and 1960s.

8. This law was passed due to pressure from the United States. After the Cuban Revolution, President John F. Kennedy's created the Alliance for Progress with the objective of avoiding the expansion of Communism in Latin America. In 1961, 8 Latin American countries, including Brazil, joined this alliance in which they promoised to implement strucutre reforms (like agrarian reform) in exchange for financial suport from the United States (Matos 2013, p. 16).

9. The economy grew an average of 11 percent between 1968 and 1974 and 7 percent between 1975 and 1980.

10. Starting in 1976 soybean production increased significantly, but the real soybean boom took place starting in the 1990s, when the Chinese economy openned up for global trade (for example, Brazil produced 500 thousand tons of soy in 1966, while the estimated soy production for 2019 is 35 million tons). <https://www.embrapa.br/soja/cultivos/soja1/historia?fbclid=IwAR1_TIGcCWs5wbvBruFkJ5rKSCSkjwp2NviHsFvCd5nfY4eLSxZhP7uYyr8> (Accessed February 2, 2021). Sugarcane also benefited from the government program Proálcool, which used sugarcane for ethanol-burning vehicles (Ondetti 2008).

11. Between 1960 and 1970 there was an average annual urban growth rate of 4.5 percent (Alvarez 1990, 45); while in 1960, 55 percent of the Brazilian population lived in rural areas, by 1980 only 32 percent of the population was rural (IBGE 1996).

12. By the mid-1970s, the guerrilla, student, and labor opposition movements had been almost completely repressed and stomped out.

13. As noted by Ondetti (2008), the rural union federation also organized some of these strikes, with the biggest strikes taking place among sugar-cane workers in Pernambuco.

14. This illustrates how the definition of landless is socially constructed, as families who owned farms of this size would not be considered landless in the poorer, northeast region of the country.

15. Poor families were not the only or main group invading indigenous land. For more discussion on the history of the indigenous populations in Brazil, see the work of scholar Darcy Ribeiro (1995, 2000).

16. The military party became the PDS (Social Democrat Party) and the opposition party, the MDB, became the PMBD (Brazilian Democratic Movement Party). Other opposition parties that formed included the PP (Popular Party), the PTB (Brazilian Labor Party) and the PDT (Democratic Workers' Party). For a detailed analysis of party formation during this period, see Alves (1985).

17. The phrase "popular movement" refers to social movements that are led by working-class or "popular" (in Portuguese poor, periphery, or grassroots) sectors of rural and urban civil society.

18. The information that follows about Salete Campigotto is from a personal interview with her on January 13, 2011, as well as a published interview with her from 2008 (Tedesco and Carini 2008).

19. A magistério program offers a secondary and teaching degree simultaneously. It is also known as nível media or, more commonly, normal médio.

20. The CPT has collected statistics on land occupations since 1987, but only started recording the organization that occupies land in 1989. In 1989, the MST was responsible for 61.2 percent of the eighty total occupations (CPT 1990).

21. In the mid-2000s the MST adopted equal gender representation within the movement. At the local level, this meant that at least one of the two NB coordinators had to be a woman.

22. This system of educational governance is referred to as a "regime of collaboration."

23. Organizers in the two communist parties, the Brazilian Communist Party (PCB) and the Communist Party of Brazil (PCdoB), were clandestine in the PMDB and pushed it to take some progressive positions.

24. All quotes or information in the book from Carmen Vedovatto are from an interview on January 5, 2011.

25. The remaining quotes or information in the book from Salete Campigotto are from an interview on January 13, 2011.

26. Field notes, September 2011.

27. Specifically, the MST drew on Soviet theorists writing between 1917 and 1931. The MST references 1931 as the moment when the Soviet Union stopped investing in the creative capacity of its population for self-governance and became a top-down industrial model similar to capitalist countries.

28. In the union movement and within political parties these debates were controversial, with deep divisions emerging between leaders who supported Trotskyism versus Stalinism, the Soviet Union versus Maoist China. Similarly, after the fall of the Berlin Wall in 1989, there was a contentious debate in Brazil about what this meant for working-class struggle. Ozai da Silva (1987) is a good resource on the political division of the left in the early and mid-1980s.

29. All quotes or information in the book from Rosali Caldart are from an interview on January 17, 2011, unless noted.

30. During this period, access to Krupskaya's work was limited to a few essays that had been translated into Spanish and then Portuguese. It was not until 2017 that a more comprehensive collection of Krupskaya's writings was translated into Portuguese.

31. In the 1980s this was the only Portuguese translation of Pistrak's writings. A second book, *Escola Comuna* (Commune School), was translated into Portuguese in 2010 (Pistrak 2010). This led to the MST's incorporation of new pedagogical practices, including the use of *complexos* (complexes) that make connections between the curriculum and students' realities. There are currently no English translations of Pistrak's works; all translations in this book are from the Portuguese texts.

32. Frederick Taylor, a US engineer, sought to improve industrial efficiency through what he called "scientific management." Scientific management involved micromanagement of all workers' tasks to improve efficiency. "Taylorism" became a prominent philosophy of industrial management.

33. After the Bolshevik Revolution there were more than 7 million orphans in the Soviet Union. The Gorky Colony was named after a Russian intellectual whom Makarenko highly respected.

34. All quotes or information in the book from Marli Zimmerman are from an interview on November 9, 2010.

35. From a presentation in an MST meeting in Caruaru, Pernambuco (Field Notes, July 2009).

36. All quotes or information in the book from Edgar Kolling are from an interview on November 18, 2010, unless noted.

37. The MST already had a national "political training" (*formação*) sector that organized courses for the political development of movement leaders.

38. This coalition included the PT, the Communist Party of Brazil, and several center-left parties, and was known as the "Frente Popular Brasil" (Brazilian Popular Front). See the Epilogue for how the Brazil Popular Front became an important actor again in 2015, during a cycle of conservative protests.

39. Students were the protagonists of these protests; see Mische (2008) for a detailed description.

40. These shifts led to the expulsion of a large Trotskyist tendency within the PT in 1992 and the founding of the first left-of-the-PT party, the PSTU (United Socialist Workers Party).

41. Ondetti (2008) argues that the tactic of occupation was why the MST continued to grow, allowing the MST to overcome the "free rider problem" as participants were fighting for private not public goods.

42. Wolford (2010b) discusses the tensions that emerged as activists brought a vision of agrarian reform based on the family-farming tradition of the largely white southern regions of Brazil to the northeastern sugar-cane regions, which had much larger African-descendent and mixed-race populations.

43. The indigenous populations led their own land struggles and had their own national organization.

44. Land redistribution is administered through the National Institute of Colonization and Agrarian Reform (INCRA), discussed more in Chapter 2. There are also some state agencies that redistribute land.

45. All data on land occupations in this book are drawn from the DataLuta 2016 report (NERA 2017), produced by the Nucleus of Research on Agrarian Reform (NERA) of the State University of São Paulo (UNESP). The only graph that draws on a different database is Figure 1.5, which shows the regional distribution of families involved in new land occupations. This database comes from ten different reports on land conflicts, produced by the Pastoral Land Commission (CPT): *Conflitos no Campo Brasil*, 1988–1998. The CPT database has slightly different numbers of land occupations and families participating than the NERA database.

46. These cooperatives also helped to financially sustain the movement, as the leadership often asked the cooperatives to donate 1–5 percent of these government loans to the movement (Ondetti 2008, 121).

47. In 2005, BioNatur became the Land and Life National Cooperative (CONATERRA).

48. Only a minority of families in settlements has actually relinquished individual land rights.

49. This definition is from the "Declaration of Nyéléni," a document approved at the first global "Forum for Food Sovereignty, which took place in Mali in 2007. <http://usfoodsovereigntyalliance.org/what-is-food-sovereignty/> (accessed April 21, 2016).

50. For more information on *La Via Campesina*, see Desmarais (2007).

51. The National Congress is not only the week-long meeting of thousands of activists but also the year of conversation and debate that happens within the other leadership collectives leading up to the congress. By the time the National Congress takes place, the movement's major strategies and priorities have been determined based on these previous discussions. The meeting of the National Congress is a moment to ratify these national priorities and celebrate the movement's victories.

52. In 2015, the MST had thirteen sectors, which in order of creation are political training (*formação* 1987), education (1987), grassroots organizing (*frente de massa* 1989), finance (1989), projects (1989), production, cooperation, and environment (1992), international relations (1993), human rights (1995), communication (1997), health (1998), culture (2000), gender (2000), and youth (2006) (Carter 2015). Some sectors are considered "collectives" as they are not formally structured in all states and their members participate in other sectors. For example, the International Relations Collective and the youth collective are not formal sectors. In 2017, the MST officially approved the creation of an LGBT collective to organize around issues of "LGBT landless" rights.

53. There are many tensions in this centralized organizing method. Ondetti (2008), for example, argues that over time the MST's leadership structure became more top-down, with decisions increasingly made by the national directorate. Furthermore, during the 1980s and 1990s, the national leadership body was primarily male and it would not be until the mid-2000s that women would win the right to equal participation in the national leadership. Nonetheless, the MST leadership considers this centralized organizational structure a necessary tool to coordinate the actions of a mass-based, nationally dispersed, and controversial movement.

54. These movements included the anti-dam movement, MMTR (rural women's movement), and DR-CUT (Central Union of Workers, Rural Department), with support from Franciscan leaders.

55. The degrees would be conferred by the private school Escola Espírito Santos, also administered by FUNDEP. The other three FUNDEP departments were a Department of Primary Education (K–8) that ran an elementary and middle school; a Department of Higher Education that brought university programs to the region; and a Department of Theology that offered religious education.

56. Teachers worked without high school degrees throughout the 1980s. However, by 1990 a law made this practice illegal and judicial bodies were cracking down on violations of this law.

57. Conflicts emerged in the course, and after the first two cohorts, the MST decided to restrict access to these programs to teachers in MST settlements and camps.

58. There were many local critics of the MST's initiatives. For example, in January 1990, during the first month of the MAG program, a local newspaper published an article claiming that the FUNDEP program in Braga was an "MST center for guerrilla training" (MST 2001, 11). FUNDEP sued the newspaper and won the case.

59. All quotes or information in the book from Elizabete Witcel are from an interview on November 15, 2010.

60. All information or quotes in the book from Vanderlúcia Simplicio are from an interview on November 9, 2010, unless noted.

61. All quotes or information in the book from Adilio Perin are from an interview on November 28, 2010.

62. All quotes or information in the book from Ivania Azevedo are from an interview on January 16, 2011.

63. Although the Ministry of Education (MEC) was not an official partner, it provided some funding.

64. The clergy later extended this contract.

65. The movement attributes this concept to the Soviet theorist Shulgin (2013); however, at this point there were not Portuguese translation of Shulgin's work.

66. Josué de Castro was a Marxist geographer who wrote *Geography of Hunger* (Castro 1952). In October 1997, Castro's daughter visited IEJC for its inauguration.

67. This collective went through different names throughout the MST's history, originally called the CAPP (Collective of Political-Pedagogical Accompaniment). I refer to this collective of activists who oversee MST programs by its current name, the CPP, to avoid confusion.

68. In 2011, the MST graduated their fifteenth MAG cohort and twelfth TAC cohort.

69. All quotes or information in the book from Cleide Almeida are from an interview on June 15, 2009.

70. Educational activists brought up a list of barriers to implementing the IEJC's pedagogies in public schools, such as the intervention of unsympathetic government officials, the shorter school days, the bureaucratic requirements for the organization of disciplines, the lack of infrastructure for gardening, and the rotation of teachers in and out of the schools each year.

71. In the 1990s, the MST also began to study the 1959 Cuban literacy campaigns and in September 1995 published the text *The Development of Education in Cuba*. The MST was also inspired by Cuba's approach to childcare, known as "infant circles." More recently, the MST has organized rural literacy programs based on the Cuban literacy program, *Sí, Se Puede* (*Sim, Eu Posso*, "Yes, we can").

72. These "mystical" cultural performances evolved from Catholic liberation theology practices. In June 1993, the MST education collective published a text called "How to

Teach Children *Mística*," to help educators attempting to incorporate this practice into their classrooms.

73. Other MST series on education include *Fazendo Escola* (Making the School, started in June 1998), *Cadernos do ITERRA* (Notebooks on ITERRA, started in 2001), and books of student artwork. There are also MST publication series on grassroots organizing, gender, health, and other topics.

74. Between 1990 and 2010, the MST published eighty-six texts, a total of 4,320 pages, describing this proposal.

CHAPTER 2

1. The landless camp was organized by a break-off group from the MST.
2. Two of the police leaders were arrested and sentenced fifteen years later, for 228 years and 158 years in prison. The governor and the 155 police officers were never sentenced (MST 2015, 47).
3. *La Via Campesina*, an international coalition of farmers' organizations fighting for food sovereignty, recognizes April 17 as the International Day of Peasant Resistance, due to this history.
4. As explained in Chapter 1, these figures represent the total number of land occupations that took place, led by dozens of different organizations. However, the MST was by far the largest and most politically powerful among them, representing at least 50 percent of the occupations.
5. A *ciranda* is a game that young children play in Brazil, where they hold hands and dance in a circle while singing. The movement adopted this name for their childcare centers as it emphasizes the pedagogically appropriate nature of the childcare.
6. The proposal was approved in November 1997 at the Third Forum of the "Provost Advisory Board of Brazilian Universities." The professors were from the University of Brasília, Federal University of Rio Grande do Sul, University of Vale dos Rios dos Sinos, Regional University of the Northeast of Rio Grande do Sul, Federal University of Sergipe, and State University of Júlio de Mesquita Filho.
7. All quotes or information in the book from Monica Molina are from an interview on November 10, 2010.
8. Wolford (2010, 2016) also argues that in order to understand the nature of INCRA and the relationships that have developed between INCRA officials and social movement activists, it is necessary to trace the history of this agency within Brazil's institutional landscape. INCRA was created on July 9, 1970, during Brazil's military dictatorship, in order to oversee the colonization of the northwestern Amazonian region of Brazil. The main goal of this recolonization program was to quell rural unrest in the northeast and southern states, by offering poor families from these regions land in the Amazon. A secondary goal for the military government was to "civilize" a part of the country over which it had little control. By the mid-1980s this process of colonization in the Amazon was slowly coming to an end. In 1987, the Brazilian Congress terminated INCRA. However, the late 1980s was also a period of widespread mobilization, with groups like the MST demanding agrarian reform. INCRA was opened again in 1989, albeit with a very different mission: "INCRA's main focus would now be on settlement rather than colonization, and instead of working on the frontier where public land seemed to be freely available, the agency would now be expected to expropriate land from large landowners in the heart of settled areas within each state" (Wolford 2016, 30). However, this shift in institutional alignment still came with very little financial commitment, as INCRA remained one of the most poorly funded and understaffed agencies in the Brazilian government (for more information, see Wolford 2010a, 2016).

9. All quotes or information in the book from Rubneuza Leandro are from an interview on July 22, 2011, unless noted.

10. Full name is the Regional University of the Northwest of the State of Rio Grande do Sul. Prior to 1985 it was the College of Philosophy, Science and Literature (FAFI). I use one name to avoid confusion.

11. All of the quotes and information in the book from Dinarte Belato are from a group interview with him and two other faculty members on November 30, 2010.

12. Similarly, Houtzager (2001) discusses how the Catholic Church was an "institutional host" to grassroots organizers during this same period in Brazil.

13. See Chapter 5 for more details on the MST's educational struggle in this region.

14. All quotes or information in the book from Ivori Moraes are from interviews on October 3, 2011, and August 27, 2016, unless noted.

15. This name was not used during this first university program in 1998; they were just re-ferred to as the MST leaders "accompanying" the program. Throughout this book, I refer to a collective of activists overseeing programs by its current name, the CPP (Political Pedagogical Collective), in order to avoid confusion.

16. All quotes or information in the book from Rita de Cascia are from an interview on January 16, 2011.

17. All quotes and information in this book form Neyta Oliveira are from a group interview on November 30, 2010.

18. Fifty-seven people were in the program, but ten dropped out of for a variety of mostly personal reasons.

19. I was able to determine everyone's status second-hand by asking other graduates from the cohort.

20. One of these regional activists passed away in 2011.

21. This was during the left-leaning administration of Governor Olívio Dutra (1999–2002); see Chapter 4.

22. All quotes or information in the book from Mauricéia Lima are from an interview on February 23, 2011.

23. All quotes or information in the book from Rosangela Nascimento are from an interview on December 18, 2011.

24. All quotes or information in the book from Bernadete Schwaab and Jussara Reolon are from an informal conversation on December 1, 2010.

25. Calculations all based on April 1998 exchange rate R$1.1366: US$1.<https://www.imf.org/external/np/fin/data/rms_mth.aspx?SelectDate=1998-04-30&reportType=REP> (accessed August 24, 2016).

26. All quotes or information in the book from Clarice dos Santos are from an interview on November 8, 2010, unless noted.

27. The reduction in PRONERA's budget in 2010 was the result of a judicial attack on the program between 2008 and 2010, which I discuss at the end of the chapter.

28. This information is from the Second National Study of Education in Areas of Agrarian Reform (INCRA 2015), the most updated study on PRONERA, which provides data for 1998–2011.

29. A graduate specialization is a two-year degree that is common in Brazil, which students take after completing a baccalaureate degree and before beginning a master's degree.

30. In Brazil, law programs are offered at the baccalaureate level, not graduate level.

31. This two-year program takes place at the MST Florestan Fernandes National School and only accepts students who participate in the international peasant organization *La Via Campesina*. In 2016, the fourth cohort was entering this program.

32. All quotes or information in the book from Bernardo Mançano Fernandes are from an interview on November 10, 2011, unless noted.

33. This information is from a phone conversation with Bernardo on July 11, 2016.

34. This arrangement had historical precedent, as the first PRONERA graduate degree program offered by the University of Brasília between 2003 and 2005 also took place at the ENFF.

35. Movement of People Displaced by Damns (MAB), Family Agricultural School (EFA) movement, the homeless movement (MTST), Rural Youth Ministry (PJR), and Small Agricultural Movement (MAP).

36. Information in this section is from my field notes from July 2009.

37. Opening Panel, Fourth PRONERA Conference (Field notes, November 2010).

38. MST, Movement of Small Farmers (MPA), Rural Youth Ministry (PJR), Pastoral Land Commission (CPT).

39. <http://portal.unemat.br/?pg=noticia/1719/T%EAm%20in%EDcio%20aulas%20 do%20curso%20de%20> (accessed November 17, 2017).

40. Congress chooses six TCU Ministers and the president chooses three TCU Ministers.

41. According to the TCU website, the TCU "audits the accounts of administrators and other persons responsible for federal public funds, assets, and other valuables, as well as the accounts of any person who may cause loss, misapplication, or other irregularities that may cause losses to the federal treasury."

42. *Acordão* 2653/2008, section b of the report, p. 9.

43. Letter from Gilda Diniz do Santos, a lawyer at INCRA, to the President of INCRA, with the subject "Acordão TCU 2653/ 2008," sent on March 26, 2009.

44. All quotes or information in the book from Leonardo Kauer are from an interview, October 25, 2010.

45. He was the director of the TCU's Parliamentary Advisory Board (ASPAR), a high-ranking official.

46. All quotes or information in the book from Paulo Medeiros are from an interview on November 10, 2010.

47. All quotes or information in the book from Jorge Martuis are from an interview on November 16, 2010.

48. Pamphlet given to me in Recife on June 10, 2009.

49. Letter to the Presidential Ministry of the Federal Audit Court, Fortaleza, July 13, 2010. Signers include a representative from the Federation of Small Farmers of Ceará, a professor at the Federal University of Ceará, a representative in PRONERA's National Pedagogical Advisory Board, a professor at the State University of Ceará, a representative from the Ministry of Education's Executive Committee for *Educação do Campo*, an INCRA bureaucrat, a representative from the State Secretary of Education of Ceará, and a member of the MST education sector in Ceará.

50. This section is drawn from my field notes from November 2010.

51. Decree 7.352, November 4, 2010. Articles 11–17 of the decree are about PRONERA. The inclusion of PRONERA in this decree was controversial. Armênio Schmidt, the Ministry of Education's Director of Diversity, told me that at the last minute INCRA officials convinced the President's advisors to also include PRONERA in the decree, which was initially only supposed to be about *Educação do Campo* (see Chapter 3 for more context). In contrast, Clarice, the coordinator of PRONERA at the time, claimed that the MEC had intentionally attempted to exclude PRONERA from being part of the decree.

52. Decree 7.352, November 4, 2010, Article 17.

53. All quotes or information in the book from Gilda Diniz dos Santos are from November 9, 2010.

54. <http://www.incra.gov.br/index.php/noticias-sala-de-imprensa/noticias/462-tcu-autoriza-execucao-do-programa-de-educacao-na-reforma-agraria> (accessed April 22, 2013).

55. Article 33 of Law 12.695/2012. This change was important, as professors have to give up a significant portion of their vacation time to teach in PRONERA programs.
56. Interview with Clarice dos Santos, September 24, 2015.
57. In the 2016 version of the PRONERA manual, the reference to the 2010 TCU judgment was no longer included, nor were there any explicit references to restrictions on social movement participation. This suggests that the regulations stemming from the 2010 judgment became more lenient over time.
58. The next two paragraphs are all from an interview with Clarice do Santos on September 24, 2015.
59. Based on January 2009 exchange rate $R2.239: US$1. <https://www.imf.org/external/np/fin/data/ rms_mth.aspx?SelectDate=2009-01-31&reportType=REP> (accessed August 25, 2016).

CHAPTER 3

1. Gramsci's concept of "common sense" refers to people's spontaneous and contradictory beliefs, their uncritical philosophical understandings of the world.
2. All quotes or information in the book from Maria Rebeca Otero Gomes are from an interview on February 14, 2014.
3. Some of these experiences included the Family Agricultural Schools (EFAs, which inspired the MST's use of the *pedagogia da alternância*), the Base Education Movement (MEB), the MST's teacher training programs, the educational activities of the Movement of People Affected by Dams (MAB), and the indigenous movement.
4. Especially important for CONTAG's growth was the Program for Assistance for the Rural Worker (PRORURAL), which was established in 1971 to provide medical and dental services for rural populations. Almost all of CONTAG union locals had partnerships with PRORURAL (Maybury-Lewis 1994, 41).
5. For more on CONTAG and the relationship between the rural union movement and other social movements during this period, see Maybury-Lewis (1994), Welch (1999), and Sauer and Welch (2015).
6. Initially, the Alternative Project for Sustainable Rural Development (PADRS).
7. All quotes or information in the book from Sônia Maria dos Santos are from an interview on March 2, 2011.
8. This is similar to Steinberg's (1999) argument that the framing literature should have a more dialogical focus that acknowledges discourse and language as an ongoing process of social communication (743).
9. Although not approved by congress, the national educational guidelines passed by the CNE have the force of law in Brazil.
10. All quotes or information in the book from Edla Soarez are from an interview on April 6, 2011.
11. All quotes or information in the book from José Wilson are from an interview on November 18, 2011.
12. Artigo 4º da resolução CNE/CEB 1, de 3 de abril de 2002.
13. This was not the first split in the PT. In 1992 a Trotskyist political current in the PT, was expelled from the party, which led to the founding of the Unified Socialist Workers Party (PSTU).
14. The *Economist* referred to this as Brazil's "take off" (November 12, 2009).
15. According to a research team at the State University of São Paulo (UNESP), by 2014 there were 126 organizations that were registered as occupying land in Brazil. Between 2000 and 2014, the MST led 50.5 percent of those occupations (2,958 of the 5,837 total occupations), with 63 percent of the total number of families (482,373 of the total 762,975 families). CONTAG organized the second most land occupation, 9 percent of the total occupations during this period (534 of the 5,837 total occupations) with 7 percent of the total number of families (54,948 of the total 762,975 families) (NERA 2015).

16. While Cardoso expropriated an unprecedented amount of land during his first term, the administration later shifted to supporting market-based agrarian reform approaches. The justification was that "market mechanisms will provide access to land without confrontations or disputes and therefore reduce social problems and federal expenses at the same time" (Sauer 2006, 182).

17. In this context, in 2007, the MST organized its 5th National Congress, with 17,500 landless activists participating from twenty-four Brazilian states (MST 2013, 57).

18. Until 2011, this secretary was known as SECAD (the Secretariat of Continual Education, Literacy, and Diversity). The term "Inclusion" was added to the name of the Secretariat in 2011, to refer to programs for students with special education needs. I refer to the Secretariat by its post-2011 acronym (SECADI) throughout the manuscript to reduce confusion.

19. In 2017, this department was called the Department of Policies for Education of the Countryside, Indigenous Education, and Ethnic-Racial Relations.

20. All information and quotes in the book from Armênio Schmidt are from an interview on November 28, 2011.

21. This advisory board was first called the *Grupo de Trabalho Permanente da Educação do Campo* (Education of the Countryside Permanent Working Group) in 2003, and became the *Coordinação Nacional para Educação do Campo* (National Coordination for Education of the Countryside) in 2004. I refer to both groups as the advisory board for *Educação do Campo*, to reduce confusion.

22. All information and quotes from Antonio Munarim are from an interview on November 28, 2011.

23. The only state government that refused to host a seminar was São Paulo.

24. Antonio Munarim gave me a copy of this letter.

25. For a longer description of this program's transfer to and trajectory in Brazil, see Tarlau (2017).

26. All quotes or information in the book from Salomão Hage are from an interview on September 22, 2015.

27. In another article I describe how a professor in the state of Bahia was able to offer an explicitly Marxist version of the *Escola Ativa* teacher trainings at her university (Tarlau 2017).

28. *Estadão* (June 3, 2011 and June 11, 2011)

29. All quotes or information in the book from Viviane Fernandes are from an interview on November 7, 2011.

30. All quotes or information in the book from Edson Anhaia are from an interview on February 7, 2014, unless noted.

31. All quotes or information in the book from Divina Lopes are from an interview on August 6, 2015.

32. A few years later, the MEC launched a new program for multigrade schools, now called *Escola da Terra* (School of the Land). For MEC officials, this was understood as a continuation of the *Escola Ativa* program; in contrast, social movement activists saw it as a new program that they had much more influence over and that adhered more closely to their educational goals (Tarlau 2017).

33. A third major program that the office for *Educação do Campo* developed, which I do not discuss, was an adult education program that allows people in rural communities to complete fifth through eighth grades, known as *Saberes da Terra* (Knowledge of the Lands).

34. The MST wrote a book about the first LEDOC program (Caldart, Fetzner, Rodrigues, and Freitas 2010).

35. Federal University of Sergipe, Federal University of Bahia, and Federal University of Minas Gerais.

36. Interview with Secretary of SECADI Paulo Gabriel Soledade Nacif, August 6, 2015. Some universities had LEDOC programs at two campuses, which counted as two university programs.
37. All quotes or information in the book from Luiz Antonio (Tonico) Pasquetti is from an interview on November 17, 2011, unless noted.
38. Informal conversation, August 7, 2015.
39. This was a change from around 9 billion dollars (according to exchange rates in January 2004) to around 60 billion dollars (according to exchange rates in January 2011).
40. Also in the mid-2000s, due to internal pressure from the women activists in the movement, the MST created an internal policy that 50 percent of the national directorate had to be female. For more information on these gender dynamics and organizational changes in the movement, see Caldeira (2009), Deere (2003), Peschanski (2007), and Wiebe (2006).
41. "Balanço da Reforma Agrária 2014 do Pimeiro Mandato da Presidental Dilma Rousseff," http://www.revistamissoes.org.br/2015/01/balanco-da-reforma-agraria-2014-e-do-primeiro-mandato-da-presidenta-dilma-rousseff/ (accessed November 15, 2017).
42. These numbers include the year 2016, although Dilma Rousseff's second term ended abruptly in May 2016 when she had to step down from office to face an impeachment trial (see Epilogue for more details).
43. Most rural schools function through "morning" and "afternoon" sessions, resulting in a four-hour school day. "Integral" schools are when one group of students uses the school for the entire day.
44. All of these goals were stated publicly at the formal launching of *ProNoCampo*, on March 20, 2012. This ceremony, including the speeches, can be watched online at <http://www.youtube.com/watch?v=hPtcdDSqcgk>.
45. Informal conversation with Vanderlúcia Simplicio, November 2011.
46. According to FONEC's founding document, this organization was "a coalition of collective groups formed to maintain autonomy in relationship to the State, with the goal of promoting a critical analysis of the public policies for *Educação do Campo*" (National Forum for Education of the Countryside, Founding Letter).
47. Many state Departments of Education created civil society advisory councils for *Educação do Campo* in the mid-2000s. In Pernambuco, the indigenous movement participates in this institutional space. However, the relationship between indigenous groups and the movement for *Educação do Campo* differs across the country.
48. All quotes or information in the book from Elisa Urbano Ramos are from an interview on July 16, 2011.

CHAPTER 4

1. The Law of Basic Educational Guidelines (LDB, 1996, Título IV, Artigo 10/11) indicates that municipal governments should "prioritize primary education" and that state governments should "ensure that primary education is offered, and with priority, provide secondary education." However, in practice, many municipal and state governments offer public education outside of their priority areas. The federal government also participates in primary and secondary education by developing a National Plan for Education (PNE), writing guidelines, and providing financial and technical assistance.
2. The estimated population for Rio Grande do Sul in 2015 is 11.2 million. <http://www.ibge.gov.br/estadosat/perfil.php?sigla=rs> (accessed July 8, 2016).
3. This study is recording nominal income, not accounting for inflation. The same study is used for all average monthly household income estimates in Chapters 4–6. <http://www.ibge.gov.br/estadosat/perfil.php?sigla=pe> (accessed August 25, 2016).

4. All US dollar estimates of 2015 average monthly household income in Chapters 4 and 5 are based on the January 2015 exchange rate $R2.6929: US$1. https://www.imf. org/external/np/fin/data/rms_mth.aspx?SelectDate=2015-01-31&reportType=REP (accessed August 25, 2016).

5. There is an extensive literature about race in Brazil and the problems with these categories and self-identification in the census (e.g., Loveman 2014; Telles 2004).

6. For more details on this European immigration, see Lesser (1999), Ribeiro (2000), and Skidmore (2010).

7. The most famous of these initiatives is the participatory budgeting system (Abers 2000; Baiocchi 2005; Goldfrank 2011a). The Porto Alegre "citizenship schools" also became an international model of educational innovation and participatory school governance (Gandin and Apple 2002).

8. The Democratic Labor Party (PDT) was also in power for one term (1991–1994).

9. These are the numbers of total land occupations in the state, including those led by other organizations; however, the MST organized the majority of these occupations.

10. All quotes or information in the book from Sister Alda Moura are from an interview on November 23, 2010.

11. In the Introduction, I reference a range of authors who document social movements' insider-outsider strategy, most significantly, scholars of the feminist movements in Latin America (Alvarez 1990) and the United States (Banaszak 2010).

12. This advisory board consists of government officials, unions, community members, and students.

13. All quotes or information in the book from Lucia Camini are from an interview on October 26, 2010.

14. All quotes or information in the book from Carlota Amado are from an interview on November 26, 2010.

15. All quotes or information in the book from Fernanda (pseudonym) are from an interview on October 11, 2011.

16. In 2011, this was approximately one-third of the state public schools on MST settlements and more than half of the high schools.

17. This information is from an interview with ex-Secretary of Education Mariza Abreu, November 1, 2010.

18. All quotes or information in the book from Eliane Muller are from an interview on January 17, 2011.

19. Governo do Estado do Rio Grande do Sul (1999). *Constituinte Escolar: Construção da Escola Democrática e Popular*. Caderno 3.

20. Projeto Político Pedagógico (PPP), Escola Joceli Correa, 2006.

21. Interview with CRE official in Santa Maria, November 25, 2010.

22. Interview with CRE official in Ijuí, November 29, 2010.

23. All quotes or information in the book from Cleusa Reichenbach are from an interview on November 27, 2010.

24. All quotes or information in the book from Izabela Braga are from an interview on November 24, 2010, unless noted.

25. All quotes and information from Mariza Abreu are from an interview on November 1, 2010.

26. Field notes, January 2011.

27. This information comes from a collection of news articles that the MST leadership in Rio Grande do Sul collected about the police violence during this period.

28. All quotes or information in the book from Luis Tesheiner are from an interview on November 17, 2010.

29. Pedro Osório, Coquerios do Sul, São Gabriel, and Nova Santa Rita.

30. All quotes or information in the book from Gilberto Thums is from an interview on November 11, 2010.
31. Public Ministry of Rio Grande do Sul Report, June 16, 2008, p. 46.
32. Ministério Público do Estado do Rio Grande do Sul, Termo de Compromisso de Ajustamento de Conduta, Procedimento Administrativo 16.315-0900/07-9, November 28, 2008.
33. These groups included the following: Justiça Global; Terra de Direitos; Rede Social de Justiça e Direitos Humanos; Associação de Advogados de Trabalhadores Rurais da Bahia; Federação dos Órgãos para Assistência Social e Educacional (FASE); Nadine Borges; Assessoria Jurídica Popular Mariana Criola; Dignitatis Assessoria Técnica e Jurídica Popular; and Gabinete de Assessoria Jurídica às Organizações Populares. <http://noticias.uol.com.br/ultnot/2008/07/24/ult23u2558.jhtm> (accessed July 10, 2015).
34. The information is this section is from field notes in July 2009. The name of the teacher is a pseudonym.
35. Field notes, July 2009.
36. Interview with Lourdes (pseudonym), CRE 8, on November 25, 2010.
37. All quotes or information in the book from Angelita da Silva are from an interview December 18, 2010.
38. The following information is from field notes in January 2011.
39. All quotes or information in the book from Nancy Pereira are from an interview on October 7, 2011.
40. List of goals for internal Department of Education document: "State Policies for *Educação do Campo* in Rio Grande do Sul, 2011 Draft."
41. Second interview with Izabela Braga, October 11, 2011.
42. MST activists learned from the experiment in Rio Grande do Sul and established Itinerant Schools in Paraná (2003), Santa Catarina (2004), Goiás (2005), Alagoas (2005), and Piauí (2008). However, in 2016 Paraná was the only state with functioning Itinerant Schools.

CHAPTER 5

1. All quotes or information in the book from Jaime Amorim are from an interview on February 16, 2011 unless noted. For more information on Jaime Amorim, see Chapter 5 of Wolford (2010b).
2. As I described in the Introduction, I chose cases with a baseline of high levels of MST activity, but where there were diverse outcomes in the MST's contentious co-governance of public schools.
3. Santa Maria is one of the ten municipalities in Pernambuco with the lowest population destiny. The estimated population in 2015 was 41,293. <http://www.cidades.ibge.gov. br/xtras/perfil.php?lang=&codmun=261260&search=pernambuco|santa-maria-da-boa-vista> (accessed July 8, 2016).
4. *Quilombos* are "maroon communities," descendants of runaway slave communities that have rights to community self-governance. There is a long and drawn-out process to become designated as a *quilombo*, as it results in receiving special benefits. There are hundreds of quilombo communities across Brazil waiting to receive official designation. For more information, see French (2009) and Leite (2012, 2015).
5. This information comes from the Santa Maria da Boa Vista Department of Culture and Tourism (Histórico de Pessoas, Departamento de Cultura e Turismo, Agosto 2003).
6. In 2015, the municipal Department of Education in Santa Maria served 6,667 students, about two-thirds in grades 1–4 and one-third in grades 5–8. There is also a network of schools in Santa Maria run by the state Department of Education, in 2015 serving 3,074 students mostly in grades 5 and above.

7. I was present in Santa Maria for two political transitions and I observed these personnel transfers taking place.

8. All quotes or information in the book from Teresneide Varjão are from an interview on April 29, 2011.

9. Erivan also became an important leader in the MST's LGBT collective that began organizing within the movement in 2015, for the recognition of "gay landless" rights. Erivan, like other gay men within the movement, found an activist home within his regional education sector and then he went on to take on more prestigious state and national leadership tasks within the movement.

10. All quotes or information in the book from Erivan Hilário are from an interview on October 25, 2011, unless noted.

11. This excerpt and the most of the following section comes from an assignment written by Erivan Hilário during his participation in the sixth PRONERA Pedagogy of Land program, in the Federal University of Rio Grande do Norte. "Quando a Vida Trasnforma a História" (When Life Transforms History).

12. This party became the Democratas (DEM) in 2007.

13. All quotes or information in the book from Leandro Duarte are from an interview on May 4, 2011.

14. All quotes or information in the book from Bernadete Barros are from an interview on May 5, 2011.

15. All quotes or information in the book from Josilene Alves Cardoso are from an interview on May 11, 2011.

16. All quotes or information in the book from Graça Gomes are from an interview on May 6, 2011.

17. MST leaders do not control how families vote, but they can encourage them to vote in certain ways. With fifteen settlements of 100–200 families—in a municipality of 40,000 people—this is significant.

18. All quotes or information in the book from Osmilda Brandão are from an interview on May 4, 2011.

19. All quotes or information in the book from Rogerio Junior Gomes are from an interview on May 11, 2011.

20. All quotes or information in the book from Elizângela Maria Gomes da Silva are from an interview on May 12, 2011.

21. All quotes or information in the book from Auzenir dos Santos are from an interview on May 6, 2011.

22. All quotes or information in the book from Rivanildo Adones are from an interview on May 6, 2011.

23. All quotes or information in the book from Návia Silva are from an interview on May 6, 2011.

24. All quotes or information in the book from Kátia Medrado are from an interview on May 9, 2011.

25. In Brazil, people who do not support the MST's actions often refer to the movement as "invading" land, rather than "occupying" the land.

26. All quotes or information in the book from Sydney Carvalho are from an interview on May 2, 2011.

27. All quotes or information in the book from Adailto Cardoso are from an interview on July 21, 2011.

28. In 2016, the MST shifted its political strategy and led a successful campaign to defeat the historically dominant family in Santa Maria in the mayoral election, a development I discuss briefly in the Epilogue.

29. For a longer history of sugarcane production in this region, see Chapter 4, Wolford (2010b).
30. Before *usinas* there was an attempt to create central mills, which largely failed.
31. This crisis was caused by the reduction in government subsidies, an increase in sugar production in other countries, and a drop in international demand with the rise of artificial sweeteners (Wolford 2010a).
32. Field notes, July 2011.
33. All quotes or information in the book from Eduardo Coutinho are from an interview on July 9, 2011.
34. The legislative assembly created a Parliamentary Inquiry Commission (CPI) to investigate Eudo's link to drug trafficking and rural assassinations. Eudo claimed that Eduardo fabricated these accusations.
35. All quotes or information in the book from Paulo Barreto are from an interview on July 6, 2011.
36. All quotes or information in the book from César Magalhães are from an interview on July 9, 2011.
37. I interviewed all of the mayors in Table 5.2, as well as all of the secretaries of education except Maria Celha Negeira de Gois and Sebastião Sales.
38. All quotes or information in the book from Elienai da Silva are from an interview on July 17, 2011.
39. All quotes or information in the book from Flavinha Tereza are from an interview on September 7, 2011, unless noted.
40. All quotes or information in the book from Ines Senna are from an interview on July 6, 2011.
41. All quotes or information in the book from Julieta Pontual are from an interview on July 6, 2011.
42. All quotes or information in the book from Brasilina Silva are from an interview on July 27, 2011.
43. All quotes or information in the book from Sonia Lopes dos Santos are from an interview on July 27, 2011.
44. All quotes or information in the book from Norma Maria Azevedo da Silva are from an interview on July 18, 2011.
45. Wolford (2010b) provides a detailed analysis of these changes in Água Preta between 1998 and 2003.
46. All quotes or information in the book from Alex Santos are from an interview on July 9, 2011.
47. All quotes or information in the book from Albertinha Tenório are from an interview on July 7, 2011.
48. All quotes or information in the book from Maria Jose da Silva are from an interview on July 7, 2011.

CHAPTER 6

1. The estimated population in 2015 was 8.9 million. http://www.ibge.gov.br/estadosat/perfil.php?sigla=ce (accessed July 8, 2016).
2. All quotes or information in the book from Joel Gomes are from an interview on September 9, 2011.
3. All quotes or information in the book from Sofia Lerche are from an interview on November 29, 2017.
4. These programs were FUNDEF and FUNDEB, respectively.
5. All quotes or information in the book from Susana (pseudonym) came from an interview on September 15, 2011.

6. Final conference document, First State Seminar for Education of the Countryside.

7. "Education of the Countryside Workshop" Agenda, December 18–22, 2006.

8. São Paulo had 41.3 million people in the 2010 census, 95.6 percent classified as urban. In 2015, São Paulo had the second highest average monthly household income in the country (after Brasília): 1,482 *reais* (about 550 US dollars in 2015).

9. For example, see this Globo report: <http://g1.globo.com/especiais/eleicoes-2010/noticia/2010/07/serra-diz-que-mst-apoia-dilma-porque-podera-fazer-mais-invasoes.html> (accessed April 1, 2010).

10. Both interviews on November 10, 2011.

11. I attempted to interview Chalita, but his secretary was never able to schedule an interview.

12. The 2010 census classified 95 percent of the population as urban (IBGE 2011). In 2014 in São Paulo there were 270 settlements with 18,932 families, among the highest number in the country (NERA 2015).

13. I also spent two months in the Pontal da Paranapanema region, the far western part of São Paulo with the highest concentration of MST settlements. I interviewed twenty-two people in this region, a combination of MST activists, teachers, and principals. This is the only region in the country where I did not observe any of the MST's pedagogical practices in the public school system, despite the large number of schools on MST settlements. For a description of this case, see Tarlau (2013).

14. All quotes or information in the book from Erivando Barbosa are from an interview on September 15, 2011.

15. According to Erivando, Cid Gomes' vice-governor was from the PT and had connections to the movement and convinced Gomes to ask for the MST's support. Cid personally came to ask the MST state leadership for support, and the movement said that they would not support him. During his second electoral campaign, Erivando said that Gomes did not bother to ask for their endorsement.

16. Gomes actually agreed to build five schools, four on MST settlements and one on a settlement affiliated with CONTAG. I only discuss the four settlements that the MST helps to co-govern.

17. All quotes or information in the book from Neidinha Lopes are from an interview on September 25, 2011.

18. All quotes or information in the book from Ana Edith are from an interview on September 15, 2011.

19. All quotes or information in the book from Simone Ramos are from an interview on September 12, 2011.

20. All quotes or information in the book from Sandra Alves are from an interview on November 22, 2011.

21. All quotes or information in the book from Ivaniza Martins are from an interview on September 8, 2011.

22. All quotes or information in the book from Rita dos Santos are from an interview on November 24, 2011.

23. All quotes or information in the book from Laura (pseudonym) are from an interview on November 23, 2011.

24. All quotes or information in the book from Beatriz (pseudonym) are from an interview on September 14, 2011.

25. All quotes or information in the book from Mariana (pseudonym) are from an interview on September 15, 2011.

26. < http://www.seduc.ce.gov.br/index.php/ouvidoria/205-desenvolvimento-da-escola/ diversidade-e-inclusao-educacional/educacao-do-campo/11295-educacao-do-campo> (accessed August 29, 2017).

27. All quotes or information in the book from Cilene Ramos are from an interview on September 8, 2011.

28. All quotes or information in the book from Camila (pseudonym) are from an interview on September 9, 2011.

29. I was giving electronic copies of each of these PPPs.

30. In 2017, the official name of the seminar (in Portuguese) was "VII Semana Pedagógica das Escolas da Ensino Médio do Campo das Áreas de Reforma Agrária do MST."

31. All quotes or information in the book Nonata Sousa are from an interview on September 13, 2011.

32. Lei #9.394 de 20 de dezembro de 1996.

33. All quotes or information in the book from Nohemy Ibanez are from an interview on September 6, 2011.

34. Most schools in Brazil, including high schools, only function in the mornings or afternoons.

35. All quotes or information in the book from Helena and Letícia (pseudonyms) came from a joint interview on September 6, 2011.

36. Field notes, November 2011.

37. Taken from the section on "objectives" in the seminar program (January 30 to February 2, 2017).

CONCLUSION

1. Quoted in Davidson (1977).

2. For some recent analysis of this policy network, see Martins and Krawczyk (2016) and Avelar and Ball (2017).

3. Importantly, Vergara-Camus (2014) argues that *both* the MST's more pragmatic relationship to the state and the EZLN's rejection of state support are strategies for building autonomy from the state and the market for their communities.

4. For example, see *Berkeley Journal of Sociology* Forum on "Power and Prefiguration," volume 58, 2014.

5. In 2005, the MST founded the Florestan Fernandes National School (ENFF) in the city of Guaranema, São Paulo, which primarily offers nonformal educational programs for activists but has also partnered with universities to offer formal educational programs. Other MST-administered education institutions include the Educar Institute (founded in 2005 in Rio Grande do Sul), the Latin American School of Agroecology (ELAA, founded in 2005 in Paraná), and the Agroecological Institute of Latin America–Amazonia branch (IALA, founded in 2009 in Pará). These latter two agroecology institutes are part of network of schools founded by the international peasant organization *La Via Campesina*. As of January 2018 IALAs had also been established in Nicaragua, Argentina, Brazil, Chile, Colombia, Ecuador, and Paraguay (McCune and Sánchez 2018).

6. Przeworski (1986) argues that socialist political parties face a choice between improving workers' immediate conditions versus investing in a long-term strategy to build socialism.

7. Sanders (2016) describes a similar process of how African American women who took over the responsibility of running the federal Head Start programs in the mid-1960s were able to gain skills and expertise that contributed to other spheres of movement organizing.

8. Oaxaca government document: "Plan para la Transformación de la Educación de Oaxaca."

EPILOGUE

1. <https://www.nybooks.com/daily/2018/03/05/blood-on-the-land-in-brazil/> (accessed November 10, 2018).<https://paraibaonline.com.br/2017/02/em-campina-bolsonaro-defende-porte-de-arma-no-brasil-e-manda-recado-ao-mst/> (accessed November 10, 2018).

2. <https://www.theguardian.com/world/2018/oct/22/brazils-jair-bolsonaro-says-he-would-put-army-on-streets-to-fight> (accessed November 10, 2018).

3. <https://www.theguardian.com/world/2015/sep/18/brazilian-congressman-rape-remark-compensation> (accessed November 10, 2018).

4. Braga refers to this as the end of *Lulismo*, the PT's "mode of regulation of class conflict."

5. Some of the following analysis comes from a blog post with Elizabeth McKenna for the University of California, Berkeley, Center for Latin American Studies blog. <https://clasberkeley.wordpress.com/ 2015/ 10/ 15/ the- myth- of- unified- unrest- in- brazil/> (accessed June 27, 2016).

6. Ninety-six percent of probabilistically sampled June protest participants claimed no affiliation with any political party and eighty-nine percent said they did not feel represented by any party. <https://www.gentedeopiniao.com.br/politica-nacional/89-dos-mani-festantes-nao-se-sentem-representados-por-partidos> (accessed February 2, 2021).

7. On June 22, 2015, the PT treasurer was convicted of bribery and money laundering and sentenced to fifteen years in jail. On August 3, 2015, Lula's former Chief of Staff, Jose Dirceú, was arrested on charges of corruption and money laundering, and after a trial on May 18, 2016, was sentenced to twenty-three years of prison.

8. The polling organization Datafolha recorded 210,000; Brazilian Military Police reported 1.1 million.

9. <http://frentebrasilpopular.com.br/conteudo/compromissos-da-militancia/> (accessed June 27, 2016).

10. For an interesting discussion of this debate, see a 2010 interview with an MST leader, reprinted in *Jacobin* in 2017, <https://www.jacobinmag.com/2017/02/brazil-pt-mst-social-movements-temer-rousseff> (accessed December 1, 2017)

11. The speaker of the house, Eduardo Cunha, led this vote for an impeachment process on April 17. Cunha himself was removed from office on May 5 for his own involvement in corruption.

12. This is a common practice and is widely understood as a pretext rather than motive for her removal.

13. Temer's appointees were from right-leaning parties that ranged from the Brazilian Social Democratic Party (PSDB), the PT's major rival at the federal level, to the Democrats (DEM), a party historically linked to the military regime. Rousseff's cabinet included women and black Brazilians from a range of left-leaning and centrist parties.

14. The PT's alliance with the PMDB began informally in 2003 during Lula's first mandate.

15. The PMDB was also allied with the PSDB during Cardoso's (1995–2002) presidency.

16. "Brazil's austerity package decried by UN as attack on poor people," *The Guardian*, December 9, 2016.

17. For just one example of this widely held opinion: <https://www.nytimes.com/2018/08/21/opinion/lula-president-brazil-corruption.html> (accessed November 10, 2018).

18. In December 2017, the PMDB reverted to its original name from the 1970s, the MDB (Democratic Brazilian Movement). Meirelles thus ran on an MDB ticket.

19. Among the articles documenting these controversial positions is: <https://theintercept.com/2018/10/28/jair-bolsonaro-elected-president-brazil/> (accessed November 10, 2018).

20. My thanks to Elizabeth McKenna for this point, made in her dissertation research on the strategic role of the evangelical church in the rise of the far-right in Brazil.

21. Among the many great analyses of Bolsonaro's use of social media is: <https://nacla.org/news/2018/11/06/specter-dictatorship-brazil> (accessed November 10, 2018).

22. <https://www.bbc.com/news/world-latin-america-45451473> (accessed November 10, 2018).

23. Specifically, I am referring to the Unified Workers' Socialist Party (PSTU), which broke with the PT in the early 1990s and has been an open antagonist of the PT ever since. In the second round of voting, the PSTU campaigned for Haddad, with a caveat that no matter who won they would oppose the government.

24. <https://www.hrw.org/world-report/2018/country-chapters/brazil> (accessed November 10, 2018).

25. <https://www.globalwitness.org/pt/campaigns/environmental-activists/at-what-cost/> (accessed November 10, 2018).

26. <https://www.brasildefato.com.br/2018/11/05/conservatives-bring-back-senate-bill-to-label-brazilian-movements-as-terrorists/> (accessed November 10, 2018).

27. <https://www.theguardian.com/world/2018/oct/30/bolsonaro-win-students-urged-report-teachers-who-complain-whatsapp > (accessed November 10, 2018).

28. <https://www.yahoo.com/news/brazil-high-court-against-police-action-public-universities-042631838.html> (accessed November 10, 2018).

29. After his election, Bolsonaro announced the creation of a new Ministry of Economy, a fusion of several different ministries, with University of Chicago–trained neoclassical economist Paulo Guedes as the Minister.

30. <https://www.mstbrazil.org/content/motion-support-occupation-old-ariadn%C3%B3polis-quilombo-plant-campo-grande> (accessed November 10, 2018).

31. This was a Brazilian Labor Party (PTB)–Workers Party (PT) ticket. The PTB was founded by populist leader Getúlio Vargas in the 1940s. In 1981, Vargas's nieces refounded the party as a centrist party. The MST considered the PTB-PT ticket to be a left coalition, given the PT's involvement and that no members of the historically powerful family were in the coalition. The movement also helped to elect the first-ever city council person from an MST settlement, a PT party member.

32. In 2012, the PT ranked third in control of municipalities, behind the PMDB with 1,022 and the PSDB with 701. In 2016, the PT had fallen to tenth place, with the PMDB still ahead with 1,038 and the PSDB with 803.

33. <https://www.bbc.com/portuguese/brasil-45700013> (accessed November 10, 2018).

34. <https://www.brasildefato.com.br/2018/10/28/joao-pedro-stedile-nos-temos-que-retomar-o-trabalho-de-base/> (accessed November 10, 2018).

35. Tendencies that began before the PT's rule (J. M. M. Pereira and Sauer 2006; Sauer and Leite 2012).

36. This university itself was created in 2009 in response to the demands of social movements.

REFERENCES

Abers, Rebecca. 2000. *Inventing Local Democracy: Grassroots Politics in Brazil*. Boulder, CO: Lynne Rienner.

Abers, Rebecca, and Margaret Keck. 2009. "Mobilizing the State: The Erratic Partner in Brazil's Participatory Water Policy." *Politics & Society* 37 (2):289–314.

Abers, Rebecca and Margaret E. Keck. 2013. *Practical Authority: Agency and Institutional Change in Brazilian Water Politics*. Oxford: Oxford University Press.

Adamson, Walter L. 1978. "Beyond 'Reform or Revolution': Notes on Political Education in Gramsci, Habermas and Arendt." *Theory and Society* 6 (3):429–460.

Altenbaugh, Richard J. 1990. *Education for Struggle: The American Labor Colleges of the 1920s and 1930s*. Philadelphia: Temple University Press.

Althusser, Luis. 1971. "Ideology and Ideological State Apparatus." In *Lenin and Philosophy and Other Essays*, 121–76. New York: Monthly Review Press.

Alvarez, Sonia. 1990. *Engendering Democracy in Brazil: Women's Movements in Transition Politics*. Princeton, NJ: Princeton University Press.

Alvarez, Sonia. 1999. "Advocating Feminism: The Latin American Feminist NGO 'Boom.'" *International Feminist Journal of Politics* 1 (2):181–209.

Alvarez, Sonia. 2009. "Beyond NGO-Ization? Reflections from Latin America." *Development* 52 (2):175–184.

Alvarez, Sonia. 2017. "Beyond the Civil Society Agenda? Participation and Practices of Governance, Governability, and Governmentality in Latin America." In *Beyond Civil Society: Activism, Participation, and Protest in Latin America*, edited by Sonia Alvarez, Jeffrey W. Rubin, Millie Thayer, Gianpaolo Baiocchi, and Agustín Laó-Montes.316–330. Durham, NC: Duke University Press.

Amenta, Edwin. 2006. *When Movements Matter: The Townsend Plan and the Rise of Social Security*. Princeton, NJ: Princeton University Press.

Amenta, Edwin, Neal Caren, Elizabeth Chiarello, and Yang Su. 2010. "The Political Consequences of Social Movements." *Annual Review of Sociology* 36:287–307.

Andrade, Marcia Regina, Maria Clara Di Pierro, Monica Castagna Molina, and Sonia Meire Santos Azevedo, eds. 2004. *A Educação Na Reforma Agrária Em Perspectiva: Uma Avaliação Do Programa Nacional de Educação Na Reforma Agrária*. Brasília: Ministério de Desenvolvimento Agrário.

Andrews, Kenneth T. 2004. *Freedom Is a Constant Struggle: The Mississippi Civil Rights Movement and Its Legacy*. Chicago: University of Chicago Press.

Anyon, Jean. 1997. *Ghetto Schooling: A Political Economy of Urban Educational Reform*. New York: Teachers College Press.

Anyon, Jean. 2005. *Radical Possibilities: Public Policy, Urban Education and a New Social Movement*. New York: Taylor & Francis Group.

Apple, Michael W. 2004. *Ideology and Curriculum*. New York: RoutledgeFalmer.

Apple, Michael W. 2006. *Educating the "Right" Way: Markets, Standards, God, and Inequality*. New York: Routledge.

Apple, Michael W. 2013. *Can Education Change Society?* New York: Routledge Taylor & Francis.

Arnove, Robert F. 1986. *Education and Revolution in Nicaragua*. Studies in Comparative Education. New York: Praeger.

Arroyo, Miguel G. 2004. "A Educação Básica e o Movimento Social Do Campo." In *Por Uma Educação Do Campo*, edited by Miguel G. Arroyo, Rosali Salete Caldart, and Monica Castagna Molina. 65–86.Petrópolis, RJ: Editor Vozes.

Auyero, Javier. 2000. *Poor People's Politics: Peronist Survival Networks and the Legacy of Evita*. Durham, NC: Duke University Press.

Auyero, Javier, and Lauren Joseph. 2007. "Introduction: Politics under the Ethnographic Microscope." In *New Perspectives on Political Ethnography*, edited by Lauren Joseph, Mathew Mahler, and Javier Auyero, 1–13. New York: Springer.

Avelar, Marina, and Stephen J. Ball. 2019. "Mapping New Philanthropy and the Heterarchical State: The Mobilization for the National Learning Standards in Brazil." *International Journal of Educational Development* 64: 65–73.

Avritzer, Leonardo. 2002. *Democracy and the Public Space in Latin America*. Princeton, NJ: Princeton University Press.

Baiocchi, Gianpaolo. 2005. *Militants and Citizens: The Politics of Participatory Democracy in Porto Alegre*. Stanford, CA: Stanford University Press.

Baiocchi, Gianpaolo, Patrick Heller, and Marcelo Kunrath Silva. 2011. *Bootstrapping Democracy: Transforming Local Governance and Civil Society in Brazil*. Stanford, CA: Stanford University Press.

Banaszak, Lee Ann. 2010. *The Women's Movement: Inside and Outside of the State*. Cambridge: Cambridge University Press.

Benford, Robert, and David A. Snow. 2000. "Framing Processes and Social Movements: An Overview and Assessment." *Annual Review of Sociology* 26:611–639.

Bergad, Laird. 2007. *The Comparative Histories of Slavery in Brazil, Cuba, and the United States*. Cambridge: Cambridge University Press.

Berryman, Phillip. 1987. *Liberation Theology: Education at Empire's End*. New York: Pantheon Books.

Bhattacharya, Tithi. 2017. "Introduction: Mapping Social Reproduction Theory." In *Social Reproduction Theory: Remapping Class, Recentering Oppression*, edited by Tithi Bhattacharya, 1–20. London: Pluto Press.

Binder, Amy. 2002. *Contentious Curricula: Afrocentrism and Creationism in American Public Schools*. Princeton, NJ: Princeton University Press.

Boggs, Carl Jr. 1977. "Revolutionary Process, Political Strategy, and the Dilemma of Power." *Theory and Society* 4 (3):359–393.

Borras Jr, Saturnino M. 2001. "State-Society Relations in Land Reform Implementation in the Philippines." *Development and Change* 32:545–575.

Bourdieu, Pierre. 2007. "The Forms of Capital." In *Sociology of Education: A Critical Reader*, edited by Alan R. Sadovnik, 83–96. New York: Routledge.

Bourdieu, Pierre, and Jean-Claude Passeron. 1990. *Reproduction in Education, Society and Culture*. London: Sage.

Bowen, James. 1962. *Soviet Education: Anton Makarenko and the Years of Experiment*. Madison: University of Wisconsin Press.

Bowles, Samuel, and Herbert Gintis. 1976. *Schooling in Capitalist America: Educational Reform and the Contradictions of Economic Life*. London: Routledge & K. Paul.

Boydston, Jeanne. 1990. *Home and Work: Housework, Wages, and the Ideology of Labor in the Early Republic*. New York: Oxford University Press.

Braga, Ruy. 2012. *A Política Do Precariado: Do Populismo à Hegemonia Lulista.* São Paulo: Boitempo Editoral.

Braga, Ruy. 2016. "The End of Lulism and the Palace Coup in Brazil." *Global Dialogue* 6 (3):10–12.

Braga, Ruy. 2014. "Precariado e Sindicalismo No Brasil ContemporâNeo: Um Olhar a Partir Da Indústria Do Call Center." *Revista Crítica de Ciências Sociais* 103:25–52.

Branford, Sue, and Jan Rocha. 2002. *Cutting the Wire: The Story of the Landless Movement in Brazil.* London: Latin America Bureau.

Braverman, Harry. 1998. *Labor and Monopoly Capital: The Degradation of Work in the Twentieth Century.* New York: Monthly Review Press.

Bray, Mark. 2003. "Control of Education: Issues and Tensions in Centralization and Decentralization." In *Comparative Education. The Dialectic of the Global and the Local,* edited by Robert F. Arnove and Carlos Alberto Torres, Second, 204–228. Lanham, MD: Rowman & Littlefield.

Breines, Wini. 1980. "Community and Organization: The New Left and Michels 'Iron Law.'" *Social Problems* 27 (4): 419–29. https://doi.org/10.3366/ajicl.2011.0005.

Breines, Wini. 1989. *Community and Organization in the New Left, 1962-1968: The Great Refusal.* New Brunswick, NJ: Rutgers University Press.

Bruno, Regina. 1997. *Senhores Da Terra, Senhores Da Guerra: A Nova Face Política Das Elites Agroindustriais No Brasil.* Rio de Janeiro: Editora Forense Universitária.

Bruns, Barbara, and Javier Luque. 2014. *Great Teachers: How to Raise Student Learning in Latin America and the Caribbean.* Washington, DC: World Bank.

Burawoy, Michael. 2003. "For a Sociological Marxism: The Complementary Convergence of Antonio Gramsci and Karl Polanyi." *Politics & Society* 31 (2):193–261.

Burgwal, Gerrit. 1995. *Struggle of the Poor: Neighborhood Organization and Clientelist Practice in a Quito Squatter Settlement.* Amsterdam: Centre for Latin American Research and Documentation.

Caldart, Rosali Salete. 2004. *Pedagogia Do Movimento Sem Terra.* São Paulo: Expressão Popular.

Caldart, Rosali Salete, Andrewa Rosana Fetzner, Romir Rodrigues, and Luiz Carlos Freitas, eds. 2010. *Caminhos Para Transformacão Da Escola: Reflexões Desde Praticas Da Licenciatura Em Educação Do Campo.* São Paulo: Expressão Popular.

Caldart, Rosali Salete, Pereira, Paulo Alentejano, and Gaudencio Frigotto, eds. 2012. *Dicionário Da Educação Do Campo.* São Paulo: Expressão Popular.

Caldeira, Rute. 2009. "The Failed Marriage between Women and the Landless People's Movement (MST) in Brazil." *Journal of International Women's Studies* 10 (4):237–258.

Camini, Isabela. 2009. *Itinerante: Na Fronteira de Uma Nova Escola.* São Paulo: Expressão Popular.

Carnoy, Martin, and Henry M. Levin. 1985. *Schooling and Work in the Democratic State.* Stanford, CA: Stanford University Press.

Carter, Miguel. 2009. "Desigualidade Social, Democracia e Reforma Agrária No Brasil." In *Combatendo a Desigualidade Social: O MST e a Reforma Agrária No Brasil,* edited by Miguel Carter, 27–78. São Paulo: Editora UNESP.

Carter, Miguel, ed. 2015. *Challenging Social Inequality: The Landless Rural Workers Movement and Agrarian Reform in Brazil.* Durham, NC: Duke University Press.

Carter, Miguel, and Horacio Martins de Carvalho. 2015. "The Struggle on the Land: Source of Growth, Innovation, and Constant Challenge for the MST." In *Challenging Social Inequality: The Landless Rural Workers Movement and Agrarian Reform in Brazil.* 229–273 Durham, NC: Duke University Press.

Castro, Josue de. 1952. *The Geography of Hunger.* New York: Little, Brown and Company.

Choudry, Aziz. 2015. *Learning Activism: The Intellectual Life of Contemporary Social Movements.* Toronto: University of Toronto Press.

Choudry, Aziz, and Dip Kapoor, eds. 2010. *Learning from the Ground Up: Global Perspectives on Social Movements and Knowledge Production.* New York: Palgrave Macmillan.

Coelho, Vera Schattan. 2007. "Brazilian Health Councils: Including the Excluded?" In *Spaces for Change?: The Politics of Citizen Participation in New Democratic Arenas,* edited by Andrea Cornwall and Vera Schattan Coelho.33–54.New York: Zed Books.

Cook, Maria Lorena. 1996. *Organizing Dissent: Unions, the State, and the Democratic Teachers' Movement in Mexico.* University Park, PA: Penn State University Press.

Cornwall, Andrew, and Vera Schattan Coelho, eds. 2007. *Spaces for Change?: The Politics of Citizen Participation in New Democratic Arenas.* New York: Zed Books.

Coutinho, Carlos Nelson. 2013. *Gramsci's Political Thought.* Chicago: Haymarket Books.

CPT. 1989. "Conflitos No Campo Brasil, 1988." Goiânia, Brazil: Comissão Pastoral da Terra. https://www.cptnacional.org.br/component/jdownloads/send/41-conflitos-no-campo-brasil-publicacao/263-conflitos-no-campo-brasil-1988?Itemid=0.

CPT. 1990. "Conflitos No Campo Brasil, 1989." Goiânia, Brazil: Comissão Pastoral da Terra. https://www.cptnacional.org.br/component/jdownloads/send/41-conflitos-no-campo-brasil-publicacao/262-conflitos-no-campo-brasil-1989-2?Itemid=0.

CPT. 1991. "Conflitos No Campo Brasil, 1990." Goiânia, Brazil: Comissão Pastoral da Terra. https://www.cptnacional.org.br/component/jdownloads/send/41-conflitos-no-campo-brasil-publicacao/260-conflitos-no-campo-brasil-1990?Itemid=0.

CPT. 1992. "Conflitos No Campo Brasil, 1991." Goiânia, Brazil: Comissão Pastoral da Terra. https://www.cptnacional.org.br/component/jdownloads/send/41-conflitos-no-campo-brasil-publicacao/259-conflitos-no-campo-brasil-1991?Itemid=0.

CPT. 1993. "Conflitos No Campo Brasil, 1992." Goiânia, Brazil: Comissão Pastoral da Terra. https://www.cptnacional.org.br/component/jdownloads/send/41-conflitos-no-campo-brasil-publicacao/258-conflitos-no-campo-brasil-1992?Itemid=0.

CPT. 1994. "Conflitos No Campo Brasil, 1993." Goiânia, Brazil: Comissão Pastoral da Terra. https://www.cptnacional.org.br/component/jdownloads/send/41-conflitos-no-campo-brasil-publicacao/257-conflitos-no-campo-brasil-1993?Itemid=0.

CPT. 1995. "Conflitos No Campo Brasil, 1994." Goiânia, Brazil: Comissão Pastoral da Terra. https://www.cptnacional.org.br/component/jdownloads/send/41-conflitos-no-campo-brasil-publicacao/256-conflitos-no-campo-brasil-1994?Itemid=0.

CPT. 1996. "Conflitos No Campo Brasil, 1995." Goiânia, Brazil: Comissão Pastoral da Terra. https://www.cptnacional.org.br/component/jdownloads/send/41-conflitos-no-campo-brasil-publicacao/255-conflitos-no-campo-brasil-1995?Itemid=0.

CPT. 1997. "Conflitos No Campo Brasil, 1996." Goiânia, Brazil: Comissão Pastoral da Terra. https://www.cptnacional.org.br/component/jdownloads/send/41-conflitos-no-campo-brasil-publicacao/254-conflitos-no-campo-brasil-1996?Itemid=0.

CPT. 1998. "Conflitos No Campo Brasil, 1997." Goiânia, Brazil: Comissão Pastoral da Terra. https://www.cptnacional.org.br/component/jdownloads/send/41-conflitos-no-campo-brasil-publicacao/253-conflitos-no-campo-brasil-1997?Itemid=0.

CPT. 1999. "Conflitos No Campo Brasil, 1998." Goiânia, Brazil: Comissão Pastoral da Terra. https://www.cptnacional.org.br/component/jdownloads/send/41-conflitos-no-campo-brasil-publicacao/252-conflitos-no-campo-brasil-1998?Itemid=0.

Dagnino, Evelina. 1998. "Culture, Citizenship, and Democracy: Changing Discourses and Practices of the Latin American Left." In *Cultures of Politics, Politics of Culture: Re-Visioning Latin American Social Movements,* edited by Sonia Alvarez, Evelina Dagnino, and Arturo Escobar,33–61. Boulder, CO: Westview Press.

Dagnino, Evelina. 2001. "Civil Society and Public Sphere in Brazil: Limits and Possibilities." Paper delivered at Latin American Studies Association Confernece. September 6-8,2001 in Washington, DC.

Dagnino, Evelina. 2007. "Citizenship: A Perverse Confluence." *Development in Practice* 17 (4–5):549–556.

Dale, Roger. 1989. *The State and Education Policy*. Buckingham, UK: Open University Press.

Darder, Antonia, Marta Baltodano, and Rodolfo D. Torres. 2003. "Critical Pedagogy: An Introduction." In *The Critical Pedagogy Reader*, edited by Antonia Darder, Marta Baltodano, and Rodolfo D. Torres,1–23. New York: RoutledgeFalmer.

Davidson, Alistair. 1977. *Antonio Gramsci: Towards an Intellectual Biography*. London: Merlin Press.

Deere, Carmen Diana. 2003. "Women's Land Rights and Rural Social Movements in the Brazilian Agrarian Reform." *Journal of Agrarian Change* 3 (1–2): 257–88.

Delgado, Guilherme Costa. 2009. "A Questão Agrária e o Agronegócio No Brasil." In *Combatendo a Desigualidade Social: O MST e a Reforma Agrária No Brasil*, 81–112. São Paulo: Editora UNESP.

Delp, Linda, ed. 2002. *Teaching for Change: Popular Education and the Labor Movement*. Los Angeles: UCLA Center for Labor Research and Education.

Desmarais, Annette Aurelie. 2007. *La Via Campesina: Globalization and the Power of Peasants*. London: Pluto Press.

Donaghy, Maureen M. 2013. *Civil Society and Participatory Governance: Municipal Councils and Social Housing Programs in Brazil*. New York: Routledge Taylor & Francis Group.

Drudy, Sheelagh. 2008. "Gender Balance/Gender Bias: The Teaching Profession and the Impact of Feminisation." *Gender and Education* 20 (4):309–323.

Duffy, Mignon. 2007. "Doing the Dirty Work: Gender, Race, and Reproductive Labor in Historical Perspective." *Gender and Society* 21 (3):313–336.

Dutschke, Rudi. 1969. "On Anti-Authoritarianism." In *The New Left Reader*, edited by Carl Oglesby, 243–253. New York: Grove Press.

Evans, Peter. 1979. *Dependent Development*. Princeton, NJ: Princeton University Press.

Evans, Peter. 2008. "Is an Alternative Globalization Possible?" *Politics & Society* 36 (2):271–305.

Fernandes, Bernardo Mançano. 1996. *MST: Formação, Territorialização Em São Paulo*. São Paulo: Hucitec Press.

Fernandes, Bernardo Mançano. 2000. *A Formação Do MST No Brasil*. São Paulo: Hucitec Press.

Fernandes, Bernardo Mançano. 2005. "Movimentos Socioterritoriais e Movimentos Socioespaciais: Contribuição Teórica Para Uma Leitura Geográfica Dos Movimentos Sociais." *Revista NERA* 8 (6):14–36.

Fernandes, Bernardo Mançano, ed. 2008. *Campesinato e Agronegócio Na América Latina: A Questão Agrária Atual*. São Paulo: Expressão Popular.

Fernandes, Bernardo Mançano. 2012. "Reforma Agrária e Educação Do Campo No Governo Lula." *Campo-Território: Revista de Geografia Agrária* 7 (14):1–23.

Fernandes, Bernardo Mançano, and João Pedro Stédile. 2002. *Brava Gente: El MST y La Lucha Por La Tierra En El Brasil*. Barcelona: VIRUS Editorial.

FONEC. 2011. "Nota Técnica Sobre o Programa Escola Ativa: Uma Análise Crítica." Seminário Nacional. Brasília: Fórum Nacional de Educação do Campo.

FONEC. 2012. "Notas Para Análise Do Momento Atual Da Educação Do Campo." Seminário Nacional. Brasília: Fórum Nacional de Educação do Campo.

Foweraker, Joe. 2001. "Grassroots Movements and Political Activism in Latin America: A Critical Comparison of Chile and Brazil." *Journal of Latin American Studies* 33:839–865.

Fox, Jonathan. 1992. *The Politics of Food in Mexico: State Power and Social Mobilization*. Ithaca, NY: Cornell University Press.

Fox, Jonathan. 2015. "Social Accountability: What Does the Evidence Really Say?" *World Development* 72:346–361.

Freire, Paulo. 2000. *Pedagogy of the Oppressed*. New York: Continuum International.

French, Jan. 2009. *Legalizing Identities: Becoming Black or Indian in Brazil's Northeast.* Chapel Hill: University of North Carolina Press.

Fung, Archon. 2001. "Accountable Autonomy: Toward Empowered Deliberation in Chicago Schools and Policing." *Politics & Society* 29 (1):73–103.

Gandin, Luis A., and Michael W. Apple. 2002. "Challenging Neo-Liberalism, Building Democracy: Creating the Citizen School in Porto Alegre, Brazil." *Journal of Education Policy* 17 (2):259–279.

Ganz, Marshall. 2000. "Resources and Resourcefulness: Strategic Capacity in the Unionization of California Agriculture, 1959–1966." *American Journal of Sociology* 105 (4):1003–1062.

Ganz, Marshall. 2010. "Leading Change: Leadership, Organization, and Social Movements." In *Handbook of Leadership Theory and Practice: A Harvard Business School Centennial Colloquium,* edited by Nitin Nohria and Rakesh Khurana,227–268. Boston: Harvard Business Press.

Ganz, Marshall, and Elizabeth McKenna. 2018. "Bringing Leadership Back In." In *The Wiley-Blackwell Companion to Social Movements,* 2nd ed., edited by David A. Snow, Sarah A. Soule, Hanspeter Kriesi, and Holly J. McCammon, 1–202. Hoboken, NJ: Wiley-Blackwell.

Gibson, Christopher L. (2019). *Movement-Driven Development: The Politics of Health and Democracy in Brazil.* Stanford: Stanford University Press.

Giroux, Henry. 2001. *Theory and Resistance in Education: Towards a Pedagogy for the Opposition.* Westport, CT: Bergin & Garvey.

Goldfrank, Benjamin. 2011a. *Deepening Local Democracy in Latin America: Participation, Decentralization, and the Left.* University Park: Pennsylvania State University Press.

Goldfrank, Benjamin. 2011b. "The Left and Participatory Democracy." In *The Resurgence of the Latin American Left,* edited by Steven Levitsky and Kenneth M. Roberts, 162–183. Baltimore, MD: Johns Hopkins University Press.

Graden, Dale Torston. 2006. *From Slavery to Freedom in Brazil: Bahia, 1835–1900.* Albuquerque: University of New Mexico Press.

Gramsci, Antonio. 1971. *The Prison Notebooks.* Edited by Quintin Hoare and Geoffrey Nowell Smith. Translated by Quintin Hoare and Geoffry Nowell Smith. New York: International Publishers.

Gramsci, Antonio. 2000. *The Antonio Gramsci Reader: Selected Writings 1916–1935.* Edited by David Forgacs. New York: New York University Press.

Grindle, Merilee S. 2004. *Despite the Odds: The Contentious Politics of Education Reform.* Princeton, NJ: Princeton University Press.

Guimarães, Juarez. 1990. "A Estratégia Da Pinça." *Teoria e Debate 12.* Guimarães, Juarez. 1990. "A Estratégia Da Pinça." *Teoria e Debate 12.*

Hall, Budd, and Thomas Turray. 2006. "A Review of the State of the Field of Adult Learning: Social Movement Learning." Canadian Council on Learning. Retrieval info: http://en.copian.ca/library/research/sotfr/socialmv/socialmv.pdf

Harbison, Ralph W., and Eric A. Hanushek. 1992. *Educational Performance of the Poor: Lessons from Rural Northeast Brazil.* New York: Oxford University Press.

Hart, Gillian. 2002. *Disabling Globalization: Places of Power in Post-Apartheid South Africa.* Berkeley: University of California Press.

Hartmann, Heidi. 1976. "Capitalism, Patriarchy, and Job Segregation by Sex." *Signs: Journal of Women and Culture in Society* 1 (3):137–169.

Heller, Patrick. 1999. *The Labor of Development: Workers and the Transformation of Capitalism in Kerala, India.* Ithaca, NY: Cornell University Press.

Heringer, Rosana. 2015. "Affirmative Action and the Expansion of Higher Education." In *Race, Politics, and Education in Brazil,* edited by Ollie A. III Johnson and Rosana Heringer, 111-131. New York: Palgrave Macmillan.

Hetland, Gabriel. 2014. "The Crooked Line: From Populist Mobilization to Participatory Democracy in Chávez-Era Venezuela." *Qualitative Sociology.* https://doi.org/10.1007/s11133-014-9285-9.

Hochstetler, Kathryn, and Margaret Keck. 2007. *Greening Brazil.* Durham, NC: Duke University Press.

Holst, John. 2001. *Social Movements, Civil Society, and Radical Adult Education.* Westport, CT: Bergin & Garvey.

hooks, bell. 1994. *Teaching to Transgress: Education as the Practice of Freedom.* New York: Routledge.

Houtzager, Peter. 1998. "State and Unions in the Transformation of the Brazilian Countryside, 1964–1979." *Latin American Research Review* 33 (2):103–142.

Houtzager, Peter. 2001. "Collective Action and Patterns of Political Authority: Rural Workers, Church, and State in Brazil." *Theory and Society* 30 (1):1–45.

Hunter, Wendy. 2011. "Brazil: The PT in Power." In *The Resurgence of the Latin American Left,* edited by Steven Levitsky and Kenneth M. Roberts, 306–324. Baltimore, MD: Johns Hopkins University Press.

IBGE. 1996. "Dados Históricos Dos Censos: População Residente, Por Situação Do Domicílio e Por Sexo—1940–1996." Anuário Estatístico do Brasil 56. Rio de Janeiro: Instituto Brasileiro de Geografia e Estatística. http://www.ibge.gov.br/home/estatistica/populacao/censohistorico/1940_1996.shtm.

IBGE. 2010. "Censo Demográfico 2010." http//:www.censo2010.ibge.gov.br.

IBGE. 2011. "Sinopse do Censo Demográfico 2010." Rio de Janeiro: Instituto Brasileiro de Geografia e Estatística.

INCRA. 2015. "II PNERA: Relatório Da II Pesquisa Nacional Sobre a Educação Na Reforma Agrária." Brasília: Instituto Nacional de Colonização e Reforma Agrária (Incra).

Jaramillo, Nathalia E., Peter McLaren, and Fernando Lázaro. 2011. "A Critical Pedagogy of Recuperation." *Policy Futures in Education* 9 (6):747–758.

Jessop, Bob. 2001. "Bringing the State Back In (Yet Again): Review, Revisions, Rejections and Redirections." *International Review of Sociology* 11 (2):149–173.

Johnson, Ollie A. III, and Rosana Heringer, eds. 2015. *Race, Politics, and Education in Brazil.* New York: Palgrave Macmillan.

Johnston, Hank. 2014. *What Is a Social Movement?* Malden, MA: Polity Press.

Kane, Liam. 2001. *Popular Education and Social Change in Latin America.* London: Latin America Bureau.

Keck, Margaret. 1992. *The Workers' Party and Democratization in Brazil.* New Haven, CT: Yale University Press.

Keck, Margaret, and Kathryn Sikkink. 1998. *Activists Beyond Borders.* Ithaca, NY: Cornell University Press.

Kitschelt, Herbert P., and Steven I. Wilkinson. 2007. "Citizen-Politician Linkages: An Introduction." In *Patrons, Clients and Policies: Patterns of Democratic Accountability and Political Competition,* edited by Herbert P. Kitschelt and Steven I. Wilkinson, 1–49. Cambridge: Cambridge University Press.

Klees, Steven, Joel Samoff, and Nelly P. Stromquist, eds. 2012. *The World Bank and Education: Critiques and Alternatives.* Rotterdam, UK: Sense Publishers.

Klein, Herbert S., and Francisco Vidal Luna. 2009. *Slavery in Brazil.* Cambridge: Cambridge University Press.

Kolling, Edgar Jorge, Ir Nery, and Monica Castagna Molina, eds. 1999. *Por Uma Educação Básica Do Campo.* Brasília: Fundação Universidade de Brasília.

Kolling, Edgar Jorge, Maria Cristina Vargas, and Rosali Salete Caldart. 2012. "MST E Educação." In *Dicionário Da Educação Do Campo,* 500–507. São Paulo: Expressão Popular.

Larrabure, Manuel, and Carlos Torchia. 2015. "The 2011 Chilean Student Movement and the Struggle for a New Left." *Latin American Perspectives* 42 (5):248–268.

Laslett, Barbara, and Johanna Brenner. 1989. "Gender and Social Reproduction: Historical Perspectives." *Annual Review of Sociology* 15:81–404.

Leach, Darcy. 2005. "The Iron Law of What Again? Conceptualizing Oligarchy Across Organizational Forms." *Sociological Theory* 23 (5):312–327.

Lebon, Nathalie. 1996. "Professionalization of Women's Health Groups in São Paulo: The Troublesome Road Towards Organizational Diversity." *Organization* 3 (4):588–609.

Leite, Ilka Boaventura. 2012. "The Transhistorical, Juridical-Formal, and Post-Utopian Quilombo." In *New Approaches to Resistance in Brazil and Mexico*, edited by John Gledhill and Patience A. Schell, 250-268. Durham, NC: Duke University Press.

Leite, Ilka Boaventura. 2015. "The Brazilian Quilombo: 'Race,' Community and Land in Space and Time." *Journal of Peasant Studies* 42 (6):1225–1240.

Lesser, Jeffrey. 1999. *Negotiating National Identity: Immigrants, Minorities, and the Struggle for Ethnicity in Brazil*. Durham, NC: Duke University Press.

Li, Tania Murray. 2007. *The Will to Improve: Governmentality, Development, and the Practice of Politics*. Durham, NC: Duke University Press.

Loveman, Mara. 2014. *National Colors: Racial Classification and the State in Latin America*. Oxford, UK: Oxford University Press.

Luedemann, Cecilia da S. 2002. *Anton Makarenko: Vida e Obra—a Pedagogia Na Revolução*. São Paulo: Expressão Popular.

Macedo, Donaldo. 2006. *Literacies of Power: What Americans Are Not Allowed to Know*. Boulder, CO: Westview Press.

Makarenko, Anton Semenovich. 2001. *The Road to Life: An Epic of Education*. Translated by Ivy Litvinov and Tatiana Litvinov. Honolulu, HI: University Press of the Pacific.

Makarenko, Anton Semenovich. 2004. *Makarenko, His Life and Work: Articles, Talks and Reminiscences*. Honolulu, HI: University Press of the Pacific.

Marcos de Anhaia, Edson. 2010. "Constituição Do Movimento de Educação Do Campo Na Luta Por Políticas de Educação." Florianópolis, Santa Catarina, Brazil: Universidade Federal de Santa Catarina.

Marcuse, Herbert. 1972. *Counter-Revolution and Revolt*. Boston: Beacon Press.

Martin, Andrew. 2008. "The Institutional Logic of Union Organizing and the Effectiveness of Social Movement Repertoires." *American Journal of Sociology* 113 (4):1067–1103.

Martins, Erika Moreira, and Nora Rut Krawczyk. 2016. "Entrepreneurial Influence in Brazilian Education Policies: The Case of Todos Pela Educação." In *World Yearbook of Education 2016: The Global Education Industry*, edited by Antoni Verger, Christopher A. Lubienski, and Gita Steiner-Khamsi, 78-79. New York: Routledge Taylor & Francis.

Matos, Jéssica Marília de Oliveira. 2013. "Terra e trabalho: uma reflexão sobre latifúndio e relações de trabalho no Brasil." Doctoral Thesis. Brasília: Universidade de Brasília.

Mauro, Gilmar. 2017. "The Coalition That Couldn't." *Jacobin*.

Maybury-Lewis, Biorn. 1994. *The Politics of the Possible: The Brazilian Rural Worker' Trade Union Movement, 1964–1985*. Philadelphia: Temple University Press.

McAdam, Doug. 1999. *Political Process and the Development of the Black Insurgency, 1930–1970*. 2nd ed. Chicago: University of Chicago Press.

McAdam, Doug, and Hilary Schaffer Boudet. 2012. *Putting Social Movements in Their Place: Explaining Opposition to Energy Projects in the United States, 2000–2005*. Cambridge: Cambridge University Press.

McCammon, Holly J., Courtney Sanders Muse, Harmony D. Newman, and Teresa M. Terrell. 2007. "Movement Framing and Discursive Opportunity Structures: The Political Successes of the U.S. Women's Jury Movements." *American Sociological Review* 72 (5):725–749.

McCune, Nils, and Marlen Sánchez. 2018. "Teaching the Territory: Agroecological Pedagogy and Popular Movements." *Agriculture and Human Values.* https://doi.org/10.1007/s10460-018-9853-9.

McEwan, Patrck J. 1998. "The Effectiveness of Multigrade Schools in Colombia." *International Journal of Educational Development* 18 (6):435–452.

McLaren, Peter. 2003. *Life in Schools: An Introduction to Critical Pedagogy in the Foundations of Education.* 4th ed. Boston: Pearson Education.

MDA. 2012. "Manual de Operação: Programa Nacional de Educação Na Reforma Agrária (PRONERA)." Ministério do Desenvolvimento Agrário (MDA). http://www.incra.gov.br/images/phocadownload/servicos/publicacao/manuais_e_procedimentos/manual_de_operacoes_do_pronera_2012.pdf.

MEC. 2004. "Referências Para Uma Política Nacional de Educação Do Campo." Caderno de Susbsídos. Brasília: Ministério da Educação.

MEC. 2010. "Escola Ativa: Projeto Base." Brasília: Ministério da Educação.

Mediratta, Kavitha, Norm Fruchter, and Anne C. Lewis. 2002. "Organizing for School Reform: How Communities Are Finding Their Voice and Reclaiming Their Public Schools." New York: New York University Institute for Education and Social Policy.

Mediratta, Kavitha, Seema Shah, and Sara McAlister. 2009. *Community Organizing for Stronger Schools: Strategies and Successes.* Cambridge, MA: Harvard Education Press.

Meek, David. 2015. "Towards a Political Ecology of Education: The Educational Politics of Scale in Southern Pará, Brazil." *Environmental Education Research* 21 (3):447–459.

Meyer, David S. 2004. "Protest and Political Opportunities." *Annual Review of Sociology* 30:125–145.

Meyer, David S., and Debra C. Minkoff. 2004. "Conceptualizing Political Opportunity." *Social Forces* 82 (4):1457–1492.

Meyer, David, and Sidney Tarrow, eds. 1997. *The Social Movement Society.* Lanham, MD: Rowman & Littlefield.

Michels, Robert. 1915. *Political Parties: A Sociological Study of the Oligarchical Tendencies of Modern Democracy.* New York: Dover.

Mische, Ann. 2008. *Partisan Publics: Communication and Contention Across Brazilian Youth Activist Networks.* Princeton, NJ: Princeton University Press.

Moe, Terry M., and Susanne Wiborg, eds. 2017. *The Comparative Politics of Education: Teachers Unions and Education Systems Around the World.* Cambridge: Cambridge University Press.

Moreira, Maria Helena Alves. 1985. *State and Opposition in Military Brazil.* Austin: University of Texas Press.

Morissawa, Mitsue. 2001. *A História Da Luta Pela Terra e o MST.* São Paulo: Expressão Popular.

MST. 1987. "Documento Do 1o Seminário Nacional de Educação Em Assentamentos Realizado Em São Mateus-ES Dias 27 a 30/07/1987."

MST. 2001. *Iterra: Memória Cronológica.* Veranópolis, Brazil: Iterra.

MST. 2003. *Educação de Jovens e Adultos.* Caderno de Educação 11. Veranópolis, Brazil: Iterra.

MST. 2007. "Assentamentos Do MST Em 2004." Movimento dos Trabalhadores Sem Terra. http://www.mst.org.br/mast/pagina.php?cd=1010.

MST. 2013. "Nosso História." *Movimento Dos Trabalhadores Rurais Sem Terra,* July 2013. http://www.mst.org.br/node/7702.

MST. 2015. *History of the MST: We Cultivate the Land and It Cultivates Us.* Veranópolis, Brazil: Iterra.

Mundy, Karen, Andy Green, Bob Lingard, and Antoni Verger, eds. 2016. *The Handbook of Global Education Policy.* Handbook of Global Policy Series. Malden, MA: Wiley-Blackwell.

Navarro, Zander. 2009. "Treze Teses Para Entender o MST." *Folha de S. Paulo,* de dezembro de 2009.

Navarro, Zander. 2010. "The Brazilian Landless Movement (MST): Critical Times." *REDES* 15 (1):196–223.

NERA. 2017. "DataLuta: Banco de Dados Da Luta Pela Terra: Relatório Brasil 2014." São Paulo: Núcleo de Estudos da Reforma (NERA), Universidade do Estado de São Paulo (UNESP). http://www2.fct.unesp.br/nera/projetos/dataluta_brasil_2016.pdf.

Neri, Marcelo. 2015. "Brazil's New Middle Classes: The Bright Side of the Poor." In *Latin America's Emerging Middle Classes*, edited by Dayton-Johnson, 70-100. London: Palgrave Macmillan.

O'Cadiz, Pilar, Pia Wong, and Carlos Alberto Torres. 1998. *Education and Democracy: Paulo Freire, Social Movements and Educational Reform in São Paulo*. Boulder, CO: Westview Press.

Offe, Claus, and Helmut Wisenthal. 1980. "Two Logics of Collective Action: Theoretical Notes on Social Class and Organizational Form." *Political Power and Social Theory* 1:67–115.

Ondetti, Gabriel. 2008. *Land, Protest, and Politics: The Landless Movement and the Struggle for Agrarian Reform in Brazil*. University Park: Pennsylvania State University Press.

Ostrom, Elinor. 1996. "Crossing the Great Divide: Coproduction, Synergy, and Development." *World Development* 24 (6):1073–1087.

Oviedo, Alexis, and Danny Wildemeersch. 2008. "Intercultural Education and Curricular Diversification: The Case of the Ecuadorian Intercultural Bilingual Education Model (MOSEIB)." *Compare* 38 (4):455–470.

Ozai da Silva, Antonio. 1987. *História Das Tendências No Brasil (Origens, Cisões e Propostas)*. São Paulo: Proposta Editorial.

Pahnke, Anthony. 2018. *Brazil's Long Revolution: Radical Achievements of the Landless Workers Movement*. Tucson: University of Arizona Press.

Paschel, Tianna S. 2016. *Becoming Black Political Subjects: Movements and Ethno-Racial Rights in Colombia and Brazil*. Princeton, NJ: Princeton University Press.

Payne, Charles. 1997. *I've Got the Light of Freedom: The Organizing Tradition and the Mississippi Freedom Struggle*. Berkeley: University of California Press.

Payne, Charles, and Carol Sills Strickland, eds. 2008. *Teach Freedom: Education for Liberation in the African-American Tradition*. New York: Teachers College Press.

Pereira, Amilcar. 2015. "From the Black Movement's Struggle to the Teaching of African and Afro-Brazilian History." In *Race, Politics, and Education in Brazil*, 59-72. New York: Palgrave Macmillan.

Pereira, Anthony. 1997. *The End of the Peasantry: The Rural Labor Movement in Northeast Brazil*. Pittsburgh: University of Pittsburgh Press.

Pereira, Joao Márcio Mendes, and Sérgio Sauer. 2006. "História e Legado Da Reforma Agrária de Mercado No Brasil." In *Capturando a Terra: Banco Mundial, Políticas Fundiárias Neoliberais e Reforma Agrária de Mercado*, edited by Sérgio Sauer and Joao Márcio Mendes Pereira, 173–206. São Paulo: Expressão Popular.

Perlstein, Daniel H. 1990. "Teaching Freedom: SNCC and the Creation of the Mississippi Freedom Schools." *History of Education Quarterly* 30 (3):297–324.

Perlstein, Daniel H.. 2004. *Justice, Justice: School Politics and the Eclipse of Liberalism*. New York: Peter Lang.

Peschanski, Joao Alexandre. 2007. "A Evolução Organizacional Do MST." Masters thesis. São Paulo: Universidade de São Paulo.

Pistrak, Moisey M. 2010. *A Escola-Comuna*. Translated by Luis Carlos de Freitas. São Paulo: Expressão Popular.

Piven, Frances Fox, and Richard Cloward. 1977. *Poor People's Movements: Why They Succeed, How They Fail*. New York: Vintage.

Piven, Frances Fox, and Richard Cloward. 1997. "Normalizing Collective Protest." In *The Breaking of the American Social Compact*, 345–374. New York: The New Press.

Plank, David. 1996. *The Means of Our Salvation: Public Education in Brazil, 1930–1995.* Boulder, CO: Westview Press.

Poletto, Evo. 2015. "Churches, the Pastoral Land Commission, and the Mobilization for Agrarian Reform." In *Challenging Social Inequality: The Landless Rural Workers Movement and Agrarian Reform in Brazil.* Durham, NC: Duke University Press.

Przeworski, Adam. 1986. *Capitalism and Social Democracy.* Cambridge: Cambridge University Press.

Psacharopoulos, George, Carlos Rojas, and Eduardo Velez. 1993. "Achievement Evaluation of Colombia's Escuela Nueva: Is Multigrade the Answer?" *Comparative Education Review* 37 (3):263–276.

Raekstad, Paul. 2018. "Revolutionary Practice and Prefigurative Politics: A Clarification and Defense." *Constellations,* 25: 359-272.

Ribeiro, Darcy. 1995. *O Povo Brasileiro: A Formação e o Sentido Do Brasil.* São Paulo: Companhia das Letras.

Ribeiro, Darcy. 2000. *The Brazilian People: The Formation and Meaning of Brazil.* Translated by Gregory Rabassa. Gainesville: University of Florida Press.

Rojas, Carlos, and Zoraida Castillo. 1988. "Evaluación Del Programa Escuela Nueva En Colombia." Bogotá: Instituto de Ser De Investigaciones.

Rojas, Fabio. 2007. *From Black Power to Black Studies: How a Radical Social Movement Became an Academic Discipline.* Baltimore, MD: Johns Hopkins University Press.

Roniger, Luis. 1994. "The Comparative Study of Clientelism and the Changing Nature of Civil Society in the Contemporary World." In *Democracy, Clientelism and Civil Society,* edited by Luis Roniger and Ayse Güens-Ayata,, 1-18. Boulder, CO: Lynne Rienner.

Rosa, Marcelo Carvalho. 2009. "Para Além Do MST: O Impacto Nos Movimentos Socias Brasileiros." In *Combatendo a Desigualdade Social: O MST e a Reforma Agrária No Brasil,* 461–477. São Paulo: Editora UNESP.

Rubin, Jeffrey W. 2017. "In the Streets and in the Institutions: Movements-in-Democracy and the Rural Women's Movement in Rio Grande Do Sul." In *Beyond Civil Society: Activism, Participation, and Protest in Latin America,* edited by Sonia Alvarez, Jeffrey W. Rubin, Millie Thayer, Gianpaolo Baiocchi, and Agustín Laó-Montes, 219-237. Durham, NC: Duke University Press.

Sahlberg, Pasi. 2016. "Global Educational Reform Movement and Its Impact on Schooling." In *Handbook of Global Education Policy,* edited by Karen Mundy, Andy Green, Robert Lingard, and Antoni Verger, 128-144. Hoboken, NJ: Wiley-Blackwell.

Samoff, Joel. 1999. "Institutionalizing International Influence." In *Comparative Education: The Dialectic of the Global and the Local,* edited by Robert F. Arnove and Carlos Alberto Torres. Lanham, MD: Rowman & Littlefield.

Sanders, Crystal R. 2016. *A Chance for Change: Head Start and Mississippi's Black Freedom Struggle.* Chapel Hill: University of North Carolina Press.

Santos, Cecilia M. 2010. "Da Delegacia Da Mulher à Lei Maria Da Penha: Absorção/Tradução de Demandas Feministas Pelo Estado." *Revista Crítica Da Ciências Sociais* 89:153–170.

Santucci, Antonio A. 2010. *Antonio Gramsci.* New York: Monthly Review Press.

Satgar, Vishwas, ed. 2014. *The Solidarity Economy Alternative: Emerging Theory and Practice.* Scottsville, South Africa: University of KwaZulu-Natal Press.

Sauer, Sérgio. 2006. "The World Bank's Market-Based Land Reform in Brazil." In *Promised Lands: Competing Visions of Agrarian Reform,* edited by Peter Rosset, Raj Patel, and Michael Courville, 177-191. Oakland, CA: Food First Books.

Sauer, Sérgio, and Sergio Pereira Leite. 2012. "Agrarian Structure, Foreign Investment in Land, and Land Prices in Brazil." *Journal of Peasant Studies* 39 (3–4):873–898.

Sauer, Sérgio, and Clifford Welch. 2015. "Rural Unions and the Struggle for Land in Brazil." *Journal of Peasant Studies,* 42 (6): 1109-1135.

Scheper-Hughes, Nancy. 1992. *Death Without Weeping: The Violence of Everyday Life in Brazil.* Berkeley: University of California Press.

Schiefelbein, Ernesto. 1991. *In Search of the School of the XXI Century: Is the Colombian Escuela Nueva the Right Pathfinder?* Santiago: Unesco/Unicef.

Scott, James. 1998. *Seeing Like a State: How Certain Schemes to Improve the Human Conditions Have Falied.* New Haven, CT: Yale University Press.

Secombe, Wally. 1974. "The Housewife and Her Labour under Capitalism." *New Left Review* 83:3–24.

Shirley, Dennis. 1997. *Community Organizing for Urban School Reform.* Austin: University of Texas Press.

Shulgin, Viktor. 2013. *Rumo Ao Politecnismo.* São Paulo: Expressão Popular.

Singer, André. 2013. "Classes e Ideologias Cruzadas." *Novos Estudos, Dossiê: Mobilizações, protestos e revoluções,* 97:23–40.

Singer, André. 2015. "Cutucando Onças Com Varas Curtas." *Novos Estudos,* 32 (2): 39-67.

Skidmore, Thomas. 2010. *Brazil: Five Centuries of Change.* 2nd ed. Oxford: Oxford University Press.

Skocpol, Theda. 1985. "Bringing the State Back In: Strategies of Analysis in Current Research." In *Bringing the State Back In,* edited by Theda Skocpol, Peter Evans, and Dietrich Rueschemeyer, 3–44. Cambridge: Cambridge University Press.

Smucker, Jonathan Matthew. 2017. *Hegemony How-To: A Roadmap for Radicals.* Chico, CA: AK Press.

Snow, David. 2004. "Social Movements as Challenges to Authority: Resistance to an Emerging Conceptual Hegemony." In *Authority in Contention,* edited by Daniel Meyers and Daniel Cress, 3–25. New York: Elsevier.

Snow, David A., Burke Rochford, Steven Worden, and Robert Benford. 1986. "Frame Alignment Processes, Micromobilization, and Movement Participation." *American Sociological Review* 51 (4):464–481.

Sobrinho, Roberto Sanches Mubarac, Adria Simone Duarte de Souza, and Célia Aparecida Bettiol. 2017. "A Educação Escolar Indígena No Brasil: Uma Análise Crítica a Partir Da Conjuntrua Dos 20 Anos de LDB." *Poiésis: Revista Do Programa de Pós-Graduação Em Educação—Mestrado, Da Universidade Do Sul de Santa Catarina—UNISUL* 11 (19):58–75.

Souza, Maria Antonia de. 2002. "Relaciones MST-Estado: Encuentros y Desencuentros En La Educación de Jóvenes y Adultos de Los Asentamientos Rurales." In *Sociedad Civil, Esfera Pública y Democratización En América Latina: Brasil,* edited by Evelina Dagnino, 200-248. Campinas, SP, Brazil: Editora Unicamp.

Steinberg, Marc. 1999. "The Talk and Back Talk of Collective Action: A Dialogic Analysis of Repertoires of Discourse among Nineteenth-Century English Cotton Spinners." *American Journal of Sociology* 105 (3):736–780.

Su, Celina. 2009. *Streetwise for Book Smarts: Grassroots Organizing and Education Reform in the Bronx.* Ithaca, NY: Cornell University Press.

Suh, Doowon. 2011. "Institutionalizing Social Movements: The Dual Strategy of the Korean Women's Movement." *The Sociological Quarterly* 52:442–471.

Tarlau, Rebecca. 2013. "Coproducing Rural Public Schools in Brazil: Contestation, Clientelism, and the Landless Workers' Movement." *Politics & Society* 41 (3):395–424.

Tarlau, Rebecca. 2017. "State Theory, Grassroots Agency, and Global Policy Transfer: The Life and Death of Colombia's Escuela Nueva in Brazil (1997–2012)." *Comparative Education Review* 61 (4):675–700.

Tarrow, Sidney. 2011. *Power in Movement.* 3rd ed. Cambridge: Cambridge University Press.

Taylor, Verta. 1989. "Social Movement Continuity: The Women's Movement in Abeyance." *American Sociological Review* 54 (5):761–775.

Tedesco, J.C., and J.J. Carini, eds. 2008. *Conflitos Agrários No Norte Gaúcho, 1980–2008*. Porto Alegre, RS, Brazil: EST Edições.

Telles, Edward E. 2004. *Race in Another America: The Significance of Skin Color in Brazil*. Princeton, NJ: Princeton University Press.

Tilly, Charles. 2008. *Contentious Performances*. Cambridge: Cambridge University Press.

Torres, Carlos Alberto. 1991. "The State, Nonformal Education, and Socialism in Cuba, Nicaragua, and Grenada." *Comparative Education Review* 35 (1):110–130.

Tuğal, Cihan. 2009. *Passive Revolution: Absorbing the Islamic Challenge to Capitalism*. Stanford, CA: Stanford University Press.

Twine, France Winddance. 2000. "Racial Ideologies and Racial Methodologies." In *Racing Research, Researching Race: Methodological Dilemmas in Critial Race Studies*, 1-34. New York: New York University Press.

Tyack, David, and William Tobin. 1994. "The Grammar of Schooling: Why Has It Been So Hard to Change?" *American Educational Research Journal* 31 (3):453–479.

Vergara-Camus, Leandro. 2014. *Land and Freedom: The MST, the Zapatistas and Peasant Alternatives to Neoliberalism*. London: Zed Books.

Voss, Kim, and Rachel Sherman. 2000. "Breaking the Iron Law of Oligarchy: Union Revitalization in the American Labor Movement." *American Journal of Sociology* 106 (2):303–349.

Wampler, Brian. 2007. *Participatory Budgeting in Brazil: Contestation, Cooperation, and Accountability*. University Park, PA: Penn State Press.

Wampler, Brian, and Leonardo Avritzer. 2004. "Participator Publics: Civil Society and New Institutions in Democratic Brazil." *Comparative Politics* 36 (3):291–312.

Warren, Mark R., and Karen L. Mapp. 2011. *A Match on Dry Grass: Community Organizing as a Catalyst for School Reform*. Oxford: Oxford University Press.

Weber, Max. 1919. "Politics as Vocation.". Lecture delivered at the University of Munich in January 28, 1919. http://anthropos-lab.net/wp/wp-content/uploads/2011/12/Weber-Politics-as-a-Vocation.pdf

Welch, Clifford. 1999. *The Seed Was Planted: The Sao Paulo Roots of the Brazil's Rural Labor Movement, 1924–1964*. University Park, PA: Penn State University Press.

Welch, Clifford. 2009. "Camponeses: Brazil's Peasant Movement in Historical Perspective (1946–2004)." *Latin American Perspectives* 36 (4):126–155.

Wiebe, Nettie. 2006. "Women Reversing Desertification: Via Campesina Takes on Aracruz Corporation in Brazil." *Canadian Woman Studies* 25 (3-4):167–172.

Wolford, Wendy. 2010a. "Participatory Democracy by Default: Land Reform, Social Movements and the State in Brazil." *Journal of Peasant Studies* 37 (1):91–109.

Wolford, Wendy. 2010b. *This Land Is Ours Now: Social Mobilization and the Meanings of Land in Brazil*. Durham, NC: Duke University Press.

Wolford, Wendy. 2016. "The Casa and the Causa: Institutional Histories and Cultural Politics in Brazilian Land Reform." *Latin American Research Review* 51 (4):24–42.

Wright, Angus, and Wendy Wolford. 2003. *To Inherit the Earth: The Landless Movement and the Struggle for a New Brazil*. Oakland, CA: Food First Books.

Wright, Erik Olin. 2010. *Envisioning Real Utopias*. London: Verso.

Wright, Erik Olin. 2013. "Transforming Capitalism Through Real Utopias." *American Sociological Review* 78 (1):1–25.

INDEX

ABAG (Brazilian Association of
    Agribusiness), 159–60
Abers, Rebecca, 12–13, 58, 154, 210, 212–
    13, 224, 244, 279, 290, 292–93
abertura. See political opening
Abreu, Kátia, 163–65
Abreu, Mariza, 194, 195–96, 198, 199,
    204, 205
acampamento. See camps
Active School. See *Escola Ativa*
adult education. 65–66, 72, 79–80, 87–101,
    106–9, 106t, 107f, 108t, 131–32,
    142, 217–18, 236–37, 246–47, 250–
    51, 288–89, 310, 354n18, 354n32.
    See also literacy programs; MAG;
    SECADI; TAC
affirmative action, 9, 110–11, 154–55, 157–
    58, 267, 289, 298–99
agrarian reform
    and CONTAG, 85–139
    difficulties in achieving and critiques of,
        17–18, 23, 193, 208, 234–35, 238–42,
        243–44, 256–57, 277, 311–12
    gains in the 1990s, 58, 132, 216–17,
        234–35, 249
    historical attempts for, 38, 46–47,
        136, 214
    and MST's educational goals, 30–31, 43,
        49–50, 56, 66–67, 69–72, 128–29, 130–
        31, 132–33, 134, 164, 166, 167–71, 177,
        180–81, 190, 199–200, 202, 209, 220,
        223, 224–25, 226, 229, 230, 237–38,
        246, 250, 252–53, 257, 258–59, 264,
        271, 277–78, 279–80, 281–84, 286–87
    MST vision for, 2–6, 7, 17–18, 29, 36
    National Program for Education in Areas
        of Agrarian Reform (*see* PRONERA)
    strategy for achieving, 193, 211–12, 229,
        293–94, 305–6, 314–15

and Workers' Party (PT), 129–30,
    140–42, 160–61
agribusiness, 16–17
    Aracruz Ceuloso, 160–61
    Cargill, 160–61
    and *Educação do Campo,* 30–31, 129–30,
        160–73, 288–89
    monocultural production, 62,
        160–61, 282
    Monsanto, 95, 160–61, 282
    MST mobilization against, 264, 281,
        282, 305–6
    pesticides, 62, 161–62, 282
    and Rousseff's administration, 159–70
    state support for, 39, 87, 104, 130, 204,
        207, 303, 315–16
    and violence, 303, 310–11, 315–16
agricultural cooperatives, 22–23, 61, 67–68,
    69, 132–33, 208, 273, 296, 316
agricultural production
    different visions of, 130–31, 132–33, 159–
        60, 240, 285
    historical development, 38–39
    incorporation in schools, 273–75, 315–16
    MST agricultural production sector
        (Production, Cooperative, and
        Environment), 61, 63, 69, 297–98
    MST support for, 2–3, 5–6, 315–16
    state support for, 61, 132–33, 135
agroecology, 23, 62, 105–6, 115–16, 132–33,
    134, 154, 177, 209, 224–25, 240, 264,
    270, 272, 278, 286–87, 315–16, 317
Agronegócio. See agribusiness
Agrotóxico. See pesticides
Água Preta (Pernambuco), 25, 31–32, 211,
    213, 214, 215f, 231–39, 291t
Alcântara, Lúcio, 251, 256
Alckmin, Geraldo, 254, 309–10
Almeida, Gualberto, 217

Alternative Project for Sustainable
    Rural Development and Solidarity.
    See PADRSS
Althusser, Louis, 19–20, 295–96
Alvarez, Sonia, 9–10, 36–37, 39–40, 43, 58,
    118, 124, 284–85
Amorim, Jaime, 214, 236, 240
Andrews, Kenneth, 8–9, 11–12, 16, 24–25,
    99, 209, 259, 284–85, 289, 290
Apple, Michael, 19–20, 21
Arraes, Miguel, 214, 233
austerity, 84, 304–9, 312–13, 315–16
auto-gestão. See self-governance
Auyero, Javier, 23–24, 216, 231
Avritzer, Leonardo, 12, 46–47

Baccalaureate and Teaching Certificate
    in Education of the Countryside.
    See LEDOC
Bahia, 39, 214–15, 217, 218, 220
Baiocchi, Gianpaolo, 12–13, 46–47, 58, 210
Banaszak, Lee Ann, 8–9, 284–85
Barros, Florêncio de Filho. See Coronel
    Barrinho
Barros, Noé, 215
Base Ecclesial Communities. See CEBs
base nucleus. See NB
Binder, Amy, 20–21
BioNatur, 61–62
black rural communities. See quilombos
BNDES (Brazilian National Development
    Bank), 160
Boggs, Carl, 11–12
Bogo, Ademar, 263
Bolsa Família. See cash-transfer program
Bolshevik Revolution, 2, 52, 53–54, 194
Bolsonaro, Jair, 303–4, 309–11,
    312–13, 315–17
Bourdieu, Pierre, 19–20, 295–96
Bowles, Samuel, 19–20, 295–96
Braga (Rio Grande do Sul), 66–73, 250
Brasília, 1–3, 25–26, 63, 85–86, 95, 109–10,
    117, 119–20, 124–25, 133, 140–41,
    144–45, 157–58, 179, 222, 250, 281,
    282–83, 316–17
Brazilian Association of Agribusiness.
    See ABAG
Brazilian Democratic Movement Party.
    See PMDB
Brazilian Federal Court of Audits. See TCU

Brazilian Homeless Movement. See MTST
Brazilian Landless Workers Movement.
    See MST
Brazilian National Development Bank.
    See BNDES
Brazilian Rural Confederation. See CNA
Brazilian Social Democratic Party. See PSDB
Brazilian Sociality Party. See PSB
Brazilian Statute on Childhood and
    Adolescence, 181
Britto, Antônio, 180
Burawoy, Michael, 6–7

Caldert, Rosali, 35, 52–53, 54, 67–68, 93, 96,
    138, 144–45, 158, 165–66, 206, 250
Camini, Isabela, 181, 184, 187
Camini, Lucia, 183–84, 199
Campigotto, Salete, 44–46, 50–54,
    166, 177
camps
    attacks against, 42–45, 49, 84–85, 181,
        194, 198, 207, 214, 313
    decision-making structure, 17–18, 36–37,
        47–48, 48f, 49, 55, 62–63, 76, 217, 218
    education in, 2–3, 29–30, 43, 49–51, 52–
        53, 54, 55–57, 64–65, 68, 74–75, 78–
        80, 86, 106–7, 130–31, 177, 180–82,
        209, 211, 217, 220, 235, 236, 249, 289,
        290–91, 297–98
    leadership development in, 47–48, 124,
        236, 293–94, 314–15
    mobile schools (see Itinerant Schools)
    numbers of, 214, 246
capitalism
    arguments for, 57
    critiques of, 2, 17, 19–20, 54, 263,
        316, 317–18
    relationship to schools, 49, 56,
        129–30, 294
    strategies against, 5, 246, 296–97,
        313–14, 316
Cardoso, Fernando Henrique, 57, 59, 70, 82–
    83, 84–87, 90, 105, 128–29, 137–38,
    139, 140, 143–45, 313
Cargill. See agribusiness
Carnoy, Martin, 20–21, 296–97
Carter, Miguel, 2–3, 63, 71–72, 159–60
Caruaru (Pernambuco), 223, 236–37, 238
cash-transfer program, 140, 208
Castro, Maria Helena, 254, 255

Catholic Church, 36, 38, 40, 41–44,
47–48, 66, 80, 89, 135, 136,
207, 259–60
CPT (Pastoral Land Commission), 41–43,
136, 207, 259–60
liberation theology, 47–48, 181–82,
207, 249–50
preferential option for the poor, 40
Ceará, 25–26, 31, 32, 68–69, 93, 100, 119,
120, 246, 292, 317
CEBs (Base Ecclesial Communities), 40,
43–45, 249–50
Central Union of Workers. *See* CUT
Chalita, Gabriel, 254–55
ciranda (childcare center), 3–4, 85–86,
94, 350n5
civil society
Gramscian definitions, 6–7, 13, 15, 20–21,
152, 193
mobilization of, 47, 122, 125–26, 128–29,
130, 137, 171, 306–7
participation in state institutions and
programs, 80–81, 110, 116–17,
119–20, 121, 140, 146–48, 153–54,
159, 161–62, 253, 311–12, 318
social movements relationship to, 17–18,
31–32, 56, 74, 213, 224, 232–33, 279,
290–91, 316–17
theories of, 9–13, 18, 58, 80–81, 146, 209,
210, 284–85, 290, 293, 298
Class Coordinating Collective of Base
Nucleuses. *See* CNBTs
clientelism, 57, 210, 216, 220
Cloward, Richard, 7–9, 16, 126, 171–72,
284–85, 288, 294–95
CNA (Brazilian Rural Confederation),
159–60, 163
CNBB (National Conference of Brazilian
Bishops), 132–33, 139
CNBTs (Class Coordinating Collective of
Base Nucleuses), 74
CNE (National Education Advisory Board),
138, 142
CNTE (National Coordination of
Educational Workers, Mexico), 299–300
cognitive liberation, 17, 344n21
co-governance
definition, 9–10, 298
and prefiguration, 12
See also contentious co-governance; triple
governance

collectivity
and leadership, 2–3, 13–14, 16–18, 31–32,
51, 63–64, 99, 114, 192–93, 213, 242–
43, 245, 271–72, 279, 290, 291–92,
293, 304 (*see also* leadership)
MST principle of, 53–54, 55, 93–94
practiced within schools and education
programs, 54–55, 69–70, 115, 125,
279, 296
in the Soviet Union, 53–55 (*see also* Anton
Makarenko)
Collor de Mello, Fernando, 57, 59
Communist Party of Brazil. *See* PCdoB
Confederation of Indigenous Nationalities in
Ecuador (CONAIE), 299–300
Congressional Investigation. *See* CPI
conscientização (consciousness–raising), 6–7, 9,
17, 19, 68–69, 72, 159–60, 163, 172–73,
197–98, 240, 274, 278–79, 296, 317–18
Constitution of 1988, 46–47, 49, 142
CONTAG (National Confederation of
Agricultural Workers)
affiliation with CUT, 136
Alternative Project for Sustainable
Rural Development and Solidarity
(PADRASS), 136–37
composition of, 135
education struggles, 119–20, 128–29,
134–39, 143–44, 150–51, 161–62, 163,
164, 171, 252–53, 287–88
founding, 38, 134–35
land occupations, 58–59
mobilizing under dictatorship, 135–36
participation in *Educação do Campo* or
PRONERA, 119–20, 128–29, 136–39,
143–45, 150–51, 161–64, 171, 252–53
state affiliate in Ceará, 252–53
state affiliate in Pernambuco, 137
contentious co-governance, 5, 13–15, 18,
19–20, 29, 32, 50, 92–93, 104, 123,
125–26, 128–29, 139, 158, 178–79,
184–85, 192, 193, 198–99, 205, 209,
210, 212–13, 223, 231, 239, 243–44,
245, 247–48, 255, 258, 263–64, 270,
274–80, 285–86, 290–94, 291t, 298,
299–300, 301–2, 314, 317–18
contentious politics, 5, 9–10, 11, 13, 16,
21, 23–25, 29, 30, 45, 82, 93–94,
98–99, 118, 124, 182, 186, 191, 209,
220, 228, 258, 285, 294–95, 300–2,
315–16, 317–18

coronéis. See *coronelismo*
Coronel Barrinho, 216, 217, 220
coronelismo, 215
Coutinho, Eduardo, 211, 232–35, 240–41
CPI (Congressional Investigation), 159–60
CPP (Political-Pedagogical Collective), 73–
   74, 93, 101, 218–19, 349n67, 351n15
CPT (Pastoral Land Commission). *See*
   Catholic Church
CRE (State Department of Education
   Regional Offices, Rio Grande do Sul),
   50, 188–90, 192, 201
CREDE (State Department of Education
   Regional Offices, Ceará), 252–53, 262–
   63, 264, 266, 268–70, 275–76
Crusius, Yeda, 193, 195, 198, 199, 201–2,
   203, 204–7, 209–10
curriculum
   and Afro-Brazilian history, 298–99
   in *Escola Ativa,* 151
   and Indigenous movements, 298–300
   in Itinerant Schools, 183, 184–85
   in LEDOC, 155
   in PRONERA programs, 91, 93, 96, 101,
      110–12, 321, 325
   in settlements, 209, 224–25, 253–54, 263,
      266–67, 272–70, 278, 347n31
   standardization of, 204, 254,
      300–1, 311–12
   state capacity to develop, 15–16
   United States, 20–21
   urban bias in, 143, 254
CUT (Central Union of Workers),
   42, 136–37

Dagnino, Evelina, 12, 46, 58, 80–81,
   292–93, 298
Dale, Roger, 20–21
Democratic Workers' Party. *See* PDT
Department of Education for Diversity and
   Citizenship, 142–43
DER (Department of Rural Education of
   FUNDEP), 66–67, 69, 70–71, 72
dos Santos, Clarice, 105, 109–10, 115,
   117–18, 122–24
Duarte, Leandro, 220, 222, 223–24,
   225, 228–30
Dutra, Olívio, 58, 179–80, 183, 188–92,
   193–94, 199, 205–6, 209
Dutschke, Rudi, 5–6

Educação do Campo (Education of the
   Countryside),
   agribusiness support for, 129–30, 160–70,
      171–72
   creation and expansion of, 128–29, 132–
      34, 170–73, 287
   definitions, 1–2, 3, 30–31, 170–71
   institutionalization in Ministry of
      Education, 128–30, 142–48, 146f, 147f,
      288–89, 292, 354n19
   institutionalization in states, 206–7,
      226–28, 230, 238–39, 241–42, 246–47,
      250–54, 258, 262–64, 265–66, 267–68,
      270, 274–80, 292, 355n47
   Operational Guidelines for a Basic
      Education in the Schools of the
      Countryside, 137–39
   presidential decree in support, 121
   São Paulo rejection of, 254–57
   See also *Escola Ativa*; LEDOC
Education for All, 282
Education of the Countryside. See *Educação
   do Campo*
education sector of the MST
   childcare provision, 3–4 (*see also
      ciranda*)
   conflicts and tensions, 102–3, 124–25
   decision-making structure,
      63–65, 239–44
   founding of, 29–30, 52–53, 55–57, 80–81,
      178, 180, 217, 236, 249
   intellectual inspirations, 51–55,
      68–69, 72–73
   leadership development, 21–22, 63–64,
      99–102, 179–80, 217, 229–30, 236–38,
      242–43, 250, 265–66, 294
   literacy initiatives, 70–72
   principal activities, 77t
   protest and mobilization, 3–5, 180–82,
      239, 295–97
   publications, 27–28, 76–80
   teacher training, 66, 72–75, 218–19,
      227–28, 241, 250–51 (*see also* teacher
      training programs of MST)
   women's participation in, 36–37, 50–51,
      297–98 (*see also* women)
   See also *Educação do Campo; escolas do
      campo*; Itinerant Schools; LEDOC;
      PRONERA; *Pedagogia da Terra*
Educational Institute of Josué de Castro.
   See IEJC

EFA (Family Agricultural Schools), 66–67
Eldorado dos Carajás massacre, 85, 87
Encruzilhada Natalino, 42–43
ENERA (National Meeting for Educators in
    Areas of Agrarian Reform), 85–86, 132,
    250, 281–83, 301
ENFF (Florestan Fernandes National
    School), 63, 112–14, 352n34, 361n5
engenho (sugarcane mill), 231, 235, 238–39
Erundina, Luiza, 58
Escola Ativa (Active School), 148,
    158–59, 289
Escola Nova Sociedade (New Society School),
    184–85, 192, 193, 204–5
Escola Sem Partido (School Without Political
    Parties), 311–12
escolas da formação (political training
    schools), 19, 55–56, 63, 88, 100, 112,
    223, 347n37, 348n52
escolas do campo (Schools of the Countryside
    [Ceará]), 247–48, 258–80, 292, 317
Escuela Nueva. See *Escola Ativa*
escuelas normales. See normal schools (Mexico)
European immigration, 37–38, 41,
    179, 351n13
Evans, Peter, 39, 313–14

Family Agricultural Schools. *See* EFA
Father Arnildo Fritzen, 44–45
fazenda (large plantation or
    land estate), 42–43, 52–53, 68, 102–3,
    195, 197, 220
Fazenda Annoni, 52–53, 68, 102–3, 195,
    199–200
Fazenda Macali, 42
Fazenda Milano, 220
Federal University of Goiás, 120–21
Federal University of Pará, 107–8, 149
Federal University of Paraíba,
    107–8, 218–19
Federal University of Rio Grande do
    Norte, 226
Federal University of Santa Catarina,
    144, 250
Federal University of Sergipe, 71, 107–8
Federal University of the Southern
    Frontier, 317
Fernandes, Bernardo Mançano, 16–17,
    110–11, 113, 127, 166–67, 170
Fifth Institutional Act (AI-5), 39

Florestan Fernandes National School.
    See ENFF
FONEC (National Forum for Education of
    the Countryside), 151, 165
food sovereignty, 62, 132–33, 136–37, 170,
    286–87, 296, 301–2, 350n3
formal education, 55–56, 65–66, 88, 93, 237,
    297, 314–15
    distinction from informal or non-formal,
    18–21, 45
Fortaleza (Ceará), 248–49, 250,
    252–53, 306–7
Foundation of Educational Development
    and Research. *See* FUNDEP
Francisco Barros High School, 264–66,
    268, 272
Franco, Itamir, 57, 59
Franco, Marielle, 316–17
Free Fare Movement. *See* MPL
Freire, Paulo, 3–4, 19, 40, 43–45, 51, 56–57,
    58, 65–66, 67–69, 70–72, 74–78, 89,
    132–33, 166, 218, 223, 224–25, 238,
    273, 306
    Pedagogy of the Oppressed, 40, 70–71, 75–
    76, 132–33, 166
Frente Brasil Popular (Brazil Popular
    Front), 306–7
    frente de massa (front of the masses), 2–3,
    277, 306–7
Frente Povo Sem Medo (People Without Fear
    Front), 306–7
FUNDEP (Foundation of Educational
    Development and Research), 66–67,
    69–71, 72, 349n55, 349n58
Fundescola, 148–49

gender
    gender inequaliy, 19–20, 21–22,
    43, 296–98
    gender parity, 2, 301–2, 346n21, 348n52,
    350n73, 355n40
    integration of gender into the curriculum,
    253–54, 273, 311–12
    MST gender sector, 2–3, 39–40, 43,
    63, 100
    See also LGBTQ participation; women
Genro, Tarso, 203, 206–7
Gintis, Herbert, 19–20, 295–96
Global Educational Reform Movement
    (GERM), 298–301

Gomes, Cid, 256, 267–68, 278
Gomes, Jetro, 226–27, 230–31
Gomes, Rogerio Junior, 223, 226
Gramsci, Antonio, 5–7, 15, 16–17, 18, 19–
    21, 29, 48, 56, 58, 67, 82–83, 123, 124,
    130, 152, 186, 193, 229, 281, 282–83,
    284, 293, 296
  frontal attack, 114–17, 178–79, 193,
    198, 209–10
  hegemony, 6, 13, 15, 57–58, 130,
    165, 294–95
  intellectual and moral leadership, 6, 16–
    18, 48, 130, 212, 239, 242, 243–44,
    270, 277, 279, 290, 293, 315–16
  organic intellectual, 16–18, 48, 67, 82–
    83, 124, 126, 130, 165, 226, 276–77,
    296, 298
  passive revolution, 130, 171, 315–16
  uptake in Brazil, 12–13
  war of position, 6–7, 58, 123, 130, 171,
    223, 229, 231, 243, 316–17, 318
    (see also long march through the
    institutions)
green revolution, 39
Guaranema (São Paulo), 112, 361n5
Guimarães, Juarez, 294–95

Hage, Salomão, 149–50, 152
hegemony. See Gramsci, Antonio
Heller, Patrick, 9, 10, 12–13, 210, 258
Henrique, Ricardo, 144–45
High School Degree and Teaching
    Certification Program. See MAG
high-stakes testing, 204, 300–1
Hilário, Erivan, 1, 146, 217–25

Ibanez, Nohemy, 272, 274, 276–77
IEJC (Educational Institute of Josué de
    Castro), 63, 65–66, 72–75, 106–7, 112,
    153–55, 177, 185, 196, 197, 200
INCRA (National Institute of
    Colonization and Agrarian Reform),
    25–26, 27, 30, 90, 104, 106, 109, 111,
    115, 116–20, 121–24, 127,
    311–12
  comparison to Ministry of Education,
    110, 288–89
  history of, 82–83, 87
  See also PRONERA; triple governance

indigenous peoples, 2, 37, 41, 161, 179, 213,
    248–49, 298–300, 303–4, 309–10, 315,
    346n15, 355n47
  and Educação do Campo, 132, 133, 142–
    43, 167, 272
  Kaingang Indians, 41
  Nonoaí reserve, 41
informal education, 3, 201–2
  definition of, 19
  literature about, 19–20
institutionalization of social movements or
    their demands,
  debates in the literature, 7–9, 11, 171–72,
    284–85, 294–95
  MST perspective on, 1, 165–70
  outcomes, 73–74, 98–101, 126,
    155–57, 161–62, 167–70, 171–72,
    248–49, 287–89
  paths to achieving, 29–31, 104, 171–72
International Monetary Fund
    (IMF), 139–40
International Relations Collective (CRI), 28
ITERRA. See IEJC
Itinerant Schools, 178–79, 181–88, 191–92,
    194–203, 205–10, 290–91

Jesus Santos, Maria de, 22–23, 35, 75–76,
    82, 100–1, 246, 249, 253, 254, 256–57,
    265, 273, 277
João Pessoa (Paraíba), 218–19
João Sem Terra High School, 259,
    265–67, 275–76
Joceli Correa High School, 188–91, 192, 205
Joseph, Lauren, 23–24

Keck, Margaret, 32, 57–58, 154, 212–13,
    224, 244, 247, 253, 278–79, 292–93
Kolling, Edgar, 55–56, 66, 85–86, 93, 99,
    110–11, 132–34, 145–46, 166–67,
    192, 250
Krupskaya, Nadezhda, 52–53, 282

La Via Campesina (LVC, The Peasant Way),
    62, 350n3, 351n31, 361n5
Lagoa do Mineiro High School, 259–60,
    264, 269–70, 276
land occupations, 2, 23–24
  of agribusinesses, 140, 160–61, 235

during PT administration (2003–2015), 139, 160–61, 208, 209–10, 290–92
during Temer administration, 310–11, 313–14
expansion nationally in 1990s, 59, 84, 85, 93, 132, 136, 178, 180–81, 184, 211, 213–14, 216–18, 220, 232, 249–50, 255, 259–60, 270–37
in the 1970s–80s, 2–3, 19, 21–22, 36, 38–49, 52–53, 159–60, 179–80, 259–60, 286
landlessness
and educational access, 49, 55, 88, 96–98, 118, 202, 272
extent in Brazil, 2, 5, 37–39, 41, 46–47
and identity, 55, 238–39, 241
and intersectional identity, 21–22
movements to eradicate, 41–44, 56–57, 83, 136, 140–41, 310–11 (*See also* CPT; CONTAG; MASTRA; MST)
repression against, 84–85, 87, 124–25, 132, 159
social construction of, 41, 346n14
See also *sem terrinha*
Lava Jato. See Operation Car Wash
LDB (National Education Law), 142, 272, 275, 355n1
Leach, Darcy, 8
leadership. *See* collectivity; education sector; leadership entries in camps; settlements; women; and youth
Leandro, Rubneuza, 55, 88, 91, 217, 227–28, 238, 240, 241
LEDOC (Baccalaureate and Teaching Certificate in Education of the Countryside), 153–59, 163, 171–72
Lenin, 52–53, 80–81, 282–83
Levin, Henry, 19, 296–97
LGBTQ participation and rights, 2–3, 21–22, 297–98, 303–4, 310, 316–17, 345n20, 348n52, 358n9
Li, Tania, 117
Liberal Front Party. *See* PFL
liberation theology. *See* Catholic Church
literacy programs, 3, 36, 38, 43–45, 65–66, 70–72, 80, 82–83, 85–89, 105–6, 130–32, 139, 177, 211–12, 218, 236–37, 250–51, 287, 317, 349n71, *See also* Freire, Paulo
long march through the institutions, 5, 10–11, 23, 32, 83–84, 124, 213, 283–84, 294–95, 298, 304, 315–16, 318

Lula (Luis Inácio da Silva), 39–40, 57, 58, 83, 104, 105–6, 109, 121, 128–29, 139–43, 159, 160, 161, 233, 239–40, 251–52, 260–62, 298–99, 307–10, 318

Maceió (Alagoas), 258, 260–62, 265, 269, 271–72
Madalena (Ceará), 249
MAG (High School Degree and Teaching Certification Program), 44, 65, 66–70, 73–74, 87–88, 131, 185, 200, 218–19, 250–51, 286
Magalhães, César, 233–34
Magalhães, Eudo, 233–34
Makarenko, Anton, 53, 54–55, 68–70, 74, 76, 273, 282
Maxim Gorky Labor Colony, 54–55
Mapp, Karen, 21
Maranhão, 148–49
maroon community. See *quilombos*
Marx, Karl, 6, 12, 19–20, 52–53, 96, 229, 260, 282, 295–96, 306, 345n27
MASTRA (Movement of Landless Workers of the Southern Region), 43
mata sul (southern forest), 231–32, 236–37, 239–40
Mauro, Gilmar, 294–95
Maxim Gorky Labor Colony. *See* Makarenko, Anton
McAdam, Doug, 11, 14–15, 17, 84–85, 124–25
MDA (Ministry of Agrarian Development), 87, 122–23, 311–12
MEC (Ministry of Education)
creation of, 142
description, 128–29, 142, 145, 146–55, 159, 166–67, 171, 254, 288–89
educational jurisdiction, 87, 97, 106, 142–44, 155, 197–98, 288–89
institutionalization of *Educação do Campo* (see *Educaçao do Campo*)
literacy programs, 236–37
MST participation in, 71–72, 143–46, 153–55, 287, 289
protests against, 1–2, 3–4, 86–87, 110, 150–52
support for common core, 311–12
Mercadente, Aloizio, 163
Meyer, David, 8–9, 14–15, 284–85
Michels, Robert, 7–9, 284–85, 288

military regime in Brazil (1964–1984), 29–
  30, 36–37, 38–43, 45–46, 70, 80, 89,
  135–36, 142, 179–80, 231, 303–4, 306,
  309–10, 312, 314–15, 350n8
Ministry of Agrarian Development. See MDA
Ministry of Education. See MEC
mística (political-cultural performance),
  27, 94–95, 103, 113, 120, 133, 143,
  154, 164, 218–19, 236–37, 270,
  271–72, 282
MNU (United Black Movement), 39–40
Molina, Monica, 86, 106
monoculture. See agribusiness
Monsanto. See agribusiness
Moraes, Ivori, 92, 94, 96–97, 101, 188,
  205–6, 207
Movement of Landless Workers of the
  Southern Region. See MASTRA
movement strategies. See social movement
  strategy
MPL (Free Fare Movement), 305
MST (Brazilian Landless Workers
  Movement)
  activist reflections, 68–69, 98–103,
    146, 165
  agricultural production sector, 61,
    69–70, 315–16
  and coalition building, 62, 118–22, 125–
    26, 128–37, 143–45, 165, 166–70,
    171, 247–48, 251–55, 278, 287–88,
    306–7, 313–14
  educational vision, 3–4, 49, 167–72
  expansion nationally, 59–63, 213–14,
    216–17, 248–49
  first land occupations, 39–44
  founding, 43
  founding of national and regional
    education sectors, 55–57, 217–19,
    236–37, 249, 251–52
  goals, 2, 282–84
  initial educational experiments, 43
  internal organization and decision-making
    structure, 2–4, 47, 62–65
  leadership development, 98–102,
    222–23, 238–40, 293–94, 296–98,
    314–16, 317–18
  literacy, 70–72
  loss of members and support,
    102–3, 239–43
  national congresses, 1–4, 62–63,
    84, 305–6

pedagogical approach, 51–55, 65,
  90–96, 264–74
and Pedagogy of Land program (see
  Pedagogia da Terra)
and PRONERA (*see* PRONERA)
publications, 75–80
relationship to the state, 5–6, 136–42,
  145, 159–86, 206–10, 220, 225–31,
  234–35, 236–37, 243, 255–64,
  274–78, 287, 290–93, 305–7,
  313–14, 316–18
teacher training programs (*see* teacher
  training programs of MST)
violence and repression against, 84–161,
  193–99, 303–4, 306–7, 310–12
MTST (Brazilian Homeless Movement),
  306–7, 309–10
multigrade schools and classrooms, 148–53,
  289. See also *Escola Ativa*
Munarim, Antonio, 1, 144–45, 146, 148, 149,
  171–72, 254–55

National Agrarian Reform Plan, 46–47
National Conference of Brazilian Bishops.
  See CNBB
National Coordination of Educational
  Workers (Mexico). See CNTE
National Education Advisory Board.
  See CNE
National Education Law. See LDB
National Forum for Education of the
  Countryside. See FONEC
National Institute of Colonization and
  Agrarian Reform. See INCRA
National Meeting for Educators in Areas of
  Agrarian Reform. See ENERA
National Program for Education in Areas of
  Agrarian Reform. See PRONERA
National Program for Education of the
  Countryside (*ProNoCampo*), 163–65
National Renewal Alliance (ARENA),
  39, 233
National Union of Municipal Secretaries of
  Education. See UNDIME
National Union of Students (UNE), 306–7
Nazaré Flor High School, 260, 264, 268,
  271–72, 275–76
NB (base nucleus), 27, 47–48, 48f, 55,
  64f, 67–68, 74, 92–93, 113–14,
  115, 271–73

neoliberalism, 29, 36, 57, 59, 61–62, 80–81, 83, 84, 130, 285, 308–9, 317–18
Neubauer da Silva, Roserly, 254
NGOs, 6–7, 58, 134, 143–44, 160, 165, 171–72, 271–72, 344n12
non-formal education, 19–20, 21, 40, 45, 55–56, 88, 93, 212–13, 217, 296, 297, 361n5
normal schools (Mexico), 299–300
núcleo de base. See NB

occupations. *See* land occupations
occupied encampments. *See* camps
Operation Car Wash, 306, 307–8
organic intellectual. *See* Gramsci, Antonio

Pará, 84–85
Paraíba, 218–19, 222
Paraná, 43, 71, 309, 312, 357n42
participatory democracy, 12–13, 18, 23, 27, 36, 46, 57–59, 72, 76, 80–81, 129, 134, 142, 144, 151, 158–59, 179–80, 183–84, 190, 206, 209, 210, 224–25, 266, 290, 292–94, 317–18
    participatory budgeting, 12, 58, 179–80, 183–84, 206
Paschel, Tianna, 9, 30–31, 39–40, 124, 140, 287, 310, 314–15
Passeron, Jean-Claude, 19–20, 295–96
Pastoral Land Commission. *See* CPT
patronage. *See* clientelism
PCdoB (Communist Party of Brazil), 306–7
PDT (Democratic Workers' Party), 233
peasant identity and culture, 5, 23, 51, 62, 67, 143, 159–60, 166, 195, 263, 266–67, 270, 273
peasant leagues, 36, 38–39, 214
The Peasant Way. See *La Via Campesina* (LVC)
pedagogia da alternância (pedagogy of alternation), 66, 90–91, 106–7, 111, 154–55, 218–19, 250, 273
Pedagogia da Terra (Pedagogy of Land bachelor's degree program), 90–103, 120, 133, 153, 191–92, 226, 229–30, 250, 268, 269–70
pedagogy of alternation. See *pedagogia da alternância*
Pedagogy of Land. See *Pedagogia da Terra*

Pedagogy of the Oppressed. See Freire, Paulo
Pernambuco, 25, 31–32, 88, 91, 102, 118–19, 136–37, 167, 211–12, 213–31, 248–49, 250–51, 291–92, 314
PFL (Liberal Front Party), 220, 223–24, 233
Pistrak, Moisey, 53–54, 73–74, 76, 273, 282
Piven, Frances Fox, 7–9, 11, 16, 126, 171–73, 284–85, 288, 294–95
PMDB (Brazilian Democratic Movement Party), 49, 163, 180, 186, 193–94, 233, 307–8, 309–10
political ethnography. *See* research methods
political opening (*abertura*), 29, 36, 39, 42, 136, 238, 239, 241
political opportunity structure, 14–15, 124–25
Political-Pedagogical Collective. *See* CPP
Political-Pedagogical Project. *See* PPP
popular education, 19, 21, 22–23, 28, 89, 166, 181–82
Porto Alegre (Rio Grande do Sul), 12–13, 58, 179–80, 186, 202
Portuguese colonialism, 37, 231–32
PPP (Political–Pedagogical Project), 190–91, 193, 228, 265–67, 276–77, 278
practical authority, 154, 212–13, 224, 244, 279, 292–93
preferential option for the poor. *See* Catholic Church
prefiguration and prefigurative politics, 5, 7, 12, 23, 29–30, 37, 67–68, 80, 90, 92, 114, 115, 126, 158–59, 273, 275, 279–80, 284–85, 292, 295, 296, 297, 301–2, 304
PRONERA (National Program for Education in Areas of Agrarian Reform)
    attacks against, 114–18, 122, 288–89, 311–12
    Baccalaureate and Teaching Certificate in Education of the Countryside (*See* LEDOC)
    creation of, 82–87, 132
    difficulties funding, 94, 119–20, 122–24, 289, 311–12
    expansion, 104–10, 142, 177, 229–30, 250–51, 289
    first baccalaureate program (*See* Pedagogia da Terra)
    geography baccalaureate program, 110–14

PRONERA (*Cont.*)
main arguments about, 30, 82–84,
124–27, 289
mobilization in defense of, 118
MST and social movement participation
in, 150, 155–57, 159, 177, 250, 286,
289 (*see also* triple governance)
placement in INCRA, 87
Territorial Development in Latin America
and the Caribbean, PRONERA
program, 108–9
See also *Pedagogia da Terra*; triple
governance
ProNoCampo, 163. *See also* National Program
for Education of the Countryside
PSB (Brazilian Sociality Party), 223–24,
226–27, 233–35, 256, 278
PSDB (Brazilian Social Democratic Party),
57, 70, 84–85, 193–94, 198, 203, 206,
251–52, 254–56, 305–6, 308–10
PSOL (Socialist and Liberty Party), 139–40,
309–10, 316–17
PT (Workers' Party)
formation, 12–13, 42, 49, 136, 249–50
internal changes, 58–59, 104, 315–16
MST relationship to, 15, 31, 129–30, 193,
203, 206–8, 256, 285, 287–88,
294–95, 313–14, 317–18
ousting from power, 32, 304–9
support for *Educação do Campo*, 129–30,
139, 149, 150, 159–65, 171–72, 206,
252–53, 278, 293–94
support for PRONERA, 83–84, 104–10,
113, 120–21, 124–25
See also agribusiness; Dutra; Lula;
participatory democracy; Rousseff
Public Ministry (Rio Grande do Sul)
MST mobilizations against, 202–3, 207
prosecution against Itinerant Schools,
199–200, 207, 209–10, 290–91

quilombos (maroon communities, black rural
communities), 132, 158, 161, 214–15,
230, 357n4

race/racial justice, 2, 9, 37–38, 39–40, 59,
110–11, 136–37, 140, 142–43, 146,
158, 214–15, 217–18, 298–99, 301–2

real utopias, 11–12, 23, 29–30, 37, 67–69,
72, 80–81, 286, 306–7
Recife (Pernambuco), 118, 138, 214, 218,
231, 237
research methods, 17–18, 23, 32, 248
comparative case study, 24–25, 292–93
political ethnography, 23–25
positionality, 28–29
relational comparison, 25, 248
Rigotto, Germano, 186, 193–94, 205–6
Rio Grande do Sul, 25, 31, 41, 42–43, 44, 50,
52, 66–67, 68–73, 87–90, 94, 95–96,
101–2, 106–7, 117, 120, 143, 177, 210,
213, 244, 250–51, 290–92
Rojas, Fabio, 9, 148–49, 172–73, 300
Rondônia, 84
Rousseff, Dilma, 129–30, 159, 282–83, 304–
9, 310–11, 317
Rui Barbosa School, 192, 204–5
rural union movement. *See* CONTAG

Santa Maria da Boa Vista (Pernambuco), 25,
31–32, 211, 213, 214–33, 239, 243–79,
291–92, 314
Santos, Milton, 282
São Francisco River, 214–15, 217
São Paulo, 25, 26, 31–32, 39–40, 58, 63,
83–84, 108–9, 110–11, 112, 113, 117–
18, 127, 166–67, 179, 196, 239–40,
254–55, 278–79, 292, 301, 303, 305,
306, 309–10
Schmidt, Armênio, 143, 145–46,
149, 254–55
Schools of the Countryside (Ceará). See
escolas do campo
SECADI (Secretariat of Continual
Education, Literacy, Diversity and
Inclusion), 142–43, 144–45, 146, 148–
50, 152, 166–67, 311–12
Secretariat of Continual Education, Literacy,
Diversity and Inclusion. *See* SECADI
self-governance, 11–12, 29, 48, 54–55, 68–
70, 74, 92–93, 114, 125, 127–28, 157,
205, 218–19, 268, 270
sem terrinha (little landless children), 1–2,
3–4, 55, 182, 202, 238–39, 250–51
SEPPIR (Special Secretariat for Policies to
Promote Racial Equality), 140
Serra, José, 254

sertão (semi-arid region), 58–59, 214, 231, 248–50, 259, 260
settlements,
  agricultural production in, 61, 69–70, 208
  attacks against, 198, 312
  creation and development of, 2, 5, 21–22, 58–59, 74, 83–84, 104, 105, 126, 140–41, 180, 214, 216–17, 218, 228, 232, 249, 316
  decision-making structure, 62–71, 93–94
  education in, 3–4, 37, 45, 46, 49, 52–53, 55–57, 63–66, 68–70, 74–75, 79–80, 85, 90, 102–3, 118, 130–31, 159, 170, 177, 178, 184–85, 187–94, 200, 204–6, 209, 217, 218, 220–30, 235–43, 251, 256–78, 289, 292, 317
  Freire visit, 70–71
  leadership development on, 18, 23, 47–49, 99, 124, 213, 291–92, 293–94, 297–98, 314–16
  MST visions for, 16–18, 48, 286–87
Sikkink, Kathryn, 32, 247, 253, 278–79, 292
Simplício, Vanderlúcia, 68–69, 82, 93, 100, 127, 157–58, 163
Skocpol, Theda, 15
Soarez, Edla, 138, 227–28, 241
social movements
  definitions, 6–7, 8–9, 11, 17
  infrastructure, 13–14, 16, 18, 29, 31–32, 82–83, 99, 100, 178, 209, 210, 243–44, 259, 279–80, 284, 290, 293, 297
  infrastructure and capacities, 7–8, 10–11, 13–14, 15–20, 29, 31–32, 67–68, 72, 81, 82–83, 99, 100, 114, 159, 178, 205–6, 209, 210, 212, 243–44, 259, 279–80, 284, 288–89, 293, 297, 301–2, 304
  internal capacity, 7–8, 10, 11, 16, 18, 19–20, 29, 67–68, 72, 81, 82–83, 114, 159, 206, 212, 284, 288–90, 301–2, 304
  in Latin America, 9–10, 12–13, 40, 42, 112, 298–300, 303–4, 310–11, 318
  outcomes, 9, 13–14, 24–25, 31–32, 126, 128, 171, 173, 248, 287–90, 292–93, 344n15, 344n17, 345n32
  theories of, 6, 7–15, 124, 134, 284–86, 289
social movement strategy, 11–12, 284, 287–88
  access–influence model, 11–12

institutional or state engagement, 5, 7–11, 12, 13–14, 15, 19–20, 23, 29–30, 32, 58, 80–81, 82–83, 171–72, 178–79, 210, 244, 245, 277–78, 279–80, 284, 285, 287–89, 294–95, 301–2, 304, 316–17
social reproduction theory, 19–21, 56, 296
social transformation,
  MST vision of, 2, 6–7, 17–18, 21, 36, 61, 74–75, 166, 260, 266, 283–84, 305–6
  relationship to schools, 19–20, 151
socialism
  critique of, 103, 164–65, 171–72, 194, 303
  historical examples, 2, 42, 52, 56–57, 58, 214, 295, 316–17
  MST's vision of, 2, 5, 54, 62, 63–64, 68, 80–81, 128, 131, 157–59, 161–62, 164–65, 227–28, 246, 296–97, 301–2, 306–7
  socialist pedagogies, 51–54, 68, 76–78, 130
  theories of, 2, 11–12, 294–95, 361n6
Socialist and Liberty Party. *See* PSOL
socio–territorial movements, 16–17
Soviet Union, 52, 53–54, 57, 347n27, 347n33
Special Secretariat for Policies to Promote Racial Equality. *See* SEPPIR
state capacity, 13–16, 18, 29, 31–32, 46, 71, 129–30, 140, 146–57, 178, 201–2, 206, 209–12, 224, 243–80, 284, 288, 290, 292–93, 310–11, 317–18, 344n18
State Department of Education Regional Offices, Ceará. *See* CREDE
State Department of Education Regional Offices, Rio Grande do Sul. *See* CRE
state-led development strategy, 18, 39, 128, 256
state-movement cooperation, 31, 143–44, 145, 178–206, 210, 274–75, 316–17, 318
  critique of, 7–8, 284–86
state–society conflict, 29, 36–37, 57, 71–72, 80–81, 83, 84–87, 124–25, 130–34, 145, 220, 318
state-society relations, theories of, 7–9, 220, 285–91, 292–95
Statute on Rural Labor, 38

Stédile, João Pedro, 41, 44–45, 93, 114, 260–
    62, 282–84, 306–7, 315–17
strategic engagement in institutions. *See*
    social movement strategy

TAC (Technical Administration of
    Cooperatives), 65–66, 69–70,
    72–73, 87–88
TAC (Term of Commitment to Adjust
    Conduct), 198–99, 207
Tarrow, Sydney, 8–9, 11, 124–25, 284–85
TCU (Brazilian Federal Court of Audits)
    critique of, 117–23, 282
    involvement in CPI, 160
    prosecution against IEJC, 115–24
    prosecution against PRONERA, 197
    structure and purpose, 125–26,
        352n40, 352n41
    teacher training programs of MST, 27, 29–
        30, 44, 56–57, 66–67, 73–74, 85, 149,
        154–55, 185, 187, 207, 212–13, 223,
        225–26, 238–39, 242–43, 247–48,
        250–51, 253–54, 270, 279, 296, 298,
        299–301; *See also* MAG
Technical Administration of Cooperatives.
    See TAC
Technical Institute of Training and Research
    in Agrarian Reform. *See* IEJC
Temer, Michel, 307–9, 310–13
Tereza, Flavinha, 236–38, 240–41
Term of Commitment to Adjust Conduct.
    See TAC
Thums, Gilberto, 196–97, 200, 203
triple governance, 30, 83–84, 104, 109. *See*
    also PRONERA

UnB (University of Brasília),
    support for MST educational initiatives,
        71–72, 86, 105–6, 132–33, 139, 153–
        54, 222, 350n6
    support for PRONERA and LEDOC
        programs, 107–8, 153–58, 352n34
UNDIME (National Union of Municipal
    Secretaries of Education), 241
UNEMAT (State University of Mato
    Grosso), 114–16, 117–18

UNESCO (United Nations Educational,
    Scientific, and Cultural Organization),
    71–72, 130–33, 139, 222, 236–37, 287
UNESP (State University of São Paulo), 83–
    84, 108–9, 110–14, 127, 166–67
UNICAMP (State University of
    Campinas), 110–11
UNICEF (United Nations Children's Fund),
    70, 71–72, 130–33, 139, 222
United Black Movement. *See* MNU
United Nations Children's Fund. *See* UNICEF
United Nations Educational, Scientific, and
    Cultural Organization. *See* UNESCO
University of Ijuí, 104, 125, 133,
    191–92, 250
    conflicts with MST, 95–99
    establishment of Pedagogy of Land
        program, 89–90
    history of, 89
    MST pedagogies in, 90
    reflections from graduates, 99–103

Vargas, Getúlio, 38, 85
Varjão, Teresneide, 146, 217–23
Veranópolis (Rio Grande do Sul), 72–73,
    106–7, 196–97
Vergara-Camus, Leandro, 7

Wampler, Brian, 12–13, 46
Warren, Mark, 21
Wilson, José, 138, 163, 164
Witcel, Elizabete, 68, 94, 96–97, 180–81,
    182–83, 185–86, 187, 191–92, 194,
    201–2, 204–5
Wolford, Wendy, 16–17, 37–39, 42–43, 232,
    239–40, 343n3
Women
    female activism in MST, 94, 146, 160–61,
        236–37, 266
    female leadership development and
        integration into the movement,
        21–22, 29, 65–66, 80, 180, 250–51,
        266, 297–98
    women's participation in MST education
        initiatives, 21–22, 37, 43, 44, 49, 50–51,
        180, 217, 296–98

women's rights movements, 2, 8–10, 46–
47, 136–37, 315–17 (*see also* gender;
LGBTQ participation and rights)
Workers' Party. *See* PT
World Bank, 130–31, 140, 148–50,
171–72, 252
Wright, Erik Olin, 23, 268–69, 343n3

youth
access to education, 3, 74–75, 80, 114,
118, 126, 131, 146, 153, 159, 163, 164–
65, 171–73, 177, 259–60
and agricultural production, 273

Children and Youth Congress, 181
leadership development and integration
into movement, 21–22, 29, 70, 72, 80,
130–31, 167, 229–30, 236–37, 250–51,
257, 279–80, 297, 314
MST youth collective, 2–3, 63
National Meeting of Adult and Youth
Educators, 237

Zimmerman, Marli, 55, 68, 101–2,
180, 185–87, 191–92, 194, 201–2
Zumbi dos Palmares, 282.
See also *quilombos*